"We, the Barbarians"

CRITICAL MEXICAN STUDIES

CRITICAL MEXICAN STUDIES
Series editor: Ignacio M. Sánchez Prado

Critical Mexican Studies is the first English-language, humanities-based, theoretically focused academic series devoted to the study of Mexico. The series is a space for innovative works in the humanities that focus on theoretical analysis, transdisciplinary interventions, and original conceptual framing.

Titles in the series:
  The Restless Dead: Necrowriting and Disappropriation
    by Cristina Rivera Garza
  History and Modern Media: A Personal Journey by John Mraz
  Toxic Loves, Impossible Futures: Feminist Living as Resistance
    by Irmgard Emmelhainz
  Drug Cartels Do Not Exist: Narcotrafficking in US and Mexican Culture
    by Oswaldo Zavala
  Unlawful Violence: Mexican Law and Cultural Production
    by Rebecca Janzen
  The Mexican Transpacific: Nikkei Writing, Visual Arts, and Performance
    by Ignacio López-Calvo
  *Monstrous Politics: Geography, Rights, and the Urban Revolution
    in Mexico City* by Ben Gerlofs
  *Robo Sacer: Necroliberalism and Cyborg Resistance in Mexican
    and Chicanx Dystopias* by David Dalton
  *Mexico, Interrupted: Labor, Idleness, and the Economic Imaginary
    of Independence* by Sergio Gutiérrez Negrón
  Serial Mexico: Storytelling across Media, from Nationhood to Now
    by Amy E. Wright
  Sonic Strategies for Performing Modern Mexico by Christina Baker
  *Subjunctive Aesthetics: Mexican Cultural Production in the Era
    of Climate Change* by Carolyn Fornoff
  *Fatefully, Faithfully Feminist: A Critical History of Women, Patriarchy
    and Mexican National Discourse* by Carlos Monsiváis, translated
    and edited by Norma Klahn and Ilana Luna
  *Biocosmism: Vitality and the Utopian Imagination in Postrevolutionary
    Mexico* by Jorge Quintana Navarrete

"We, the Barbarians"
Three Mexican Writers
in the Twenty-First Century

Mabel Moraña

Translated by Stephanie L. Kirk

VANDERBILT UNIVERSITY PRESS
Nashville, Tennessee

Copyright 2024 Vanderbilt University Press
All rights reserved
First printing 2024

Originally published as *"Nosotros, los bárbaros": Tres narradores mexicanos en el siglo XXI*. Mexico City: Bonilla Artigas Editores, 2021.

Library of Congress Cataloging-in-Publication Data

Names: Moraña, Mabel, author. | Kirk, Stephanie L., translator.
Title: "We, the barbarians" : three Mexican writers in the twenty-first century / Mabel Moraña ; translated by Stephanie L. Kirk.
Other titles: "Nosotros, los bárbaros." English
Description: Nashville, Tennessee : Vanderbilt University Press, 2024. | Series: Critical Mexican studies | Includes bibliographical references and index.
Identifiers: LCCN 2023054129 | ISBN 9780826506696 (paperback) | ISBN 9780826506702 (hardcover) | ISBN 9780826506719 (epub) | ISBN 9780826506726 (pdf)
Subjects: LCSH: Mexican fiction--21st century--History and criticism. | Herrera, Yuri, 1970---Criticism and interpretation. | Melchor, Fernanda, 1982---Criticism and interpretation. | Luiselli, Valeria, 1983---Criticism and interpretation. | LCGFT: Literary criticism.
Classification: LCC PQ7203.2 .M6713 2024 | DDC 863/.709972--dc23/eng/20240214
LC record available at https://lccn.loc.gov/2023054129

Contents

Acknowledgments — vii

INTRODUCTION — 1

1 Yuri Herrera: A Distilled and Elliptical Art — 11

    Children's Stories, *Talud*, and *Diez planetas*: The Science of Fiction

    Testimonial Virtuosity in *El incendio de la mina El Bordo*

    Trabajos del Reino: First as Tragedy, then as Farce; The *Corrido* as Social Text

    Señales que precederán al fin del mundo: A Voyage into Silence and the Journey as Paradigm; Becomings; Tradition/Modernity and the Function of Myth; "We, the Barbarians" and the Place of Enunciation

    La transmigración de los cuerpos: Social Space and the Place of Death; The Body as Commodity; Community/Immunity

2 Fernanda Melchor: Necro-Aesthetics and the "Truth of the Body" — 129

    (Thankfully) *This Is Not Miami*: Chronicle and Border Narrative; Regional Identities.

"Youth, Divine Treasure" in *Falsa liebre*: Mapping Subjectivity; Perversion, Excess, and Gender

Temporada de huracanes or the Whirlwind of Language; The Black Hole of the Witch; Patriarchy and Witchcraft; Secrets and Gossip; (Anti)Modernity and Community in La Matosa

3 Valeria Luiselli: The Unbearable Lightness of Being 205

Displacements, Dispositifs, and Gestures in *Papeles falsos*; The Exoskeleton and the Seeing Eye; The Map and the Hole; Liminality and Name Dropping

Los ingrávidos: Owen and I (or Vice Versa?); The Metaphyiscs of Presence; Translation and Simulacrum.

The (Irritating) *Historia de mis dientes*; The Aura of the Object; The Auction House and the Negotiation of Meaning

Los niños perdidos (un ensayo en cuarenta preguntas); The Migrant's Via Crucis and the Theater of Belonging; Microhistory and Literature

Lost Children Archive: Word and Silence; Archive and Narration; Border Semiotics and Autofiction; Luiselli's Use of Children; Elegaic Discourse

Notes 293

Acknowledgments

I would like to express my gratitude to Bonilla Artigas Editores in Mexico for allowing the publication of the English version of my book, and to Vanderbilt University Press for including it in the Critical Mexican Studies series. Also, my appreciation to Stephanie Kirk for her hard work in translating this text.

M. M.

Introduction

In these political and socially turbulent times, of unchecked financial and economic vicissitudes and devastating visions of death provoked by systemic violence, migration policies, and global public health challenges, it is important to note that literature is not a priority. As the new millennium advances, literature only—or perhaps, primarily—begins to establish itself as a term of relative interest when we connect it to an area of urgent debate and potential social transformation. Only then can we see the link between literary production and its reception (albeit with certain mediations) to the domains of politics and ethics, social critique, the representation of subjects and the regulation of the subjective. These connections are of particular relevance in an age of intense focus on the object: its production and exchange, transactions, methods of circulation, use value and exchange value. I believe we have yet to reach the point where all aesthetic value or all poetics must necessarily be subordinated to the exigencies of reality. Instead, the secret is found in the forms that this articulation produces, in the elegance of its setting, the effectiveness of silence, the strength of its reserve and, finally, in the way in which both word and idea are permeated by the real, without self-denial, asserting themselves and their inalienable right to polysemy, to modesty, and to redundancy.

I was drawn to this book's brief corpus by a similar question to the one that informed my study of Peruvian authors (*Arguedas / Vargas Llosa: Dilemas y ensamblajes*): an interrogation of the impulses that have crystallized in different aesthetic projects and that offer a kaleidoscopic vision of both national cultures and collective imaginaries.[1] Owing to the different levels of output between the Mexican authors of this book and the Peruvians of my earlier work, the degree of maturity of their literary oeuvre, and their individual relevance and prominence within their era, this book's analysis is less complex than the previous one. It was, however, a similarly intriguing exercise in terms of the discussion of the authors' parallel aesthetics and their creation of highly differentiated and even opposing fictional worlds. In this book, I chose not to analyze the divergences and convergences among the authors' respective literary works, since this brief corpus, unlike the Andean one, does not lend itself to a detailed engagement with political and ideological contexts (the Cuban Revolution and *Senderismo* in the case of Peru) or existential circumstances (the Nobel Prize, suicide) that create obvious antagonisms. Nevertheless, I was seduced by the strategies each author deploys from their literary arsenal, to confront an era rich in conflict but lacking in ways to challenge the necropolitical horizons of our globalized world.

Some of the points of analysis that distinguish this study are evident. The first is each text's locus of enunciation, both in geocultural terms but also in political and ideological ones. In this way, the narration becomes a form of symbolic production that reveals the tension between the specific moment of development that bisects national culture as well as late capitalism's cultural transnationalization. In different ways, each of the three Mexican authors I study here (Yuri Herrera, Fernanda Melchor, and Valeria Luiselli) negotiates the tension between localism and regionalism. As my analysis will underscore, Herrera's most effective literary tool is his aesthetic refinement. Guided by techniques of narrative economy that burnish his writing and free it from the splinters and roughness of afterthoughts and digressions, his narrative glides along precisely and sharply, as if shaped by a chisel. His plots and characters evoke in-between frontier spaces, the starkness of the desert landscape and the region's complex simplicity. He eschews realism, instead embracing how the imaginary reveals our historical moments to us, drawing on the undoubtedly discordant, contradictory, disparate, and self-interested versions and visions that invade the public sphere.

Herrera's literary works are not located in the elusive scenarios of the *real*, but instead in the unencumbered space of the imaginary, where reality has found its way into images, sounds, and above all, atmospheres. This allows for an internalization of personalized versions drawn from news stories and *corridos*, distinguishing between what they say and what we perceive has happened. Even in its immanence, this content is alien and beyond the reach of the ordinary individual in terms of language, rationality, and memory. Herrera's terse, contained, and laconic prose is inhabited by echoes and traces and at the same time, is completely distinctive. He invokes drug cartels, death, and love in depraved contexts where the archetypal alienated and vulnerable subjectivities of unique and unforgettable characters take refuge. Herrera's writing is sensual, circumspect, and knows exactly when to draw the line.

Fernanda Melchor's narrative production, above all her novels, seems to catch even the author herself by surprise. Incontrollable, relentlessly dark, morbidly crammed with sounds, images, and words, her writing transmits the jagged breathing of her characters along with overflowing inner worlds that spill out onto the page. The rebellious heir of the distant reverberations of the funereal Baroque, her texts are like excavations that penetrate the mass graves of our collective unconscious. The subjectivities of her characters, what Barthes would call "paper beings," appear to be fashioned from a rough and abrasive material.[2] Perhaps for this reason they push incessantly at the borders of the text, spilling over into the social and textual margins, colliding with the syntax, and reconquering language. Her settings are like barebones theater sets in a low-budget stage show—in which the actors heroically but fruitlessly attempt to conceal the precarious nature of their environment. And thus, these characters both embrace and reject stereotypes, drawing on and then abandoning creative formulas, trespassing into excess and ornamentalism, drawing on elements of the *novela negra*, of the gothic, of the Neo Baroque and appropriating, and sporadically recycling, different aesthetics without ever settling on a particular one. Often young, her characters are victims of an unintelligible and inaccessible world, venturing into, and then fleeing different poetic territories. They are restless, evanescent, malleable, and melancholy.

Valeria Luiselli's work is of a different ilk. Her writing is calculated and cerebral as well as hypothermic. Even her textual engagement with affect seems to respond to a plan she previously sketched out on a yellow writing pad, with arrows and circles detailing how to proceed, when to stop, at what point the ghost should enter, the cat leave, the Middle Child speak. Her writing reveals a suitable amount of moderate and tacit feminism; metaliterary references to a childhood of travel, of experiences and mythical places; instructions on how to proceed through the text. Featuring interminable lists of people to be cited, unusual places and details that describe an outdated, old-fashioned bohemian lifestyle, her works feature judicious helpings of humor and irony. Luiselli's writing complies with the demands of the market: a sprinkling of *tropicalismo* (*ma non troppo*) filtered through a convincing academic style and cleverly subsumed into market-driven themes whose pulse she takes from New York City. Luiselli's literature consists of gestures that serve principally to carefully outline the shape of her own image. Autofiction extends throughout her works like a self-sustaining thread. In Luiselli's work, there exists an apparent and unresolved tension between exteriority and national culture that, in my view, provides a point of interest. Another characteristic is her desire to identify issues that connect albeit obliquely with present-day problems. Tempered by the nonexistent sounds of the Native Americans and by those of her own children who seek their parents' attention, she scatters the theme of children lost in the desert among audiobooks, drawings, and daily anecdotes. This gesture of looking back in time over the richness of Mexican culture from the outside, from a space of safety—as Osvaldo Zavala has skillfully analyzed—offers an interesting perspective as nationalism disintegrates into global scenarios and then, like a kaleidoscope, (re)consolidates into different forms of cultural citizenship.[3]

Thus, we arrive at three very different models of intellectual positioning through which we can glimpse the ghost of nationalism in a variety of forms. As I have shown, the locus of enunciation speaks to a series of situationally dependent possibilities and decisions, conceiving of the act of literary creation as intellectual labor, or rather as the production of fictional discourses that emerge from concrete subjects connected to specific circumstances of cultural production. These authors' poetics emerge from radically different existential territories and involve divergent understandings of the role of the body as well as the impact of affect, class, race, and gender, the value of language as identity, desire, and belief. These poetics constitute alternative forms of social consciousness and offer distinct approaches to the relationship between fiction and reality, imagination and rationality, knowledge, feeling and power, as well as nation and postnational spaces.

Yuri Herrera's works speak to the experience of a poetically distilled life, capable of lyrically upholding the myths that crowd the popular imaginary, without turning his writing into a thesis on Mexican history nor a repository for the horrors of our age. Instead, Herrera lets his writing glide over reality's rough surface illuminating the subjective side of social processes and the price we pay for survival. His writing imprints an indelible trace upon the narrated material, a shadow that we glimpse through his characters' way of life, the beliefs they hold, the subcultures to which they belong and through which he processes the daily life of the nation.

From the settings in Veracruz that frame the stories of young people tormented by violence and precariousness, the question of the nation provides a gory and, at the same time, wildly imaginative presence, as Melchor demonstrates in a prose that, at times, seems to be on a psychedelic trip but that nonetheless maintains an unnerving connection with lived reality. In Melchor's world, the margin assumes the role of main protagonist, providing a vestigial, variegated, and profusely visual space in an original voice. Herrera's characters also dwell on the periphery, but Melchor engages much more dramatically with this space in the dynamic layers of her characters' psychology and emotionality and their actions, which she presents with a raw and flagrant immediacy. Melchor tends toward excess, Herrera to restraint. In this excess, her positioning at the limit(s) approaches a mythical transcendence and brushes up against abstraction, although her fictitious beings possess a profound and coherent verisimilitude. Her characters are both straightforward and profound, terse, convincing, and carefully calibrated.

For Luiselli, the nation becomes a specter. Her utilization of ghostliness makes her world less credible and adds an at times excessive element of immutability and literariness. In any case, the national question acts as a magnet through its canonical referents, its hidden urban corners, as well as contemporary scenes that begin in the testimonial vein and end up in the realms of the novel. In Luiselli's prose, ghosts wander through a clearly compartmentalized cultural space (elitist and institutional on the one hand and popular and/or mass media driven on the other). These ghosts speak to a national(ist) legacy that is transmitted from generation to generation within an intellectual sector that has become, to a great extent, transnational in nature and whose sterile contact with the perversities of reality achieves a new synthesis of Mexican history's dense and conflictive nature. Although Herrera also writes from an external US enclave, his positionality does not seem to have tempered his relationship with the raw material of his work. Distanced from constant contact with Mexico City's absorbent nucleus, his provincial origins, his capacity to capture the experience of peripheral spaces and decode the border's epistemic challenges have resulted in an impeccable use of language, an eloquence of expression, and even in the use of gestures the reader can imagine accompanying border language: the beating heart of the landscape and the characters' thoughts and feelings.

These three authors have individually identified secure and richly deserved ways of inserting themselves into the global cultural market, cultivated through the outstanding exercise of their profession and through their unfaltering desire to innovate and to communicate an authentic and distinct voice within a multicultural public space that imposes its own rules and expectations. Each of the three authors has won over a public whose interest will continue to define itself as their work develops and embarks on future paths. Despite these marked differences, the authors I study here offer the reader a radically distinct version of Mexico from José Revuelta's dynamic and inexorable vision or Carlos Fuentes's cosmopolitan Mexicanness, or the Contemporáneos' avant-garde experimentalism or the Generación del Crack's groundbreaking narrative project. Elements from these previous authors and movements linger, however, and are distilled into this generation's aesthetics. Nonetheless, the succinct and intense Juan Rulfo hovers over their contemporary poetics in the form of an unbeaten and inescapable ghost.

Some critics have said that Luiselli's texts are "born translated" or "born to be translated" not only because, in some cases, they appear first in English but also because she incorporates themes and designs framework for a public that is not necessarily Mexican. We could say something similar about Herrera's texts although, in his case, the strategy he employs to insert his work into transnational forms of circulation and consumption appears much less deliberate. Perhaps unconsciously, Herrera, a writer who has earned a lasting place in the Mexican canon, engages a public that extends beyond Mexico's national limits. In Melchor's case, her translatability appears to be more complex, at both a cultural as well as a linguistic level, since the question of intelligibility takes on a deeper dimension. It invokes the need for contextual comprehension and, above all, intuitively submerges the reader into everything that translation cannot capture, but that the texture of the narrative relentlessly communicates.

Most striking in the case of these authors are their specific readings of modernity, not only as a multi-faceted system of social organization, cultural distribution, and political directionality, but also as an epistemic platform that organizes knowledge as well as forms of cognitive privilege and the level of access to and integration in public spaces and symbolic goods. The three authors approach the problem of social decentralization and displacement in different ways, displaying disparate techniques for the administering of distance from the principal centers of late capitalism and the cultural flows they generated. In their works, language covers a spectrum that ranges from an appropriation of colloquial turns that regionalizes literary discourse and symbolically intercedes in it (Melchor, Herrera) to the use of the most conventional and standardized forms that reveal the authors' command of literary expression. This language is used as a tool, adjusted to, and informed by the incorporation of canonical references and borrowings from other languages that reflect the discourse's cosmopolitan tendencies and its interest in the globalized world (Luiselli). This tension between localism and globalism reveals vital aspects of contemporary systems. At this level, the gradual weakening of the nation-State as the primary platform of cultural analysis is counteracted by the empowering of local vernaculars and regional imaginaries and with a return to the representation of belief systems and sensibilities that denote distinct social and economic locations. In this way, light is shed upon national fragments, retrenchments, hybridizations, and incongruities. Highlighting the local/global dialectic, these paradoxical instabilities increase nostalgia for a world that is gradually dissolving into standardization and recover voices that, demanding a history that is more inclusive, diverse, and open to other ways of understanding the social and the political, resonate in global spaces.

The writers analyzed in this book expand variously and in contrasting ways upon notions of community, identity, gender and affect, as well as concepts of homeland, border and citizenship centering or displacing the inescapable themes of inequality, and social (in)justice, subjective or socially imposed forms of guilt and redemption, of desire, nostalgia, and corporality. Their fictional worlds are interwoven with grotesque, sentimental, and lyrical elements. On occasion, their work features concrete segments of contemporary modes of socialization, and on others, it ventures into mythical territory. In all three cases, Herrera, Melchor, and Luiselli's first literary ventures all engage in different ways with the chronicle. In his reconstruction of the fire in the El Bordo mine, Herrera reveals the construction of a specific version of the truth to uncover the role of those responsible for the disaster. Melchor's journalistic pen exposes episodes in and around Veracruz in which elements of the *crónica roja* or "yellow journalism" mix with the *nota social* or society pages. In the news stories and articles that make up *Papeles falsos*, Luiselli brings to the surface aspects and tones that characterized her previous works such as a propensity for urban or suburban circuits traversed in the manner of a flâneur, dilettantism, constant reference to important personages from the world of culture, or travel to iconic places (the San Michele cemetery, writers' graves, urban sorties that uncover secret or transitional spaces of special significance).

Each author also maintains a deeply significant relationship with literary tradition, making explicit connections to the aesthetic of the Contemporáneos or Generación del Crack in the case of Luiselli, or the narco novel or border narratives that some see in Herrera and that he develops, in a very different style, to authors such as Homero Aridjis, Heriberto Yépez, Elmer Mendoza, Daniel Sada, and Orfa Alarcón, among many others. For her part, Melchor has been compared to Flannery O'Connor, for her predilection for the grotesque and the dark corners of human behavior. Her style has also been associated with US "Southern Gothic" authors. Moreover, because of her interest in questions of gender (masculinity, homosexuality, and feminism), Melchor is considered the heir to contributions made from mid-century on by authors such as Josefina Vicens (*El libro vacío*, 1958) and Inés Arrendondo. More recent parallels can be found between her work and that of Cristina Rivera Garza (*Ningún reloj cuenta esto*, 2002; *La muerte me da*, 2007) as well as with some aspects of Ana Clavel's writing.

However, beyond potential literary legacies and aesthetic adaptations, we cannot understand literature written today in and around Mexico as an autonomous sphere that is circumscribed by a sealed and self-sufficient literary field. Effectively, no type of symbolic creation can ignore the presence of necro-culture rooted not only in Mexico but also transnationally, connected to drug trafficking and other types of organized crime and also derived and, in many cases, generated by transnationalized State control in which "law enforcement" has taken a leading role for decades. Violence influences artistic creativity by not only affecting the way of life and material conditions of cultural production but also by bearing on the collective imaginary, penetrating the social world, and imperiling its citizens. Violence manifests itself when the State fails to safeguard human rights, neglects the distribution of natural resources and the implementation of social justice.

No one has made a more important contribution to an understanding of the necropolitical landscape than Sayak Valencia with her characterization of political, economic, and social systems as "gore capitalism," a regime that brutalizes bodies and devastates lives using its resources to wield authority, generate fear, and turn power into spectacle.[4] Likewise, Rossana Reguillo and José Manuel Valenzuela have worked on similar topics for decades, offering insight into youth culture, which is well represented in Melchor's work, and on the themes of the border and narco culture that resurface in Herrera's.[5] In the same way that this materiality is translated into the proliferation of corpses, mutilations, kidnappings, and rapes, late capitalism, supported by neoliberal politics, also imposes itself through epistemic models that obfuscate social conscience, naturalize aggression, and legitimize impunity. We can demarcate Felix Guattari's "existential territories" according to these parameters. The experience suppresses emotion, images, and ways of conceiving of social and communal life and then reemerges in the symbolic register of literature, the cadences of language and the images that make the unspeakable visible.

The three authors I address in this book pay constant attention to the body as the space where the social contract, social control, desire, sacrifice, and the onrush of violence are all concentrated. Violence here is both systematic and structural, criminal, and employed by the subject in a transgressive act of self-destruction or self-sacrifice. Nevertheless, the body is also the repository of contradictory and subtle emotions, of volcanic and devastating passions, of repressed feelings and incurable frustration, of unremitting struggle and resistance. Images of the body multiply in the writing of these three authors. In Herrera's work, we encounter the nomadic and border body, vulnerable to violence or contagion, obfuscated by sex, or undertaking a mythical journey, a body that seeks redemption, or is sacrificed with impunity in the mines in the service of foreign capital. In Melchor's unrelenting writing, we also encounter the multiplying body, sunk into perversion and promiscuity in permanent search of the moment when the senses are dulled and the world switches off, subsumed into malevolence, where the collective unconscious and its subliminal forms invade life. Finally, in Luiselli's texts, we encounter the body of the child migrant, imagined, or recreated from testimonials, fatally injured in the same lands that were wrested from their ancestors, who dwells in rumors or stories. This is the shadow-body, a ghost unto itself that populates the crevices of the present.

All of this occurs in different linguistic manifestations, like the tributaries of a single river that lead to the multiple waterways of literature that absorb them, combine them, and release them—exuberant and independent—into global spaces. Slang, regionalisms, figures of colloquial speech, literary words, influences from other languages, childhood idioms, neologisms, quotations, curse words together with terms from ancient languages all find their way into dialogues, descriptions, and narrative developments, creating spaces of lexical and semantic convergence that conceptualize their issues and linger in the collective imaginary. A similar operation occurs with scenes that dramatize the movements and speeches of singular characters who remain with the reader long after they finish the book and who become incorporated into the rich Mexican repertoire of unforgettable and unerring paper beings that resist classification and exposition.

Modernity, patriarchy, marginality, violence, consumerism, instrumental rationality, productivity, and necro-aesthetics are all some of the concepts that these three authors contribute to the political, philosophical, and poetic explorations of our time. Their work represents ideologemes that epitomize nuclei of meaning that we must decode because they define our way of being in the world of late capitalism. The contraction of the space/time we live in, the proliferation of virtual worlds, the simultaneity and dismantling of the structures that distributed power during modernity all present epistemic challenges and not just twenty-first century social and political divergences. There is no aesthetics without politics; every ideology is simultaneously a messianic or diabolic poetics, directed toward either life or death, but with its languages and artistic images condensed and now also digitalized, incumbent upon us to decipher. The work of the three authors studied here points us toward these shared horizons through captivating and, of course, polemical, and meticulous readings of the present.

CHAPTER 1
Yuri Herrera
A Distilled and Elliptical Art

Children's Stories: Preparing Readers

Talud and Other Stories: Telling the Tale

Diez planetas: The Science of Fiction

Testimonial Virtuosity in *El incendio de la mina El Bordo*
    Microcosms
    Human Bodies versus Legal Bodies

Trabajos del reino: First as Tragedy, then as Farce
    Tragedy, Myth, Fable, and Farce
    Axes and Paradigms
    What's in a Name?
    The Word, a Glimmer
    The *Corrido* as Social Text
    Courtly Theater: Dialogic Scenes

Señales que precederán al fin del mundo: A Voyage into Silence
    Journey as Paradigm
    Word, Language, Time, Writing: Symbolic Displacements
    Becomings
    Tradition/Modernity and the Function of Myth
    "We, the Barbarians": From Enunciated to Enunciation

La transmigración de los cuerpos: "Symbolic Exchange and Death"
    Mediation and Mandate
    El Alfaqueque and "The Accursed Share"
    Social Space and the Place of Death
    Body as Commodity
    Community/Immunity

Born in 1970 in Actopan, Hidalgo, Yuri Herrera embarked on his literary career at an early age, writing experimental short stories on topics related to science fiction, power, and national identity. The prizes and awards that Herrera has won up to now demonstrate that his originality and virtuosity have not escaped national and international notice.[1] Carefully rooted in popular culture and in the language of the sociocultural environments with which his literature engages, his style has piqued the global imagination, earning him a place in the transnational market and in the academic world in Latin America, Europe, and the US. Positioning his aesthetics in the symbolic territory of transnationalized Mexican literature while simultaneously distancing himself from stereotypical engagements with themes of drug trafficking and violence, Herrera lays out a sophisticated and lyrical poetics in which his localism avoids folkloric touches. The spaces, subjectivities, and symbolic processes that characterize Herrera's work emerge in a variety of representation styles ranging from science fiction to myth, from *testimonio* to fictionalized social and biographical themes, where imagination and memory become indistinguishable. Herrera's linguistic mastery does not overwhelm or besiege the reader. His use of ellipses, hesitation, silences, and suggestions keep the reader on tenterhooks throughout a self-assured and alluringly meted out, contained, and palimpsestic narrative.

In my opinion, until now Yuri Herrera's work has had at least two definitive impacts on the field of narrative and literary criticism not only in Mexico but also in Latin America. Firstly, he has elevated creative writing to a level that few authors of his or previous generations have attained. Secondly, he has called into question the critical and theoretical analytical models that have faltered in recent years in their attempt to insert texts that have come about precisely as a rejection of previous understandings of writings and the role of literature in a global cultural context dominated by audiovisual media into familiar and usually hackneyed or stereotypical paradigms. These mismatches are evident not only in relation to Herrera's work but also, more generally, in their engagement with the work of other writers who began their publishing career in the seventies and eighties. However, Herrera's writing offers the clearest example of these discrepancies. For the most part, critical engagement with his work has been limited to simple commentary, textual interpretation, or the application of conventional critical models that are insufficient to deal with the material under analysis.

For decades, modern understandings of literature revolved around movements or styles that served to classify heterogeneous materials by sorting them into predictable and restrictive categories. Among these, the question of realism in all its varieties, including magical realism and dirty realism, is particularly relevant. Something similar occurs with subgenres such as the *novela negra* or the detective novel, science fiction, melodrama, and *testimonio*, which are reduced to a series of formulas and mechanisms. Many of these conceptions of literature are based on their fidelity to objective details or define themselves through their divergence from the mimetic pact, taking the perception of what is exterior to the subject as their point of reference, as if materiality were not interiorized and (con)founded in our inner life.

Critical orientations previously used to assess Yuri Herrera's work have frequently emerged as inadequate templates for tackling it beyond a superficial identification with some of its features. Subsuming it into the categories of border literature or literature of violence or necrowriting can offer only tentative, obvious, and unevenly salient understandings of his style and literary motifs and places reductive pressure on texts that go beyond the aforementioned templates. Thus, critics have resorted to repetitive comments, paraphrase, clichés and to citing from reviews or interviews, avoiding a deep engagement with an author who clearly stands out in the field of Hispanic letters.

Herrera's excellence comes chiefly from the degree of aesthetic and ideological refinement of the issues that his narrative assumes and the mechanisms with which he chooses to develop them. In discussing how he distills his intensely precise and aesthetically powerful forms of literary representation into his work, we find repeated instances that lead us to 1) a deeply felt observation of the social question and its conceptual elaboration; and 2) an observation of the social that goes from the conceptual level to an interiorized or figured form that becomes part of the collective imaginary. By way of an example, we find the movement from the experience of a multifaceted border culture and its real and symbolic negotiations to the way in which such experience is socially conceptualized through ideas and opinions about violence, the north/south contrast, and the impact of gender and race in frontier spaces, etc. In contrast to many writers who draw on the realm of the social through information gathered from reports on past or current events, journalism, and popular opinion, Herrera incorporates this first level of understanding and interpretation into his work thus focusing on the second phase of this process. This instance corresponds to the form in which concepts and experiences of the border, its communities, its social organization etc., are appropriated at a symbolic level, crystallized into myths, legends, folkloric tales, and anecdotal or invented narratives of border crossing. For Herrera, the relationship that these materials display with different aspects of Mexican history is more significant.[2] In my view, Yuri Herrera operates exclusively at a level in which empirical, experiential, conceptual, ideological elements have been reduced and subsumed into a repository of knowledge, beliefs, and images that constitute the political and cultural Mexican unconscious at both the regional and national level. His work represents a process of distillation that, as with a good liqueur, incorporates key ingredients that then dissipate, remaining only as an echo or memory, both present and spectral, which cedes the foreground to the final product.

Just as the direct experience of conflictive Mexican reality retreats from the foreground—while still being internalized—Herrera also subsumes official forms of perceiving and interpreting national history and society into his decantation process. Serving as plankton that nourishes the texts without necessarily appearing on the narrative's terse surface, he critically assimilates elements originating in the discourse of power, as well as in the elaborations of the mass media, in the materials provided by cultural history or in the techniques extracted from Latin American literary history (vestiges of Borges, echoes of Rulfo). In my view, Herrera does not engage with Mexican history and reality per se, but rather with the aesthetic and ideological crystallizations inspired by the Mexican political and social realities found on the outskirts of big cities. Herrera dwells in marginal, border, and in-between territories in which a mythical and fictitious culture flourishes and in which everyday life is inseparable from belief and fantasy. In such articulations, there is no distinction between invention and experience, so closely intertwined are the two. Herrera's writing retrieves the indistinguishable contours of individual and collective subjectivity, revealing a dimension in which elements of modernity, tradition, the vernacular and the foreign, the urban and the rural intermingle and mutually impact each other. In some cases, Yuri Herrera's fiction delivers a lightning bolt of singularity and in others a complex vision of the communal, that is, of a fortuitous conjunction of beings, places, and points of view, neither real or unreal, but instead purely possible, virtual, and dazzling, which come together in the literary chronotype.

Given the refinement of socio-political and cultural elements present in Herrera's works, the question of mediation acquires specific importance both in the traits his characters possess as well as in novelistic scenes and situations. Intermediation dramatizes the processes of social transformation that inform the use of plot, collective avatars and *becomings* that he mobilizes in the text. Through this method, his fictional world becomes a dynamic, autonomous, hybridized, and unique space/time continuum. Lobo, Makina and Alfaqueque, key characters in Herrera's first 3 novels, serve as connective links between otherwise disconnected territories. Each of his plots places an emphasis on these intermediate positionalities, providing not only a specific and unexpected perspective on fictional events and situations, but also underscoring the importance of intermediate and marginal spaces as cognitive interstices per se. These spaces promote a type of *border gnosis*, a displaced and border knowledge that those who, from a peripheral location and specific viewpoint, perceive and operate upon an imagined reality. In my opinion, these displacements constitute one of the distinctive contributions and traits of Herrera's literary works.

CHILDREN'S STORIES: PREPARING READERS

Two children's books form an alternative part of Yuri Herrera's narrative production. In them, we see the convergence of his interest in popular culture, comic strips and illustrations, as well as the relationship between affect and knowledge, and his vision of Mexican society as a space of strong historical-anthropological density that eliminates the possibility of reducing the national question to a single aspect. *¡Éste es mi nahual!* (This is my Nahual) is a comic book illustrated by Humberto Aguirre ("Jans") that tells the story of a lost child who encounters a magical being who then offers him protection throughout his life.[3] On the back of the book, Herrera describes the story in the following terms:

> This is the story of Lucio, a kid who loved comic strips, spicy salsa, and running like the wind. Lucio didn't have much to worry about, until one day, when he wasn't paying attention, he gets lost in the city. To try and find his way home he calls upon a magical being to help him. And so begins an adventure in which he finds a new way of seeing the world.[4]

Intended for children between the ages of approximately four and nine, the book features colorful and humorous images that visually narrate the story alongside his lively and agile writing. Neither the visual or written storylines takes primacy over the other but are instead complementary, relating a story that optimistically implies that every child can feel supported by a presence that's only visible to them if they believe in it and that is there to care for him or her when things get tough.

¡Éste es mi nahual! describes Lucio's happy discovery of a magical being, a dog in his case, that will guide him onto the right path. As relayed to him by his grandfather, belief in the existence of a nahual is presented as a historical and cultural legacy passed from generation to generation, acquiring the force of urban legend in modern times. The *nahual*, also known in Mesoamerica as a *nagual* or *nawal*, is a being with magical powers that can transform into an animal to influence the lives of human beings for both good and bad according to its nature. In the form it assumes, the *nahual* behaves as a sort of other "I," revealing itself to the person it protects with disguises or shape shifting appearances that obscure its identity. Supposedly, everyone is assigned a *nahual* from birth (like the "guardian angel" of the Christian tradition who cares for and protects a designated person). The *nahual* also endows its charge with a special power, sharpening his or her senses, or bestowing a special attribute upon him or her with which to navigate life. Pre-Hispanic in origin, so-called *nagualismo* is connected to shamanic powers and rituals, establishing a belief that not only connects different historical and cultural periods but also different life forms (human and animal) and helps to configure a holistic vision of the universe. The book describes Lucio's adventures when he is lost as he searches for his *duende* to help get him out of trouble. Some of his encounters (a dove that becomes multicolored to cheer up a little girl, a lizard that scares an abusive man by getting under his clothes) provide humorous interludes that promote the idea of justice and the protection of children. Accessible and practical, the story is both didactic and comforting.

Five years later in 2012, Herrera published a second children's book, this time aimed at older children between ten and thirteen. Featuring the work of illustrator Patricio Betteo, Herrera's book *Los ojos de Lía* (Lia's Eyes) constitutes an attempt to interpret social and political contemporary Mexican topics for children.[5] At stake in this challenging task is the creation of a literary pact that, adapted to the expectations and possibilities offered by this specific and complex sector of the reading public, still allows for the channeling of problems and scenarios that are hard to grasp, even for adults. Additional challenges include the processes of meaning production specific to this type of literature given that the articulation of intellectual, social, and political content must take into consideration the development of affect as well as a limited and still-developing infantile collective experience. The theme of

Los ojos de Lía is violence, specifically its impact on the subjectivity of young people who witness the transformation of their world through situations and processes they struggle to comprehend and to which they are unwilling observers. Noteworthy here are Herrera's efforts to communicate how acts of violence are ingrained in social reality and how they invade and destroy daily life. Young people's atomized world is the result of the materialization of their imaginations through their exposure to the breakdown of idealized models of social order, family harmony, and community operations. At this level of their development, children seem to have lost their *nahuals* and instead find themselves vulnerable to the harshness of "uncivil society."

In analyzing this book, Christian Sperling situates his reading directly within the Mexican literary national market, making direct reference to the representation of trauma in the production of meaning.[6] In this sense, the question of violence as a symbolic commodity presents an inevitable introduction to the disintegration of the social fabric, and the impact that these processes bring to the subject. The problem of how to educate and even inform children about these extreme situations is enormously relevant to the fields of education, the media, arts, and parenting. As Sperling observes, one of the merits of Herrera's story is its semiotic value in visually illustrating a phenomenon that is not only conceptual but also demands the absorption of an explicit and grotesque version of reality. In addition, the story engages primarily with Lía's psychological and emotional transformation as she becomes aware of the changes taking place in public spaces, with events encroaching upon her social circle and affecting her personally. The story demonstrates how children process violent incidents as if they were films, finding humor in some of the most lurid details. In this way, young people psychologically and emotionally adapt to narratives that radically modify their daily reality. The manifestation of trauma via this fragmentation of the domestic sphere, in which everything hitherto considered as pertaining to the family shatters into pieces, shows the breakdown of social values and sensitivity and their replacement with catastrophe, danger, the fragmentation of the world, emotional dispersion, and the overbearing presence of spectral symbols that reinforce the constant proximity of death. Sperling categorizes Herrera's story as a "therapeutic narrative" since the trauma at the heart of the text is overcome at the end, when the experience of violence appears to have been processed.[7]

Proposing an integrated solution is problematic, as it appears to validate the status quo. As Sperling points out, in *Los ojos de Lía*, a circular narrative brings the girl back to where she started, reinstating her stability.[8] The viability of such a solution is, of course, open to debate, but what better alternative exists for children at the age of the text's target audience? As Sperling explains, Mexican narrative has tried out a series of alternatives (madness, silence, a breakdown in memory, the disintegration of the subject, the "black page").[9] Nowadays, we find ourselves confronted with the challenge of representing the unrepresentable, and of integrating into daily life what we cannot integrate into the known experience of daily life. While never harmonious, the latter has begun to be tolerated. Similar questions have been raised in general around the topic of trauma (the Holocaust, slavery, rape, grief, death, torture etc.), or situations that surpass representational capacity both in terms of physical suffering as well as the harm they cause to the subject's emotional and intellectual structure. In the case of young people, perhaps the only thing to which we can realistically aspire is to act to radically transform politics and the political and raise people's threshold of suffering so, as during wartime when people learn to live with tragedy without necessarily accepting its existence, they can better withstand the onslaught of a wholesale necro-social situation. We must put into place psychological defense mechanisms that permit survival but that also are cognizant of the risk of normalizing horror and of extending society's threshold of suffering as it loses contact with human principles. The representation of violence in the media and the exploitation of its grotesque and excessive nature (condensed into the commercial formula "if it bleeds it sells") speaks to information's ethical problem of how the popular imagination is configured. Sperling questions whether a similar use of commercialized violence is not present in Herrera's story since the book takes the phenomenon of violence in the juvenile imaginary as its organizing principle.[10]

Herrera's story ends on an idealized and "therapeutic" note that allows the girl to cope with the present and perhaps prepare herself for what might happen in the future. However, for the author, this ending is not a definitive response to crisis nor a way of confronting trauma. These themes require a deep social, political, psychological, and emotional engagement. So, *Los ojos de Lía* presents young people with an initial introduction to the theme of violence and promotes a sustained family discussion around the most pressing aspects of the ongoing crisis with which Mexico and the wider world are struggling. Interestingly, the story engages with a series of topics that the author's novels will explore in more depth, more sophistication and in multiple registers. These include how to best translate social experiences to the symbolic register along with the profound disconnect experienced by the public sphere in all its manifestations. These include the organization and role of the "ideological apparatus of the State," communitarian narratives, and instances that demand a political reinvention and consequently a social rearticulation of the social foundations that, at this point, are unimaginable.

TALUD AND OTHER STORIES: TELLING THE TALE

Herrera wrote the short stories brought together under the title *Talud* over a period of several decades beginning in 1987, publishing them in different Mexican magazines and newspapers.[11] With his growing popularity, these first youthful writings offer an opportunity to glimpse certain aspects of his work's thematic and compositional development. The book's title refers to a pre-Hispanic architectural style that features sloping panels that rest on vertical planes, typical of the construction of pyramids, temples, and buildings from Teotihuacán and other Mesoamerican regions. The reference forges a cultural connection between Herrera's stories and the time and space that speaks both to Mexico's dense historicity as well as the texts' own architecture. Both wide-ranging and brief, the stories collected in *Talud* thematize different aspects of Mexican popular culture, demonstrated through references to beliefs, linguistic forms, regional customs, and domestic rituals. Herrera's characters possess a common and constant striving for material betterment and personal fulfillment that detaches them from the boundaries of reality and propels them toward a dream state. Concentric circles develop from Herrera's depiction of daily life, from which we can perceive the blurred horizons of possibility. Frequently overwhelmed by frustration and lack, his characters channel all their thoughts and actions in the direction of this dream.[12] Herrera's plots are simple, and the short tales do not engage in character development. From these bare outlines of personalities and social roles, some of the stylistic traits that characterize his later work emerge: the provision of minimal information to the reader, who must grasp situations and moods for him or herself; the economical use of literary devices; the rejection of hackneyed images; a preference for working-class figures who live outside of big cities and for the labyrinths that the imagination concocts to offset the harshness of reality. The affective world takes priority over all others and poses a series of questions such as How do we distinguish love from madness? (as in the story "El hilo de tu voz." The thread of your voice); What is the difference between a *luchador* and a vigilante? ("Las llaves secretas del corazón," The secret keys to the heart); What darkness dwells in the heart of the common man? ("Por el poder investido en mí," By the power invested in me). Many of his stories can be summed up with an almost elemental question that gets to the heart of the story, and which serves as a fictional way of reflecting on human nature and social interaction.

Herrera's stories take a gamble on the reader's identification with the feelings and habitat of common experience, that is, with a non-dominant social stratum where subjects bereft of political or economic power and possessing only modest symbolic capital dwell. In these social environs, conventional concepts regarding power and the family, customary definitions of success and failure, human interactions shaped by habit and unsuccessful relationships between individuals and institutions constitute collective experiences that the writer processes in idiosyncratic ways. In other words, from his earliest stories, Herrera brings to bear the relevance of both individual and collective behaviors, ideas, and values in which his characters' singularity and their unique subjective forms and socialization are embodied. These ideological ways of understanding and acting within a given social space find a particularly productive territory for exploration and poetic representation in the theme of social self-recognition. It is precisely in this intersection of public and private space where a series of social models crystalize, expressing both directly and indirectly the myth of modern Mexican-ness, the legacy of Aztlán, pre-Hispanic traditions, popular beliefs, collective rituals, the behaviors and values of the community, ideas about the border, the vision of el Norte, political power, and the importance of the family, individuality, and society.

In the twelve short stories that make up *Talud* there is an irony informed more by humor and suspicion than simply acerbity, although the latter is also present in some cases, thus revealing more about the observer than the observed reality. People's capacity to believe, to search, to throw themselves into situations that lead inevitably to misfortune and unease, provides fertile ground not for a self-important exploration of human nature in all its supposed universality, but rather in the particularity and contingence that flourishes in marginalized communities and peripheral areas completely lacking in any privilege except that which allows imagination and desire to fly unfettered. Like Romero in the story entitled "Por el poder investido en mi" Herrera's characters know that "si algo hace perder el tiempo es la esperanza" (nothing is a bigger waste of time than hope).[13] Standing before a couple of newly-weds, the same character thinks: "Ponen los ojos en blanco ... como si el matrimonio no fuera un camino sin desviaciones hacia el odio mutuo" (they roll their eyes ... as if marriage was anything else but a straight road to mutual hatred).[14] When confronted with the spectacle of daily life, the narrator can analyze social performances as if they were a funhouse mirror, while failing to realize that he is the most pathetic and out of place of all.

At times, brief glimmers foreshadow the style that Herrera's novels will take to a level the short stories cannot achieve. At the beginning of "El origen de las especies" (Origin of the species) Herrera evokes a gloomy setting: "Más que el catre o el bulbo con manchas hepáticas colgando del techo, lo que más lo deprimía era la elaborada carpetita de plástico sobre el buró" (even more than the cot or the liver-spotted bulb hanging from the ceiling, the most depressing thing was the embroidered plastic folder on the bureau).[15] Perceptions and subjectivities come together in minimalist descriptive sketches that describe the nature of a place assumed to be mediocre, isolating and unwelcoming and that imprints itself also on the person who dwells in this no-man's land: "Por el rabillo del ojo pudo ver de nuevo la sonrisa torva que ponía el agente Félix cuando no lo miraban de frente: como si desapareciera todo él y sólo quedaran sus colmillos afilados y brillantes resplandeciendo ante el sufrimiento del mundo" (From the corner of his eye he again spied the grim smile that Agent Felix wore when you didn't look at him directly: as if he his being disappeared and all that remained were his sharp and sparkling canines, gleaming in the face of the world's suffering).[16] In a rapid-fire prose that explores a sensibility broken down by emotional frustration, "El hilo de tu voz" succeeds in transmitting both anxiety and obsession. Interior reality imposes itself upon common experience and communication becomes saturated with obstacles beyond which the subject withers away alone, inflamed by a possibility that is out of reach. Traversing the story's meagre pages, fragility is at bursting point, encountering the reader at the very border where dream and hallucination converge.

Symbolizing the ambiguous identity of subjects who are caught between social acceptance and a need to fit in that results in their depersonalization, the transformations that the characters or the fictional situations undergo in Herrera's work are one of its strongest aspects. We find an imaginary lover who becomes a real attacker ("El hilo de tu voz"); the protagonist of "Los otros" (The others) who surrenders to destabilizing jealousy; the wrestler who becomes a secret vigilante and hunts down abusers; the liminal state of someone living both as a zombie and an anxious adolescent in "Los mejores años de su muerte" (The best years of his death). Their unstable in-between positioning exemplifies the crisis of crystallized and rigid forms of modern identity where subjectivity finds itself under pressure and ends up shattering interpersonal relationships. In this regard, "La decadencia de la familia Wilde" (The decline of the Wilde family) focuses on how a family's potential lineage influences the invisible routes that will determine their place in society.

"Los andamios paralelos" (Parallel scaffolds) is one of the most ambitious of the stories in this brief collection. Clearly drawing inspiration from

Jorge Luis Borges, it explores the ontological breakdown of reality and artificiality that facilitates an exploration of alternative temporalities and possible futures. The story's very execution, its exploratory Borgesian language and structure makes it effective. Incorporating the Argentine master's traits ("La historia era absurda, pero algo en su extravagancia le confería una virtud verosímil de la que carecen los cuentos de borrachos" [the story was absurd, but something in its extravagance imbued it with the verisimilitude of the stories that drunks tell]), its reworking allows Mexican-ness to naturally surface, making what could have been parodic into an example of intertextuality.[17] The story takes place in a *pulquería* named El Reloj de Arena and, without dominating the plot, it incorporates a reworking of the topic of the aleph and some autobiographical references. Except for a superfluous last paragraph, the story offers an incisive demonstration of narrative skill where brevity and lyricism combine to produce a pristine and intriguing narrative of visual and verbal images. Less effective, to my mind, are stories like "Alegoría de la biblioteca" (An allegory of the library), where the echoes of Borges produce a more trifling tale than those previously mentioned, or "Poemas de las formas intermoleculares" (Poems of Intermolecular Forms) whose creative structures are less elevated than those of Herrera's more significant narratives. Stories such as "Las llaves secretas del corazón," "Los otros," "Por el poder investido en mi" "El lúser" (The Loser), "Augurios" (Omens), and "La fiesta del Sábado" (Saturday's Party) engage with male subjectivity and human connections, revealing masculinity to be a vulnerable condition always on the brink of aggression or self-destruction, and functioning as a generally failed way of negotiating social recognition.

Herrera's "science fiction" stories explore aspects of alternative perceptions of reality with less success than "Los andamios paralelos." "Ficha técnica" (Datasheet), a short text published in 2014 in the literary magazine *Buen Salvaje*, plots other dimensions of existence and feeling that allow individuals to experience paranormal phenomena and promote a rethinking of the human condition ("exnormales"). In "Poemas de las formas intermoleculares" the liquid corporality of extraterrestrial beings becomes a part of everyday life. In other stories, Herrera evokes images that possess metaphorical value—garbage, for example, as in "Los últimos" (The Last Ones), promoting devastating visions of a consumed world: "el mar se había comido la tierra y la basura se había comido el mar" (the sea had eaten the land, and the garbage had eaten the sea) and where all that remains is waste, lack, and loneliness.[18]

Herrera uses topics such as dehumanization, cosmic isolation, and the use of anomaly as alternative ways to access different levels of reality, as well as animalization and animism to forge new routes toward spaces and experiences that go beyond the norm. Yet, in my opinion, and as his excellent later work demonstrates, we do not encounter his gift as an acute observer of both the real and the imaginary here. Apart from a few isolated examples, the texts gathered in *Talud* and other stories from the same period appear lightweight and juvenile even though each of them contains a glimmer of the polished skill and sensitivity he will later display in his novels. If we consider them as testing ground for the literary devices he will employ in his major works, the short stories give us a taste of some of their fundamental aspects, such as his constant engagement with the dynamics of transformation and transition as well as in the evolutions that expose human nature and its tenuous ties to other life forms, including supernatural beings.

The metamorphosis of a minor *lucha libre* wrestler into an anonymous vigilante, the individuals who are forced to disguise themselves as animals in public, the hierarchical mutation of humans into animals in "Los objetos" and other similar stories destabilize our certainties about the world and open the door to doubt, ambiguity, and confusion. He does not address these aspects in depth, as if merely raising them in the tentative and provisional narrative of the short story were enough. The same can be said of "El mirador de muertos" (Lookout of the dead), a tale that turns on the relationship between life and the act of narration or, in other words, on the idea of how the human is made visible, something that the short story symbolizes through the idea of invisible bodies, and of stories that offer a postmortem vision of the subject.

Herrera imagines the relationship between identity and narrative as an unstable bond constantly open to negotiation. Self-awareness and social interaction are both closely linked to desire but his engagement with this impulse capitulates to the genre's brevity and the narrator's angry tone. Characters, frequently male, come up against social conventions, hierarchies, and their own limits, constantly confronting small daily setbacks that speak to human vulnerability in the face of society and the self. "The Law Is the Law" demonstrates the corruption of police power; "Un arte de monstruos" (An art of monsters) depicts artistic creativity as the product of unusual sources as well as the violence that consumes individuals. The world associated with science fiction provides a space for Herrera's rather trivial exploration of transcendence and he depicts the border between life and death with a light humor that the reader can address by engaging thoughtfully but not necessarily seriously with the texts or by treating them as mere entertainment. For Herrera, humor:

is, in the first place, a manifestation of skepticism regarding our understanding of rules, language, and our emotions; it's a critical exercise and it's a game that calls into question how we understand that which we call normality (social, linguistic, sexual etc.). In this sense, it's a question of not only looking critically at what we're making fun of or with what we're playing but also investigating ourselves, finding out what seriousness lives inside us and using it for play.[19]

On several occasions, Yuri Herrera has described how he believes the imagination works in present day contexts, conceiving of it as a mechanism for social transformation that undergoes a process of defamiliarization from our perceptions and certainties. Herrera, perhaps, sees the imagination as an apparatus—in the Foucauldian sense of the *dispositif*—that sanctions a form of power that can subvert reality and colonize it with perspectives that de-automatize how we interpret *what is*, subjecting it to a scrutiny of possibilities and alternatives that innovatively mobilize social and political energy. In "El músculo del futuro" (Future muscle), Herrera indicates that:

> The imagination is a break with order, the order of external things, and the conception of one's own order; the imagination is the reconciliation of the world with our own fears and desires; the imagination is an intimate declaration of sovereignty that we can all make over the universe. What we call reality is not an unmovable object but rather the material we mold with our imagination. Every place in the world is just waiting over and over for us to give it a new name, like new human beings do.[20]

Imagination, then, is an appropriation of the world, making it part of our own internal reality, not as surrender but instead in the spirit of someone who takes possession of reality and molds it according to his or her desires and needs, eschewing the passivity and fatalism implied in accepting its premises as ontological and determining qualities. This does not imply a privatization of the concept of the real based on individualism or the solipsism of the subject, nor the stubborn denial of the circumstances that the medium imposes upon us, but rather the possibility of a new way of seeing that dismantles the mechanisms of power and false conscience and instead suggests alternative routes. The imaginaries that we share indicate a collectivization of symbolic forms as a means of common and eventually transformative action over the social, natural, and subjective scene.

If fantasy, like magic, superstition, or mysticism, can act as a form of evasion or subterfuge that eludes reality, it can also be directed toward the imagination of new forms of social organization and subjective interconnection. In this way, Herrera utilizes fantastic characters, situations, and settings (strange, unreal, supernatural, anomalous, paranormal) to shift normative visions. In the literary chronotype, normative visions are bisected by strange and dissonant elements that dismantle hegemonic discourse along with the regularized ways we generate meaning. Herrera thus carries out certain incursions that intersect historical discourse ("Alegoría de la biblioteca") and the fictional worlds of Borges and Cortázar ("Casa tomada") and permits discreet echoes of Juan Rulfo's universe to permeate his terse and explosive prose. Herrera imbues his stories with questions of the strange, the hallucinatory, or the fantastic and an odd and unsettling quality, which facilitates a turn toward reality, i.e., an angle from which common perspectives are deformed, revealing improbable dimensions and indescribable ways of shaping the "known" world.

DIEZ PLANETAS: THE SCIENCE OF FICTION

At various moments, Yuri Herrera has referred to the theme of alienation in the face of language and the innovative and transgressive power of the word. In an interview with Carmen de Eusebio, he offers a point of entry to the theme of exile that he presents the reader in the short story collection, *Diez planetas* (*Ten Planets*), through fantastical situations and characters.[21] The shift in literary quality from *Talud* to *Diez planetas* is striking and can be attributed to an improvement in the sharpness of the diction that reveals the literary progress Herrera achieved in the two-year interval between collections.[22] This literary maturity is also displayed in the selection of themes and in the lyrical depth that mitigates the banality of science fiction mainstays such as the weird or the unusual. In Herrera's hands, the word finds new literary life, giving the impression that something *extra*ordinary is making its way into reality. He creates a new artefact through linguistic mechanisms that generate signifiers, images, and alternative worlds. As an intervening element in the dominant versions of reality, as well as in the definition of the political, language allows for a deep penetration into the very nature of knowledge and into the exhaustion of interpretative paradigms. For Herrera, words are events, that is, an always-extraordinary occurrence that denotes a *happening*, a subtle or spectacular transformation of both daily life and the symbolic universe.

The fantasy element of science fiction ratifies literature's capacity to insert strange and anti-normative elements into reality, confirming "la idea de que cada personaje es tan extraordinario como un marciano, que cada situación precisa su propio planeta, y que cada amanecer debe ser visto con la fascinación con la que contemplamos las estrellas"[23] (the idea that everyone is as remarkable as a Martian, that each situation needs its own planet, that each dawn should be greeted with the same fascination with which we study the stars). This work of defamiliarization is one of the genre's characteristics that nowadays draws not only on the uncertainty caused by the collapse of the so called "grand narratives" but also on the advance of the posthuman in different areas of philosophy, biotechnology, and social organization in the context of globalization. Thus, although the very nature of literary construction consists of inserting the imaginary into daily life, the use of the fantastic applied here to dominions impacted by technology or by unpredictable spatio-temporal coordinates intensifies this effect, symbolizing the estrangement of the world and allegorizing the search for new horizons of reality and knowledge unfettered by ordinary ways of perceiving.

The characters and situations that set the tone in *Diez planetas* fall within the category of so-called "soft science fiction," whose theme of technological innovation and futuristic elaboration Herrera presents without much scientific engagement. In my opinion, the way the genre has been and is being reconceived by Latin American authors reinforces nostalgia for the great masters from H. G. Wells (*Time Machine*, 1895, and *Invisible Man*, 1897) and Italo Calvino (*Cosmicomics*, 1965) to the scientific lyricism of Ray Bradbury (*Fahrenheit 451*, 1953), and from there to the dazzling imagination of Stanislaw Lem's *Solaris* (1961) and finally to more recent works by Haruki Murakami and Marcel Theroux. Also worthy of mention are authors like Isaac Asimov, whose story "Nightfall" (1941) is considered one of the best in the history of the genre.

The upheaval provoked by the weakening of modern thought has motivated a reactivation of the concepts of monstrosity and the supernatural as forms of imaginary anthropology that reconfigure notions of otherness and alienation. The reader also witnesses an apparent reengagement with questions of subjectivity. Interiority, referenced in different stories as the soul or the mind, the emotions, memory, or even bodily interiority becomes a testing ground for humanity's ability to tolerate and adapt to the acceleration, compression, and simultaneity that characterize the global world.[24] This involves not only inserting subjective and material forms into a technological world but also devising dystopic versions of a reality that has surpassed the limits of conventional realism and is resistant to cloying versions of magical realism. Confronted with the fluidity that has almost completely blurred the division between "high" culture, popular culture and mass culture, science fiction offers alternative and deregulated spaces that speak to the absence that a desacralized world presents to the collective imagination and to cultural anxiety.

Science fiction allows for the representation of previously unthinkable ways of articulating ecological, feminist, and social concerns like migration, xenophobia, and value distortion. The genre also channels expressions of disavowal, irony, and skepticism, and displays concrete critiques of a wide variety of themes like state politics, nationalism, discrimination, environmental pollution, the urban world, the acceleration of life, consumerism, and many other challenges of the contemporary world. In this way, science fiction lends itself to reflective ways of reading such as exploring utopian or prophetic ideas, reviving ancestral myths and legends, or reworking history through fictionalization.

Many decades ago, at its most ambitious, science fiction outlined the thematic contours of a genre that not only critically comprehended and confronted social reality but also foreshadowed the paths that progress would take. As a forward-looking genre, this type of literature speculated on and allegorized the contradictions and effects of scientific advancement. Opting for imaginative reality, science fiction became immersed in the themes of futurism and technology, identifying a repertoire of topics including time travel, extraterrestrial life, the existence of parallel universes, the discovery of new space/time dimensions, the conquest of the universe, the animistic connection between objects and beings, technological hybridization of human beings, the mixing of humans with other species, and postapocalyptic existence. Alternatively, these tendencies can be combined with primeval or ancestral myths that offer temporal and geocultural dimensions. Seeking to harness the relationship between humanism, science, and utopian/dystopian visions, some authors employ the genre to revisit classical antiquity where the empirical and the mythical comes together in marvelous articulations of the monstrous and the diabolical. Thomas More's *Utopia* (1516) provides an antecedent for this paradigm, where fiction and satire combine to project social and political ideals onto a non-existent world that represents the limits of the real world and signals the need for its improvement. Later, incorporating elements from psychoanalysis (Carl Jung in particular), cultural anthropology, religious thought, and scientism, syncretic versions appeared that allowed for the rethinking of social and political questions from other innovative, esoteric, anti-normative, and emancipated rationalism to classic realism. Feminism and criticism connected to queer, transgender, and other theories have productively intersected with science fiction, exploring different possibilities for reframing identities connected to gender, sexuality, and corporality, moving beyond contemporary regulations and conventions.

Contemporary science fiction, however, particularly that produced in the Hispanic world, has frequently downplayed some of the critical facets (particularly sarcasm and fantastical lyricism) that characterized some of science fiction's best examples from the nineteenth century onward. In this regard, Herrera's texts are no exception. The poeticization and social critique that inform Herrera's texts, specifically in his second collection of short stories, hovers over the strongest stories like an unfinished impulse in search of an ending.

Some of Herrera's science fiction writings seem like they are trying to escape classification and stylistic conventions, to take refuge in the fertile territory of language. Their primary focus on science's imaginative element and on reality's blurred borders appears, to my mind, rigorously distilled by Herrera in his novels, where the dismantling of limits and certainties is elliptically incorporated into plots and characters. The texts are organized around a questioning of the symbolic configuration of the world and the location of the human condition within the immeasurable confusion of universality. For their part, the novels organically incorporate the inquisitive spirit of these issues into their characters' very speech and the trajectories that detail their fictional lives. In the novels, the thematic articulation of this fictional universe's contingency empowers the aesthetic as an expressive register of human reflection and intuition.

Diez planetas brings together tales that revolve around fantastic situations of interplanetary exile, the animation of objects and intergalactic displacements with an antirealist expressiveness endowed with a level of innocence and a desire for experimentation. In many cases, this expressiveness fades during the representation of the fantastical event and in the development of the element at the center of the plot (the house that takes on human characteristics, the bacteria that leads an amazing life inside a person, etc.). Abstracting and conceptualizing the different plots, we quickly find more weighty themes. "La ciencia de la extinción" ("The Science of Extinction) portrays a nameless world where human understanding of reality is threatened by the absence of language and by memory loss.[25] In the silence, the world disappears, an idea Herrera explores in other texts (his novel *Señales que precederán al fin del mundo* [Signs that will precede the end of the world] for example), as the flipside to the centrality of language.[26] "Los conspiradores" ("The Conspirators") penetrates the identity-based antagonism that connects existence and territoriality, transforming language into an element of power that dissolves conflict since words themselves possess the potential to colonize and dominate. Language and power manifest themselves as the nucleus of the clash of civilizations, permitting a reflection on humanity from the vantage point of language. Short stories such as "El obituarita" ("The Obituarist") focus on the existence of identity theft after death in a world marked by invisibility where the value of the written word persists as an essential element of social configuration. Obituaries are ritualistic and commemorative scriptural forms as well as mechanisms of power. As they memorialize a life, they define the dead person; for this reason, souls desire to control this discourse even at the expense of appropriating the evidence that reveals the deceased's true personality.

In "El cosmonauta" ("The Cosmonaut"), Herrera revisits the act of representing subjectivity in exceptional circumstances. The story revolves around the incommensurability of truth that cannot be translated into words. The main character possesses a gift: he can read nostrils like a map that reveals any subject's network of experiences since through them breathe the remnants of the landscape within which each individual lives their life. In this way, the narrator comes to grips with a world of signs that gives the presence of the Other away through the particles that reveal moments in their lifecycle:

> A lover's fragrance, the scrape of their shoes, the stench of their desire for another person; the bile that follows an outburst, the density of being buried in a chest, the changes of landscape on the way to hide the chest, the damp stone beneath which the chest was abandoned. No matter how far the thing travels from a place, the nose hooks in and preserves its trace as if it were a coordinate.[27]

When the narrator applies his interpretative powers to the cosmonaut who possesses the secret of interplanetary experience, he reaches a limit that, in its essence, is reminiscent of the enigma posed in Borges's "El etnógrafo" ("The Ethnographer"): the existence of a truth that has been located after a long and difficult search but should remain untold.[28] "La consolidación anímica" (Consolidation of Spirits) depicts a postapocalyptic world where a desert-like planet has become an "espacio embrujado" (haunted space) where souls congregate and create all types of turmoil: "riña ectoplasmática" (ectoplasmic quarrels), "duelo de alaridos satánicos" (dueling satanic howls), "levitación ininterrumpida de muebles" (continual furniture levitation), a "madre errante en busca de sus hijos" (a wandering mother in search of her children) who encounters a poltergeist and similar circumstances in which excess must be controlled and resolved through the correct bureaucratic channels.[29] In "Los objetos" ("The Objects") Herrera explores aspects of subjectivity in automated worlds or in places where the animal and the human converge. Whether he is exploring technological interference or the porous boundaries between living things, or between living things and objects—like in Julio Cortázar's celebrated "Casa tomada"—an emotional quality persists in the stories that appears in tense and dehumanized atmospheres that suddenly find themselves imbued with life, recalling previously unthought ways of sensitivity and consciousness.

Herrera sets his short stories in contingent spaces of posthuman survival from where he projects an implicit criticism and nostalgia for the world left behind. But, as we know, even the most intrepid imagination can only rearticulate elements that form part of the subject's experience or construct absurd or shocking totalities made up of traces of his/her world that may reproduce, reverse themselves or break into fragments, but always return to history and reality: "En Marte no hay oficinas de gobierno. En Marte el Estado es más una serie de sobreentendidos que una serie de libros o de escritorios. Es la regularidad de los rituales, las reglas tácitas, las negociaciones apenas gesticuladas" (On Mars, there are no government offices. On Mars, the State is more a series of understandings than a series of books or desks. It is a matter of regular rituals, tacit rules, barely there negotiations).[30] "La otra teoría" ("The Other Theory") details a version of the earth as a flat entity that exists only to feed its Creator—a mouth ready to devour it, or a dragon's eye who can wipe out the universe in one blink. Herrera's relativist ways of understanding existence, truth, experience, and human life decenter our long-held certainties and values and replace them with mysterious, ironic, futile, or poetic possibilities. In "Los últimos" ("The Last Ones"), Herrera explores the theme of planetary desolation, extraterrestrial life, and solitude through the relationship of space and place, where bodies seek shelter in nooks and crannies and life clings to tiny spaces in a universe devoid of hope. Similarly, in "Músculo vivo" ("Living Muscle"), fantastic beings emerge from imaginative combinations of recycled materials and minor events stimulate the posthuman world. In the works, the universe's transformations inevitably engender desolation and silence. Unusual forms of self-consciousness survive, making the testimony of the witness (human, object, or microscopic element) the vantage point from where to recount the end of the Anthropocene. We find a similar ending in "Catálogo de la diversidad humana" ("Inventory of Human Diversity"), where questions of taxonomy, language, and names bring echoes of Borges and interrogate the reliability of categories and identities.

In these short stories, communication appears as a constant theme, operating as a guide to intersubjective relationships and as a key that opens the door to knowledge and gives meaning to both sensibility and reason. The latter is at the center of "Anexo 15, numeral 2. La exploración del Agente Probii" ("Appendix 15, Number 2: The Exploration of Agent Probii"), where the disappearance of language as shared patrimony combines with the transformation of "reality" on an unstable planet where human survivors have sought refuge. Each person speaks to themselves in their own language, unfurling it like a fan made up of syntactical, lexical, and phonic forms that transform communication into a Babelic convergence of symbolic registers disconnected from words. Copulation is the lingua franca and from it "se convienen relaciones, se organizan fiestas, se revelan secretos, se heredan recetas, se detallan instrucciones" (relationships are formed, parties organized, secrets revealed, instructions given).[31] Individual language constitutes an impassable space, an act of espionage or a desire for demonic possession that takes Agent Probii's life. The expansion plans of the ninth planet's residents seem to foreshadow the imposition of orgies as a form of universal communication.

If linguistic and other forms of communication are common in the stories that make up *Diez planetas*, so too is the reflection on (re)writing as an exercise in which the role of the author is constantly called into question. The author's function is impugned, appropriated, copied, etc. through the creation of parodic versions that implicitly bring up themes of the aura and of originality. Although the ideas and the literary devices Herrera employs are not new, the persistent desire to question the role of high culture as a privileged representational space is noteworthy. "Zorg, autor del *Quijote*" ("Zorg, Author of the *Quixote*") intertwines the extra-human with literature's capacity to bridge time and cultural space. As in Borges's work, the text could potentially give rise to a deep reflexivity on questions of authorship and on the longevity of classics throughout history, although in Herrera's short story the Otherness of the unusual characters that drive the plot puts the question of poetics and the material conditions of production and dissemination of literature into perspective. The practice of literature allows for the exploration of the possibilities of existence through which Herrera frames some of the issues he raises, such as the conditions in which knowledge is produced and the nature of reality: "Zorg escribía historias de seres fantásticos encerrados en una u otra manera en los límites de su cuerpo, en límites geográficos, en límites epistemológicos" (Zorg wrote stories about fantastic beings trapped in one way or another within bodily, geographical and epistemological limits).³²

Zorg's texts engage kitsch and drama as well as hybrid forms that parody genres and thus point to their exhaustion or their historical specificity. But he directs most of his efforts to an entertaining and irreverent rewriting of *Don Quixote*, which poses the question of the possible recontextualizations of the classics, their cultural purpose, changes in their reception, and the effectiveness of established languages in a Babelic world. The character of Pirg, who "trabajaba en un cubil propagador de historias" (worked in a story producing den) initially reacts to the manuscript of the *Quijote* "un título corto, al grano, pegador" (a short and sweet title, with a kick) with a disdain that later becomes curiosity and professional interest.³³ He is worried, above all, about Don Quixote's reasons for setting out on adventures in a world that doesn't understand him:

> The easiest thing is to say that someone acts simply because he's been hurt or he's been called upon, but then a character becomes nothing more than the noise that an object produces if we touch it, and then what? Your character, on the other hand, constructs his own motives. Like when Sancho asks him why he does crazy things or if Dulcinea has given him cause to feel jealous, and Don Quixote says "There is the point . . . and that is the beauty of this business of mine; no thanks to a knight-errant for going mad when he has cause; the thing is to turn crazy without any provocation, and let my lady know, if I do this in the dry, what I would do in the moist?"³⁴

This rediscovery of Cervantes's work occurs in a decentralized context that demystifies it while reinscribing it within a textuality transformed by neologisms that defamiliarize the cultural space and de-automatize the reading of the classic work, opening it up to a new sensorium from which, nonetheless, narrative commonplaces come into play. The reader/editor (Pirg) addresses the causal relation in fiction, the way in which this principle of logic dialogs with the characters' subjectivity and with the construction of imagined worlds. The question of fiction's deterministic quality, on the one hand, and the fictional character's internal logic, on the other are central questions of Cervantes's text. This logic is inscribed within the represented world, to which the author does not belong, and whose "truths" correspond to systems with which they are incompatible. Herrera's short story alludes to other aspects that Pirg suggests about Don Quixote's horse, Rocinante, and some of the other scenes including acceptance of Zorg's suggestion of adding spaceships to the narrative since "el anacronismo [acercará el texto] al realismo sucio" (the anachronism [brings the text closer] to dirty realism).³⁵ This intervention into the classic text points to a deeper reflection on literature's survival, the loss of the aura, and the demystification of authorship. Modernity had originally connected these concepts, which, now faced with the postmodern influence of the market on the production and consumption of symbolic goods, are being reconsidered.

This story employs a methodology that also appears in other pieces of this narrative series, such as in "El cosmonauta," where the first five pages function as an unnecessary introduction to the story. The topic of the nostril as a map and the examples of what the protagonist discovers as he interprets his findings seem to belong to a different story, with a thematic center and development that could easily have gone another way. The author seems to be aware of the weak transition between the two parts when he clarifies "todo esto es para explicar qué es lo que sucedió con el cosmonauta" (all of this serves to explain what happened to the cosmonaut).³⁶ In "Zorg, autor del *Quijote*" the introduction also appears as something separate from the rest, as it includes prior events that have no bearing on the main story of the rewriting of Cervantes's text and seems to be dependent on these prior events rather than being introduced by them. In both cases, a more "humanistic" principal theme is inscribed within formulaic science fiction terms, revealing the discontinuity not as a literary device within the text but rather as a problem of literary composition. Although putting contexts and diverse symbolic elaboration into dialogue is a promising notion, it fails to work here as Herrera tries to adapt the story artificially to the conventions of the genre. We never see this internal disconnect in the novels nor can it be attributed to the genre of science fiction, which lends itself to clear-cut uses of connected themes, styles, lexical choices, etc. It seems obvious that the author is much more comfortable dealing with modern thematics than with the wide-open spaces of post-humanistic speculation.

Darko Suvin has theorized science fiction as a literature of "cognitive estrangement," inseparable from imperialism and its colonization of lands and imaginaries.³⁷ The genre began to flourish in the nineteenth century during the decades of imperial expansion, and its development can be attributed to similar colonialist objectives: the discovery and seizure of new galactic lands and spaces, the struggle for hegemony, the othering of beings deemed non-human, the usurping of resources, the glorification of the heroism of the conquistador, and the debasement of the conquered. According to Carl Freedman, science fiction as a genre is characterized by the dialectic between estrangement and cognition.[38] If the question of estrangement is located in the possibility of realities other than daily life where it questions the normalization of reality, the cognitive aspect is connected to an attempt to understand and rationalize new dimensions from their points of convergence as well as divergence from the empirical world we recognize as our own.[39] According to Suvin, if this dialectic is not present and the cognitive aspect is minimal, estrangement becomes a mere defamiliarization of reality, that is, a generic form of fantasy that avoids a deep dive into the issues it presents. In this case, science fiction becomes, as he points out, a "sub-literature of mystification."[40] According to Freedman, academia's denigration of science fiction is a consequence of its commercial popularity and of its prosaic character as well as a critical preference for more bourgeois forms of subjectivity favored by novels of different genres (realist, sentimental, historical). In contrast, science fiction is an expression of an identity crisis as well as the subject's alienating experience of deterritorialization that catapults him or her out of his or her natural habitats. At a time when objects take primacy over subjects, when space and time are compressed, when simultaneities and ruptures exist between the individual and the environment, science fiction of sufficient quality and depth can represent the loss of certainty that marks the end of modernity and the beginning of postmodernity, and the age when extreme interconnection coexists alongside alienation and the isolation of the subject.

Eric D. Smith describes science fiction as being "born from the imperialist collision of cultural identities taking as its thematic and formal substance imperialism's spatial dislocations, science fiction seems to be the ideal instrument with which to critically understand the transition from postcolonialism to globalization."[41] From this vantage point, as Smith explains, science fiction becomes a generator of "new cartographies of hope" since, in experimental terms, it explores utopian scenes in which science is emancipatory and subalternity reversible.[42] However, the genre also facilitates other operations that assimilate a postmodern ethos such as the transitoriness and transitional dynamics that are key to Herrera's work. In this regard, we should also include the representation of difference or what we might call the "vanishing point" that colors and disturbs sameness and allows for the appreciation of non-normative ways of knowledge and social existence. While modernity revolves around the formation and consolidation of identities, postmodernity consecrates and celebrates difference as a way of representing the Other and its forms of social existence.

As an academic trained not only in aesthetics but also in political science, Herrera possesses a clear understanding of the deceptiveness of power and of how ideology permeates and shapes our social fabric. In his writing, he invokes multiple types of borders that do not offer fortuitous options but rather the vindication of the concept of space-limit, laden with meaning, fundamentally hybrid, where principles of identity and cultural essentialism come under pressure. Space, the human body, affectivity, the relationship between the finite and the infinite, present and eternity, the here and there (and beyond), all represent borders (spatial, temporal, existential, organic, conceptual, etc.) that science fiction explores through images and concepts that go beyond the quotidian perception of reality. Language also operates as a border between ideas and communication, between objects and representations and between silence and legibility. Words traverse spaces and conquer territories, but they also serve as instruments for subduing collective thought, homogenizing it through false consciousness, clichés, or farcical official discourse.

In her study of Spanish-language science fiction, Yolanda Molina-Gavilán highlights the genre's multifaceted nature which, she explains, can be conceived of as a true "mitología de nuestro tiempo" (mythology of our time) from where society confronts its collective fears that would be difficult to express from the perspective of pure instrumental rationality.[43] As he demonstrates in his novels, Herrera knows that different versions of truth exist in parallel as well as convergent and divergent forms that seek support from language, images and beliefs and which respond to very different forms of the circulation and dissemination of popular knowledge. The short stories that make up *Diez planetas* display many points of access for penetrating both our society's emptiness as well as transitional intercultural processes, the conflicting coexistence of species and the theme of language as key to unlocking the mystery of the human condition and its infinite materializations.

TESTIMONIAL VIRTUOSITY IN *EL INCENDIO DE LA MINA EL BORDO*

MICROCOSMS

The chronicle *El incendio de la mina El Bordo* (*A Silent Fury: The El Bordo Mine Fire*) offers a spine-chilling account of a real event which, despite its historical distance, has consumed Yuri Herrera since he was a student.[44] In impeccable prose, the author/narrator lays out a story that hews closely to the facts but that also includes the presence, voices and stories of the miners and their families, as well as the points of view of others, such as journalists and community members, who participated in the rescue effort, the disposal of the bodies, and the drafting of reports and official accounts. The author/narrator's proximity to the facts is crucial here and turns the narrative into a type of writing in which the architect of the story, involved through his archival investigations and interviews only after the fact in an event that took place a century earlier, uncovers previously untold, displaced, or discarded versions of the tragic event. Although the author cannot position himself as a witness, his work, like his pledge of objectivity and narrative intentionality, situates him within the subgenre of testimonial literature.

Divided into eight parts ("El Bordo," "Ese día" / "That Day," "La espera" / "The Wait," "Los sobrevivientes" / "The Survivors," "El incendio de las mujeres" / "The Women's Fire," "El informe pericial" / "The Expert Report," "La fosa" / "The Grave," and "Los muchos días siguientes" / "The Many Days That Followed"), Herrera's text opens with a concise explanation of the narrative's focus: "El Bordo se incendió la mañana del 10 de marzo de 1920. Murieron, por lo menos, ochenta y siete personas" (El Bordo caught fire on the morning of March 10, 1920. At least eighty-seven people were killed).[45] His narrative reworks previous versions that were produced for different purposes. During his undergraduate studies at the UNAM, as well as during his doctorate at UC Berkeley, Herrera dove into what happened at El Bordo, studying the attendant discourses and interpretations, and analyzing the accounts and interpretations of the catastrophe in a work entitled "Los demonios de la mímesis: Textualidad de una tragedia en el México posrevolucionario" (The demons of mimesis: Textuality of a tragedy in post-revolutionary Mexico).[46] Following these earlier explorations, Herrera's chronicle was published ten years after his first novel *Trabajos del reino* had cemented him as one of the most important voices in contemporary Latin American literature. Perhaps because the book surpasses the bounds of fiction and because it connects the author to his work as a journalist, and by extension, to the history and politics of Mexico, it has not received much critical attention beyond a few small articles and reviews. However, this book in many ways offers the perfect introduction to Herrera's later works.

To begin with, this exemplary account forges an intimate connection between reality and writing, posing important questions about the way in which visions and versions of a fact, whether oral or written, achieve the status of an event through a narration that both inserts itself into the collective imaginary and modifies it. Among the issues represented in *El incendio de la mina El Bordo* we find many that will appear in the author's later works, from a variety of ideological and aesthetic perspectives. The first of these is the relationship between truth and discourse. The second pertains to the importance of intermedial events in which systems of domination are revealed through direct application, like a monstrous machine that feeds on beings who have been put into deadly motion by its gears. Thirdly, taking commonality as its epistemic priority, the narrative offers a contrast with the discourse of power, as a way of naturalizing the effects of exploitation and systemic violence at the level of popular culture. Thus, the narrative reveals the possible complicity of language, its cooptation by authoritarianism, as well as its capacity for liberation.

In official usage, language is essential for constructing the rhetoric of hegemony and for the processes of cultural institutionalization (via documents, archives, declarations etc.), it functions to organize the dispersion and the ephemeral nature of orality and delineate certain versions of the events through documentation. The power of words thus emerges along divergent lines, making language a battleground whose tensions are magnified at the social and political level. Orality captures what is immediate and spontaneous, testimonial, and anecdotic, in other words everything that makes up the history of a community, producing a provisional and ephemeral stratum that should be captured before it falls into oblivion. In this regard, *El incendio de la mina El Bordo* serves as a negotiation between both levels: it feeds on stories, opinions, and memories, testimonials, and experiences, but in order to persist and to challenge official narratives, it also retreats toward the permanence writing offers. The book therefore operates as a denunciation of a chapter of Mexican history that exposes the biopolitical strategies of capitalist modernity along with the impact they wield on the configuration of subjectivities and on the very lives of the subjects to whom they are directed.

Although the event referenced in the text occurred more than a century ago, it is engraved in the history of national infamy thanks to the memorialization efforts of people like Herrera. His new recounting of the events that led to the death of at least eighty-seven miners alongside the incalculable emotional, physical, and psychological harm suffered by others, prevents oblivion from diluting it. In "Los demonios de la mimesis" Herrera alludes to other authors who recount what happened at El Bordo and whose texts serve as antecedents for his own chronicle. One of these is his fellow Hidalgan, Rodolfo Benavides, whose *El doble nueve* (The Double Nine) of 1949 offers a faithful chronicle of the historical event but changes dates, names, and protagonists, although the principal facts of the Pachuca fire are still recognizable.[47] The principal contribution of Benavides's text is the inclusion of the testimonials that document what happened and that offer information about the miners' lives, the challenges of their work, and the subjective repercussions that this harsh labor regime had on them and their families. Herrera engages in a critical analysis of *El doble nueve*, both in terms of the characterization of the miners and that of the "gringos," the description of the different spaces and work conditions, as well as attitudes toward death. He also refers to elements of gender throughout the text. For example, in his doctoral thesis he writes:

> *El doble nueve* is a novel about men. Evil men, gringos; destroyed men, miners; despicable men, public officials. With one exception, women are in the background, scarcely outlined, presented as a group. There is no interest in their individuality since their role in the novel—even the one who is a protagonist—is clearly established: they are a symbol of purity and emotional support, a necessary element for the reproduction of social life and of men. And they are, of course, objects of desire and the source of conflict.[48]

Herrera's analysis of questions of memory, power, and representation (to mention just a few of the aspects he studies) demonstrates his clear understanding of the text's literary devices and of the intellectual and emotional effects triggered by the final literary product, something that will also be instrumental in the construction of his fictional texts. The second source used by Herrera is Félix Castillo García's unpublished manuscript, presented as "a mining tale" under the title "La quemazón de la mina del Bordo." As Herrera explains, this characterization avoids designating the events as a crime, an accident, or a tragedy and instead offers the witnesses' version of what happened including technical information such as work schedules and tasks, as well as a glossary that explains the terminology that describes specific jobs, tools, and places within the mine.

Herrera's own narration emphasizes the importance of "mediations" with regard to societal configurations. The miners are the bridge between raw material and profit, taking us back to a time when primitive accumulation created the conditions for the development and dominance of capital. As Marx makes clear, through their labor, life and profit are tightly connected and interdependent. Mining represents a form of millenarian exploitation and subjugation that, since colonial times, has levied a predatory impact on the environment and on the lives of individuals and communities. The extraction of natural resources is carried out using forms of "modern" slavery that, via the façade of salaried work, obscures the tremendous exploitation and the physical deterioration that the miners endure because of their working conditions and the lack of workplace safety, not to mention the harm caused to the environment. The miner is an example of the typical zombie-like worker referred to in *Das Capital*, exploited by the system that consumes not only his or her physical strength but also his or her emotional, psychological, and intellectual forces, free time, family life, and consciousness. Laboring for minimum wage, the miner is condemned to live in poverty and debt, inhabiting spaces of death in which his health is seriously compromised without any alternative or possibility of change. With its rigid stratification deep inside the earth, the location of the mine perfectly symbolizes human action upon nature. It represents the invasive *ethos* of the Anthropocene, the age in which humanity has irreversibly imposed itself upon the natural world, through devastating actions that affect the land, the fauna and flora as well as bodies of water, causing climatic change and transforming cycles of productivity at a planetary level. As a microcosm, the mine's spatial organization constitutes an anti-world in which the hierarchies and systems of exploitation of the world of others reproduce themselves, inverted symmetrically, victimizing those without recourse to social justice. The strata or "floors" that indicate the different levels of penetration into the earth, the underground work, the tunnels, the lack of space, clean air and water, the danger of accidents and overcrowded conditions for the workers all speak clearly to a process of dehumanization that values profit over life and the object over the subject.

The miners are treated as beasts of burden that dig deep into the earth's crust like invisible forces, clearly indicating the instrumentalization of the subject who burrows into the inner earth in search of riches to benefit the State and multi-national companies. The processes of accumulation and capital reproduction give rise to multiple forms of human alienation and subsume the subject into profit. The question of profit or earnings that looms over Western social organization began with overseas conquest and colonization and extended into the era of liberal and republican modernity. Yuri Herrera's detailed archival research, compilation of witness testimony and collection of information about different versions of the fire at the mine, offers an opposing way of accessing reality in which he juxtaposes the rapacious excavation of the land with his own excavation of the historical and cultural events, recovering facts and presenting them as a vindication of the victims, a rewriting of the official version and an homage to the dead. Herrera takes us into the deepest tunnels and through his writing recreates the lack of air, the feelings of contamination, confinement, and being trapped that we imagine the individuals in the mine suffering. The voice Herrera employs to tell this tale together with the flawless way he orchestrates the story represents the text's greatest achievement.

His voice is taut with a seasoned and restrained indignation that expresses itself laconically, aware that the narrative's strength resides in its authenticity, belonging, in turn, to a domain that is both inside as well as outside language. This truth takes root in lived experience, in a bare and impactful reality made apparent by the bodies that demonstrate irrefutable proof of the existence of necro-politics.

Millenarian exploitation, power's control of life and death, the plundering of nature and the exploitation of the poor all represent the historical truth of necro-politics. Employing neither pathos nor melodrama and with Herrera's characteristic restraint, the fire in the mine takes a toll on both reason and affect. The reader shares the grief and anger, identifying with the impotence of the masses, moving cautiously through an atmosphere charged with the smell of sulfur, dust suspended in the air, smoke and gas emanating from the earth that reveals the wound in its entrails, and the loss of human life to unnecessary immolation, urged on by the forces of unforgiveable perversion that worship at the altar of capital. This halo of blame and impunity traverses the text as a whole and emanates from it. Herrera understands how to convey the theme of social injustice and speaks about the victims with genuine solidarity, shored up through his own experience and refined through detailed documentary evidence. Herrera's narration is archeological in nature. It uncovers a story of which, as he explains, "quedan pocos rastros" (traces of this history are few).[49] The fragments of information in the documents that describe the event distinguish between the "hombres favoritos" (favored men) and those who "desde siempre estuvieron condenados" (were doomed from the outset).[50] What appears to be a question of fate is connected nonetheless to something far more pedestrian: the class structures and biopolitical dominance that have been part of the history of the Americas since the "Discovery" and have been underwritten by national politics of all eras. Like an omen, a series of absences and silences herald the coming catastrophe: the warning bells did not go off, no one saw the flames, but the smell of burning wood and the warm air gave it away. Herrera's textual logic lays out the rules for how the decisions about who should live and who should die were made in a type of accelerated temporality, intensified by the fire's implacable progress. The mine's different levels randomly indicate different degrees of understanding. The men's names evoke distinguishing marks—Delfino Rendón, Agustín Hernández, Edmundo Olascoaga, Antonio López de Nava, José Linares—and are repeated throughout the text, personalizing those who were not just cheap labor but, instead, flesh and blood beings, with families, personal stories, and feelings of solidarity for their unfortunate companions. The cages that bring the men to the surface extract some from the earth but leave many behind, and also bring evidence of death: "Cisneros dijo haber visto una masa encefálica en una de las sogas de las chalupas, y jirones de ropa, seguramente de alguien que al ver la chalupa pasar intentó prenderla en su vuelta a la superficie" (Cisneros said he'd seen brain matter and shredded clothing on one of the cage ropes, no doubt that of someone who'd seen the passing car and attempted to catch it).[51] This climate of death gestures toward the inadequate security measures that should have protected the workers and contrasts with the event's sterile official reports that seek to downplay the catastrophe.

A web of ambiguity, speculation, and vacillation produces a discourse of impunity, furnishing justifications, normalizations of events, presumptions, and inconsistencies that lead to a fateful decision: "veinte minutos después de estar operándose la salvación de los mineros, de improviso los directores dieron la orden de suspender los movimientos y fueron cerradas las entradas de la mina" (twenty minutes after the miners' rescue began, out of the blue the supervisors gave the order to halt operation, and the entrances were closed).[52] The decision seals the fate of the trapped miners, whose number has never been fully established. We do know, however, that five minutes of inhaling the gases from the mine and the smoke from the fire would have been enough to kill any human being, so the search for survivors was called off. Six days later, after unsealing the exits, the death toll rose to eighty-seven, "no diez ni cuarenta y dos, [y] que en el nivel 207 había siete mineros vivos" (not ten or forty-two—but that seven of the miners on level 207 were still alive).[53] The actions and declarations of mayors, judges, directors, and the mine company's managers, as well as journalists, photographers, and others, present a sequence of accounts about the situation, based on speculations or unfounded interpretations, such as those that suggest that the miners were unfazed by death because they were used to danger or that some were even willing to pretend to be dead so that their families could receive compensation. Speculation swirled around the causes of the fire, with some insinuating that it could have started because of the carelessness of the workers themselves.

Culprits, heroes, and victims begin to emerge from what seems to be a true descent into the circles of hell. Darkness, asphyxiation, terror, isolation, and the despair of those who remained in the different levels of the burning mine resemble the illustration of a mythical punishment that allegorizes the downfall of humanity at the end of days. Herrera draws on archival as well as journalistic information (articles, editorials, and photographs) and presents it with a concise objectivity that reveals the callousness and baseness that speaks to the lack of human connection between the different segments of the population that come together around the catastrophe at the mine. The sections entitled "La espera," "Los sobrevivientes" recreate the chaotic response to the disaster, and the reader becomes involved in the tension and mayhem that explain the unnecessary loss of lives. A master narrative of the events is interiorized as "truth," and then repeated as if to underscore its studied coherence. Nevertheless, in the only photographic testimony that exists we discover clear indications of subjects shaken by their experiences and by the obligation to suppress their feelings. The body communicates its dilemmas using its own language of gestures, silences, and signs that Herrera undertakes to decipher:

> In the photo you can see all seven survivors, barefoot, impeccably dressed in white, with their hands in their laps except for one, whose right arm rests on a fellow miner's. All are clean-shaven or have neatly trimmed mustaches and gaze into the camera. They don't look like they just escaped from hell: the week of underground starvation is not reflected in their expressions or on their bodies, with the exception of one, the first man on the left, who seems to betray a silent fury: lips clamped together, brows arched. But again, no one recorded what they thought or felt at that moment.[54]

As if part of a semiotic exercise, the placement of the bodies denotes an orchestration and misrepresentation: the creation of order that forestalls any cracks or violation of its inherent artificiality. The words and images do not decode the events.

The victims were not only alone in the mine but also trapped in the area that surrounded it. There too were the miners' families, primarily their wives and children, additional prisoners of a system that offered no way out nor recognition of the humanity of those who sustained it. The question of gender surfaces in multiple ways when attention is focused on these female symbols of humanity and domesticity, the subsistence of daily life and the vulnerability of the mining community. As superstition dictates, women are bad omens in the mines and as such had to be kept away from the entrances through which the bodies and body parts were brought. However, the daily and material victimization of women extended also to their public humiliation since they were interrogated about intimate aspects of their relationships with the miners in order to receive compensation and forced to lay out details of their lives, including their marital status and previous traumas. Their responses to these interrogations were to be endorsed by male witnesses that authenticated their declarations and decided their truth since a woman's word alone has no value. The narrator emphasizes the point that neither the woman nor many of the men of the community could sign their name, let alone defend their rights or revolt against the exploitative working conditions. As the text indicates, "en el expediente de la investigación las mujeres aparecen como seres incompletos, callados, sin voluntad ni fortaleza" (But the women in the case file seem to be incomplete, silent beings, lacking in strength and determination).[55] The case of María Luz Barrios is typical. Twenty signatures are required to corroborate her words. "Twenty" reiterates the narrator, emphasizing the system's irrational cruelty toward vulnerable subjects who have been beaten down by tragedy.[56]

HUMAN BODIES VERSUS LEGAL BODIES

From his first engagement with this topic, in his approach to the fire, Herrera has undertaken to analyze the way in which the legal narratives intervene in the formation of collective memory. In this way, his analysis's independent perspective succeeds in calling attention to the fissures, gaps, and contradictions present in official discourse, impugning the manipulated versions put out by the mine authorities, official experts, and lawyers. He discovers evidence of worker exploitation and a cover up of the catastrophe. The expert reports, carried out after the cleanup of the mine which eliminated evidence as to what had happened, are deployed as a series of knowledge and practices in which information provided by doctors, engineers, photographers, and translators complements one another to produce a report that removes responsibility from those in charge of the mine. The narrator indicates that this "expertise" circulated throughout the mine's officialdom: "Los secretarios del juzgado son traductores de voces: escuchan a ciudadanos sin calificación para dialogar con la ley y convierten su voz singular, pedestre, en una voz universal y neutral que pueda encajar en los códigos con que funciona el proceso."[57] Unsurprisingly, the legal investigation ended, and the report was filed away without assigning accountability for the disaster and even insinuating that fault lay with one of the miners.

Herrera's chronicle, however, does not confine itself to referencing alternative information about the event or the circumstances that surrounded the miners' death, some of whom were as young as fourteen, but instead also offers information about their lives and the poverty-level wages they earned. Hewing closely to testimonies and archival documents, the authorial voice reserves the right to explicitly bring to light salient aspects of the narrative: "Vale la pena subrayar algunas cosas que impresionan al perito: que los mineros pueden usar los baños sin tener que pagar por ello . . . (de verdad dijo esto)" (It is worth highlighting some of the things the inspector finds impressive: that the miners can use the bathroom without having to pay; that state-of-the-art technology allows the miners not to risk accidents or hazards to their health [he honestly said that]).[58] He refuses to validate or ignore flagrant aspects of official discourse without signaling their importance for understanding the facts. For example, the clarifications in the text that accompany the declarations of José Linares, who was "the last man out" are instructive here. The narrator draws attention to the manipulation of witness statements, emphasizing the time and date they were recorded. He follows his intervention with a paragraph that begins: "Tres cosas dice este testigo" (this witness states three things), in which he underlines the essential parts of Linares's witness statement, and the way in which his claims were contradicted or devalued.[59] The narrator, then, is closely engaged with his text and with the chief goal of clarifying the case's circumstances and challenges. Finally, Herrera's book opens the graves to examine the recurrent theme of bodies and the treatment they receive at the hands of the State government and the mining company. The burial of all the bodies in a common grave "es un último gesto de la Compañía para dejar claro lo que antes practicaba en términos de explotación laboral: que todos esos cuerpos, vivos y no vivos, eran de su propiedad" (it's a final gesture on the part of the company that makes it clear what had previously been carried out via worker exploitation: that all these bodies, living or dead, were Company property).[60] The strategies of exploitation and disposition of the bodies of the workers show clearly how they are perceived as cogs in a productivist and dehumanizing system that never stops to examine the value of life or the repercussions of these deaths on families and the community. With brutal descriptions, that do not shy away from grotesque elements that reveal gruesome facts, Herrera's text refers to the forms that grief would have assumed, were it not mediated by the Company's authoritarianism. The intervention of the Company gives a Kafkaesque twist to the circumstances that depersonalize the facts and control them from above, as if by the strings of an anonymous invisible and ruthless power.

"Los muchos días siguientes" takes a semiotic look at Parque Hidalgo, the kiosk and the signs, the complicity of the texts inscribed there (none of which were explicitly dedicated to the deceased miners) and their possible interpretations. Above all, in his text Herrera includes the way in which the region's silence is gradually replaced with resistance and trade union organizing, presenting a productive way to interiorize what was learned. He exposes the struggle between the workers' activism and the way in which the media interprets these elements of ideological mobilization in Pachuca as well as how they try to absorb them into the notion of a "espacio de concordia" (a place of harmony), which has been constructed around the mine.[61] The last pages record, one by one, the workers' efforts to organize and their protests: the strike of 1923; objections to the firings of 1930 and the formation of the Alianza de Trabajadores Mineros, the organization of the Sindicato Industrial de Obreros y Empleados Mineros, Metalúrgicos y Similares de la República Mexicana, that became the Sindicato Nacional de Trabajadores Mineros, Metalúrgicos, Siderúrgicos y Similares de la República Mexicana in 1934; and the establishment of cooperatives, etc. until 1947 when "ante la dificultad cada vez mayor para encontrar plata, los inversionistas y administradores estadounidenses abandonan las minas del Estado" (as a result of the increasing difficulty in finding silver, American investors and administrators abandon mines in the state of Hidalgo).[62]

In 1950, the State took part ownership of the mines, and after more accidents (1965), strikes (1980), and vigorous calls for workplace safety, at the end of the 1980s they were privatized and then gradually closed and finally dismantled. Before engaging with Herrera's other works, I recommend the reader begin with *El incendio*. In this early work he displays great maturity, and his narrative intuition comes to the fore. Above all, in *El incendio* we see the author's sensitivity, his commitment to and his concern with the complex theme of truth and the question of the simulacrum that his fictional works scrutinize poetically and politically.

TRABAJOS DEL REINO: FIRST AS TRAGEDY, THEN AS FARCE

TRAGEDY, MYTH, FABLE, AND FARCE

Forceful and complex, Yuri Herrera's first novel represents one of the most sophisticated contributions to Latin American literature.[63] Working from the principle of the collective imaginary, as I laid out at the beginning of this study, and not from the raw material of a social and political framework and less still from its emblematic occurrences, the author here confronts a diverse array of beliefs, images, symbols, and concepts that constitute an aesthetic and ideological raw material that can be molded through literature to assume new forms and meanings.

The text positions the mythical space of the cartel at its nerve center. However, it avoids explicitly engaging with the phenomenon of drug trafficking—one of late capitalism's quintessential aspects—in which the logic of the system that has disseminated its lessons to all social levels is perversely imitated. In effect, drug trafficking considers itself to be an interiorization of the pragmatics of accumulation and of the reproduction of capital, conquest, and the transnationalization of markets that have been globally consolidated since the conquest. These examples of primitive accumulation that include the annexation of territory and the appropriation of resources, subjects, and natural and civilizing spaces, find their counterpart in this clandestine form of transnationalized exchange that expands beyond the sale of drugs. Drug trafficking has undergone transformation, and the business today includes the protection rackets focused on people and property by the gangs ravaging the country, the illegal extraction and selling of natural resources, territorial control as well as kidnapping and forcible recruitment of individuals for different jobs and organizations. Using the same perversity employed by capitalism to subsume life to the logic of profit, drug trafficking has inflicted a regime of terror and pillaging, devastating individuals and communities with the evident complicity of the government *du jour*. These activities provide cover for the State's own militarization processes, population control, and appropriation of lands and resources. Along with a discursive proliferation that underwrites the despotic and bloody exercise of power, the macrosystem of global capitalism and its clandestine imitation seek similar ends: the excessive enrichment of the leaders, by whatever means, and the exploitation of those who sacrifice their vital energies and community ties. As Marx warned in his studies on the relationship between capital and work, the human body becomes a cog in a machine (like in the El Bordo mine) that sucks the subject dry while celebrating and fetishizing the object. In the collective imaginary, a type of popular revanchism interprets this parallelism as a form of civil disobedience that unmasks the corruptibility of political power and demonstrates the hypocrisy of its claims to consolidate some type of social order upon radical inequality and political and economic injustice. Without a doubt, people have reacted with horror to the devastating methods employed by drug traffickers whom they primarily blame for the creation of social chaos and regimes of terror. However, the folklorization of this parallel structure of power and profit allows us to interpret, with a degree of condemnation, the farcical nature of the myth that these narco empires are autonomous national and transnational spaces.

The tragic failure of democracies, the concurrent rise of global capital, and the constant official valuing of the object over the subject, invites a curious and even inevitably admiring look at the level of organization that is attributed to the cartels, the power of their leaders, the supposed ostentation of their haciendas, and, above all, their procurement of everything that capitalistic modernity values as great achievements: capital accumulation, luxury, individualism and the attainment of a Hollywood-type life style with no rules or restrictions. Celebrated maximum security prison breaks, the earning of money beyond the exploitative confines of a minimum wage job, and the power of criminals that can bring the State to its knees are enough to provoke the glorification of a counterculture that intrigues and nourishes the popular imagination. This perception of narcos (the capos, their actions, their possessions, and their symbolic power) varies according to social class, accentuating the fascination for the narco as (anti)hero and even as a redemptive figure for the working classes.[64] Constructed as an image of antihegemonic masculinity, the narco boss adheres also to existing models of machismo, rebellion against the system, rejection of fear and an embrace of bravery.

In David Thelen's interview with Carlos Monsiváis, the Mexican chronicler emphasizes the link between the narco paradigm and entertainment industry models, particularly film, songs, and television series that referenced the way of life and personality of narco bosses as copies of characters embodied by John Wayne and Randolph Scott in US cinema.[65] For Monsiváis, films such as *Scarface* embody a type of outlaw based on the deployment of a countercultural habitus that simultaneously inspired fascination and repulsion. Concentrated in these types of characters and the narratives in which they appear are a series of psychological, social, and affective registers that are inscribed as alternatives to the dominant types deemed to be archetypes of middle-class American life. According to Monsiváis:

> The drug consumers in the States are a reality, but the fundamental role of narcos occupies the popular Mexican mind: you see it in the songs, in films, you see it in ways of life. John Wayne has even influenced the narcos' style of walking. Narcos think they go into the cities like John Wayne or Randolph Scott into the saloons. . . . The culture industry has affected more than you can believe. The narcos tried to be norteños in a sense new in Mexico, one that didn't exist before the 1960s, norteños like John Wayne or the Marlboro man or Clint Eastwood or a Vietnam vet turned FBI (Federal Bureau of Investigation) man. It may not be conscious, but the narcos' walk, their outfits, their idea of a he-man, the obsession with guns—all come from American western movies. John Wayne and his gun. And the narco is a he-man with a lot of guns.[66]

As Beatriz Sarlo has indicated, "con el imaginario no se discute" (you can't argue with the collective imaginary) not because its "reasons" cannot be challenged but because its very constitution is more concerned with imagination, need, and desire than with logic and the principles of reality. It matters little in these constructions that the models that come together to configure the narco myth are connected to a greater or lesser degree to reality. From the point of view of the subjectivities to which this imaginary is directed, what matters here is that this imaginary fulfills a compensatory function. The images of the hero and the bandit are always conflated because both exist in opposition to the power of the police, the restrictions of the law, the punishment meted out by the system, and the authoritarianism of the State. According to these imaginative formulations, the narco capos lead a life of adventure and luxury, full of parties, violence, vices, and debauchery, all of which is celebrated in the media and in the entertainment industry (TV, cinema, video games etc.), where the most glittering characters garner fame and social recognition. Although the narco's crimes inspire terror and feed on a lack of public safety and vulnerability, they also tend to be easily relativized since they focus on individuals that embody collective aspirations and who come from low-income backgrounds with which many people identify. Although these configurations are not assimilated by everyone, they nonetheless represent mythical-poetic emblems that circulate fable-like at a collective level.[67] As Jorge Alan Sánchez Godoy has explained:

> Narcoculture has succeeded to a great degree in permeating society with its habits and values, delegitimizing pre-existing social institutions. Therefore, its manifestation represents a much more extensive conglomeration than previous critics have asserted. This includes a mafia sector that not only fights back from the trenches of a "subculture" but also brings together a multiplicity of actors and expressions that (re)build, reproduce and legitimize daily this imaginary construction drawn from roughhewn roots.[68]

In *Trabajos del reino*, Herrera takes up this angle in order to creatively approximate the collective construction of Mexican narcoculture, not to reveal the truth about narcos but rather to articulate their lies and to explore the plot of fictitious threads that the narco myth has spawned in a country where, in the words of Roger Bartra, "las redes imaginarias del poder político" (the imaginary networks of political power) are both intricate and murky. No truth about the narco can destroy its mythical nature, but revealing its lies, its farcical ethos, and intense megalomania—its performative nature, its theatrical identity—can demonstrate the way in which its culture works, in general, as a phenomenon of belief, or even an ideology or a construction and dissemination of false consciousness.

Using the realm of fiction, *Trabajos del reino* constructs and deconstructs this myth. The figure of the narco articulates one among many stereotypes that have risen up in the popular imagination in relation to the subculture connected to drug trafficking and associated criminal activities that are also mixed with different borderland types: the "mojado" or "wetback," the "pollero" or "coyote" who get irregular migrants across the border, the cartel "capo," "el halcón" or cartel spy or lookout, the "mulas" or "mules." These images, which are all constructed from a breakdown of traits, poses, languages, and even physical characteristics whose profiles, including racist and sexist elements, are reproduced repeatedly to form an authentic semiotic repertoire that nurtures serialized narratives on the topics of narcotrafficking and border crossing.[69] The animalization of these identities in the form of traits or explicit functions holds interest in and of itself, since it speaks to the essential attributes of each element's role in the drug trafficking organizational network and more generally in criminal gangs, naturalizing these elements as if they were part of the subject's assigned identity: the mule carries the drugs, the chicken farmer (*pollero*) guides the chicks/migrants (*pollos*) etc. However, as García Godoy cogently states, such considerations and ideological formalizations must be placed in historical context since narco imaginaries vary according to regions and time periods, giving rise to a wide spectrum of value attribution to the characters and activities involved. In this sense,

> The narcocorrido is in constant evolution. At first, it possessed a close relationship (albeit somewhat reconfigured) to the archetype of bandolero and regional popular hero (as in the figures of Heraclio Bernal and Jesús Malverde). These figures symbolized a form of resistance to State power and exalted the representation of this brave challenger of authority and skillful transgressor of the law. However, the question of drug contraband was only ever inferred indirectly. It is only in the eighties when "the sociogram of the brave man completely disappeared from corridos about narcos and was replaced by direct references to drug trafficking (Héau and Giménez 651). Accordingly, the Sinaloan narcocorrido eliminates all social and political connotations, dissolving its connection to the people and the traditional epic in order to immerse itself in a new hedonistic, utilitarian and individualist enterprise.[70]

Taking into account substantial aesthetic, ideological, and historical differences, similar processes are at work in other genres of literature focused on subcultures (the picaresque, the Far West, the mafia) where the imaginary construction of characters, situations, social spaces, etc., surpasses and alters the referents that spawned them, crystalizing certain of their traits that then represent them as original. Something equivalent occurs with the representations of the power relations that these subcultures wield in the fictional world. The relationship between the characters who form part of these alternative constructions, and the dominant culture has also been stereotyped, although in some cases the complexity of the sociocultural conditions that formed such phenomena produced rich and illuminating narratives. Figures such as the sicario, or the drug dealer are often linked to national identities (Mexican, Colombian, gringo) that cinema and television equip with characteristics that rely on differences in language, customs, and behavior that are in turn linked to the commercialization of illicit substances or other forms of illegal conduct. These simplifications facilitate the popularization of cultural products making them easy to assimilate and serialize by a variety of publics. At an ideological level, the imaginary integrates, re-elaborates, and sublimates elements that form part of the social conscience, which is itself impacted by dominant ideas that are then disseminated and socially reproduced. Undoubtedly, these processes suggest the presence of distortions that reduce, simplify, hyperbolize, idealize, or demonize collective experiences. These operations carry out specific social functions (compensation, revenge, distraction, negation, pseudo-explanation etc.) and are interiorized as truths that do not require substantiation.

In addition, governmental strategies that directly engage with the topic of drug traffickers serve only to obscure the true causes of the current situation and the complicity of businesspeople and politicians in organized crime's operations. The struggle against drug trafficking allows official discourse to legitimize the constant state of civil war in the nation, using the rhetoric of good versus evil to obscure the State's inability to govern. At the same time, public opinion is distracted from other types of crimes or political and economic actions that go unpunished, while the conflict over routes, territories, and drug marketplaces occupies the front page of newspapers and television. In a presentation and article entitled "Semántica del luminol," Yuri Herrera makes explicit reference to all these themes, invoking the image of a Mexico surrounded by yellow crime scene tape to codify and categorize the evidence.[71] According to Herrera, in a country where maps and statistics are used to control information about crimes committed with impunity, in 2011 the government forbade the public performance of *narcocorridos* because they were seen to venerate the figure of the capo as a hero, giving rise to collective support for the narcos' "exploits." As the author explains, "La censura no detiene la violencia, sólo aspira a controlar cómo es simbolizada" (Censorship does not stop violence, it just attempts to control how it is symbolized").[72] The political and no longer uniquely social, ethical and security concerns caused by drug trafficking become manifest when we compare the situation during the period of the PRI during which "el narco funcionaba a través de cacicazgos regionales coordinados por un capo que organizaba, conciliaba y `negociaba con el gobierno central" (Narcos were structured into regional "cacicazgos" coordinated by a capo that organized, paid off, and negotiated with the central government).[73] Later, as Herrera points out, "este acuerdo se rompió, y con la atomización de los grandes grupos vino una disputa por los territorios de cultivo, industrialización y transporte de los estupefacientes" (this agreement broke down and, with the splintering of the big groups, disputes over drug crop cultivation, the industrialization and transport of narcotics) and violence became more generalized.[74]

While official policy promotes widespread impunity, it simultaneously tries to control the imaginary via the censure of the *narcocorrido* for supposedly worsening the security crisis, threatening to imprison people who produce this type of popular music and the stations or entertainment venues that broadcast it. In addition to being a literary and aesthetic project, it thus becomes clear that *Trabajos del reino* is also a political reflection on popular culture and power, including the issue of censorship. It highlights the hypocrisy and the complicity of the State in the existence of narcoculture and its protection of the parallel economic structure. Today, the State functions as a true social, political, and economic laboratory in which parastatal, transnational forms of capital accumulation and conquest marketing are put to the test. In this conference presentation, Herrera referenced British writer and journalist Ed Vullamy's opinion on Mexico, which bears repeating here:

> Mexico's war does not only belong to the postpolitical, postmoral world. It belongs to the world of belligerent hyper-materialism, in which the only ideology left—which the leaders of "legitimate" politics, business and banking preach by example—is greed. Narco-cartels are not pastiches of global corporations, nor are they errant bastards of the global economy—they are pioneers of it. They point, in their business logic and modus operandi, to how the legal economy will arrange itself next. The Mexican cartels epitomised the North American free trade agreement long before it was dreamed up, and they thrive upon it.[75]

For Herrera, literature offers the possibility of forging an alternative discourse on a social reality that can, in turn, destabilize dominant discourses and penetrate the complexities of social conflict from the symbolic realm.[76]

AXES AND PARADIGMS

As a semiotic space, the world of the novel proposes a series of scenarios that illuminate the tension related to the habitus of characters, their lifestyles, and the conflicts that drive their interactions in this fictional universe. While avoiding the construction of a polarized and rigid world, tensions such as tradition/modernity, center/periphery, hegemony/subalternity, art/power underly the narrative. This fictional world is instead a fluid albeit stratified space, in which emotional interactions and material transactions take place that revitalize and give meaning to the theatricality of the novel's narration.

Trabajos del reino works along two principal axes. In the first, it imagines the cartel as a space of absolute power that resembles a monarchy both metaphorically and hyperbolically, with a capo who wields complete control over a hierarchical and autonomous structure that is personalized and based on territorial control. Possessing an aura that elevates him beyond most people, the figure of el Rey/the King invokes desire, not only as the location of material power (the possession of goods, jewels, authority, centrality, prestige) but also as a generator of meaning. The second axis is Herrera's insertion of the main character Lobo—a composer and singer of *corridos*—into the plot as an interstitial and connective figure. As previously indicated, the theme of mediation is essential to Yuri Herrera's literature and his principal characters always feature a connective quality at the level of cultural tradition (Lobo), quest (Makina), or negotiation (Alfaqueque). In *Trabajos del reino*, the singer links two worlds that can be broken down to different levels: the world of art; popular culture as an open communication project; the cartel as an enclosed and clandestine social nucleus; the symbolic space of absolute power; and the regional celebratory narrative of the *corrido*, in which the leader's victories are both praised and simplified.

The narrative's dramatic intensification can be found in the intersection of two symbolic orders and systems: the capitalist worship of money and material power and the idea of art as the exercise of "organic" potentiality with respect to power (the ability to legitimize, consecrate, and disseminate meanings and rework empirical experiences as literature). However, although the sphere of artistic creation relies on a commodified system of patronage, it also follows its own logic propelled by the myth of art's autonomy—the symbolic register as a codification that responds to humanistic themes (ideas of authorship, creation, message, art, language) whose sublimity redeems the actions and raises them to the level of fable. We thus find ourselves confronted with two ideological registers in the production of a *false consciousness* that can translate the narco tragedy into the language of farce, an outlandish and heightened form assumed by the logic of reproduction and commodification of life during biocapitalism.

The dynamic between reality and simulacrum traverses the novel at different levels, going beyond anecdote and gesturing instead to a reflection on modernity and to the role that symbolic languages play in relation to values that are rooted in contingency and reformulations of power. Based on the corrupt centrality of the State, power transmits itself in the form of myth and is embodied in different "objects," reaching the outer limits of the system. In this sense, the figure of el Rey hovers over the totality of the story and dominates it, even at times when he is not at the forefront of the action and who appears embedded from the novel's opening lines. Drawing on legendary models of local *caudillos* and *caciques* and of cinematographic images used to glamourize the spectacle of machismo in the mythical spaces of lawless lands, at the beginning of the novel el Rey appears as a "miracle" who stands out in the regional landscape.[77] The first encounter between Lobo and el Rey takes place in a cantina where the capo appears as the magnetic center of an alternative world that forms a contrast with the precarious and marginal lives that surround him. El Rey dwells in spaces that lie beyond State institutions (although thanks to corruption and complicity there are elements of them enthroned in the narcosphere). He places himself outside the law, operating within a closed circle of simulacrum and artificiality. Described at the opening of the novel as a man whose blood is different to others, of domineering gestures and flashy clothing, el Rey is a lighthouse that emits a strong beam and who can reconfigure time and space. On seeing him, Lobo thought: "Pensó que desde ahora los calendarios carecían de sentido por una nueva razón: ninguna otra fecha significaba nada, sólo esta, porque, por fin, había topado con su lugar en el mundo; y porque había escuchado mentar un secreto que, carajo, qué ganas tenía de guardar" (that from now on there was a new reason why calendars were senseless: no date means a thing besides this one. Because finally he'd found his place in the world. And because he'd heard something about a secret, which he damned well wanted to keep).[78]

Space and time are reconfigured and the secret (associated with farce, simulation, appearance, simulacrum) represents knowledge that is codified as power, and that demarcates the circle that Lobo, also described in the novel as the Artist/el Artista, wants to occupy. El Rey is a figure to whom the concept of "charismatic authority" applies, something that Sánchez Godoy brings up via Freud's ideas on the behavior of the massman, since el Rey embodies a hierarchical figure that his social circle both resists and venerates creating, at a communitarian level, a form that "desviada de la cohesión social" (diverging from social cohesion) produces a collective mimesis based on magnetism and loyalty.[79] Explaining this configuration of collective imaginaries, Sánchez Godoy also shows that drug traffickers were stigmatized and marginalized when they first appeared in urban locales, which helped consolidate the basis of ethical and aesthetic codes and the logic of power that we attribute to them today, since the initial stigma was transformed into countercultural heroism.[80]

Seen through Lobo's enthralled gaze, el Rey is a blinding light that reorders the world. The novel lays out a series of factors to support his leadership: blood (of a different kind as befits his condition of monarch), opulence (the jewelry that capos use to denote their status), performance (the theatricalization of his power, including his authority, charisma, and violence), and his complete confidence in money matters which he demonstrates when he pays for el Artista's services during the wake that ends in the death of the drunk who had shortchanged him. El Rey's physicality represents another important element: "su majestad labrada en pómulos de piedra" (majesty chiseled into his cheekbones).[81] All of this consolidates his place as the central generator of power and affect and defines his aura, confirming his exceptional status as someone able to reformulate power relations and order the imagined universe, following the outline of the Hollywood model that shapes the construction of popular myths:

> The one time Lobo had gone to the pictures he saw a movie with a man like this: strong, sumptuous, dominating the things of the world. He was a King, and around him everything became meaningful. Men gave their lives for him, women gave birth for him; he protected and bestowed, and in the kingdom, through his grace, each and every subject had a precise place. But those accompanying this King were more than vassals. This was his Court.[82]

Power occupies the seat of honor and represents a force that is contingent on those who orbit around the shining lighthouse that disposes of both time and space. Lobo demonstrates this through his discarding of traditional calendars that organized normal methods of time keeping. In the presence of the capo, the world takes on an alternative meaning: "Pensó que desde ahora los calendarios carecían de sentido por una nueva razón: ninguna otra fecha significaba nada, sólo esta, porque, por fin, había topado con su lugar en el mundo" (He thought from now on there was a new reason why calendars were senseless: no date means a thing besides this one. Because finally he'd found his place in the world).[83] In the same vein, Herrera writes: "Nunca reparó en esa cosa absurda, el calendario, porque los días se parecían todos: rondar entre las mesas, ofrecer canciones, extender la mano, llenarse los bolsillos de monedas.... Finales y caprichos, así eran la huella más notable para ordenar el tiempo. En eso se le iba."[84]

Lobo witnesses el Rey's magical meddling in the known reality through his transformation of the places colonized by the cartel. Before the arrival of the monarch, Lobo remembers a place as "un basural, una trampa de infección y desperdicios" (a dump, a hellhole of waste and infection).[85] In contrast, narco-style represents a camp exoticism that diversifies provincial uniformity, inserting the mirage of a luxurious and empty otherness that the singer describes like a circus parade:

> People from far and wider, from every corner of the earth, people from beyond the desert. Word of God there were even some who had seen the sea. And women who walked like leopards, and giant Warriors, their faces decorated with scars; there were Indians and blacks; he even saw a dwarf.... He heard tell of mountains, of jungles, of gulfs, of summits, in singsong accents entirely new to him: yesses like shesses, words with no esses, some whose tone soared up so high and sank so low it seemed each sentence was a journey.[86]

The singer's voracious gaze collects sensations and sounds, experiencing the world as filtered through el Rey's anomalous powers of seduction. He succeeds in attracting a wide range of residual subjects cowed by the prospect of what Lobo calls el Rey's prosperous domain, toward a nucleus magnetized by the dirty money of his clandestine transactions, which is located beyond all ethical reach and focused on the constant production of profit as he adheres to the obvious lessons of capitalism. With his alienated consciousness, however, Lobo only sees power's carnivalization, its flamboyant and multiform paraphernalia, from which derives the illusion of autonomy that presents the narco as a microcosm of plenitude in a world dominated by inequality and exploitation. Appearing to possess absolute and autonomous power, the cartel presents itself as a utopian prospect. Situated in a no-man's land, beyond the reach of calendars and maps and the control of official power, a war machine outside the State, the cartel is an assemblage that displays its mechanical strength by vampirically sucking the blood of its members: capos, devotees, workers, jesters who surround the power base with a halo that legitimizes it as a producer of signifiers. In contrast to the grind of daily routine, in spatial-temporal terms el Rey confirms the existence of the miracle of transforming dirt into gold: "Éstas eran las cosas que fijaban la altura de un rey: el hombre vino a posarse entre los simples y convirtió lo sucio en esplendor" (The royalty of a king determined these things: the man had settled among simple folk and turned the filth to splendor).[87]

If first *costumbrismo* and then magic realism (albeit in a different register) succeeded in producing exportable Latin American images, narco-culture represents without a doubt a new aesthetic and ideological constellation that translates the reproduction of farcical (grotesque) capitalism into the symbolic realm, revealing how social and economic peripheries assimilate and reproduce the system's rules and principles on their own terms. In these terms, *Trabajos del reino* is a novel of both sentimental education and sentimental development as well as a novel of *political* education in which the singer moves from a state of false consciousness to a form of enlightenment in which understanding, grief, and disenchantment are mixed. Art operates as the mediating element between alienation from reality and an understanding of it. Art aesthetically codifies a fragmented world that resists totalization. Art moves from patronage to a measure of autonomy, however it cannot embark on an emancipatory and celebratory circuit, since its trajectory is one of dependence and protectionism, of gratuitousness and neglect. Like a floating signifier, the postmodern minstrel's music and song is subjected to the hierarchical structures of the narco-system and by the end of the novel becomes a commodity without a market or possibility of exchange, searching for a sociocultural space in which to seek shelter.

El Rey's mythical representation remains firmly integrated into the paradigm of power. Meanwhile, Lobo/el Artista occupies a subaltern place constructed as the flipside to the grotesque hegemony of the capo, in which the former is dependent, alienated, and serves only to obey and venerate. Lobo is a sensitive and naïve character, with a history of marginalization and burdened by unfulfilled desires. For him, the Word is an instrument of connection and personal expression but also a resource for knowledge and transformation. His search for economic and social stability is less than his desire to find a public, to define a social role in which singing operates like a narrative that focuses and disseminates a version of reality for others to consume. Popular and eventually populist, singing is the vehicle for the communication and socialization of ideas around which the narco-community congregates, providing a more select community than that of the cantinas and dive bars but also a more watchful and cohesive one as it circulates around the crucial element of the local monarch. The act of singing filters and naturalizes the narco's violence and perverse acts, converting them into adventures in an example of popular (anti)heroism that blurs their negativity and transforms them into rebellious and self-legitimizing adventures onto which the audience can project their own frustrations and retaliations.

The *corrido* is a soundbox in which echoes of banditry or *caciquismo* merge into exemplary figures that embody archetypal values including pragmatism, loyalty, bravery, lack of fear of death, love for the land and the maternal figure, the woman, and the pueblo, and in which the measure of a man is cultivated as a myth of masculinity and power. In this sense—and if sufficiently formalized—the *corrido* can be defined according to concrete parameters. As Carlos Monsiváis has pointed out, the "encomiendas categóricas" (categorical mandates) to which the *corrido* responded, and which at its zenith thematized the possibilities of the Mexican Revolution were to: "cantar a la gente de un pueblo que se reconoce en la violencia, consagrar héroes y leyendas, sostener la idea de la historia como duelo de caudillos, promover un arquetipo de la poesía popular, implantar el orgullo de la tropa, seleccionar las batallas memorables, destacar la figura de Pancho Villa, hacer las veces de memoria sintética de la Revolución" (Sing of a people who identify with violence, consecrate heroes and legends, promote the idea of history as a duel between *caudillos*, promote the archetype of popular poetry, implant the pride of the troop, select the memorable battles, highlight the figure of Pancho Villa, synthesize the memory of the Revolution).[88] Accordingly, the composer/singer's activity possesses a function that goes beyond contingency and becomes a collectivized performance embedded in the memory of the community. In *Trabajos del reino*, in addition, Lobo possesses a catalyzing role. His final composition serves as a watershed moment in el Rey's journey from his zenith to his fall. The song represents an iconic moment of public recognition as well as an acknowledgment of failure. The art of the singer and composer of *corridos* evolves from its initial contractual character (the marking of formal celebrations) to unleash a process that leads to the irrevocable truth of the cartel's destruction: a moment of poetic justice, the restoring of an "order" in which corruption and inequality nonetheless continue to be the norm.

Lobo occupies the typical role of mediator in *translating* signifiers from one system of signs to another in an exercise that incorporates elements of parody, reductionism, and adulation. The "reality" of drug trafficking remains buried beneath many layers of a constructed imagination. The novel penetrates these layers without explaining them, allowing the reader to reconstruct the terms of the simulacrum and identify its literary devices. The characters are actors in a dialogic scene, carnivalesque but held to strict limits by the economy and effectiveness of the language. From the beginning, the novel's sober and terse discourse makes an impression, unfolding while the reader is carried along by the narrative thread while immersing him or herself in the twists and turns of an existential landscape marked by interludes, reticence, and sarcasm.

In the sense I referred to earlier, we can conceive of *Trabajos del reino* as a bildungsroman, as an inward journey in which the character navigates different stages until he reaches a more exact understanding of the world in which he moves. Deeply marked by affect, his compositions incorporate psychological, social, emotional, sexual, and intellectual elements that converge to communicate values and life lessons. In a parallel and symmetrical development to his lyrics, Lobo's own personal transformation incorporates all these elements, as he becomes the parodic "organic intellectual" of the narco world. The narco universe of power attracts literary representation not only because its authority radiates a polysemy difficult to locate in other themes but also because the rituals that surround this power serve to intensify its aura. Absolute power communicates something unique and exceptional, where everything seems possible in a space filled with celebrations and conflicts, festivities, and tragedies. At the same time, the framework of power always appears as a multi-faceted game that is both ephemeral and eternal, solid and fragile, always hiding behind masks, tricks and betrayals, intrigues, and plots, and always subject to constant resignifications.

Fragmentary, kaleidoscopic, succinct, and profound, the novel rapidly transits through moments of the construction and deconstruction of a universe that contains within it the seeds of its own destruction. This process is narrated from the excentric viewpoint of a character who, credulous, alienated, and peripheral to the center of power, represents the field of vision from which the novelistic universe is deconstructed and reinterpreted. Lobo represents an artist in search of a patron as well as the historical category of the artist who executes commissions that lead to the creation of masterworks but who now has been coopted and degraded by the demands of the neoliberal market. In the novel, explicitly located in late-stage modernity, Herrera defends artistic production as an emancipated space in which aesthetic values are viewed from idealistic and romantic perspectives. He highlights the minimal space that exists between power and creative freedom in our global age. The novel explores how the remnants of art's auratic influence are superimposed onto the processes of commodification of the symbolic product in which the reproducibility of artistic works (the recordings el Rey promises Lobo, for example) are transformed into an irresistible reward. The reestablishment of "order" at the end of the novel might be perceived as a concession to the status quo were it not for the fact that the reader perceives the prevailing calm as both unstable and fleeting, providing only temporary cover for the violence and corruption that have survived the debacle.[89]

According to Sánchez Godoy, the stigmatization of narcoculture at its origins led to a symbolic construction in which axiological codes, mechanisms of legitimation, power logics and different forms of aesthetic and mythical-religious forms of expression were articulated as integral pieces of the imaginary world of drug trafficking, lending it an air of a counter-culture that resists and transgresses state culture. With the rise of urbanization and the insertion of drug trafficking into cities at all levels of society, narcoculture came to be considered as "legitimadora de un universo absorbido por un hedonismo a ultranza, un individualismo, un utilitarismo y una búsqueda de prestigio social" (a legitimizing function of a universe obsessed with extreme hedonism, individuality, utilitarianism and the search for social prestige).[90] We can see a mix of both instances in *Trabajos del reino* where the cartel's rural penetration and its modus operandi begin to trickle down into less programmatic stages at the community level. If power, in and of itself, is an intricate system of signs, the singer fulfills the function of capturing its ethos and translating it into a catchy tune for special occasions. The goal is to normalize a schematic version of events in the community's imaginary until the experience develops to the extent where awareness distorts the commercial pact of the commissioned work of art.

WHAT'S IN A NAME?

In the field of language philosophy, the proper name has been studied as a dispositive of (self) recognition and as significant link between language and reality. Names form part of the way individuals are socialized but also refer to the subject who is named or the project through which the appellation is assigned. Names that are historic, commonplace, funny, fashionable, melodramatic, or inspired by cultural, biblical, or mythological meaning, have connotations whose significance connects to the subject in different ways. It has been proven that when the meaning of a name is very well known, the individual unconsciously expends a great deal of his/her energy in "living up" to it and in making his/her life correspond to the personality, attributes, and expectations associated with it. Consequently, the elimination of a name is significant and is integral to the semiotics of the text. The subject is thus reduced to a sign or a letter. A nameless character is seen above all as a device or tool, an actant or agent that simply moves through the narrative terrain. For some authors, an unnamed character is like a point on a cultural map, a localization that exists without need for biographical or characterological details.

In *Trabajos del reino*, as in Yuri Herrera's other novels, characters are not given names because the author wants to primarily emphasize their functionality in the narrative and in the world that he or she shares with others and which he or she helps configure. Unlike the works of other authors who use this mechanism to connect a person's anonymity to dehumanization and alienation (in Kafka, for example), Herrera abstracts the moment of personalization, offering a postmodern, attenuated, and commonplace view of this procedure that is devoid of higher meaning. In Herrera's narrative, the context alone fleshes out the characters who are presented with subtlety, boldly sketched, but without an abundance of details as if they had been born to inhabit their assigned roles. Each character embodies a fictional epiphenomenon, and then vanishes toward the imaginary horizon from where they first came.[91]

An extensive analysis of the question of naming could be developed, contextualizing each case within its literary genre (science fiction, narconarrative) etc. that would frame the omission of the name within a specific site of meaning. In the case of *Trabajos del reino*, Herrera builds the novel on the foundation of spaces and characters that embody recognizable attributes that are both laden with meaning and defined by their specific purpose. Each one's iconic value epitomizes a standardized but also empty framework that his use of anecdotes fills with specific content. Herrera names everything in a hyperbolic and aspirational sense. "El Reino" (the Kingdom), "la Corte" (the Court), "el Rey" (the King), "el Artista" (the Artist), "el Palacio" (the Palace), "la Niña" (the Girl), "el Periodista" (the Journalist) are all names that gesture toward desire (and to the way in which each person defines their existential territory) and to the symbolic and emotional field that defines this desire. This subjective projection adheres to the subject/object, covering it with a celebratory aura and both consecrating and naming it. The narrative development reveals that no character lives up to his or her name, that is, the narrative exposes the kingdom as a simulacrum and as the representative space of a power anchored in farce.

From the royal kingdom that serves as a parodic referent in the novel, to the authoritarian and self-contained space of the cartel, the story is first a tragedy and then a farce. However, since reality is a phenomenon of belief that operates primarily within the circle of faith that contains it, the characters' vision is more important than that of the reader. Farce, simulacrum, and the theatricalized elements of the plot all serve to demonstrate the persistence of power as both the inevitable origin of collective imaginaries and, in its updated and degraded version, a criminal space immune to ethical principles. As in all monarchies, in Herrera's "kingdom" ostentation, personalism, and megalomania lurk. The court is a closed and structured space where the concept of sovereignty operates as a simulacrum, replete with vulnerability and contingency. Eminently ideological, power is experienced as both eternal and absolute, the producer of a false consciousness where, confined by the general performance that surrounds them, characters exist and hold meaning.

Throughout the novel, the image of the body as a metaphorical form that assists in the materialization of power is developed at a variety of levels. Not only are the bodies of el Rey (his authoritarianism, his sexual limitations, his aura) and el Artista (his needs, his desires) brought to bear on the novel but the social and the communitarian body appear too. The duality of life/death and all intermediate instances (precariousness, wounds/injuries, torture, putrefaction) develops the idea of sovereignty from the angle of biopolitics, explaining that power is strengthened when it embeds itself in the social body and weakened when the latter is attacked. Drawing on the work of Roberto Esposito, Carlos Ávila has pointed out the organic relationship between power and corporality, explaining how the social body interiorizes endogenous harm and attacks it from within by infiltrating and transgressing immunitarian barriers.[92]

In *Trabajos del reino*, the capo initiates the fall when he meddles in el Rey's dominions and violence ensues. El Traidor / the Traitor's mysterious identity gives rise to a palace intrigue that leaves several deaths in its wake. Lobo infiltrates the other capo's court, becoming an alien element that pollutes the enemy cartel's socio-criminal body. Defenseless against exogenous elements, (unattainable) purity seems to be the only way for the microsocial body to survive. The narration's fable-like style aligns with the categorization of the characters whose attributes surpass the singularity of the given name and cede to the nickname's anonymity and the social representativeness that distinguishes it. Within this structure, everyone has a role to play that gives their presence meaning within the selective and limited space of the Court. The given name is, as I have already shown, a convention based on the social group that shares it. In *Trabajos del reino*, a field of connotations that strengthen the clandestine nature of the group's social network, where everyone's alias shields and protects him, replaces the purely allegorical value of a name. Names are the way society engages with the meaning of individuality as a link between sign and referent. In Herrera's novel, however, this singularity is sacrificed for function. The cartel, like a war machine that exists beyond the reach of the state, operates by either destroying or penetrating institutional protocols to disqualify and denaturalize it. Presided over by the capo, the cartel fulfills its authoritarian principle by delegating specific functions and by the stratified order imposed on them.

The novel's effectiveness, its delicate lyricism, is located in the development of the space between the nickname and the fictional character it designates, that is, in the development of a subjectivity that exists, like a floating signifier, in the fictional microcosmos. By problematizing the binary relationship between sign and referent, the novel opens a space of signification for the characters to fill line by line. The nickname of "Lobo" that the character has had since he was very young functions as a hyperbolic attribute replaced by the nickname "el Cantante" or "el Artista" that explains his role upon joining the cartel. As Carlos Ávila has pointed out, el Artista emerges in the novel as the "wolf-man," a hybrid being, simultaneously rational and instinctual, who is elevated to the status of "Artist" but who gradually returns to being Lobo during the narrative arc. According to Ávila, "el hombre-lobo [tiene una] condición sacrificial . . . porque abarca a la bestia y al hombre, porque habita ambos mundos y al mismo tiempo no pertenece a ninguno de los dos" (the wolf-man possesses a sacrificial quality . . . because it incorporates both man and beast, and because he inhabits both worlds while belonging to neither).[93]

José Eduardo Serrato Córdova has noted the presence of narco world stereotypes in the novel that also feature in the *corrido*. The topics of the capo's despotic power, betrayal, the underlings' blind loyalty, beautiful and compliant women that surround the bosses, all contribute to the clichéd nature of the entourage that accentuates the farcical nature of the fictional representation. The characters, backdrops, props, values, and plots are all predictable, as in a mafia film or a western. Nevertheless, the originality and quality of the work do not stem from there but instead from the way in which Herrera fills these models with content that overflows them and equips them with new meaning.[94]

Among the female characters, the three most integral to the plot embody the roles modernity has designated to women—la Niña, la Cualquiera y la Bruja (the Girl, the Commoner, the Witch)—and are all filtered through the Artist's eyes. The first, an unattached adolescent, is marked by her availability, belonging to anyone "de quien lo precise" (whoever needs her).[95] To the Artist, she is a shadowy figure, "con un aroma de mujer distinta" (the scent of a different sort of woman).[96] The second "se le figuró como una ráfaga de insolencia, unos ojos que lo consumían y lo arrojaban; luego fue una armonía del largo cabello amarrado y la espalda curva como un rizo que comienza; y después una escarcha súbita congelándole las entrañas" (hit him like a gust of insolence, eyes that devoured him then spat him out; then it was harmony, long hair pulled back and a spine that curved in the start of a curl; and then a sudden frost that numbed his gut).[97] The third is the capo's wife, "una mujer de vestido largo y largo cabello entrecano; recia, de un aire virulento" (a woman with long gray hair and a long dress; badass, with a blistering air).[98] Displaying innocence, aggressive eroticism, authority, and power, and interpellating the artist in different ways, these women appear as varied dimensions of a complex female image that covers the stages of adolescence, adulthood, and middle age. Three types, three stages, three functions: the female figure is endowed with a savage eroticism and a strength of character that disrupts the masculine impulse, reorienting it, derailing it, empowering it or expelling it from its habitus.

El Rey, el Joyero/the Jeweler, el Doctor, el Periodista, el Artista, la Bruja, el Gerente/the Manager, el Heredero/the Heir, and el Traidor ritualize the socialization of the narco-cosmos, revealing it as a compartmentalized space, defined in terms of its exceptionality. The cartel's sovereignty assimilates authority to the monopoly of legitimate violence, which it brandishes to preserve order, and its hegemonic political territoriality that runs parallel to the State's and defies its laws and operating principles. The final flight through crevices, passages, and tunnels and the appearance of a decapitated peacock as the grotesque expression of the cartel's unsustainable artificiality, offer the flipside to the lyricism that imbues the opening of the novel when we first encounter the cartel. Chaotic and farcical, the novel's denouement includes el Rey's final reflection when he admonishes the Artist for his betrayal by implicitly portraying him in his compositions as weak and infertile, "no se trata solamente de ser poderoso, sino de parecerlo, y de que los de más lo crean"; "Hay que serlo y hay que parecerlo . . . y yo lo soy . . . pero necesito que mi gente lo crea, y ese, pendejito, ese era tu trabajo" (It's not enough to be a badass, right. You have to *be* one and you have to *look* like one. And I am . . . but I need my people to believe it, and *that*, you little shit, is your job).[99]

In the kingdom, art loses ground when it rejects its role as an ideological tool and when it dismantles its pact with power and instead flashes with the brief light of truth. El Rey's failure to prolong his legacy through an heir capable of continuing his lineage and la Cualquiera's simultaneous impregnation by el Artista create a counterpoint that speaks to the power of sexual fertility as both a manifestation of masculinity as well as a mechanism for transcendence and an extension of life. This turn of events leaves el Rey in a situation of tactical inferiority that foreshadows his dethroning. El Artista, on the other hand, remains open to some kind of future in which singing and aesthetic representation occupy a complicated but secure place as a form of freedom and consciousness and as a manifestation of cultural and political intervention into reality. Power is thus not only an accumulation of concrete and symbolic resources but also a form of belief that draws strength from rituals and myths, from legends and ceremonies and from accolades and tactical silences. El Artista moves away from his moral goal, thus contributing to the destruction of the kingdom and his own position in it. After enduring an unexpected event worthy of a *corrido* that would tell the tale of the tragedy and farce of a king and his kingdom, he ends up fleeing to save his life but remains in control of his own destiny.

THE WORD, A GLIMMER

The magical nature of words becomes obvious from the book's first pages where Herrera alludes to language as Lobo's only way of counteracting the hostility of his childhood land (dust, sun, and silences). From his schooldays on, he registered the hidden harmony that joined words and sounds and his mastery over language becomes a way of life "al ofrecer rimas a cambio de lástima y centavos" (offering rhymes in exchange for pity, for coins).[100] His own refrains and his "public words" (posters, diaries, lyrics) provide a refuge until playing the accordion helps him promote the idea of song as a way of relaying the experience of others, or in other words, as a simulacrum of the subjectivity that would act as "un espejo de la vida que le contaban" (a mirror held up to lives overheard).[101] His direct experience of the cartel's power and of palace life provide Lobo's first intense experiences, equipping him with the creative impulse and with a delight in the act of poetry: "Cantó la historia con la fe con que se cantan los himnos y con la certeza de los pregones, pero más que todo, la hizo sentir pegajosa, para que la gente la aprendiera con la cintura y las piernas y pudiera repetirla después" (He sung his song with the faith of a hymn, the certainty of a sermon, and above all he made sure it was catchy so people would learn it with their feet and their hips, and so they, too, would sing it later).[102] The act of singing becomes corporal, and Lobo uses it as a way of materializing ideas and sensations. These assume a physical form in the audience, buoyed by the affective atmosphere that celebrates the capos' criminal epic. As José Manuel Valenzuela observes in *Jefe de jefes: Corridos y narcocultura en México*: "El estilo de vida asociado al poder del narcotráfco se despoja de elementos morales que funcionaron cuando las dimensiones del consumo se vinculaban con los medios que lo posibilitaban" (The lifestyle associated with narco power is stripped of the moral elements that operated when consumption was connected to the means that made it possible).[103] In the novel, ethics and aesthetics merge in the pragmatics of song, burying a conflict that is central to the fictional world and that will end with an alliance between art and power. Lobo's didactic process incorporates a movement from alienation to consciousness.[104]

El Artista is not the only one for whom truth is a flexible material that can be shaped to adapt to the demands of the Court: "Para entretener a los necios con mentiras limpias el Periodista tenía que hacerlas parecer verdades. Las noticias verdaderas eran cosa de él, materia de corrido, y había tantas por cantar que bien podía olvidar las que no servían al Rey."[105] The process of thematic, lexical, and rhetorical selection in the *corridos* involves a rigorous filtering of reality to compose a narrative whose principles, in terms of genre, are overseen by those in power. For the singer, however, language's very magic is what molds reality. In this configuration of desire, and as a pathway to its attainment, el Artista conceives of words as intermediary tools, something that begins in his own childhood. In the gloomy silence of his family house, he had grown up with a precarious and anxious relationship to language: "Por ello a Lobo las palabras se le fueron acumulando en los labios y luego en las manos" (That was why the words started to pile up, first in Lobo's mouth and then in his hands).[106] Moreover, with his minimal formal education he could not discern its possibilities. Only later, in the streets: "aprende a habitar el mundo a través de las palabras públicas: los carteles, los diarios en las esquinas, los letreros" (inhabiting the world through its public words: posters, papers sold on street corners, sign) until the accordion teaches him how to "colorear sonidos" (shape the sounds).[107]

At this point in his education, truth is a utilitarian option. At the end of the first third of the novel, immediately after the appearance of the glittering image of la Cualquiera, Herrera dedicates two pages to a description from the narrator's point of view of el Artista's perception of the world, which includes the light of knowledge, expression, the accumulation of sensations, and a whirlwind of signifiers. The linguistic signs fertilize his mind. El Artista's relationship with these elements is sensual and almost mystical:

> Milling the sheets between rolls of insomnia, they signal, scratching at the wasted white of the paper, at his eyes. And what was each sheet if not a working tool, like a saw for someone who builds tables, a gat for someone

who takes lives? Ah, but never this bluff of sand, the spirit and ambition to uncover. So many letters there. They are. There they are. They are a glimmer. How they jostle together and overflow, soaking each other and enveloping his eyes in an uproar of reasons.[108]

For el Artista language is still open to debate and exists in the space between truth and lies, between certainty and volubility. For him, words represent neither a mere intellectual exercise nor a pure sensory stimulation. He identifies this fertilizing and illuminating function with life and therefore in opposition to death. In a phase preceding el Artista's full coming to consciousness, the word takes on the character of a truth that inclines toward Eros and not Thanatos, and the simulacrum begins to resemble complicity and death.

Words are a "un despeñadero de arena . . . son un destello . . . Bronca de signos que se atan. Son una luz constante" (Bluff of sand. They are a glimmer. An uproar of signs bound together. A constant light).[109] The last phrase appears four times in the two short pages, like a tapping noise that registers the euphoria of his constant discovery of language: "Un resplandor diverso cada una, cada una diciendo el nombre verdadero a su modo. Hasta las más mentirosas, hasta las más veleidosas. . . . Son una luz constante. . . . Son un faro que se derrama sobre las piedras a su merced, son una linterna que se pasea, se detiene, acaricia la tierra y le descubre cómo acabalar el servicio que le ha tocado" (Each with its own radiance, each speaking the true name in its own way. Even the most false, even the most fickle. . . . They are a constant light. . . . They are the lighthouse flare cast over stones at his command, they are a lantern that searches, then stops and caresses the earth, and they show him the way to make the most of the service that is his to render).[110]

The metaphorical proliferation is both sensuous and affective, almost erotic. Ignited by the cartel's secrets, and the mystery that surrounds its members, the creation of the el Artista diverges from reality, from the value of truth and from morality and justice. It loses itself in the sensuality of sound, and in the delinquent and untiring accumulation of signifiers that go beyond the limits of communication to constitute a devastating aesthetic experience that verges on the sublime. Beyond the pragmatism of the transmission of information, the expression of feeling and the exchange of ideas, the word is a ludic tool that plays with the limits of secrecy, exposing it without betraying it. Only the love scene with la Cualquiera is relayed with as much sensuality as the description of el Artista's encounter with the word, a moment of plenitude in which the limit is reached and named. He is only woken from his linguistic delirium by a list of bodies, torture, and betrayals although it will be through language that he will attain understanding of the contradictions that the illusory image that surrounds power has encountered. La Niña says it clearly in the middle of the novel, before she throws him out "Ellos son unos hijos de la chingada y . . . tú eres un payaso" (They're badass motherfuckers and you're nothing but a clown), thus confirming the degraded and expendable nature of art that is subjected to power.[111] However, el Artista requires other instances of clarification before, at the end of the novel, he is able to say:

> Who was the King? An all powerful. A ray of light who had lit up the margins because it couldn't be any other way as long as it weren't revealed what he was. A sad sack, a man betrayed. A single drop in the sea of men with stories. A man with no power over the terse fabric inside the artist's head. (The Artist allowed himself to feel the power of an order different from that of the Court, the skill with which he detached words from things and created his own sovereign texture and volume. A separate reality).[112]

To allow for an ethical ending—where the capo's power falls and with it the symbolic mechanism el Artista controls, capable of filtering reality and consecrating it in song—we gradually and believably witness his efforts to undermine el Rey's carefully constructed mythical stature. The opaque density of truth inserts itself between art and power, favoring the simulacrum over creativity. Creativity, power, and song all feed on the myth until the sovereign's necro-politics collide with the social forces that precipitate his loss of hegemony. Language then becomes a series of floating signifiers and silence, as in *Señales que precederán al fin del mundo*, persisting in an open space, ready to inaugurate a new beginning. The signs of language are in this instance impregnated with nostalgic lyricism: "Decir cuate, sueño, cántaro, tierra, percusión. Decir cualquier cosa. Escuchar la suma de todos los silencios. Nombrar la holgura que promete. Y luego callar" (To say homeboy, daydream, decanter, meadowland, rhythm. To say anything. To listen to the sum of every silence. To give a name to the space full of promise. And then to fall silent).[113]

The poetic evocation of language—both phonetic and semantic—constitutes a deepening of its value as an instrument of penetration into reality, essential for the process of its construction and for grasping it and sharing it. As an element that creates community, language communicates epistemic value: a narrative of feelings that permits a recognition, interpretation, and integration of the real into the imaginary, transforming it into an existential territory and a space for the generation of life and meaning. El Artista's music cannot extend its reach to el Heredero in order to consecrate the cartel's dynastic principle. Its myth corroded, the protagonists in the narco-saga fall one by one, under their own weight. Now that he has fallen from grace, el Rey savagely tells el Artista: "Tú eres un soplido, una puta caja de música, una cosa que se rompe y ya, pendejo" (You're a piece of fluff, a fucking music box, a thing that gets smashed, you piece of shit).[114] When the court collapses, ceding to the "forces of order" but more so to its own internal tensions, the Artist's only recourse is to return to the in between space he had left, enriched only by misfortune and by his experience of ephemerality and loss.

THE CORRIDO AS SOCIAL TEXT

The theme of music serves as an element of the transfiguration and displacement of sociocultural content in both the novel and generally in the world it represents. Herrera executes the transition from experience to discourse and, more specifically, to popular culture's symbolic register in various ways, reconfiguring the meaning attributed to celebration, simplifying them in accordance with a logic of parodic heroism, masculinity (machismo), and control. In addition, the mechanisms underpinning the *corrido*'s creation naturalize the events being celebrated and render them part of daily life.[115] As Valenzuela points out: "El corrido mantiene su función tradicional como crónica, registro, referente axiológico, historia subalterna y recuento de asuntos de interés social que se cuentan cantando" (The *corrido* preserves its traditional function as chronicle, record of activities, axiological referent, subaltern history and subject of social interest told through song).[116]

The *corrido* brings together individual experience and collective identity through the assimilation of events to the outlines of a paradigmatic, celebratory, and hyperbolic narrative. The *corrido*'s sanctifying aims always crown a basic conflict: antagonism between gangs or individuals, opposition to the leadership, triumph over adverse circumstances and "limit situations." This act of assimilation requires simplification and the adaption of facts to the genre's formalized codes. The subject celebrated in the *corrido* confronts adverse societal conditions, fighting inequality and systemic violence with individual strengths that are always strongly imbued with passion and emotion.

Various scholars have analyzed the *corrido* as a transformation of the Peninsular *romances*, above all in its incorporation of elements of violence and social critique, ethno-racial elements, community spaces (pueblo, border, neighborhood, gang), and the acknowledgment of inequality, precarity, marginality.[117] The *corrido* is disseminated in a variety of spaces according to its themes and level of explanation of events and protagonists: public for the commercial promotion of popular culture, and private for spaces frequented by people—often members of criminal gangs or cartels, etc.—directly connected to the *corridos*' themes. In this way and depending on the case, the mediating insertion of the *corrido* provides a mytho-poetic nexus between legality and covertness, status quo and popular subversion, public space and subjectivity, life, and death. The *narcocorrido* seems to have invigorated this form of popular composition, which, shaped by processes of modernization, has weakened during the decades of the last century. Providing new antiheroic protagonists and scenes of extreme violence in contexts also marked by the erosion of the State, the tragic emotion that Américo Paredes had referenced with respect to the *corrido* finds new channels in the genre's renewal.[118] The *narcocorrido* incites anti-governmental vengeance and exalts paradoxical but effective forms of capitalistic goals that do not require participation in its productivism and discipline. The mythologizing of power, which is one of the characteristics of the *corrido*, finds a singular form of expression in *Trabajos del reino*, in the character of Lobo who provides a transition between the two registers. The first, paradoxically, draws on the lineage of ancient regimes of individual and absolute power, whose pomp and aura of monarchical investiture place the figure of the capo in a superior self-proclaimed and supposedly inaccessible space. The second corresponds to the dimension of popular culture found in the chorus that acknowledges, admires, respects, and celebrates power. A dialectic exists between empirical material and oral narrative that mutually determine and mold each other. Again, in Herrera's work the mediating function acquires a primordial relevance since within it lies the force that unleashes reactions and substantial changes in the relational economy of history. In *Trabajos del reino*, the attribution of truth—one of the *corrido*'s principal traits—stands out. The genre establishes a reception pact based on its supposed condition as a form of popular testimony of situations and events that occur at the heart of the community. El Artista began to exercise his métier by paying tribute to el Rey, but the genre's adulatory value also possesses a functional aspect, and el Rey attempts to take advantage of it as a way of penetrating the enemy space, since both he and the rival capo possess the same weakness for praise. Before making the incursion into the enemy cartel, el Artista clearly understands the death drive it contains: "Están muertos. Todos ellos están muertos. Los otros. Tosen y escupen y sudan su muerte podrida con engaño pagado de sí mismo, como si cagaran diamantes. Sonríen, los dientes pelados cual cadáveres, cual cadáveres, calculan que nada malo les puede pasar." (They're dead. All of them, dead. The others. They cough and spit and sweat their deaths, rotted through with self-satisfied deceit. As if they shat diamonds. They grin with bare teeth, like corpses; like corpses, they figure nothing bad can happen to them).[119] An awareness of the simulacrum leads directly to the perception of impending death. Without the simulacrum, the cartel's structure cannot sustain its illusion of power. Herrera presents the corrosion of its dominance as the materialization of an irreversible necrosis. The false consciousness that el Artista's work helped disseminate and consolidate gives rise to a critical and disenchanted recognition of a weak and disappointing reality.

First as an incursion into the imaginary, and then as a device that channels a truth regime into the world of the simulacrum, the *corrido* succeeds in destabilizing the systemic logic of the represented world. The truth succeeds in unsettling the cartel's self-consecrating order as well as its hegemonic discourse and unmasks the fissures and the weakening of power. It is a potentially self-destructive act of awareness since in dis-assembling the system of power, el Artista's function within it is also dismantled. However, paradoxically, this dismantling occurs in the act of its own disruption.

Only one *corrido* actually appears in the novel, when the singer points out el Rey's inability to hold onto his absolutist regime of personalized power: "Yo sé que aunque calles quieres / que ya no estemos jodidos / ni que fueras de vil palo / somos tus únicos hijos" (Tho you don't say it, King, I know / You don't want us getting shot / Cause you're not made of stone / And we're the only sons you got).[120] The reproach contained in el Artista's words is not directed to el Rey but rather to the Father, that is, to the figure of the Protector charged with symbolic feelings and emotions based on the betrayal the subalterns feel at the patriarch's decline. Their recrimination is not directly political nor economic but rather subjective, affective, and existential, an opportune counterpart to accolades produced by commission in other eras. Alienated from the order upon which he depends, el Artist flees, while the kingdom collapses under the weight of its own contradictions. El Artist refuses to become part of el Heredero's dynastic power and, in a perfect circle, returns to his origins, albeit as a different man, enriched by his experiences and apprenticeship. Like a Chinese box, Lobo's misfortune is embedded within the cartel's story, both at its peak and at its decline.

At the same time, the creation of power formulates a story embedded within the nation's greater reality. The "order" imposed by the State (in this case the police) submits to the cyst-like world of the cartel, which results in a relative and fleeting victory. As an autonomous project embedded within the logic of capitalism, the cartel views its loss of sovereignty eschatologically, like rot. There is nothing outside of capitalism, and it contains within it the seeds of its own destruction. El Artista's ground zero perspective puts into relief the events that have happened since he met el Rey to the moment just before his fall, as if they were a dream that takes place in a space outside of the law, morality, and critical judgment that Lobo perceives as a blinding light that poeticizes history in all its avatars. As critics have noted, the naturalization of violence removes the limits between different social actors, projects, and procedures since the criminal practices involves agents of the State as well as those from the worlds of organized and common crime. As Valenzuela has indicated, "El marco axiológico se ha desdibujado ante los ojos de importantes sectores sociales de nuestro país, para quienes no existe diferencia cualitativa entre narcos, policías y judiciales" (The axiological framework has blurred the vision of important social sectors in our country, for whom there is no qualitative distinction between narcos, police, and the legal system).[121] In this context, many forms of popular culture express imaginaries that transform tragedy into farce, with the latter understood as a process distanced from its referents through an ironic, parodic, and even comic construction of social drama.

However, nothing shapes el Artista's apprenticeship more than the audience that begins to push back on the coarseness of his themes and the general sense of his messages. The novel dramatizes the moments of mediation in which he traffics in his symbolic product. Between art and public, media is the tool that commercializes and is one of the springs of the wide and complex mechanism of cultural production-dissemination-reproduction. This works as a two-way street that delivers the Artist to the overwhelming opinion of the consumers: "No querían sus canciones. Los loros de la radio decían que no, que sus letras eran léperas, que sus héroes eran malos. O decían que sí, pero no: que los versos les gustaban, pero ya había orden de callar el tema ... fachada pa los gringos, y chitón temporal mientras se sosegaban los anunciantes" (They didn't want his songs. Jockeys at the station said his words were coarse, his good guys were bad. Or they said yes, but no; they liked the lyrics but had orders to shut his groove down ... a show for the gringos, temporary hush-hush till the advertisers cool down).[122]

Concisely, the novel exposes the pressure exerted by the market, the transnationalization and commercialization of cultural goods and consumer demands as examples of the condemnation or consecration of local products. *Trabajos del Reino* also underscores art's ideological value, where in addition to its expressive, lyrical, and socializing sheen, it must also assume a relationship with reality in order to understand the political implications of defamation and panegyric, deciding on life and death actions, and negotiating messages for a wider and more diverse public than the cartel's captive audience. El Rey is told of the problem ("Lo de siempre: que no se puede hablar bien de usted a la gente" [same old story: they mustn't be seen speaking well of you to the people]) and suggests a behind-the-scenes scheme to bring el Artista's merchandise to a new public: "Ni se preocupen, aquí el Gerente va a arreglar con unos amigos para que muevan su música en la calle . . . Al cabo así es como hacemos negocios, ¿no?" (Don't you worry about it, the manager here will arrange things with our friends to move your music on the street . . . . After all, isn't that the way we do business?).[123] The informal economy works alongside the official one, opening up underground channels for a wider and less mediated audience for his products. El Artista finds himself torn between here and there, us and them, life and death in a world increasingly defined in antagonistic opposing terms: "Tienen una pesadilla los otros: los de acá, los buenos, son la pesadilla; la peste de acá, el ruido de acá, la figura de acá. Pero acá es más de veras, acá está la carne viva, el grito recio" (They have a nightmare, the others: the men here—the good guys—are their nightmare; the smell here, the noise here, the hustle here. But here it's more real, in the flesh, alive and kicking).[124]

This Manichean distribution of values reveals a highly emotionalized conscience, radicalized by anger, desiring to harm in order to "sentir su espanto, pues, porque el susto de los otros alimenta bien, remacha que la carne de los buenos es brava y necesaria, que hace bulto y zarandea las cosas" (feel their fear, right, because their fear is what you feed off and makes clear that the flesh of the good is brave and necessary, that is shakes things up and fills the space).[125] Imbued with the cartel's death drive, el Artista inhabits a tumultuous and perturbed space:

> They should be snatched up by the hair and have their faces rubbed in that vile truth, that ruthless putrid truthful truth, let them be lured in by it. They should be stuck on the spikes of our sun, drowned in the ruction of our nights, have our songs inserted under their fingernails, be lain bare with our skins. They should be tanned and hided. And caned. . . . They'd rather just hear the pretty part, but the songs we sing don't ask their say-so. A corrido ain't a painting that hangs on the wall. It's a name and its a weapon.[126]

El Artista's worldview stems from his frustration with the instability of his position as an organic element of the cartel, harnessed to the values and interests of an organization that is beginning to reveal its fissures and contradictions. Within the polarized sociocultural context of the Court the *corrido* acquires a combative character, displacing it from the festive space to the field of struggle itself in which the organization's loyalties, strategies, values, and interests must be defined. Later, Lobo will tell el Periodista that more than gossip or storytelling, his songs fulfill a social function: "El corrido no es nomás verdadero, es bonito y hace justicia" (The *corrido* isn't only true; they're also beautiful and just).[127] But the journalist remains unconvinced since his task is to manage information and use language in a utilitarian and direct fashion. He recommends that the artist keeps his option between his passion and his obligations open, that he seeks an audience beyond the powerful.

El Artista begins to write *corridos* for the enemy capo and finds out that life on "the other side" of things is suspiciously similar to that in the original Court and he undergoes a rude awakening: "Tuvo una visión minuciosa del rostro del Rey, como con una lupa le vio la consistencia floja de la piel, de una constitución tan precaria como la de cualquiera de las personas en este lugar. Disimuló que el hallazgo lo fulminaba" (The King's face appeared to him in all its detail, as if under a magnifying glass, and he saw how flaccid the skin, how precarious his constitution, like that of anyone here in this place. He pretended not to be thunderstruck by the discovery).[128]

The only *corrido* included in the novel recounts the disintegration of the cartel and the diminishing of its power. Capo/king/father is revealed as a sentimentalized construct that interiorizes the powerful figure in intimate and painful decline. With his defeat a cycle comes to an end, the calendar returns to real time, the exceptionality of the miracle is now over: "A partir de ahora ningún rey le daba nombre a sus meses" (From here on out, no king named his months).[129]

COURTLY THEATER: DIALOGIC SCENES

If we are to accept, as Herrera proposes, the subversive and emancipatory value of the imagination, *Trabajos del reino* should be viewed as an exploration of the effects of liberty on the restrictive space of sovereign power. In the novel, the movement from submission to rebellion, from enlightenment to recognition, from simulacrum to truth, proceeds at an appropriately slow rate, marked by pivotal moments that detail el Artista's various stages of apprenticeship.

The question of space is fundamental to the novel as it foregrounds various arenas of life and death, of domesticity and celebration, of entertainment and violence. The spatial distribution that correspond to various moments in the fictional timeline show the progression from Lobo's initial poverty in "una casa endeble donde nadie cruzaba palabras" (a sorry house where no one exchanged words) and the "territorio hostil" (hostile territory) of the street where the singer tried his hand at "coloreando sonidos" (shaping the sounds) to earn a living, to the magnificence of the idealized and exotic palace inhabited by eccentric characters, as if in a variety show.[130] Between the two poles are cantinas, *antros* and marginal corners that operate as intermediate, temporary, and hostile places in which the singer initially familiarizes himself with popular usage, attitudes, and values. In these settings, his skill with words and his understanding of people's moods and desires finds admirers.

Public spaces provide the backdrop for the singer to hone his skills for bigger venues. Song represents one more element in a complex sociocultural, ideological, and political performance that expands out into concentric circles from the power nucleus of el Rey to the Court and the community. The community visits the palace, paying homage to its inhabitants, and requesting their help with lives that have been rendered precarious and subordinate by systems of exclusion and that the cartel imitates and radicalizes in a despotic exercise of narco-*caciquismo*. The cartel is self-contained, demarcating a unique space of celebration and crime, of intrigue and torture. As within any palace environment, the threads of adulation, appearance and ostentation are woven into the daily narrative. The public and private spheres where narco-sociability is developed are both autonomous and overlapping. Their interrelation makes it clear that subaltern subjects belong to el Rey, who exercises his all-encompassing power through necropolitics that mimic the mechanisms of the authoritarian state. However, within the controlled space of the kingdom, his command over life and death only permits him certain access to discourse, emotions, and thoughts. Despite their secondary role in the world of narco-power, women emit a transformative and reflexive energy around the reality that absorbs them as essential parts of the order and contribute in great part to the theatricalization of the palace microcosm where all alliances must be viewed as transitory and deceptive.

The novel's continual references to the kingdom are nothing more than the parodic allegory of a centralized power that defines itself as an enduring dynastical political-social autarky consecrated by religion. The novel's farcical underpinnings promote an ironic reading in which collective belief nonetheless incorporates a transcendent element that, built on false consciousness, sees narco-power as the materialization of a superhuman capacity that Lobo himself defines at the beginning of the novel:

> The royalty of a king determined these things: the man had settled among simple folk and turned the filth to splendor. Approached from afar, the Palace exploded from the edge of the desert in a vast pageantry of gardens, gates, and walls. A gleaming city on the fringes of a city in squalor, a city that seemed to reproduce its misfortune on street after street. Here the people who came and went thrust their shoulders back with the air of those who know that theirs is a prosperous dominion.[131]

As the author has pointed out in several interviews, the novel's fictional setting evokes Ciudad Juárez. The dialogical relationship between poverty and luxury, daily life and exceptionality, center and periphery, finds an unstable, provisional, and farcical synthesis in the narco-oasis that unscrupulously and defiantly exposes its ill-gotten abundance as proof of its superiority and autonomy. The Pantagruelian banquet hosted by the cartel satiates more than just hunger, with "the desire to be other" that more than one member of the court and the community strives for. But above all, the experience of space dazzles the singer, like an entry point into a territory that must be conquered, and over which rights must be won. Lobo loses himself in the palace, traversing it "como un gato en casa ajena" (like a cat in a new house).[132] The place's deceptive simplicity and its grandiosity disconcerts him, and he uses a little mirror to secretly look at "los muebles labrados, las puertas de metal, los candelabros" (carved furniture, metal doors, candelabras) and the "gente de las ciudades, trajeados de portafolio, policías en busca de su cuota. . . . Era como ser invisible" (visitors from the cities, suits with briefcases, officers of the law who'd come for their kickback. . . . It was like being invisible).[133]

A baroque and courtly topic and symbol of trompe l'oeil, the mirror motif adds artificiality, caution, and perhaps hypocrisy to the Artista's curiosity, offering him a rearview vantage point (he looks through the mirror "over his shoulder") inverting the image, enhancing the distorted vision el Artista takes in as real. Other allusions to distorted reality are connected to his vision. After using the glasses prescribed by el Doctor, he realizes that there's no difference between one cartel and another and their routines etc. are identical. He thus comes to understand that his role as witness involves not only seeing the masks but also penetrating them. He perceives not only reality but also a value judgement he develops as an observer, the work of reason, intuition, and morality. Truth lies in wait at every corner, and it prevails as a scruple, and a self-imposed task that refashions its place in the world. Nearing his end, el Rey himself is refashioned through his masks, as a simulacrum: "El Artista leyó en el pie de foto que el Rey había sido capturado cuando 'intimaba' con tres mujeres. Simón, pensó. He ahí una historia para ser cantada, no la que el Rey había representado con gracia hasta el final, sino la otra, la de las máscaras, la del egoísmo, la de la miseria" (The Artist read in the caption at the bottom of the photo that the King had been captured during an "intimate encounter" with three women. Right, he thought. There's a story to be sung, not the role the King had played with grace until the end, but the other tale, the one about masks, and egotism, and misery).[134]

Like a Chinese box, the novel is a theatricalization that contains within itself additional simulacra and other disguises that corresponds to attributes or people (in the theatrical sense of "character" or "social role" that a person assumes), which complicates the id-entity of each actor, transforming him or her into another force (avatar or imposter). As a form of symbolic representation, the song feeds on simulacrum and on the parody or burlesque constructs that are superimposed onto reality until they replace it in the collective imagination.

The kingdom thus functions as the cartel's farcical reality, representing it as a centralized and hierarchical organization. It possesses a totalizing meaning in that each part of the system is represented by typified characters and by paradigmatic loci and situations. The kingdom does not represent the cartel but rather the *myth* of the cartel—the ideological edifice that underpins the idea of a clandestine organization as a (war) machine existing outside of the state, albeit intimately incorporated into its apparatus. The novel reveals these connections with references to the police that come to the palace to pick up their bribes and to the soldiers who sit at the table with the capo at the end of the novel to help find him a way out. Based on the analogies Herrera makes between kingdom/cartel and capo/king, *Trabajos del reino* possesses cognitive value not in terms of sustaining a premeditated anachronism but instead by installing a double meaning that takes the obvious differences between the terms that the allegory approximates and the exaltation of similarities for granted, relegating literalness to the background. El Rey's ambit is ex-centric, not only because it sits at social and territorial margins but also because it expresses a strange reality where he assigns himself and his surroundings unusual attributes like the animals that speak to the hyperbolic consumerism facilitated by drug trafficking:

> They went out to the grounds, strolled by a fountain in whose center stood a god spitting water through its mouth, carried on to a maze of shrubs that spelled out the King's name.... Then she gazed out at the perimeter, the electrified fence, the desert.... They walked to where the King's collection was. There were snakes, tigers, crocodiles, an ostrich, and in a bigger cage, almost its own garden, a peacock.[135]

The setting decenters the cartel, theatrically placing it in a luxurious and exotic space that compensates for its humble origins, its violence, illegality, and the sowing of death and destruction that underscores the pretentious paraphernalia that surrounds the capo and his entourage, who are represented as characters in a glorious saga of bullies and killers. These contrasts shore up the look of a low-budget film that fulfills the delusions of grandeur of sex workers and assassins. Decorated like the country house of a European noble but with the over-the-top and eclectic taste of the nouveau riche, the palace oozes artifice, bad taste, excess, and ill-gotten gains. The retaining wall that surrounds it speaks to the violence that underpins it and presages its fall.

The lyrics inscribed into the landscape that hide the unspoken name of el Rey, the lack of direct allusion to narcos, its corrupt and necro-maniacal world, and the omission of the key words that reference drug trafficking all contribute to the elusive and elliptical style that characterize Herrera's novel. Marked by omissions and tacit understandings, the novel is articulated via the structure the reader builds as the narrative progresses, releasing the allegory's exact meaning, built on the careful articulation of images and silences, of reticence and voids as significant as the poetic language that surrounds them, consistent with the clandestine world in which the plot unfolds. The novel grows in sentimentality, producing an affective space that absorbs the erasure of political parody. As the nucleus of a centralized and hegemonic power, wielded with populist and despotic traits, the fall of the monarchical regime's empties out the world. Disappeared from the authoritarian regime's nerve center, the precarious community disperses and withdraws to its places of origin: the margins, the underground, subaltern places, the system's periphery, the cracks, the between spaces of a torn and unraveling storyline. The spatial transition hurries the action to its end, disbanding the cartel and uncovering the instability of its furtive and marginal position as well as the weakness in its network of relationships that connected the palace's situational community, a true den of capos and peons that lived an illusion of power and sovereignty. People no longer wander through gardens and salons with delight and amazement but instead stampede among corpses, betrayals, and threats as they try to save themselves. Artificially sustained by the regime, human interactions cannot survive its downfall. El Rey was the producer of meaning, organizer of the collective calendars, giver of significance to time and space, the controller of affect, stipends, and punishments. His fall shows the fragility and self-sanctification of the power that bound it all together. Dispersion reigns in the palace where, toward the end, there is no sign of the sovereign's ghostly shadow.

In the city where el Artista arrives and from which he then flees on his way elsewhere, "había cambiado la estación y un polen denso y dorado flotaba en el ambiente" (the season had changed, and a dense golden pollen floated in the air) as if inaugurating a beginning or revealing, in an almost cinematographic way, an ending.[136] Sentimentalized and contained, the ending again underlines the idea that *Trabajos del reino* is not a narconarrative but rather a bildungsroman freed from the genre's formal qualities and defying hermetic classification and compartmentalization in a process of symbolic production that skillfully explores the popular imagination. The "differential inclusion" implemented by the cartel reproduces the logic of migration politics. The border's function is not to exclude, but to selectively include. Within this selective inclusion, el Artista occupied both sides of the electric fence, he was absorbed; at first, he was accepted and appropriated and afterward he was excluded to facilitate the reestablishment of the underground world's autocratic order. His exit from the kingdom returns it to the chaotic space of the narco-world that will continue to exist without him, refashioning itself through new avatars. Lobo, for his part, recovers his image and acknowledges his pain, his sadness, his body, his love: "El dolor le palpitaba en las sienes mas no abominó de él. Era suyo. Si era la muerte, era suya. Era dueño de cada parte de sí, de sus palabras, de la ciudad que ya no precisaban buscar, de su amor, de su paciencia y de la resolución de volver a la sangre de Ella, en la que había sentido, como un manantial, su propia sangre." (Pain hammered his temples, but he did not curse it. It was his. If it was death, it was his. He owned every part of himself, of his words, of the city he no longer had to find, of his love, and his patience, and the determination to return to her blood, in which, like a wellspring, he'd recognized his own).[137] As Lombardo explains, "La novela finaliza, entonces, con un nuevo reparto de lo sensible, con una nueva lógica de lo visible y lo invisible, de la palabra y del ruido, del tiempo y del espacio" (the novel ends with a new distribution of feelings, with a new logic of the visible and the invisible, of words and noises, time and space).[138]

While *Trabajos del reino*'s use of precise and economical diction, its selective colloquialism, its opportune use of regional language, and its moments of inestimable lyricism are exceptional, perhaps even more so are its silences, discretion, and ellipses. All the words that el Artista does not sing, and the unexpressed love and hate remain unspoken in Herrera's novel but are nonetheless present in the atmosphere of his narrative as well as in gestures, in spaces and decorations.

SEÑALES QUE PRECEDERÁN AL FIN DEL MUNDO: A VOYAGE INTO SILENCE

If *Trabajos del reino* builds on plot points located in primarily closed, circumscribed, and controlled spaces, placing the principal character in a problematic context that tests his moral, affective, and ideological resources, Yuri Herrera's second novel uses different forms of displacement as its principal key. Through both space and time, the emblematic character of Makina will, from the perspective of her own movements, explain the appearance of elements that constitute a geocultural landscape of historical, social, and political meaning. In a different way to the first novel, *Señales que precederán al fin del mundo* works as an exposé that returns insistently to the question of institutions and to the principles that charge them with meaning.[139] Topics as diverse as family, land ownership, the border, the army, and sports are just some of the issues with which the narrative engages to call the reader's attention to the forms and places around which society organizes itself. As part of a precarious and dysfunctional ordering, the places traversed by the novel mark moments that connect to a bigger story that encompasses and goes beyond Makina's journey.

Conceived of as a grand narrative, in the novel the social functions as a reality that, particularly in marginal areas still operates as the debate between tradition and modernity, between the ancestral and the new, and between the primitive and the contemporary. Rather than following a linear progression, these moments must be understood in terms of their complex and conflictive simultaneity or as fluid and coexistent realities that make up the fabric of the community. Embedded in the social characteristics of the cultural and historical context that frames the novel are other elements that point to the representation of violence, machismo, inequality, social injustice, corruption, and selfishness as both individual and collective features. The novel offers a profound exploration of the limit between life and death. This issue is illustrated in the demarcation that separates Mexico from the US and, in the most abstract of terms, in the representation of community life, necro-politics, alienation, and consciousness.

JOURNEY AS PARADIGM

The unforeseen event around which the novel is organized illuminates a series of peripheral and border spaces that straddle languages, cultures, national territory, cultural domains and subjective parameters outside of big urban centers. As Martín Lombardo has pointed out,

> This is a literature of communal margins. Not only because its characters are marginal nor because some of them are immigrants but rather because it examines the majority of the community from the spaces where the community begins to erase its borders and create other kinds of communal links. The novel examines the entire community from its borders.[140]

The presence of material or symbolic limits introduces the themes of authority and transgression as well as the movement of characters across both fictional space and narrative plot. The act of crossing borders, whatever these might be, also assumes relevance in terms of who crosses, who facilitates it, what the risks and the cost might be, what transformations are unleashed by the crossing, who guards the thresholds, and who controls movement. Also interesting is Lombardo's observation that Yuri Herrera's contemplation of power demonstrates the survival of what has been repressed, despite the constraints placed upon it: "lo reprimido es aquello que circula bajo otra forma, en muchos casos, bajo la forma del secreto" (The repressed is that which circulates in another form, in many cases in the form of a secret). In this sense "el poder aparece como una tensión de fuerzas productiva: incita, suscita, produce" (power appears as productive tension: it incites, provokes, produces).[141]

In Herrera's novel, the motif of the journey always accompanies the theme of the hero and assumes an original approach to the question of limits (finish lines, extremes, boundaries) by centering the move toward Mictlan, the land of the dead in Nahua cosmogony, in the character of Makina. As Joseph Campbell indicates in *The Hero with a Thousand Faces*, the hero's journey is motivated by the search for things to aid the collective good.[142] The quest is marked by obstacles that parody life itself with its external barriers and internal encumbrances.[143] Identified as the hero, the main character represents collective desires and values. Directly or metaphorically, the hero's journey is always a descent during which he or she must confront a series of challenges that put their bravery and their ability to survive to the test. These cultural elements give Herrera's novel a strong foundation which, building on the references to life and death, and the purpose of Makina's journey and the challenges she faces, creates an intense nucleus around which the plot unfolds. As a kinetic character defined by movement, Makina must be considered in relation to the verb *jarchar*, coined by Herrera, with which he describes the action of leaving, and of dwelling in intermediate spaces between the places of departure and arrival. In other words, the neologism describes a dynamic and interstitial activity that connects social, cultural, and subjective spaces.

In medieval times, the *jarcha* itself provided a lyrical nexus between two cultures—Arabic and Christian—that relied on oral culture to be deciphered. In this sense, the Mozarab *jarcha* holds within itself the secret of its meaning as well as culture's essential impurity; its explicit value exists in its combinatory decodifying of sounds, feelings, and rituals. Built on and sustained by the border between civilizations in conflict over many centuries, the *jarcha* represents a symbolic act of mediation, a move toward the adventure of intercultural meaning and the intercultural sign. Makina's movements are subtle links in time and space that traverse history and its different levels of transparency and opacity. The *jarcha* is a sign that becomes intelligible and that announces, perhaps, the end of the world or at least the end of the world that el Norte threatens to subsume or of a present that is lived in the past, and in cultures suppressed by colonialism. In Herrera's poetics, *jarchar* means to leave a place, to go off, cross a threshold, launch oneself down a path, take a risk.

The term Herrera invents is itself a signal that points to other transhistorical and intriguing levels of poetic interpretation. The nature of the novel connects it to topics of great weight in our time including migration, border, (de)territorialization, communication, and language. The search for the other and the journey undertaken to locate him/her is one of the matrixes of the folkloric tales Vladimir Propp analyzes in *Morphology of the Folktale* where he identifies functions that are repeated as motifs in the tales, recombining and configuring a paradigmatic structure for these types of narratives.[144] Many of the functions Propp identifies can be found in *Señales que precederán al fin del mundo*: absence, quest, recognition, errand, mediation, magic elements, struggle, and return etc. For this reason, the plot is developed in well-defined stages or steps, following a standardized, incremental, and teleological schema.

Literature of all periods has explored the allegorical value of the journey, from the *Odyssey* and the *Aeneid* and Biblical texts, moving through

Don Quijote de la Mancha to Jack Kerouac, Antonio Tabucchi, and many others. The closest literary manifestations to *Señales que precederán al fin del mundo* of mythical displacement are Rulfo's *El llano en llamas* and *Pedro Páramo*, along with proliferating contemporary accounts of border crossing. All these texts feed into Makina's quest, referring to other journeys without invoking them directly. In these types of travel narratives, the route the main character undertakes allows for an exploration of variety and difference, inequality and exteriority, the world, affectivity, psychology, and memory. The constant decentralizing of the hero allows the reader to observe his/her behavior, reactions, resources, and fears. Journeys represent insatiable desire, the drive toward the ideal and toward utopia, fear of death, and the absence of the Father. According to Jung, the journey always implies the search for shadows (secrets, the unknown, enigmas, evil), forms part of initiation rites, and entails transformation and danger. It also assumes pilgrimage, purification, and catharsis and is permeated with the idea of return. Detachment and alienation reinforce the traveler's individuality and his/her vital force, forcing him/her to connect with unexpected beings, situations, and spaces that to a great extent give life to subconscious fears and impulses. Overcoming obstacles makes the traveler stronger, revealing his or her identity and deepening his/her understanding of his/her origins and goals.

Makina's itinerary becomes increasingly complex as it progresses. She moves from her provincial life sheltered by her community to Mexico City, and from there to the border and onto the US in a route that a complex combination of economic and social factors has transformed into a mythical journey in search of happiness. The dramatic reality of Central American migration is subsumed into the character's representativeness who, in this sense, is part of what the novel describes as mass exodus.[145] The US is viewed as both the land of opportunity and as a place of cultural loss and even alienation and dehumanization. The levels of difficulty that Makina encounters put her to the test spiritually and physically, pushing her beyond her limits. The experience she derives from the journey makes her grow, change, and adapt to the circumstances that challenge her patience and her physicality, as well as her ability to improvise, withstand, and recover creatively from the obstacles she encounters.

In Mexican literature, land is always at the crux of everything. In Herrera's novel the question unfolds in multiple meanings, extending to family inheritance and the territory that is traversed, the land that is left behind and the space that must be conquered. It touches the very heart of the rural question and constitutes the principal axis of Mexican history (and Latin American history in general) because of the conquest and subsequent dispossessions of natural resources suffered by autochthonous peoples. The land usurped through colonialism, struggles for land ownership during Independence and modernity, constant political programs in pursuit of agrarian reform and the theme of land as the central aim of the Mexican Revolution, followed by Cárdenas's land reform, constitute instances that speak to the symbolic and material value of territory as an element of survival, identity, and political mobilization. Consequently, land has been a constant presence in the popular imagination and in literary and visual representations of Mexicans. However, Makina's journey in search of land does not result in its attainment but instead in the loss of territoriality, community, and family ties.[146] At the end, the world is dissolving, and silence pervades the space of language, indicating an irreversible emptying. Makina's gradual descent ends in the loss of time and space, in a dimension without time, without recognizable places to anchor herself. Her identity has been erased and replaced with another, in a moment that seems to comprise total alienation or perhaps even death.

Obviously, this subjective dimension is fundamental to the novel. However, the way in which this interiority coincides with the spatial displacement that blurs the borders between territorial mobilization and internal/interior journey comprises one of the narrative's great strengths. Makina's enters material, emotional, social, and spiritual labyrinths that are connected to the geography she traverses both in terms of life experiences as well as the instances the soul undergoes during its journey. But in this confluence of dimensions, the social clearly predominates as the strata that determines material conditions and the characters' forms and degrees of social consciousness. Inequality, precarity, machismo, the processes of commercialization, commodification, and dehumanization operate at all the world levels she traverses, extending from south to north in a journey marked by feelings of danger, loss, and alienation.

Herrera builds the novel on a series of binary elements that, while not indicating a polarized world, promote reflection concerning the dynamics and negotiations between them. Man/woman, transcendence/materiality, Mexico/USA, language/silence—all create tensions and flows of meaning that enable plot development and slowly reveal Makina's subjectivity. She goes from one extreme to the other, deploying different communicative strategies, aided by her instincts and by the experience she has accumulated in a masculine world. The men who control Makina's journey, despicable in varying degrees, function almost as a diffuse and collective character, as a category of *actant*, in which individuals are scarcely distinguishable between themselves, fulfilling the same role of controlling their respective territories, affirming their symbolic capital, and exchanging merchandise. Only some characteristics of their individual appearances make them stand out during Makina's travels: "El señor Dobleú era un espectáculo feliz de redondeces pálidas surcadas por venitas azules" (Mr. Double-U was a joyful sight to see, all pale roundness with tiny blue veins).[147] Señor H, described as "una serpiente disfrazada de hombre" (a snake disguised as a man) is presented in the novel as being all "relumbrón de oro y camisa estampada de pájaros" (bird-print shirt and glimmering gold).[148] Señor Q presents himself as an individual not predisposed to violence and is dressed in black from head to toe. In a prophetic tone, he informs Makina of what she will encounter on her journey. Señor P, involved in a struggle over territory with Señor H, is armed with "un cuchillo largo y estrecho . . . que palmeaba constantemente" (a long thin knife . . . that . . . he patted nonstop).[149] He looks lasciviously at Makina but does not attack her. Herrera complements his depersonalization of the "señores" with that of their subalterns who are even less distinguishable between themselves: "Todos los esbirros se parecían, ninguno tenía nombre. . . . El esbirro .45 hacía pareja con el señor Hache contra los esbirros .38" (His thugs all looked alike and none had a name. Thug .45 was on Mr. H's side playing against the two Thugs .38).[150] Makina thus confronts a hostile and compartmentalized world dominated by machismo, drug trafficking, and borderland hybridization in which the signs preceding the end of the world proliferate.

WORD, LANGUAGE, TIME, WRITING: SYMBOLIC DISPLACEMENTS

Makina is not only defined by spatial displacement but also by her ability to move between diverse cultural territories. In her journey, toward (re)totalization, Makina's transitional character unifies symbolic spaces; in different languages she communicates the need to connect, to recognize the presence and absence of the Other, as well as the enigma of social interactions that announce both the end and the beginning of the world. Following the logic of the mediations I've already mentioned as being constants in Herrera's work, the theme of communication is essential in *Señales*. The apocalyptical element alluded to in the novel's title presages extraordinary situations and scenarios. Makina embodies the role of language, implying the possibility of transgressing borders, crossing imaginaries, and connecting existential spaces. Before she embarked on her journey, she worked not only as an operator, connecting phone messages in her town; but she also spoke three languages—the vernacular, the national or Latin language (Spanish), and *gabacho* or the language of the el Norte (English). Makina (*máquina*, machine) offers a covert link to technology and the processes of automation. Her control of the technology of communication possesses an obvious symbolic value that places it at the center of exchanges and collective mediations, awarding it an almost magical power over the signs that bring the community together and link it to the outside world. As Nathan Richardson points out "Makina is, then, at once, a consequence of language, a weapon of language, and a language weapon herself."[151] Above all, it is in the realm of interpersonal relationships where Makina achieves the most success, displaying a savoir faire learned through direct contact with a hostile and slippery reality. The novel includes references to situations in which the girl is shown interceding in practical questions, mediating disagreements, and facilitating reconciliations. As she learned early on during her work as a phone operator, an ethics of discretion and community service underwrites the politics of language: "Una no hurga bajo las enaguas de los demás. / Una no se pregunta sobre las encomiendas de los demas./ Una no escoge cuáles mensajes lleva y cuáles deja pudrir. / Una es la puerta, no la que cruza la puerta" (You don't lift other people's petticoats. / You don't stop to wonder about other people's business. / You don't decide which messages to deliver and which to let rot. / You are the door, not the one who walks through it).[152]

Standing at this threshold, Makina observes and (dis)covers an encoded world that portends its own destruction. One of the omens that announces this process is perhaps related to the fall of language as an informative and expressive link and with its transformation into an electronically regulated, depersonalized, and prodigious tool. It is worth emphasizing that this communicative function confers upon Makina the privilege of rational centralization with which she organizes community interactions as well as her own memory. In his studies on the body, memory and spirit, Henri Bergson explains:

> the brain is no more than a kind of central telephonic exchange: its office is to allow communication, or to delay it. It adds nothing to what it receives; but, as all the organs of perception send it to their ultimate prolongations, and as all the motor mechanisms of the spinal cord and of the medulla oblongata have in it their accredited representatives, it really constitutes a centre, where the peripheral excitation gets into relation with this or that motor mechanism, chosen and no longer prescribed.[153]

Makina's centrality is evident not only from her leading role in the fictional world but also because, through her own mobility, she deploys the different strata of this universe in surrounding layers that possess different degrees of proximity and connection to her. These concentric and increasingly peripheral circles deposit language, rationality of myth, the simultaneously tenuous and secure connection between life and death, and above all, the linguistic, visual, poetic, and emblematic sign that generates meaning. Makina uses language as an instrument of solidarity with the migrants she meets before crossing the river (the "gente huida"). She deciphers a letter for an illiterate old man in which his son explains how to find him once he makes the crossing; she teaches a boy how to say soap in *gabacho* and she explains to another that on the other side you're not permitted to cook on the sidewalk.[154] When she referees a couple's fight on the switchboard, Makina retransmits the lovers' words, translating their angry sentiments into less antagonistic formulations leading to their reconciliation.[155]

Perhaps the most intriguing aspect of her character, however, is the fact that she embodies the link between life and death. The novel opens with her declaration "I'm dead" when the earth collapses beneath her feet, swallowing up people and cars. This phrase initiates the route that she will take from her town to Mexico City and from there to the US, forcing her to confront criminal situations, dangerous journeys through rivers and deserts, mountains, highways, suburbs, and military bases that place her at risk of violence, climate extremes, checkpoints and threats and warning signs of an inevitable and terrible destiny. In addition to ethno-racial and gendered borders, she must transgress numerous emotional, physical, and social boundaries. From the names of mountains and valleys, her personal geography is replete with signs that seem to announce that, regarding the subject/object of inequality, prejudice, and poverty, the border is all encompassing.

The mixture of languages indicates that Makina's world is not only multicultural but also, frequently, Babel-like. The mixture of signs speaks to the complexity and richness of humanity, to the temporality of individual positions, to the variability of affect and the futility of earthly connection. These are the components of an inevitable adventure in which the great dramas of human existence are displaced onto fruitless power struggles. In the final instance, everything is part of the same subjective and cosmic mass that is both internal and transcendent and that constitutes existence.

The journey from Mexico to the USA embodies a utopian dream with the attainment of el Norte framed as a place of privilege and opportunities. Other versions of the "el Norte" myth define it as a place where you lose your soul, your language, your family ties, your homeland, and your contact with nature. Thus, we see the materialization of the possibility of a new beginning, as well as the beginnings of the alienation of the self and the sacrifice of interiority. As in *Trabajos del reino*, most of the characters are referred to indirectly either by their initials (Señor Hache, Señor Dobleú or simply Señor Q, Señor P, etc.) or their nicknames (Chucho). Seen from Makina's viewpoint, even cities receive personalized names, (the Ciudadcita, the Gran Chilango, Gringolandia, or the Gabacho), subsuming popular feelings into language that assimilates places and situations to emotionalized imaginaries.

Makina experiences a world devoid of meaning, one that swallows itself up, putting its borders, its content, its inhabitants, as well as its own history into crisis. Corroded by its extractivist ambitions, Makina's hometown is collapsing into the netherworld: "earth's insanity." Often subsumed in the narrator's voice, the only subjectivity and the only gaze seems to be her own. Although she is not, Makina comes across as a one-dimensional character who lacks the depth that comes from references made by other characters or from the narrative discourse itself that the reader can scrutinize. Herrera exaggerates Makina's role as mediator, to the point where her most important character trait is her ability to fulfill the stages that have been laid out. Mobilization, physicality, and hope combine to motivate her to persevere and move forward.

The reader interprets the character as an essential link in a vital trajectory that is, in some ways, universal. As Makina herself describes it, she is not the person who comes through the door but instead she is the door itself or rather the threshold, or intermediate space, the fissure in time through which she filters a story that could have been buried in the region's perforated land but instead comes to the surface and is put into words. She is the intermediate point that both separates and unites, she is the border, the line that divides two worlds, that transgresses or not, but that impacts life forever. Like Lobo in *Trabajos del reino*, Makina must fulfill an errand: find her brother who, like him, left in search of the Promised Land that, in both cases, was as much material as symbolic. Both characters work then, according to a mandate, responding to an order that to a certain extent defines them. It is in these circumstances that Makina leaves her house as the novel begins: "Mejor me apuro a cumplir este encargo" (Best be on with my errand).[156] This situation is reinforced when Sr. Hache exacts payment for the contacts he has made by giving her another task: "Nomás te voy a pedir que lleves algo, una cosita de nada" (All I ask is that you deliver something for me, an itty bitty little thing).[157]

As Herrera explains, this situation has antecedents: "Con el señor Q Makina tenía su propia historia: dos años atrás había chambeado como emisaria de urgencias en las negociaciones que él y el señor Hache sostuvieron. . . . Recaditos a media noche . . . palabras trasmitidas por Makina sobre entregado a un cacique pueblerino" (With Mr. Q. Makina had her own backstory: two years ago she'd worked as a messenger doing emergency negotiations he and Mr. Aitch held. . . . Midnight messages . . . an envelope slipped to a small-town cacique).[158] For both Lobo and Makina crossing implies a decisive moment. Both characters abandon the known world carrying with them only the symbolic capital of words (song, communication, *corrido* lyrics, knowledge of other languages). But in both cases the use of language is a performative activity that implies theatricality and the use of masks as well as expressive actions that can connect the system's dots: movements on a stage, tricks behind the scenes, simulacra and a strategic engagement with challenges and dangers.

Both characters are defined by the crossing (in the case of Lobo, from legality to illicitness) that determines and transforms them. Both describe a circle and lose something of themselves as their story unfolds. In the emblematic river crossing, Chucho, the coyote who guides Makina and other migrants during a large part of their journey, resembles the mythical personage of Charon who ferries the dead across the river Styx into the underworld. Although Charon's name is not invoked in the novel, the evocation of Hades underscores the idea that Makina has been dead since the beginning of the novel and that her journey is in fact the descent into the stages that lead to the hereafter—the space of silence. Chucho disavows the mere condition of *pollero* or coyote when the American rancher tells him that this will be his last trip: "No soy pollero, dijo Chucho. Já, si te he visto cruzando gente, dijo aquél. Y ya te atrapé en el acto. No, si no niego el acto, dijo Chucho. Pero no soy un pollero" ("I'm no coyote," Chucho said. "Ha! I seen you crossing folks," the man said. "And looks like now I caught you in the act." "Not the act I'm denying," said Chucho, "tho I'm no Coyote").[159]

In the cultural economy of late capitalism, where the ancestral dimension combines with technology, automatization, and the search for access to the "other side" as a form of utopia and salvation, nothing is as it seems. Crossing to the other side—to the land of the dead—presupposes traversing the border, crossing the river, moving toward the consumer society that begins by appropriating the migrant's identity, erasing his/her memory, obscuring his/her place of origin.

BECOMINGS

Makina is from a town that teeters on the edge of destruction, or that has already been destroyed, and she heads off to the other limit, where, on many levels, her brother embodies the simulacrum. In other words, he represents the disappearance of the *original* in the search for the *second*, degraded version. El Norte is assimilated into the underworld, along with the loss of identity, the utilization of the subject and its incorporation into the apparatus of an invisible but omnipresent State. Not only does her brother inhabit an alienated identity, but he is also alienated from himself. *I am other*. Paradoxically, the illusion of the Promised Land has deterritorialized him, and worse still, has dehumanized him. Transformed into a zombie by the false reality that sustains him, his relationship with Makina—the link that initiates her journey and sustains the narrative—no longer holds meaning. A new emptiness deepens the already existing nothingness and communicates to the reader, as in the earlier *Trabajos del reino*, that there only exists various levels of nothingness: relative and definitive nothingness, contingent and eternal nothingness, earthly and transcendent nothingness, and emotional, intellectual, and existential nothingness. The role of writing fulfills a particularly important role in *Señales que precederán al fin del mundo*, since it acts as the counterpart to the world of orality, images and signs that sustain the plot. Makina, the machine or *máquina* that assembles individuals, spaces, and situations, will use her written knowledge to help some immigrants. But toward the end of the novel, the files of US bureaucracy contain her sentence of death, giving her "otro nombre y otra ciudad de nacimiento . . . , nuevos números, nuevo oficio, nuevo hogar" (another name, another birthplace. Her photo, new numbers, new trade, new home) Makina's reaction "Me han desollado" (I've been skinned) places her in a Kafkaesque situation regarding the anonymous power of the State, which deprives her of her humanity, reinventing her life story and determining her destiny.[160] It represents another form of the death she references at the beginning of her odyssey. The circle closes because, in her world, rather than traversing different lives, subjects traverse different deaths in a cycle that returns them to their origins. El Norte is synonymous with dehumanization, farce, and writing. The latter is a vehicle for alienation and for the destruction of vernacular forces and personal roots.

    The temptation to interpret Makina's name as a reference to *máquina* or machine and to attribute the novel's meaning to this motif risks promoting the idea that the character possesses an automatic and essentialized function in which she fulfills her designated role without the slightest degree of consciousness. However, we can connect Makina to *máquina* if we understand the meaning of the word, in Deleuzian terms, as an assemblage or as a system of relations that works both on the inside by way of the components that give it meaning and coherence (the control of linguistic systems, beliefs, emotional and family aspects) as well as on the outside by way of expressive and material forms such as (re)actions, gestures, and decisions. Makina focuses on herself and displays multiple meanings that, as we have seen, possess a mythical dimension. At the same time, and despite her permanent (de)(re)territorialization, her character maintains unity, coherence, and intensity. She emanates a clear sense of directionality, purpose, and character and an inclination toward restitution and (re)totalization. This drive ensures her wholeness and her connections to the outside.

Within the novel's geopolitics the limits of the fictional world are not only territorial, spatial, and cartographic but also essentially political in the same way that borders are not lines drawn like scars—to use a well-known metaphor used in scholarship on migration—to divide territories. The delimitations that Makina crosses are distributions of power as well as social and ideological horizons within which reside relationships of domination, hierarchies, and codes. While not overlapping exactly with national horizons, these relationships tend to appear within the framework of the nation-State as the conventional way to understand the relationship between power and culture today. Makina's world is deeply rooted in colonial depredation and, in a complementary fashion, leans into the void of its own historical extinction. The underlying dynamic between modernity and tradition, center, and margin, North and South, is skillfully contained within the narrative's structural framework without transforming it into an anti-imperialist indictment and without again delving into the well-established memories of grievances that have occupied and continue to occupy more explicit forms of political and cultural denunciation and testimonialism. As part of an inescapable social landscape, we find South to North displacement in the novel's plot that, like in *Trabajos del reino*, "interroga a la comunidad entera a partir de sus bordes" (interrogates the entire community from its borders).[161]

Makina's evasive corporality gradually provides evidence of her progressive dematerialization. Her entry into the US can be interpreted as either rebirth or death, but nonetheless marks a cutoff point that places the character in a transcendental dimension, without removing her from ordinary life. From her initial declaration, the character descends into the underworld in stages. She crosses the river (a symbolic element that represents the separation between life and death) where she appears to drown, and continues through the desert, where she is shot, although her injury does not prevent her from continuing her journey. If we accept that the character is on a journey through the various levels of Mictlán, this interpretation of the novel, with its echoes of Juan Rulfo, confirms her descent is indeed eschatological. As Richardson points out, "Read this way, Makina's quest is not simply a shadow of an earlier archetype, but the journey of a dead soul, already separated from the body, toward its final resting place in the underworld."[162]

In a revealing interview with Aaron Bady, Herrera himself indicates that Makina's border character moves in this interstitial and Dantescan space that the Mexican tradition identifies with Mictlán, descending through the nine levels that contain challenges that strip the character of parts of herself, until she arrives at pure silence: "That place is the place of re-creation. In this world, you didn't die and disappear, and you weren't reincarnated: You came to this place of silence to somehow be part of a re-creation."[163]

Neither Makina's archetypal character, nor her dubious corporality nor even her name (suggestive of a posthuman (id)entity), succeed in minimizing her consistency nor her poetic profile, although the reader does witness her progressive dematerialization. Her journey follows an itinerary of prophetic signs whose apocalyptic message corresponds to el Norte, the place of alienation and silence (the loss of the mother tongue, for example) of dehumanization and utter deterritorialization.[164]

What Richardson rightly characterizes as a restorative trajectory and as an archetypal journey keeps open the possibility of a timely reading of the migration drama, the progressive devaluation of poverty, the constant search for the Other, and capitalism's alienating attractions. For me, this is where the novel's excellence lies. It can be seen as a type of tacit continuation of Rulfo's short story "Nos han dado la tierra," with the journey stemming from the constant scarcity of natural resources, depredation, and the desire to find one's own place where one can survive and where family and communitarian life can continue. In both cases, no reference is made to the right to land but instead to land that has been granted—an anonymous and misleading act that never materializes.

Makina's two dimensions—the worldly and the transcendent—masterfully come together to give the concisely and powerfully configured character a succinct and moving profile. Her journey is a drive that moves from fragmentation to totalization, from the attempt to recover something she has never really had and a person from her past she no longer recognizes. Although she completes the nine levels of the underworld, the subaltern subject still carries the weight of the effects of social fragmentation, political alienation, and economic precarity. The subject confronts the obstacles that put it to the test, imbuing it with a mythical and paradigmatic quality. The series of trials and the oscillation to and from deprivation is the destiny of the subaltern who is faced with three choices:

alienation in el Norte and depersonalization; the return to the silence of dispossession; or rebirth, thus beginning the interminable journey anew.

TRADITION/MODERNITY AND THE FUNCTION OF MYTH

Multiple and simultaneous journeys (territorial displacements as well as interior explorations) make Makina's character a vector around which the fictional world is organized. The world unfurls like the setting of a theatrical plot and like the symbolic materialization of a vernacular cosmogony. The latter possesses secrets that surpass language's capacity and belong only to silence. Makina's embarks on a hermeneutic journey that deciphers signs from which we can interpret the historical and civilizing process that, in turn, leads to the exhaustion of a universe of feeling that the weight of modernity continues to absorb. The narrative, with Makina at its center, relies on the protagonist's condition as a subject displaced from both her ancestral world as well as from modernity as we understand it in the contemporary world. As an intermediary and intermediate character, Makina is in various ways the incarnation of the Malinche, a woman caught between two civilizations, charged with the mission of communicating with both worlds. She was the translator of languages and cultural meanings, the ancestral subject in the face of the empire.

Makina is driven by ambiguity, or even more precisely, by a bivalence that manifests itself on many fronts. As she walks toward Mictlán—the mythological and transcendent land of the dead—the reader tends to view her character as the embodiment of a spectrality that is shown through the world of dreams, an imagined or parallel world. Identified with el Norte, this mythical land (USA for Central American migrants) must be conquered by way of tasks or challenges like the descent into hell. In this journey, the soul, the sense of identity, and the meaning of life that are embedded in community and family ties, as well as one's own land and beliefs, are lost. The border is the dividing land, and the characters who surround Makina on her route and crossing represent different moments on her journey to find her brother, who perhaps is also dead, or at least alienated by simulacra and the requirements the commercial paradise has imposed upon him.

In an interview with Diego Erlan, Herrera himself explains that *Señales que precederán al fin del mundo* offers two possible readings: one more literal in which, during her journey to find her brother, Makina discovers the world, and another more, profound and allegorical, reading in which she travels through the land of the dead without fully realizing what has happened to her.¹⁶⁵ At times, as at the beginning of the novel, her understanding surfaces: "Estoy muerta, se dijo Makina, cuando todas las cosas respingaron" (I'm dead, Makina said to herself when everything lurched).¹⁶⁶ We can, however, appreciate the connection between the temporalities that coexist and interrelate in the narrative's present in the plot's back and forth, its overlay, and, at times, the parallelism between two readings.

In this sense, Makina's temporal journey possesses an obvious civilizing connotation. The relationship between the ancestral and the modern involves connections between primitivism and technological advancement, the primordial and the future, community and post-citizenship. The novel locates two of its fundamental elements in the between-space that these dualities bring forth, and that can be encapsulated by the binary tradition/modernity. On the one hand, we find the theme of myth, an ideological formation based on fable and belief. On the other hand, migration, the emblematic displacement of individuals whose mere existence and mobility serve to document the decline of the national as a primary instance of the articulation of sociability in the modern world. In both cases, although the registers are different, the organizing principle is the crossing of real or imagined borders between two worlds.

Nowadays, the subject finds itself situated in a civilizing state in which the values and social practices connected to solidarity and intersubjective communication are weakening and undoing the social fabric, giving way to forms of alienation that seem to announce the end of the known world. In this panorama characterized by deterioration and collapse that exemplifies the beginning of the novel with the world's sinking, practices such as pilgrimages, omens, and the discovery of the apocalypse remerge as premodern signs of a world that is returning to cyclical time. In this world, the word once again becomes silent so that new forms of life can revitalize the arid space of inequality and grief. In the novel's allegorical landscape, el Norte is the place of surrender: an anti-utopia that works in both the literal and figurative sense of desired destiny. The US is the magnetic north for all those who, exhausted by precarity and violence, go in search of a life of opportunity beyond the context of their origins. In their journey to their north, the migrant does not realize that she/he heads toward more of the same: insecurity, discrimination, and aggression directed toward the displaced, the "illegal," the nomad, the Other. Reintegration—if achieved—implies the renunciation of one's own values, one's language and the beliefs and forms of the known life. It is a journey without return, after which the world will always be Other.

The appeal to myth represents a recognition of the crisis of instrumental reason upon which the project of modernity is based. Makina's journey advances toward Mictlán, which is referenced in the ethnographic work of Bernardino de Sahagún (1499–1590), published centuries after his death under the name *El México antiguo*. In this work, based on tradition and oral tales transmitted to him by informants, the different stages of the journey are described in different sections whose titles are referenced in Herrera's work. The chapters' epigrammatic titles indicate enigmatic moments in the journey, alluding to the mythical levels and describing nature as something both supernatural and sublime, possessing an almost cosmic force. Santiago Navarro Pastor has analyzed the relationship between the journey to Mictlán and Makina's to el Norte, a connection that Herrera, himself a student of Aztec cultural traditions, admits exists.[167] Comparing these stages with Cecilio Robelo's observations in his *Diccionario de Mitología Náhuatl*, we can see that the nine levels of descent in the novel follow almost exactly the mythical and eschatological scale.[168] This reinforces the reading of Makina as a protagonist who penetrates the land of the dead.[169] This interpretation is also borne out by multiple textual references, the allusions to spectrality for example, or the character's lack of corporality such as when the bullet wound disappears as if it had never happened, or when she drowns in the Río Bravo but recovers without it leaving a trace, etc. All of this relativizes Makina's corporeality, transforming her into a dual and polysemic subject.

Makina's adventure is not only one of belief and spirituality, but also a knowledge exercise, motivated by existential, intuitive, and affective elements and by traditional and modern wisdom (for example, like the mastery of language and the practice of translation that connects her to the Malinche but that also projects her toward a transcultural future). No form of knowledge, whether it be modern or ancient, is disposable as we navigate the erratic history of the present where different levels of social systems and regimes of truth yield. The novel appears to not only carry out a fierce critique of present day necropolitics but also introduces a call to recover cultural roots, aspects displaced by modernity, and subjective ties that exist in elements capable of protecting the individual from consumerism's depersonalization, from competitiveness and alienation, thus returning the subject to its human condition.

The contrast between the intercommunicative style used at the switchboard where Makina works and new technology is highlighted by the cellphone that someone arrogantly shows her in her village after returning from el Norte: "Ni modo, chamaca, un día te tenías que quedar sin trabajo, observa y aprende" (Tough luck, kid, it had to happen: you're going to be out of a job. Watch and learn). The cellphone is revealed to be an element that puts popular ingenuity to the test, when it fails to connect the way he thought it would: "Pero luego de los tit tit siguió sólo silencio, un silencio especialmente pesado porque parecía que todos aguantaban la respiración para no estropear el prodigio" (But the peep-peeps were followed only by silence, a silence that was especially weighty because it seemed as if everyone was holding their breath so as not to spoil the wondrous trick).[170] This situation places Makina a few steps ahead of her interlocutor "¿No será que también te faltó comprar las torres?" (Maybe you should have bought a few cell towers, too?).[171] But fundamental here is the increase in indications of modernity that appear as she makes her way toward el Norte. These gradual changes mark the coming of a different world, displacing the old one. The language shift indicates a transition from the telluric to the cosmopolitan and displays the simultaneity of registers that coexist in modernity's peripheral spaces where premodern traits and vernacular cosmovisions linger. In all aspects, *Señales que precederán al fin del mundo* promotes a syncretic cultural reality that corresponds to the social formations of border regions. The point of crossing between countries represents a zone of exchange and hybridity that deauthorizes any claim to ethno-racial, religious, or civilizing purity. The coexistence of asymmetrical registers (some that are dominant, others that are dominated) reveal the historic struggle between different epistemes, forms of life and social organization, conceptions of the world, and political and economic understanding.

Giovanna Rivero has referred to the representation of a "novum" episteme in relation to Makina's character that serves as a true dispositive that channels unheard of forms of cognition and imagination in which converge principles connected to different binary systems.[172] In this sense, for Rivero, Makina=Máquina or machine represents technological elements that, as in the textual and ideological contexts of science fiction, prepare us for a different reality that is beyond our familiar paradigms. According to Rivero, "Sintetizando, el mito como antípoda y antídoto de lo real cumple la misma función de ruptura del novum tecnológico" (Synthetically speaking, in its capacity as the real's antipode and antidote, myth represents a rupture with "novum" technology). It's appearance defamiliarizes the known world, proposing new connections that illuminate other zones of the real: "En otras palabras, el mito funciona como un novum porque en su recursividad administra simultáneamente la creatividad para amoldar su esquema a los eventos del azar y la subjetividad para otorgarle sentido al tiempo como un fluir exento de historicidad" (In other words, myth functions as a novum because in its recursiveness it simultaneously provides creativity for adapting its outlines to chance events and subjectivity for endowing time with meaning as an ahistorical flow).[173]

Makina moves in a parallel time to history, coexisting without completely coinciding with it, relating to the real through superpositions, folds and slippages of meaning and presence, of words and silence. She discovers other dimensions of the real, other colors that the eye cannot see, sounds that become muted at her step. Although the connection Rivero makes between Makina and science fiction seems excessive to me, I share her thoughts on the novel's utopian composition, in which modern, Western knowledge and ancestral cosmogonies indicate the move away from national projects and toward a vision of the migrant as a new subject of future history that replaces sovereignty, hegemony, and citizenship. Rivero sees Makina as "mesías de una nueva 'verdad' histórica posnacional y posmexicana, concretamente, pero también post-imperial. El suyo es un doble viaje: el viaje político del mártir y el viaje religioso de la sacerdotisa" (a messiah of a new concretely post national and post Mexican historical truth, that is also post-imperial. Hers is a double journey: the political journey of the martyr and the religious journey of the priestess).[174] Rivero continues in this vein: "De allí que otra posibilidad de interpretación para esta propuesta de Yuri Herrera sea el que Makina ocupa no únicamente el lugar de Marina o Malinche, sino el de una traducción sincrética entre el Cristianismo y la femineidad "chingada" del México prehispánico: Makina es también la Virgen de Guadalupe, invencible, rizomática, utópica" (Thus, another possible interpretation of the novel is that Makina fulfills the role not only of Marina or Malinche, but also that of a syncretic translation between Christianity and the "chingada" [fucked] femininity of pre-Hispanic Mexico: Makina is also the invincible, rhizomatic and utopian Virgin of Guadalupe).[175]

In this regard, Malinche and the Virgin of Guadalupe can be understood as the same figure whose historical density goes beyond the traditional topic of the quest and instead intensifies it as an investigation of the very meaning of history, of modernity and of el Norte, toward which displaced migrants voyage. At the same time, Makina's own displacement in the chapters that detail the stages of the descent into the underworld occurs in a concrete social space that is recognizable as peripheral and marginal, situated in an intermediate site between her village and Mexico City as well as between the megalopolis and US border. The characters who she passes and the spaces she traverses signal the route of the migrants. Makina is constructed as a paradigmatic character who follows in the footsteps of many others and confronts similar obstacles. Machismo, systemic violence due to inequality, sharp contrasts in social circumstances between classes, opportunism, criminality, and the general precarity of life are all characteristics of a heterogeneous and unforeseeable space that is seen from the perspective of a person who is subject to its conditions and suffers constant abuse and disparagement.

In the realm of material culture, Makina reflects on the backpacks people carry on the journeys in which they supposedly include affective objects of personal and cultural meaning, together with essential items. Anthropologist Jason De León has studied the objects that migrants take with them, to inquire into the travelers' subjectivity and the way they prepare to take on the unpredictable hardships of the migrant trail. In *The Land of Open Graves: Living and Dying on the Migrant Trail* (2015), De León analyzes these types of traces that display migrants' vulnerabilities, their beliefs as well as their most prized possessions, at least those that they can carry on their journey. The elements that De León describes replicate the vestiges that Makina observes among the things that other travelers leave behind: "Amuletos, cartas, a veces un violín huapanguero, a veces un arpa jaranera. Chamarras . . . porque les habían dicho que allá si algo había era hielo, aunque el viaje lo plagaran desiertos. Metían su poco dinero en los calzones y una navaja en el bolsillo de atrás. Fotos, fotos, fotos" (Amulets, letters, sometimes a *huapango* violin, sometimes a *jaranera* harp. Jackets . . . because they'd been told that if there was one thing they could be sure of over there, it was the freezing cold, even if it was desert all the way. They hid what little money they had in their underwear and stuck a knife in their back pocket. Photos, photos, photos).[176]

The elemental value of what migrants carry and the affective charge of almost everything they pack for their journey demonstrates the connection to their homeland and their family, the love for the music of their region, as well as the feeling of danger and uncertainty that also goes with them. In her own luggage, Makina carries a flash light, a white blouse and one with colorful embroidery "por si se atravesaba pachanga" (in case she came across any parties), "tres braguitas para andar siempre con una limpia, aunque tardara en hallar lavadero" (three pairs of panties so she'd always have a clean one even if it took a while to find a washhouse) a "latin-anglo" dictionary, a picture her little sister had drawn, a bar of *xithé* soap, a lipstick, and some sweets.[177] The objects portray a basic and modest life as well as her optimistic goals for an uncertain but easily imagined immediate future. They also indicate a plan to go back "Ella se iba para nomás volver, por eso llevó apenas estas cosas" (She was coming right back, that's why that was all she took).[178] Makina makes her way toward a depersonalized, commodified, and anonymous world. The signs preceding the end of the universe are multiplying and accelerating since she arriving at "el lugar donde el viento corta como navaja" (the place where the wind cuts like a knife) and where the first indication of the cultural change she perceives is the hybridized use of language by Americanized Latin Americans: "Son paisanos y son gabachos y cada cosa con una intensidad rabiosa . . . tienen gestos que revelan una memoria antiquísima y asombros de gente nueva" (they are homegrown and they are anglo and both things with rabid intensity . . . their gestures and tastes reveal both ancient memory and the wonderment of a new people).[179] In their speech they mix traits of both cultures, creating an intermediate condition like her own:

> Malleable, erasable, permeable; a hinge pivoting between two like but distant souls, and then two more, and then two more, never exactly the same ones; something more that serves as a link. . . . More than the midpoint between homegrown and anglo their tongue is a nebulous territory between what is dying out and what is not yet born. But not a hetacomb. Makina senses in their tongue not a sudden absence but a shrewd metamorphosis, a self-defensive shift.[180]

With an evident desire to not discredit Spanglish's hybridity which at times is unsettled and enriched by the use of terms, syntactical and phonetic structures of native languages, we see how the narrator situates Makina's interpretation of the linguistic changes that chart the move toward modernity (if by this we understand the superposition of socio-economic and cultural structures that are assimilated into the ideology of progress, cosmopolitanism, technologization and transnationalism).

The novel unequivocally communicates the social cost that modernization imposes on native cultures and on the social formations that are peripheral to capitalism's center. Traditional society is buffeted by aggressive manifestations of land grabs (privatization of terrains, extractivism, commercial exploitation of natural resources) that drive a wedge between the individual and nature and subsume the communitarian into the logic of capitalistic accumulation. Communication (telephones, writing, languages)—so lavishly displayed in *Señales que precederán al fin del mundo*—situates the transition that is slowly but surely leaving behind personalized forms of social relations in the realm of the symbolic and sign. Makina enters a space dominated not only by silence—perhaps the result of the communicative confusion of the world—but also by the commodification of life and dehumanized modes of coexistence.

The theme of power is omnipresent throughout her journey, manifesting itself in the superposition of traditional forms of *caciquismo*, clientelism, machismo, and opportunism onto more depersonalized relationships of dominance that derive from the hegemony of capital, social inequity, and systemic violence. This is evident in the concept of borderization and in the transgressions of limits, facilitated by a complex network of intermediation in which figures from drug lords to their minions, corrupt border guards, coyotes, and occasional actors play a role. Border areas beyond any others represent the processes in which forms of traditional and modern power overlap and co-exist, capturing in their net the lives of individuals and communities who move blindly in a world that seems hell-bent on self-destruction.

For Makina, some elements clearly signal cultural difference and the enigmatic forms that life "on the other side" assumes. In the fourth section entitled "El cerro de obsidiana," Makina reflects on how the community will communicate without her mediation as switchboard operator, the American city begins to emerge, revealing its hostility. The "no entry" signs reveal inaccessible spaces, and the multiplicity of special offers that fulfill no need overwhelm her. This mercantile paradise is exhausting and a simulacrum. In the "llano de concreto y varilla" (the concrete and steel-girder plain), which forms a sharp contrast to the nature and landscape of her homeland, Makina sees her Central American compatriots who seem to recognize her as one of them but who do not approach her:

> Out on the concrete and steel-girder plain, though, she sensed another presence straight off, scattered about like bolts fallen from a window: on street corners, on scaffolding, on sidewalks; fleeting looks of recognition quickly concealed and then evasive. They were her compatriots, her homegrown, armed with work: builders, florists, loaders, drivers; just playing it sly so as not to let on to any shared objective, and instead just, just, just: just there to take orders. They were the same as back home but with less whistling and no begging.[181]

Working low-skilled jobs or within the informal economy, migrants are characterized by their subordination to the system and by the domestication of their cultural habits. Work instils new biopolitical dynamics that impact lifestyles, language use, interpersonal relationships, and bodily expression. The idealized world of el Norte operates as an exploitative, disciplinary, and repressive panopticon.

For her part, Makina inspires mistrust in the controlling society where she has recently arrived, carrying a package that immediately marks her as "illegal": "Makina vio a dos tipos en un coche negro con rines plateados. Son tiras, se están maliciando quién es usté, continuó. Vamos a caminar hasta que se distraigan. . . . El auto . . . no tardó en regresar y los siguió a distancia" (Makina saw two guys in a black ride with silver rims. Cops, wondering who you are, he went on. We're going to walk till they get sidetracked. . . . The car . . . soon returned to follow them at a distance).[182] The stadium that she encounters during her journey and where she will find "señor Pe" is so immense that it looks like a black hill, filled with thousands of seats in this color folded in front of a green diamond: "un cerro de obsidiana erizado de pedernales, reluciente y afilado" (an obisidian mound barbed with flint, sharp and glimmering).[183] In this setting, at once playful and corporate, Makina finds herself surrounded by several Black men who are accompanying the man who will collect the package. It is an iconic and enigmatic place that assumes the identity of the society to which she is headed and where, as her guide tells her: "Los gabachos juegan un juego con el que cada semana celebran quienes son" (Every week the Anglos play a game to celebrate who they are).[184] The way he explains the game to her presents it as a meaningless pastime, extraneous and disconnected from the body and with other participants. It can be interpreted as a symbolic search for identity affirmation and as a childish and baffling ritual. Work and play operate in counterpoint and indicate distinct if not contrary ways of socialization and use of bodily, physical, and affective energy. The Other's gaze re-builds the elements of the cultural landscape from the other side, using the protagonist's displacement as an opportunity to make a cultural and ideological counterpoint based on the distancing brought on by her condition as a stranger.

Further on, Makina witnesses a gay wedding whose ceremonies seem beautiful but also baffling to her: "Lo que no entendió era por qué era tan importante el anillo, el oficial, los padrinos" (What she couldn't understand was why the ring, the official, the godparents mattered so).[185] She's surprised that these "otros modos de quererse" (other ways to love), end up "haciendo lo mismo" (just the same), imitating "a los que siempre los han despreciado" (people who had always despised them). She speculates that perhaps "la gente se cansa de ser distinta" (being different gets old after a while) and that they want to finally "parecerse a los demás" (fit in).[186] Makina finds new places, customs and forms of socialization shaped by modernity simultaneously enigmatic and dazzling and without doubt challenging for her imagination and rationality formed by the thought structures of her own culture. Does she see the signs preceding the end of the world? At the very least she sees signs that the communitarian and telluric world, rooted in ancestral traditions and beliefs, is being left behind in the face of the advance of consumer society, political control of space, the proliferation of borderization, and the dynamics of technology.

In the clash of traditional and modern ways of being, the former category is implicitly defined as personalized modalities, forms of community networks, limited access to goods and services, the rural/city contrast, affective relationships, and a focus on family, land, and mother tongue. The second category speaks particularly to the imprint of technological processes on society, the acceleration of life, new forms of subjective alienation, the loss of a relationship with nature, the importance of consumption, and social depersonalization. However, this dualism is not presented rigidly, although in some cases the contrast is evident and radicalized. At other times, the novel represents scenarios in which we witness overlaps or rather the coexistence of tradition and modern forms that give rise to hybrid, conflictive, and often unsettling manifestations.

The subjects' mentality, along with their values and their reactions to everyday challenges reveal the persistence of structures of coloniality that are manifested in the treatment of the themes of race and ethnicity, the form that gender violence assumes and in the subjugation of huge sectors of the population by the dominant system, rendering them invisible and vulnerable. The divisions between nations as well as the question of borders, distinctions between North/South, rural/urban, localism/cosmopolitanism are products of modernity, although some date back to the colonial eras. In the same way, the forms power assumes also have colonial antecedents while at the same time revealing the distribution of spaces of authority and social repression that are specific to the contemporary period. [187]

In this sense, *Señales que precederán al fin del mundo* functions as a transhistorical journey that traverses instances of socio-political structuring that both comprise and go beyond the novel's temporality. Thus, the novel presents a wide-ranging reflection on forms of social organization, the construction of identities, the function of power, and the politics of life and death in postcolonial contexts. With the presence of Makina putting them into motion, different forms of violence and power extend throughout the text. We see, for example, the representation of power that perpetuates the inequality of the status quo manifested through patriarchy, societal control, the military and war, the marking out of borders, etc. However, in my opinion, the novel does not emphasize a rigid compartmentalization of social space but instead the communicating vessels that are erected and that create a flow that contaminates the hierarchical domains. In this sense, the novel is a symbolic form from which the author reveals the (in)human and social aspects of these processes and the effect they wield over familiar subjectivities and ways of life. The journey to el Norte is a gradual descent into the land of the dead or toward a form of death that requires a redefinition of life from the point of view of silence and grief for everything that has been lost. If the place of silence coincides with the possibility of a new beginning (a new identity, new name, another birthplace, a new home, an unusual way of being-in-common) the novel's last page makes it clear that Makina—this assemblage in which life and death are (con)fused—feels that the new beginning has stripped her of her skin ("Me han desollado, musitó" (I've been skinned, she whispered).[188] In the final dimension where time no longer exists, "no tenía reloj, nadie tenía reloj" (she didn't have a watch, nobody had a watch), panic gives way to the understanding that this is not a catastrophe ("entendió que lo que le sucedía no era un cataclismo; what was happening was not a cataclysm) although the images she has of Mexico, from her small town to the capital city, are beginning to fade in her mind.[189] And she concludes: "Estoy lista, cuando todas las cosas del mundo quedaron en silencio" (and when everything in the world fell silent [she] finally said to herself I'm ready).[190] But what is she ready for? To dwell in the land of the dead to where she has been descending since the narrative's beginning, or to confront her rebirth in another world, that has only just begun to display its challenges?

"WE, THE BARBARIANS": FROM ENUNCIATED TO ENUNCIATION

As we know, the symbolic value of the frontier, exceeds—if it fits at all—its material meaning, whether that be in the category of frontier fortification (wall, fence, barbed wire fence, barrier, electric fence) or abstraction, where an imaginary' line suggests the beginning and end of artificially divided territories to supposedly safeguard possessions and rights. This is suggested by the principles of sovereignty, private property, political and administrative domains, or similar types of demarcations that are always invoked as a way of legitimizing the ever-increasing practice of borderizing.

Described as an open wound, scar, fissure, fracture, or boundary etc, the border operates not only politically and socially but also subjectively, that is at the level of intellect and affect. It simultaneously activates the imagination and memory, exacerbates desire, stimulates the processes of idealization, overwhelms, intimidates, and defies. The border puts strategies of control to the test, promotes deception, dis-identity, falsification, daring, and reassesses the questions of rights, citizenship as well as the principles put forward as ways of legitimizing the repression of the other, that for its part, looks to transgress the law, one way or another.

As a plot driven by the detection of apocalyptic signs that herald the dismantling of familiar ways of life, or the act of being-in-common, *Señales que precederán al fin del mundo* situates one of its key moments, and in my opinion, one of the key moments in all of Herrera's work up until now, in the critical spaces of the border. The novel exalts movement by land as an individual and collective right, bound as it is to the human instinct for survival and the tendency of communities to regroup and redefine themselves. Aspects that are represented explicitly, such as identity and immigration, appear hand in hand in contemporary scenarios of inequality, territoriality, necropolitics, and privilege. Together with the essential theme of the border, communication (language, orality) defines Makina's character, and both axes converge in the scene that takes place when she leaves the military barracks and is treated harshly by the border guard. The reconfiguring of the nineteenth-century dualism of civilization vs barbarism is triggered here as a cliché that is repurposed every time there's a desire to diminish the Other in the face of the Europeanized version of civilization. This version is also used to sustain and legitimize colonialism and slavery, justifying centuries of colonialism and supporting a conception of democracy as limited and exclusionary participation that has always victimized and marginalized working-class people. Makina uses this formula as her response to the border guard who imposes the repressive norms of a system that operates as a regime of permanent authority that encompasses all aspects of life: "Si quieren venir, se forman y piden permiso, si quieren ir al médico, se forman y piden permiso, si quieren dirigirme la puta palabra, se forman y piden permiso. Se forman y piden permiso. Así hacemos las cosas aquí, la gente civilizada. No brincándonos bardas ni haciendo túneles" (You want to come here, fall in and ask permission, you want to go to the doctor, fall in and ask permission, you want to say a fucking word to me, fall in and ask permission. Civilized, that's the way we do things around here! We don't jump fences and we don't dig tunnels).[191]

Disciplinary society exposes principles that contrast with the space where the action takes place: a vacant lot with a pool of black, standing water. The degraded representation of the nation endows the guard's speech with a grotesque, ridiculous, out of place and meaningless discourse. The frontier, as such, dismantles binarisms (while generating them) and paradoxically possesses a character that is both regulatory and anti-normative since it demarcates a time that generates transgressive behaviors, hybridizations, and simulacra. In the border guard's speech, regulation and secrecy are the same as authoritarianism and subversion, civilization and barbarism and order and chaos. But his perspective is impacted by his position within a regime that is not universal. The scene exposes the relativity of these localizations where Makina and the immigrants are assembled as if they constitute one marginalized and collective subject oppressed by precarity and misfortune and whose rights are unknown, and whose body is exposed to abuse and humiliation. This is not, however, a passive subject but instead one who is formed around a project of reterritorialization and survival. Unless attention is paid to the causes of this mobilization, it is seen as a product of insubordination and barbarism and as behavior that stands in opposition to a system that privileges some subjects to the detriment of others, depending on what side of the line they find themselves.

Language and writing in their different manifestations are strongly present in this situation. The poetry that one of the migrants carries among his paltry belongings annoys the guard who conceives of it as a "romantic" and disposable element that exists in lieu of documents and money. The guard tells the man to write down what he's done wrong in his notebook, forcing him to put writing in the service of order, giving language a utilitarian value. But Makina takes up the challenge, writing an ironic text, almost a manifesto, on the back of the poem in which she gives the voice to the immigrants, parodying the terms in which people in el Norte see them:

> We are to blame for this destruction, we who don't speak your tongue and don't know how to keep quiet either. We who didn't come by boat, who dirty up your doorsteps with our dust, who break your barbed wire. We who came to take your jobs, who dream of wiping your shit, who long to work all hours. We who fill your shiny clean sheets with the smell of food, who brought you violence you'd never known, who deliver your dope, who deserve to be chained by neck and feet. We who are happy to die for you, what else could we do? We, the ones who are waiting for who knows what. We, the dark, the short, the greasy, the shifty, the fat, the anemic. We, the barbarians.[192]

Through Makina, language continues to play a crucial role not only as a scriptural gesture that, upon being obeyed, paradoxically expresses rebellion and resistance but also as an enunciative act in which various functions come together, such as the denotative, the connotative, the vindicative, the descriptive, the defensive, the identifying. The opposition "us and them" is the axis upon which the parodic *mea culpa* turns and in which the immigrant's voice ironically promotes popular opinion that blames them for contaminating both the nation's private spaces as well as el Norte's ordered existence, openly advocating xenophobic and racist positions.[193] This position expresses the dominant concept in migration politics, through which US citizens' human rights are situated above those of foreigners, primarily criminalizing their social condition when border crossing occurs without the required documentation. This attitude relegates the Other to the degrading status of "illegal alien"—an undesirable subject who is disposable, residual, and even dangerous, as well as unsanitary, contagious, and idle.

Makina deploys a sarcastic discourse whose origins lie in the rhetoric of conquest and whose principal objective was to legitimize the usurpation and eventual genocide of the "New World's" Native populations based on the superiority of those who displayed military, economic and epistemic power. Given this, Makina's earlier-cited paragraph imbues the scenario of contemporary migration with historical density as she follows the guard's orders: "Pon los ojos en el papel y escribe por qué crees que estás en la mierda, por qué crees que tu culo está en las manos de este oficial patriota. ¿O no sabes que has hecho mal? Sí lo sabes. Escribe" (Keep your eyes on the paper and write what you think you're up the creek, why you think your ass is in the hands of this patriotic officer. Or don't you know what you did wrong? Sure you do. Write).[194] The police officer's coarse language contrasts with the protagonist's succinct and powerful message, in the same way that the guard's desire to humiliate the migrants is the opposite of the text's meaning, which exudes dignity.

Other dualisms in the text connect to the concept of "us and them," which frames Makina's thinking. Vernacular cultures/colonization, language/silence, order/chaos among others underscore the confrontation between not only two ways of life that meet up and face off at the border but also two ways of social and political insertion of individuals and communities in their respective surroundings. It is important to note that Makina's text does not refer to the totality of US society but to official attitudes toward immigrants. It is precisely this blatant opposition of racist, xenophobic, and discriminatory clichés that strengthens the text's parodic function. It is, moreover, the fact that it is the same border guard who reads Makina's text out loud that creates the parodic situation that exposes the irony of her delivery, preserving the statement's ideological and social force. This makes it a true manifesto in which the chief rhetorical device, the inversion of meaning of attributes generally assigned to immigrants, throws the impact back onto the aggressor, personified in the figure of the border guard.

The points mentioned in the text draw on linguistic differences as a cultural and communicative stumbling block but also encompass a series of historical, economic, and social aspects. Makina refers to colonialism as the origin of the usurping of lands and resources that belonged to Native peoples. She also refers to the abuses and humiliations the immigrant is subject to in the workplace as well as to the stereotypes that draw on his/her supposed tendency toward disorder as well as the precariousness of his/her existence due to deterritorialization. To the violence suffered by the immigrant, who is pursued and victimized, we must add that which is additionally inflicted on the great numbers of Latinos who fight in US wars, as if they were confrontations that somehow affected them personally. The end of the passage mentions the immigrant's despair as well as his/her corporality that reveals traces that are used as indications of inferiority and that incur hatred and scorn in el Norte. In the final phrase, in which reference is made to barbarism, the narrative returns to the topic of civilization in whose name the Other receives treatment that is inhumane, unjust, and bereft of solidarity, recalling Benjamin's idea that ideas of progress and civilization should be submitted to critical discussion since "there is no document of civilization which is not at the same time a document of barbarism."[195] On strategically accepting the disparaging of immigrants as "true," Makina calls attention to those who consider themselves as superior, demonstrating the relativity of their values and their xenophobic beliefs.

The text's movement from the enunciation that Makina expresses in writing as a response to the guard's speech itself constitutes an eloquent form of communication directed toward the construction of social conscience. Makina articulates the immigrant's position in the face of the scorn and inequity they experience in the social and working conditions of the "other side." With this vision she astutely tackles the alienated conscience of the border guard who is himself subject to the regime of surveillance and abuse of authority that underpins the system. The ironic inversion of clichés and stereotypes used against migrants is employed as a device with which to display these subjects' self-awareness, which is then translated into resistance and survival mechanisms in the face of degrading and unjust situations. Language thus arrives at a climax of political and ideological expressiveness where the individual and the public, the personal and the communal, the written and the oral converge. The border serves as a trigger point for behaviors and reactions that respond to the radicalization of differences and the amplifying of inequalities. In the face of the obvious asymmetries in terms of power relations and with its role as an essential element in the formation and deployment of subjectivities, language becomes an essential weapon to penetrate the networks of the society of control and dismantle binarisms, antagonisms, and euphemisms, bringing the profound meaning behind social conflict to the surface.

The enunciation's clear political value demonstrates the representative nature of the character of Makina who reaches maximum expression at this point, acting to deconstruct the ideological apparatus that stands in opposition to her and that finds its most brutal materialization at the border. Makina's entire journey, as well as the very place where she reads the text, take place in an empty and desolate space between one country and another, and represents a displacement not just of space and time but also of the imaginary—the forms in which we conceive of and act out the social, the communal, and the political. As I have already mentioned, the intermediate or in-between spaces, instances of articulation and dismantling, of assembly and repose, are the poetic landscape through which Herrera's work moves, where language's emblematic value acquires plenitude, and where the word sharpens its links with the real.

LA TRANSMIGRACIÓN DE LOS CUERPOS: "SYMBOLIC EXCHANGE AND DEATH"

MEDIATION AND MANDATE

A plague of unknown origin attacks an anonymous city, creating an atmosphere of delirium and death that has laid claim to public space from the novel's beginning.[196] Violence, crime, fear, and grief reign over this lawless place, where the borders between life and death, health and illness are disintegrating. Negative emotions as much as physical suffering possess an infectious quality, proliferating in an anomalous and corrupt state of exception that overpowers the inhabitants' psychological defenses. These conditions inspire mistrust and aggression and intensify the skepticism and anxiety felt by a population exhausted by instability.

As Yuri Herrera has explained, nowadays we find ourselves plagued by an epidemic that disseminates hate and fear. Despite this necro-poetic climate and the piling up of episodes that illustrate different forms of social conflict, *La transmigración de los cuerpos* is nonetheless a nimble and humorous novel, full of characters who represent a wide swathe of regional society, and that appears to have been painted with a palette of brilliant colors. This setting, however, takes the reader on another trip to the apocalypse.[197] The deserted city constitutes a space of death where the invisible enemy (the epidemic, but also intrinsic violence, precarity, and the lack of state response) awaits, attacks, and triumphs. However, people carry on with their lives, above all those who form part of the inner circle, all of whom are colorful, and have nicknames that distinguish them and insert them into a novelistic theatricality.

The narrative's central element is the human body: its vulnerability, its misfortune, its defenselessness, its symbolic value; along with its appetites, needs, and desires. As a victim of disease, abuses of power, and social chaos, and of itself, the body represents the platform in which the struggle for life is made manifest and upon which all highly emotionalized community-based conflicts are resolved. Additionally, forces converge on the social body, revealing that the destruction of the social fabric goes beyond the surface. Narco violence, unchecked disease, chaotic healthcare, scarcity, and a lack of social regulation penetrate the tumultuous depths of systemic logic for which violence and illness provide eloquent metaphors. The presence of the military in the public sphere exposes the failure of the law and the adherence to a state of exception that harbors State violence as part of the power's machinery.[198]

All this may lead us to believe that the *La transmigración de los cuerpos* is a dark and dramatic novel, somber and infused with a moralistic and skeptical realism. Nothing could be further from the truth. The light and at times almost joyful narrative tone offers a playful counterpart to the themes developed within the context of a mix-up between two families that involves an exchange of corpses. The tale unfolds in a farcical way, with echoes of Shakespearean antagonisms between Montagues and Capulets and with a diction and development that, especially in the opening pages, evokes García Márquez's noteworthy opening of *El coronel no tiene quien le escriba*.[199] A group of secondary characters revolving around the central figure of el Alfaqueque / the Redeemer possess distinctive features, backstories, and frame narratives that make up the communal microcosm.

Repetitions, symmetries, and inversions are tools Herrera uses frequently in his novels and some are used in different ways on more than one occasion such as the meetings between el Alfaqueque and la Tres Veces Rubia / Three Times Blonde. In addition, various episodes illustrate the former's involvement in community matters and the fame he gained as a healer. These mediations reveal the character's talent for finding just the right response for every situation as a way of deescalating enmities, disagreements, and disputes. This aspect, among others, further demonstrates el Alfaqueque's similarity to Makina, the protagonist of *Señales que precederán al fin del mundo*, who is distinguished by her facility with languages and by her communication skills as the community telephone operator.

El Alfaqueque is also a strategic user of language, which helps him navigate daily transactions which he resolves using his powers of persuasion, adapting his discourse to its receiver, and suspending judgment on the disputes he mediates: "el Alfaqueque verbeaba lo que fuera necesario para que la gente siguiera complicándose como mejor le pareciera, no tendría chamba si se ponía a juzgar los vicios de cada cual. El verbo es ergonómico, decía. Sólo hay que saber calzarlo con cada persona." (Often, people were really just waiting for someone to talk them down, offer a way out of the fight. That was why when he talked sweet he really worked his word. The word is ergonomic, he said. You just have to know how to shape it to each person).[200]

But although el Alfaqueque's role is primarily a linguistic one it also extends to behaviors and attitudes: "Lo suyo no era tanto ser bravo como entender qué clase de audacia pedía cada brete. Ser humilde y dejar que el otro pensara que las palabras que decía eran las suyas propias" (His talent lay not so much in being brutal as in knowing what kind of courage every fix requires).[201] The character defines himself in terms of his chief attributes: "Verbo y verga" (Talk and cock) which sums up, in his opinion, his impact on the world: rhetoric and sex, ways of intervening and transforming the status quo and substantially shifting reality.[202]

El Alfaqueque's control of language is also connected, albeit differently, to Lobo's in *Trabajos del reino*. Lobo uses the lyrics of his *corridos* to capture and interpret the interactions and fluctuations of cartel power. The three central characters in Herrera's trilogy work on command, using language as a means of social insertion and as an instrument for navigating conflict that requires the mediation and negotiation of material and symbolic aspects. The three protagonists act to fulfill commissions (the *corridos*, the search for the brother, the exchange of corpses) in which we paradoxly find the character's essence. More than the other two novels, *La transmigración de los cuerpos* privileges the picaresque but without abandoning its implicit focus on themes connected to life and death. The biopolitical makeup of the social surroundings places the reader at the center of a situation that, lightly and free of portentousness and moralizing, incorporates elements that are both aggressive and defensive, earthly, and transcendent, as well as questions of immunity and contagion. The central character, however, reaches conclusions and learns life lessons from the situations he encounters that he expresses, via the narrator, with a mixture of resignation, modesty, and irony. He points out, for example, that "la gente toda es como estrellas muertas: lo que nos llega de ellas es distinto de la cosa, que ya ha desaparecido o ya ha cambiado, así sea un segundo después de la emisión de luz o de mala obra" (people, all people, are like dark stars: what we see is different from the thing itself, which has already disappeared, already changed, even a single second after the light or evil has been discharged).[203] He is presented as a character whose personal understanding and experience embody a synthesis of the fictional world. The "black dog" who prowls alongside him like a living symbol of shame or remorse, accompanies him as if it were a permanent reminder of his actions. It was when he failed to act in defense of someone when:

> And that was the precise instant he first felt the presence of the black dog, who would never again leave him, who might sometimes slip out of sight but would always be there. He learned to live with the cur, at times even to conjure him. Yes, sometimes something inside of him broke, but that's what made it possible to go places and make decisions he could never make on his own. His black dog was a dark mass that allowed him to do certain things, to not feel certain things, he was physical, as real as a bone you don't know you have until its almost jutting through your skin.[204]

As far as we know, the soul transmigrates from a dead to a living body and then comes alive with the incorporation of the spirit, in a process not unlike metempsychosis, reincarnation, or palingenesis. Modern authors such as James Joyce, Edgar Allan Poe, and Marcel Proust have taken up this topic and used it metaphorically and generally esoterically so as to highlight continuities, transhistorical links between characters or mysterious exchanges between the domains of life and death. In Herrera's novel, however, it is corpses and not souls that must reestablish themselves within the body social.

Two uses of the term "transmigrate" converge in these operations: on the one hand, the passage of the soul from one body to another, here transfigured in the "restoration" of the corpses and on the other the word "transmigration" (migrate by means of) denotes, in today's parlance, the movement of individuals and communities across spaces and borders. A transmigrant is she or he who crosses a territory that is not their final destination but rather a moment in their migratory journey. The term (trans)migration is literally used in this way to mean territorial displacement. In this sense, the word alludes to the mobility between the spaces that the individual traverses in search of rebirth and resettlement. This means the reinvention of personal history, the securing of the necessary means for survival and work, and the conditions that permit a new beginning or new origin that is associated with reterritorialization and border crossing as Herrera shows in

Trabajos del reino. Told with humor and linguistic skill, *La transmigración de los cuerpos* closes Herrera's trilogy in which he has revealed, with particular mastery, the afflicted social pact of the Mexican margins, particularly in the north of the country where rampant waves of organized crime, poverty, and the spectral shadow of the border weigh heavily upon society.

EL ALFAQUEQUE AND "THE ACCURSED SHARE"

Central to *La transmigración de los cuerpos* is the oppositional but also continuous relationship between both dead and living bodies as well as individual and social bodies. At the same time the novel, whose narrative foregrounds atmosphere, is organized into levels that build on each other in an efficient and never overwhelming narrative flow. Contagion, curfew, lack, and violence render the narrative a catastrophic palimpsest that pushes existential conditions to their extreme and impacts interpersonal relationships.

In Herrera's novels (as in Rulfo's) the theme of the quest occupies an important place. The principal characters are developed in relationship to the revelation of a type of truth. During this period, lives harden and define themselves, testing the relationship between the characters and the fictional reality. This idealistic link that the author introduces between the protagonist and his habitat makes the implicit suggestion that the character's life experience is a pathway toward illuminating, exemplary, and reliable knowledge about both the human condition and the actual nature of the real. Although the fictional universes that these characters inhabit share a fragmentary and unstable quality bordering on the apocalyptical, the search for truth represents a reordering drive that reestablishes some form of totalization or at least a rearticulation of forces that allow for the continuity of life, albeit under new material and subjective conditions.

If in *Trabajos del reino* el Artista penetrates the dark corners of power where he learns its tricks and perversities, in Herrera's second novel Makina enters the underworld in order to disentangle the truth surrounding her brother's whereabouts as well as what happened to the land she supposedly inherited. But this is not all. Her voyage is also directed toward a more transcendent truth and incorporates forms of survival that can challenge the destruction of the world and achieve a rebirth which can be understood in terms of the transition from silence to language. As far as el Alfaqueque is concerned, his mediating role places him in the space between life and death. It is from this position that the narrative traverses the shadowy world of affect (hate, grief, mistrust, desire).[205] The character explores the singular experience of death in a general climate of necropolitics, where two bodies, taken by warring families, are transformed into symbolic merchandise, and must be recovered in a mission of symmetrical restitution.

The term "Alfaqueque," of Arabic origin, refers to the rescuing of captive Christians in Muslim lands that was entrusted to the monarch's representatives. It was an honorable task, given only to the most dependable of men and required bravery and selflessness as well as a gift for diplomacy, astuteness, and knowledge of both cultures. A mastery of eloquence and rhetoric as well as the capacity to convince others and manage delicate situations between adversaries were essential for this type of emissary who would carry out a task that later was assigned to members of the religious orders.

El Alfaqueque is a sort of community referee, charged with resolving feuds, facilitating the making of amends and rescuing low-level kidnap victims all of which are tasks that go beyond his previous occupation as a minor administrative official ("tinterillo" or "pencil pusher") in a local court. As in *Trabajos del reino*, a novel that portrays a decadent and parodic version of a monarchy to capture the ostentatious lifestyle as extravagantly displayed by a Mexican drug cartel, *La transmigracion de los cuerpos* offers an ironic imitation of el Alfaqueque's original role, now embodied in the form of a provincial fixer who, while dealing with his own personal troubles, sorts out everyday disputes. We can also find this combination of the archaic and the modern as generator of meaning in *Señales que precederán al fin del mundo* particularly in the reworking of the pre-Hispanic myths connected to the afterlife (Mictlán).[206] Georg Lukács's definition of the characteristics of the modern novel as the adventures of the average or "mediocre" hero in search of authentic values in a degraded world is put to the test in Herrera's novel which is set at the margins of a country that is peripheral with respect to European point of reference where this representational model was created. As if confirming that the postcolonial world reinvents the tragedies of absolute power as farce, Herrera's novels give new meaning to power paradigms and sovereignty, repurposing traces of mimicry, farce, and the carnivalesque.[207] At the time, Lukács also emphasized the nostalgic character of the novel (above all the historical novel) and the idea that, between subject and object, the novel's methodology allows for the imposition of mediations that overcome empiricism's immediacy and contingency.

In accordance with the theme of the fluctuation between tragedy and farce, in its opening pages the novel introduces the central character, el Alfaqueque, in a sexual encounter with la Tres Veces Rubia, a woman who is desired and "possessed" at that moment by her admirer during the epidemic that adds elements of tension, comedy, and peculiarity to these scenes. Told with humor and irony, the novel establishes the dynamic between desire and death via a register that rapidly deescalates the drama. Sexuality, emphatically life-affirming and deviating from the daily routines of work and rationality, is the flip side of a public scenario that is dominated by the unsettling presence of corpses and traversed by a threatening virus. The fight over and sacrilegious manipulation of bodies represents a particular form of transgression that, following Georges Bataille's reasoning, falls within the concept of the squandering of social forces that speaks to energy wasted in unproductive actions. According to Bataille, there is a continuity between sex and death since both are crucial for the liberation of energy that the author understands in terms of "waste," or rather the dissipation of vital capital: "Sexuality and death are simply the culminating points of the holiday; nature celebrates, with the inexhaustible multitude of living beings, both of them, signifying the boundless wastage of nature's resources as opposed to the urge to live on, characteristic of every living creature.[208]

This notion of non-procreative sex and death as excess or as "antieconomy" confers the notion of something sumptuous and excessive in both experiences. Death and sex, in this sense, represent what Bataille calls "the accursed share." With this expression he refers to all that is surplus or squandered, whose use exceeds life's primary functions. In this sense, eroticism is the excess of reproductive sexuality and the surplus whose only investment is pleasure. Death is "the wasting of vital energy," with the goal of making room for subsequent generations while cutting short the lives of others. For this reason, for Baudrillard, death represents a paradoxical "symbolic challenge." Death as well as eroticism function according to a concept of continuity/discontinuity. This dynamic ensures the possibility of life even at the cost of others' lives. As a character who is essentially marked by limits, el Alfaqueque moves seamlessly between both extremes. His narrative placement signals moments of crisis that occur when an excess of social energy transforms into aggression or the transgression of limits and threatens the community's survival and stability. In these contexts, the word serves to restore moderation, operating as a form of catharsis. In a symmetrical fashion, sex possesses the same function for the character. Suspending language, sex possesses a liberating function and constitutes a tool for relating with the world and confirming the role of life as it pertains to death. Hence the slogan "verbo y verga" (talk and cock) expressed with the resounding cheek of street parlance, that gestures pragmatically to social equilibrium. As el Alfaqueque explains, in an attempt to win over la Tres Veces Rubia, in the same way that the word functions to build consensus, love is the best remedy against aggression.

SOCIAL SPACE AND THE PLACE OF DEATH

Imaginary spaces conceived of as afterlives appear frequently in Mexican literature and operate as a leitmotif in Herrera's work. The paradigmatic treatment of this work is found in Juan Rulfo's work, particularly in *Pedro Páramo* (1955), which tells of the afterlife of a town devastated by a social and existential crisis and that *Señales que precederán al fin del mundo* will take up later. In the fictions that draw on this cosmovision, the spaces of life and death run parallel but at times places and moments converge, intercept, and shape each other. As the place of romantic encounters, crimes, routines and exceptional moments, pleasure and grief, personal hell and paradise, social space is a mix of both. Hybridized and palimpsestic, social space is a politic realm (the place of the polis), created as the result of superposition and displacements as well as absences and presences. In this way it functions as a metaphor of states of mind and conflict but also as the habitat that responds to the impulses of the characters that interact with their surroundings in a singular and creative fashion.

Herrera's elision of Mexico City in his trilogy is well-known. Although some of its echoes and characteristics appear enshrined in some scenarios, the city's overcrowding, pace, and cultural diversity—elements that are so present in the works of other authors—are clearly and efficiently substituted for hybrid and patently decentralized environments in which the human and geocultural landscape of border or semi-rural zones are prioritized. Herrera recognizes the presence of two combined spatial models in *La transmigración de los cuerpos*. One is the capital city, from which he draws on the elements of simultaneity and acceleration, the isolation of people in their houses, and fear as social factor. To this he adds elements that are specific to the city of Pachuca, including allusions to "El corredor de las caricias" where brothels and nocturnal haunts are located.[209] Beyond these vectors, the key here is the notion of common space invaded by the presence of destabilizing factors (the virus, the Egyptian mosquito that causes the infections, the dead bodies left in the street due to illness or violence, the lack of commercial activity, and the state of emergency). These factors bear witness to an accelerated process of dehumanization, achieved through spatial depopulation and through the objectification of living beings. The significance of the corpse as an emblematic object, laden with messages, is evident in *La transmigración de los cuerpos*.

Western thought has always maintained a pure connection between corpse and truth, since death—and by extension the corpse—connects the individual to transcendent knowledge. The soul that has passed through the death-trance possesses knowledge (of the hereafter, the existence of God, of the recently abandoned world) but only a frustrated relationship with the truth can be established through the corpse, which increases its value as an object of fascination. Since all cultures venerate the corpse, to profane it represents an act of abominable sacrilege. In *La transmigración de los cuerpos* the centrality of bodies acts as the catalyst for the narrative and the misplacement of the corpses that have been appropriated by the warring families (who end up being related to one another), those bodies serve as the text's center and set its moment of crisis into motion. *La transmigración de los cuerpos* is a deliberately redundant text, saturated with death. In this context, the prominent presence of human remains provides a conspicuous biopolitical sign that illustrates the increasingly diminished value ascribed to life.

Bodies combine symbolic value with material depreciation since they're treated as waste products that disrupt community life, exposing its dysfunctionality. The reader cannot but connect this necro-landscape to Mexico's own situation of the last few decades where murders, kidnappings, mass graves, the incineration of bodies, and crimes (femicides, organ harvesting, etc.) have become a daily experience. In this way, recognizing the emblematic value that the body (whether dead or alive) possesses in Mexico overlaps with the most violent forms of its profanation.[210]

In *La transmigración de los cuerpos*, the corpse maintains a symbolic connection with el Alfaqueque since they both represent intermediate and ambiguous instances and functions that are vicarious in nature. Like the character, the corpse in and of itself occupies an intermediate location in the novel's structure and in the collective imaginary. It belongs equally to life and death and embodies both presence and absence. It finds itself located in a physical and symbolic in-between place since death endows the body with a new materiality. It belongs to an orbit that is both private (intimate) and public, a dialectic that can be clearly observed in funerals and burials or when ashes are scattered. The dead body puts a series of emotions and conceptualizations into motion, among which the idea of death as a state of exception predominates. In effect, although expected for every living being, death is always experienced as something unexpected and catastrophic and denotes details that render it a unique and paradigmatic event. The manner of death is essential since, according to many belief systems, this circumstance determines the soul's fate more than life itself. Understood as an "event," death is always perceived as something unique, unexpected, and surprising, as shown by the reactions and ceremonies that form part of the grieving process (description of the circumstances of the deceased's demise, the family's seclusion, acts of remembrance, epitaphs, etc.).

El Alfaqueque accumulates experience of dealing with dead bodies and with the aggressions to which they are subject in a social space dominated by chaos and the loss of civility even before the epidemic. For example, the novel refers to el Alfaqueque's intervention to reprimand some kids who were mocking bodies at a funeral home, drawing on them and taking photographs. We also see him attempting to figure out whether la Muñe / Baby Girl's body has been desecrated and arranging it to make it more presentable for her family. In this way, the simulacrum and the manipulation of corporality are submitted to regimes of legitimization whose borders are both ambiguous and shifting.

The characters that surround el Alfaqueque and, of course, he himself, move habitually in the realm of the abject, but the situation evoked in the novel seems to exceed even previous thresholds and to disrupt certain communitarian standards. Detecting a dehumanization process that is evident in the way we treat dead bodies, el Alfaqueque asks himself: "¿Cuándo dejamos de enterrar con nuestras propias manos a los que amamos? ¿Qué carajos puede esperarse de gente como uno?" (When did we stop burying those we love with our own hands? he thought. From people like us, what the hell can we expect?).[211] Society's relationship with the corpse is an aspect that goes beyond the story underlying Herrera's narrative and gestures toward Mexico's general situation, where death has invaded both urban and rural, central and border spaces as a means of intimidation by both organized crime and the government along with the sensationalist assistance of a large part of the media.

Although el Alfaqueque's is familiar with death, his observation on the treatment of dead bodies possesses wider resonance. In *Symbolic Exchange and Death*, Jean Baudrillard explains that along with the expulsion to which society condemned the insane, misfits, and members of races deemed to be inferior, society also enacts another expulsion from the collective imaginary upon the dead and upon death itself, as corpses are, according to Baudrillard, "thrown out of the symbolic circulation" of society:

> There is an irreversible evolution from savage societies to our own; little by little, *the dead cease to exist*. . . . They are no longer beings with a full role to

play, worthy partners in exchange, and we make this obvious by exiling them further and further away from the group of the living. In the domestic intimacy of the cemetery, the first grouping remains in the heart of the village or town, becoming the first ghetto, prefiguring every future ghetto, but are thrown further and further from the center toward the periphery, finally having nowhere to go at all, as in the new town of the contemporary metropolis, where there are no longer any provisions for the dead, either in mental or in physical space. Even madmen, delinquents and misfits can find a welcome in the new towns, that is, in the rationality of a modern society. Only the death-function cannot be programmed and localized.[212]

According to Baudrillard, death has lost its "normality" and, moreover, "to be dead is an unthinking anomaly. . . . Death is a delinquency and an incurable deviancy."[213] The idea that the dead do not inhabit a clear and defined place within our social structure shows the dissemination of death within a society that Baudrillard deems inhabited by "survivors." The treatment of life and death as, at times, indistinguishable zones and, at others, as forms of the human that stalk each other, connects to the concept of abjection. The dead body constitutes a radical disruption of the order of the real, considered as something that is eminently impure and transgressive. The corpse ("or *cadaver*: *cadere*, to fall") as Julia Kristeva reminds us, is the final descent: "the corpse [is] the most sickening of wastes, is a border that has encroached upon everything . . . [it] is the outmost of abjection."[214] This occurs not only because the dead body implies material dissolution but also because the violence that leads to this dissolution (to the total loss of limits without which the subject cannot sustain itself) makes a spectacle of this destruction, creating an aesthetic upon the ruins and upon the waste of the social being. As part of this life cycle, the corpse is seen as an anomaly that is difficult to assimilate within the order of the real. It represents the dominion of abjection "the place where meaning collapses."[215]

Faced with a world that is falling apart, where characters represent subjects consumed by the experience of daily violence of diverse origins and an all-encompassing and incessant nature, Yuri Herrera's novel operates at a farcical remove, like humor itself, brings the referent closer and simultaneously distances it. But as we can see, el Alfaqueque also represents aspects of the collective conscience and his reflections capture the ongoing situation in many respects, such as when he perceives the change in the way of life, the increasing loss of community feeling, the social breakdown that goes beyond the public health crisis and instead takes root at the very heart of society. This creates conditions of personal decline that can be seen in the attitudes of the characters, their interrelationships, and the way they address daily challenges. The gallery of characters featured in the novel presents personalities affected by precarious living conditions and violence. Owing to these conditions, they have mobilized picaresque strategies which, at times, often include aggression and criminality. Such behaviors channel resentment, frustration, their need for vengeance, and the impulse to intimidate the other and/or to defend personal territories whatever the cost.

The novel presents another important aspect, connected to the question of productivity in social space, or rather, with the forms of material work needed to sustain the community that seems to float in a dimension isolated from normal rhythms while teetering on the brink of destitution. The novel's plot develops in a theatricalized and dynamic style, marked with anecdotes, dialogues, the characters' brief memories, and short reflections, all done with a light touch. This all occurs, however, against a more lasting background of disorder and lack, aggravated by the mass infection and other related circumstances. The space of death has totally replaced productive activity, leaving the coast clear for intense symbolic and almost carnivalesque (in the Bakhtinian sense) exchanges that channel collective energy.

The epidemic, militarization, and civil violence constitute layers upon which the profanation of bodies, as the radical disturbance of the social order, is inscribed, adding a strongly anti-normative element that worsens the collective situation. In the face of these conditions, el Alfaqueque's diplomatic activity is fundamental and represents the only form of "work" that occurs in a community paralyzed by disease.[216] But his transactions and movements in the provincial scene take place against the backdrop of a besieged city and a bewildered community, where commerce, bureaucracy, and production itself are paralyzed. In creating a material and symbolic exchange from which the unstable collective order can be reorganized, albeit in a delimited fashion, el Alfaqueque's activity generates the only type of transaction to take place in this space. His mediation is the only form of productivity in a world turned upside down, where the exchange of the dead represents a sign of life. This serves to emphasize the exceptional nature of such an activity: the fictional world has rid itself of the dimension of labor, configuring an elemental and primary space. Betina Keizman describes el Alfaqueque's contribution to the community, pointing out that:

> As an intermediary, el Alfaqueque is the worker of right now, someone who does not seek profit in material objects but instead searches for symbolic and performative things. He's a low-end worker, someone who traffics in small

ideas that emerge and then get used up and vanish like soap bubbles. . . . In some ways, the character of el Alfaqueque is transversal, on the one hand he offers his employers face to face service, a real "skin trade" (or personal service, according to John O'Neill) . . . that provides a balm for the troubles that assail his clients. Paradoxically, they are insubstantial attentions: favors, agreements, advice, something that often belongs to the symbolic order.[217]

What Keizman's observation ignores is that el Alfaqueque's multidirectionality represents a break with vertical state and institutional power. El Alfaqueque acts where the unproductive State has failed, although his work occurs at intangible levels, in the sense that he avoids the radicalization of conflicts that would otherwise worsen antagonisms within the community and exact a high social cost. In this sense, as has already been pointed out, his work represents an updated but degraded form of the primary function of the diplomat, in sync with the dismantling of the social and the breakdown of the political. Continuing her argument, Keizman adds that el Alfaqueque embodies the work paradigm of the new millennium in terms of the production of immateriality/production of meanings, relocation, precarity, and short-term contacts for specific projects. As a good gig worker and disposable subject, he lives contingently, even during the exceptional circumstances of the epidemic.[218]

BODY AS COMMODITY

In the novel, the body functions as a semiotic unit—as an image that insistently reappears in different guises that are rendered extreme because of their proximity to death, illness, and eroticism. The body is the object of exchanges, negotiations, deceptions, and cover-ups. Constantly manipulated, moved back and forth, spruced up and central to family conflicts and entanglements, the body almost never appears in the novel as normal and balanced. The public health situation places the entire community—the social body—in a state of alert and emergency, exposing its vulnerability and subjecting the population to needs and tensions caused by shortages and uncertainty. Subjected to forms of power—institutional and personalized, governmental, patriarchal—and connected to different forms of violence, the body is constantly subordinated to conditions bordering on panic, threats, curfew, reprisals, and abandonment. Consequently, the atmosphere in *La transmigración de los cuerpos* intensifies around affect that guides improvised and hasty actions, directed toward reestablishing the unstable balance of daily provincial life.

The epidemic metaphorically illustrates the opaque but definitive threats that are enshrined within the social fabric itself, invisible and destructive. It is as if the regime's necro-politics had transmogrified, under the exotic guise of the "Egyptian mosquito," sources of illness, agony, and inevitable death. This creates a parenthesis within normality, eliminating any trace of productive work, altering routines and daily relationships, and installing exceptionality as a sign of the increasing and unstoppable corrosion of social networks. The community is on tenterhooks, overwhelmed not only by the epidemic but also by the failed public health response and by the erratic presence of the military that only serves to intensify the panic.

From the beginning of the novel, an atmosphere of terror and general devastation brought on by the disease emerges. El Alfaqueque notes that not even the wind runs through the streets where things "parecían abandonadas de sí mismas" (felt much more present when they looked so abandoned).[219] The state of exception transforms the community into a lawless land of public announcements that people interpret and discuss, while fear of the unexpected and the unknown assumes control over social space. This all takes place behind closed doors, with each house transformed into a small prison for its inhabitants, who can hear the army out on the streets, putting surveillance into operation and enforcing regulations.

Inscribed on subjectivities, actions, thoughts, and comments is what Rossana Reguillo calls the "construcción social del miedo" (social construction of fear). The fictional social context takes its inspiration from the lived experiences of residents of Mexico City in 2009 during the spread of swine flu (H1N1) when President Felipe Calderón shut down commerce in the city and imposed public health measures that brought urban activity to a halt. In the novel, the army's unnerving presence on the streets to ensure compliance with the curfew also possesses grim echoes of the omnipresence of the armed forces in Mexico brought on by the war against drugs that Calderón declared in 2006, expanding and intensifying violence, increasing neoliberal policies, and augmenting privatization and social inequality. Under these restrictions, public space becomes a battle ground penetrated by social dynamics that exceed regulations and express themselves in a disordered fashion, revealing overwhelming passions such as sexual desire, the need for vengeance, filial devotion, feelings of machismo, mistrust, and an attraction to violence, longstanding feuds, and warring family clans. The Fonsecas and the Castros represent an individualized nucleus that stands in opposition to the town's collective and anonymous backdrop as well as to the government forces that have suspended community life. The characters' names and nicknames emphasize the plot's frivolity, where extravagant characters and situations contrast with tragic elements, disease, death, vengeance, and distrust of authority. Taken as a whole, the novel presents a gallery of characters from a comedy of intrigue who are nonetheless embedded in a reality of dramatic contrasts and tragic overtones. Among the characters are el Delfín / the Dolphin (a Fonseca family member, whose nickname is a reference to his perforated septum caused by cocaine use) and el Ñandertal / the Neanderthal, a crude individual who carries out minor illegal activities, and of whom it is said "era grandote y apantallador, caminaba como si estuviera permanentemente saliendo de una sala de terapia intensiva, desplazando con lentitud cada músculo" (huge and hulking, a man who walked like he was forever on his way out of the ICU, moving each muscle with considerable care).[220] We also find el Menonita / the Mennonite who "ya no usaba overol de mezclilla ni sombrero holandés, pero sí botas de jale y camisa a cuadros. La barba rojiza se le fugaba por los lados del tapabocas" (no longer wore the denim overalls and straw hat but the workboots and plaid shirt were still there. His red beard spilled out the side of his facemask) and la Ingobernable / the Unruly, member of the Fonseca family etc.[221]

The dead bodies snatched by the warring families are Romeo Fonseca, killed when a car ran him down, although "se le notaba un dolor de antes" (you could tell there was prior pain) and La Muñe, from the Castro family whose body is "read" by Vicky, the nurse, who analyzes the traces of her dying moments.[222] As Herrera explains toward the end of the novel, the subtext of the fight between the two families stems from their interrelationships. In the case of the Castro family, there is a hint of an aristocratic background that gives them delusions of grandeur and that offers a contrast with their shabby present-day circumstances in which their former power has diminished to the control of a regional boss: "Los Castro habían sido hidalgos y señores en algún siglo en algún castillo del otro lado del mundo, ahí estaba ese escudo a colores para demostrarlo. En eso eran diferentes de los Fonseca: lo único que los Castro conservaban de su vida anterior era lo que habían buscado muchas vidas atrás" (The Castros had been noblemen and lords in some century or other in some castle or other on the opposite side of the world—and there was the colorful coat of arms to prove it. They were different from the marshaled up from many generations back).[223]

In the case of the Fonsecas, el Delfín's nickname also evokes the name of the French heir to the throne, and as such also offers a nod to a debased former lineage now reduced to an ironic provincial mediocrity. The scheming embedded in the plot reveals the web of secrets, farcical situations and simulations ignited by the deaths of Romeo and la Muñe. Amid all this, el Alfaqueque's verbal skills opens doors for him and, during his negotiations, allows many of the hidden reasons for this inter-family hatred to come to light. The Fonsecas' house, known as "la casa de Las Pericas" / the Las Pericas place:

> [the Las Pericas place] was huge and white with a big wooden veranda, as if someone had been willing to give up their old house in the tropics, despite now living on a hill a thousand klicks from the sea. . . . As soon as he stepped through the door he was dazzled by a huge room with a dozen high windows and on the table lay Baby Girl.[224]

El Alfaqueque compares the two families, discovering both similarities and differences that explain their mutual antagonism:

> The Castros had been putting on airs for years and Baby Girl cramped their style. Now the Fonsecas, too, had struck it rich, but about style they couldn't care less. So different and so the same, the Castros and the Fonsecas. Poor as dirt a couple of decades ago, now too big for their boots, and neither had moved out of the barrio.[225]

The events that introduce the corpse first highlight the staging and then, as part of the theatrical paraphernalia, the body lying on the table, building an anomalous image of domestic space that is also a place of death. In an existential tone, el Alfaqueque reflects on the fact that "la gente toda es como estrellas muertas: lo que nos llega de ellas es distinto de la cosa, que ya ha desaparecido o ya ha cambiado, así sea un segundo después de la emisión de luz o de la mala obra" (people, all people, are like dark stars: what we see is different from the thing itself, which has already disappeared, already changed, even a single second after the light or evil has been discharged).[226]

His awareness of the transitory nature of life goes hand in hand with and intensifies the corpse's tense and bloody image in its isolation and finality. One of el Alfaqueque's thoughts at the end of the novel possesses a similar tone when he reflects: "A lo mejor después ellos mismos serían sólo la cicatriz de alguien más, sin nombre, sin epitafio, nomás una raya en la piel" (Maybe they themselves would one day be nothing but someone's scar, nameless, no epitaph, just a line on the skin).[227] Emotionally exhausted by his role as mediator and by the general climate of death and neglect, the character offers a melancholy perspective on the situation and on the life that humans try to prolong only so as to cheat death. In a similar fashion, he meditates on silence, which is a theme that recurs throughout all of Yuri Herrera's work:

> It was hard and yet formless, that silence. How to describe what isn't there? What name can you give to something that doesn't exist, yet exists for that reason precisely? Kings of the kingpins, those who had invented the zero, he thought, had given it a name and even slipped into a line of numbers, as tho it could stay put, obedient. But once in a while, like at that moment, there before Baby Girl, zero rosed up and swallowed everything.[228]

The characters form part of an entourage that frequently surrounds el Alfaqueque, who relies on them to mediate in community matters, and they often end up involved in each other's issues. The descriptions are visual and expressive, revealing the twists and turns of an informal everyday life that is marked by improvisation as well as the bonds that come from shared history. Public space serves as the backdrop for the development of transactions, agreements, conflicts, and negotiations in which the materiality of the exchanges is as strong as the values and emotions at play in the real and symbolic trafficking.

Women embody a function that is both connective and triggering. They put actions into play and are simultaneously objects of desire, rejection, or male protection, but they are not protagonists in the decisively male world of the novel. Their character and individuality stand out, however, in the novel's theatrical narrative. The most important female characters are la Tres Veces Rubia, la Ingobernable y la Muñe. The latter, dead at the novel's outset, is described twice, first in life: "El Alfaqueque recordó cuando conoció a la Muñe en una chamba que le encargó el papá de ella: ñenga ñenga, callada, de ojos bonitos pero bien tristes, tenía pelo largo, siempre cuidadosamente cepillado. Daban ganas de quererla, pero como que las ganas se pasaban pronto" (The Redeemer recalled the first time he'd met Baby Girl on a job he did for her dad: itty bitty thing, quiet, long hair always carefully brushed, pretty face but eyes so sad. The kind of girl you wanted to love, really truly, but then the urge passed kind of fast).[229] In the second description, she is now dead: "Vio a la Muñe pálida, ceniza, tenía un rastro de sangre entre la nariz y la boca, las manos crispadas y la cara triste. Estaba tan pequeña y tan callada y al mismo tiempo se sentía como el corazón frío de la casa, como si aun así la sostuviera" (He saw Baby Girl there, pale, ashen, a trail of blood between her nose and mouth, hands clenched and face exceedingly sad. She was so small and so still, but at the same time seemed like the heart of the house, cold yet somehow keeping it alive).[230]

La Tres Veces Rubia, described as "un milagro de piel viva" (a burning miracle of flesh), is the object of el Alfaqueque's desire and is viewed above all through the erotic scenes she shares with the protagonist.[231] Hypersexualized, she represents a space of passion, where life is configured as pleasure, in counterpoint to the town's death drive. Vicky is another of the female characters, a nurse who helps el Alfaqueque "to get a read" on bodies, as in the case of la Muñe, to find out how she died as well as discover any possible abuse the body might have suffered at the hands of the enemy family. All the characters enshrine bodily traits that define them not only as individuals but also as marginal lifeforms that have adapted to the conditions around them and to the exceptional circumstances of the public health crisis. All of them are in direct contact with death caused by the disease and by the constant disputes and situations that arise from a lawless space subordinated to precarity and violence.

The obvious absence of a benevolent State that protects its citizenry is palpable and corresponds to the popular notion of the hollowing out of political and social institutions and their replacement with chaotic forms of co-existence and social regulation. Far from contradicting this assertion, the presence of the military serves to underscore it, since force is only exercised because of the official inability to maintain order and the well-being of a community that is beset by problems and by popular dynamics that hover at the margins of law and order.

COMMUNITY/IMMUNITY

The novel overtly engages with the paradigm of community/immunity developed by Roberto Esposito as part of his reflections on biopolitics.[232] According to this model, community (communitas) is conceived of as "aquello que liga a sus miembros en un empeño donativo del uno al otro y, por tanto, como aquello que abre al individuo hacia la alteridad" (that which joins its members in a gesture of giving and therefore something that opens the individual to alterity).[233] Both aspects, that which constitutes a cohesive force of social formation, and that which disposes the subjects toward Otherness, are well-represented in *La transmigración de los cuerpos*, where the assignment of immanence/transcendence to subjects is manifested through dialectical movements that find synthetic or redemptive movement in el Alfaqueque's actions. According to Esposito, "Si la comunidad determina la apertura de las barreras de protección de la identidad individual, la inmunidad constituye el intento de reconstruirla en una forma defensiva y ofensiva contra todo elemento externo capaz de amenazarla" (If the community determines the opening of the protective barriers of individual identity, immunity for its part constitutes the attempts to reconstruct it in a defensive and offensive manner against all threatening external elements).[234]

In *La transmigración de los cuerpos*, the threats to the community appear both literally in the form of contagion as well as metaphorically in the removal of bodies from their respective families, at moments when customary funeral rituals underscore social belonging (to community and family) and the loss of the deceased, allowing for the process of grief. In this sense, and in Esposito's terms, the novel inscribes itself at the exact intersection of biology and law, in the concrete forms of the characters' actions and reactions, and in their direct interventions into the biological life of the inhabitants of the fictional world.

The descriptions of the disease that cause the public health crisis in the town create a graphically revealed eschatological atmosphere, both in terms of the symptoms of infection that attack the lungs as well as the government's failure to control the situation. The novel describes those infected with the disease as spitting up blood, fainting or stricken by a rapid physical decline, along with intense pain that leads to anguish and death. Along with feelings of fear and repugnance that the signs of infection provoke, we see people's skepticism of the official communiques, and a rejection of the need to isolate, socially distance and avoid public spaces. The shortages and the confusing messages the population receives provides proof that the community is unprotected and that thresholds of resistance are breaking down in the face of danger. The exchange as well as the itineraries of the cadavers that have been taken hostage extend the horror beyond the limits of family and personal misfortune, impacting the funeral rites and the grief, demonstrating the lack of respect for the dead body. The warring families' dispute modifies the limits the regulations enforce, superimposing a dynamic that surpasses both the ordinances and the fear of contagion. The social energy that swirls around the exchange of bodies circulates above and beyond the risks, fears, and restrictions, placing the needs of the family above governmental authority. The evident absence of police in the case of the kidnapping of the corpses reveals society that fends for itself, neither possessing nor desiring outside help, given the disconnect between the population and government institutions, deepened by mistrust in the regime, in corruption and the inoperative nature of the State apparatus in the region.

Defined as a "historia de muertos solitarios" (a story of solitary deaths) the novel demonstrates a multiplicity of behaviors toward the cadavers (the desecration of bodies after death, soldiers opening up coffins, the treatment of the corpse as an object of exchange and negotiation) and reveals what philosophers before Esposito (Nancy, Agamben, Blanchot) have highlighted regarding the question of community: the existence of "alteridad constitutiva que la diferencia incluso de sí misma, sustrayéndola a toda connotación identitaria" (a constitutive alterity, that differentiates the community even from itself, impeding any possible connotation of identity).[235] In effect, the community displays its internal fissures, its antagonisms and ruptures, all of which are elements the inhabitants hold in common, beyond their disputes.

For Esposito, who defines the notion of community based on the will to politicize the concept, the paradigm of immunity consists of the exact opposite of community. Immunity is not a question of subsuming oneself into the community but instead the reverse: in removing the common conditions, in developing resistance (antibodies) in order to avoid being vanquished by otherness (the external virus), in other words, acquiring a form of exceptionality with respect to norms. In Herrera's novel, the community is determined to create immunity against the virus that causes the illness (the Egyptian mosquito?) and each family unit reacts in the same way to an exterior threat, although in reality the agent destroying the social fabric comes from the inside. The idea of the "Egyptian mosquito" attributes a foreign and exotic character to the biological threat that splinters the community, as if it were an act of terrorism that can repeat itself ad infinitum, revealing the individual and collective vulnerability.

In the same way that the army patrols enforcing the city's curfew engenders more fear than the disease itself, the antagonism between the families creates as much or perhaps more harm than the sickness that afflicts them. None of these internal elements of congenital violence are acknowledged as self-destructive, despite their increasingly paralyzing effect. Referring to the idea he expressed in the earlier quote, Esposito clarifies:

> This can be true for singular individuals, but also for the communities, taken in this case in their specific dimension, immunized against all foreign elements that appear as exterior threats. This is the implied conflict of immunological dynamics—already typical in modernity and nowadays increasingly extended to all domains of individual and collective experience, either real or imaginary. Even if immunity is necessary for the conservation of life, once it goes beyond a certain limit, it is constricted by a cage of sorts, in which our freedom and even the meaning of our existence end up getting lost, along with our existence's opening to its own exteriority, which has been called communitas. . . . If immunity tends to enclose our existence in circles or uncommunicated spaces, community, more than a bigger siege, is

the passage that, in cutting the lines of the limit, again reassembles human experience, liberating it from its obsession with security.[236]

In biopolitical terms, Herrera's narrative represents a fictional exploration of the way in which the imagined community absorbs otherness (exogenous elements, alterity, heterogeneity, Otherness) and the forms in which the self, or rather, the commons, relates to the exterior that delimits and thus constitutes the place of the subject. In the novel, the theme of security appears in different forms, such as in the question of health safeguards, the state of exception, militarization, the defense of life and death, the "ownership" of a corpse, the protection of familial rights, of affective territories, and the day-to-day spaces of power and their public and private constituencies. In the name of protecting the people, power harnesses collective fear and transforms it into a symbolic prison. Esposito situates the immunity paradigm, "en su doble variante biológica y jurídica" (in its double biological and legal variant) as the point where the spheres of life and politics intersect.[237] The concepts of "ownership," "the common" and "the immune" are differential dominions within a social totality, traversed by what Esposito calls the "dynamic of appropriation" that can be applied to the original arrogation of objects or products derived from natural resources like that of "determinados seres humanos reducidos al estatuto de cosa por parte de aquellos que proclaman ser sus propietarios" (certain human beings reduced to the status of things by those who claim them as their property).[238] In this process of commodification of the corpse (that, in turn, is the commodified form of a human being), the novel disposes of the theatrical movements of the imagined community, configuring the reappropriation of the dead body—strengthened as a biopolitical icon—as the nucleus of the narrative action. *La transmigración de los cuerpos* presents the process by which the task of reestablishing order is privatized. The interfamily conflict surrounding the bodies reveals a community that is in the process of absorbing the conspicuously absent State's functions. El Alfaqueque's skill consists precisely in moving among the interstices that exist in the enclosed spaces of the private, the immune and the common good. The character acts from within this chaos, moving strategically until he achieves an acceptable status quo within circumstances marked by the state of exception and militarization.[239]

CHAPTER 2
Fernanda Melchor
Necro-Aesthetics and the "Truth of the Body"

(Thankfully) *This Is Not Miami*
  Chronicle, Border Narrative, and the Villa Rica of la Vera Cruz
  Regional Identities: Heterogeneity and Consistency
  Lights, Fire, and Shadows

"Youth, Divine Treasure" in *Falsa liebre*
  The Devastation of Society
  Mapping Subjectivity
  Perversion, Excess, and Gender

Temporada de huracanes or the Whirlwind of Language
  The Problem with Truth
  The Witch's Black Hole
  Patriarchy and Witchcraft
  Between Private and Public Life: Secrets and Gossip
  (Anti)Modernity and Community in La Matosa

When Fernanda Melchor (Veracruz, 1982) published *Temporada de huracanes* (*Hurricane Season*) she had already written a series of chronicles and narratives, entitled *Aquí no es Miami* (*This Is Not Miami*) and a novel, *Falsa liebre* (False hare), both published in 2013, that had immediately caught critics' attention.[1] Both publications revealed the young author's clear upward trajectory into the Mexican literary canon.[2] As per her literary training, her chronicles demonstrate a predictable penchant for the situations and settings of life in Veracruz. For its part, *Falsa liebre* displays a thematic repertoire seen in other authors of her generation: violence, social decline, the collapse of the traditional family, marginality, an interest in peripheral social spaces, nature as a complex and aggressive entity and the vulnerability of youth.

To mobilize these themes, which she will develop more thoroughly in *Temporada de huracanes*—albeit with a different scope and perspective—Melchor uses a varied and highly expressive language, imbued with regionalisms, colloquialisms, and coarse phrasing that fit the situations and visual settings that make up the substance of her writing. All these literary mechanisms speak to a countercultural thrust that has become a cliché in Latin American literature as it searches for ways to channel its social despair and political frustration, rejecting the tropes and rules imposed by high culture, and denouncing the legacy of an unequal and deficient modernity. Beyond this, Melchor's poetics seem to be oriented less toward the symbolic elaboration of social contexts, which is a characteristic of Latin American literature, and instead toward the ampler register of the civilizational crisis that is profoundly impacting peripheral areas.

The porousness of the limits separating the lettered tradition from popular culture that animates Melchor's prose reveals the existence of a stratified and exclusionary society where intersubjective connections, and the transgression of cultural boundaries, brings an inevitable charge of material and symbolic violence in its wake. The inclusion of themes, narrative strategies, settings, and figures drawn from subaltern social spaces along with rhetorical topics replete with elements of mass culture and urban subcultures offer a counterpoint to the bourgeois novel's most formal legacies:

its representations of the "problematic hero" and its recidivist returns to the space and time of official history and the celebration of instrumental reason and modernity.

Like the literary production of many well-known twenty-first-century writers, Melchor's writing focuses instead on the failure of the social project along with its ruptures and perversities, not because there are so many idols yet to be destroyed, but rather because it is a mission that these authors, born around the end of the Cold War, seem to claim as their own.[3] In this way, Melchor engages the subversive representation of a world where the echoes of ideals and inaudible or deafening utopian discourses are, in any case, only useless remnants of social environments that precipitate a prolonged and painful process of deterioration.

In Fernanda Melchor's world, *death regimes* manifest themselves in all their forms. In the universe she creates, we clearly perceive the effects of necropolitics: the regulations that control the right to life and death, the invoking of lands that encompass secret cemeteries and mass graves, the actions of the agents of social destruction, and the absence of State control and the complicity of organized crime. Her writing offers an expression of the necro-poetics that bear witness to these themes and shifts in sensibility with a language replete with insults, crude allusions to body parts, dismemberment, murders, tortures, rapes, and domestic violence that all exceed the parameters of the human condition, civilization, self-respect, and respect for others.

As if this were not enough, Melchor's work also explores the subtler impacts of the progressive tearing of the social fabric that manifests itself in the corrosion of values, the degradation of behavior, and the narrowing of individual and collective horizons. In her literary corpus, Melchor creates a poetics of excess in which the reader simultaneously confronts the limits and contamination of language. She lodges multiple indications of the signs of irrepresentability in the register of language—that which proliferates in signs but whose meaning either evaporates or multiplies ad infinitum—providing evidence of the exhaustion of the means of communication in the face of an excessive reality whose outbursts dominate the existential landscape of our times.

Melchor's necro-aesthetic draws upon a series of mechanisms with which she demonstrates the exhaustion of the social as well as the weakening of the political, employing corporality as a representational platform in which symbolic and material elements come together on multiple levels. This bodily illustration not only includes grotesque representations of somatic aspects and functions, often depicted as repellent, sordid, and unusual, but also a mixed portrait of places (overcrowded spaces, hidden corners, a hodgepodge of elements and beings, hoarding, elusiveness, and ambiguous identities). Rather than occupying their own spaces, characters traverse social cracks and urban fissures as well as transitory places in which putting down roots and belonging are impossible: the port, the esplanade, beaches, and alleyways. Inhabited by "disposable" beings, these are intermediate, residual, and dark spaces, ideal for criminality, drugs, violent coupling, furtiveness, and flight. Within them, beauty, culture, order, and pleasure are forbidden. They function as sites of sacrifice and victimization in which aggression and impunity run parallel in indivisible complicity.

Fernanda Melchor's aesthetics both use and abuse the mechanisms of dirty realism, employing them to communicate horror and emotional reactions that bring fearsome repercussions in their wake. Habits and behaviors come together to position the body as a site of terror and rejection in its disarticulation of the norms of human regulation and its substitution of deformities, unpleasant characters, and situations as well as unexpected and unacceptable relationships that negatively affect the reader's sensibility, pushing tolerance to its limits. She seeks to illustrate the surrender of civility and the destruction of life in the face of incomprehensible and/or uncontrollable factors that have led to a deviation from security protocols and human rights.

She also presents deformity, hybridity, ambiguity, anomaly, and ugliness as alternatives that facilitate narrative theatricality, staging and visualizing aspects that wound the recipient down to the last detail. Faced with the horror of reality, the collective imaginary has incorporated the experience of violence within itself, normalizing unusual examples of violations of human behavior. To cross this threshold and cause a reaction to such actions the level of grotesque display must hyperbolically increase until it attains a type of pornography of violence and of the surroundings and peoples that are associated with it. When the word is the only element that serves these purposes, language becomes an instrument that must be taken to its extremes, both at a lexical as well as at a semantic and syntactic level. In *Temporada de huracanes*, Melchor employs syntactical rupture, collage, onomatopoeia, elimination of punctuation, rapid shifts in viewpoint, an insistence on ambiguity. Her characters are developed as individuals with volatile personalities and undefined, hybrid identities. Melchor depicts processes of animalization, automatization, and psychological deterioration that point to the idea of human debasement as an irreversible deviation from nature and culture. All these mechanisms appear at one moment or another in Melchor's novels. Already aware of spectacular and performative elements, detectable in scenes of death in exceptional criminal contexts as illustrated in *Aquí no es Miami*, she displays an interest in combining aesthetic features of the *crónica roja* with questions of emotion.

In *Los muertos indóciles: Necroescrituras y desapropiación*, Cristina Rivera Garza refers to the radicalization of horror in the northern hemisphere, particularly in Mexico in the cities of Tamaulipas, Culiacán, Morelia, and Veracruz and poses the question:

> What does it mean to write, today, in such a context? What are the challenges for writing, when professional precariousness and gruesome deaths are the stuff of everyday life? Which aesthetic and ethical dialogues does the act of writing hurl us into when we are quite literally surrounded by corpses?[4]

And she adds: "Si la escritura se pretende crítica del estado de las cosas, ¿cómo es posible, desde y con la escritura, desarticular la gramática del poder depredador del neoliberalismo exacerbado y sus mortales máquinas de guerra?" (If writing is supposed to critique the status quo, then how is it possible—through writing and with writing—to dissociate the grammar of predatory power from aggravated neoliberalism and its deadly war machines?)[5]

Language is an instrument that not only translates experience into discourse but also, via the latter, impacts the processes of the formation of social conscience. The symbolic representation of violence explores the imaginary and experiments with possible forms of understanding the internal rationality of destructive impulses, linking them to the systematic disarticulation from where we derive the principles and resources for the control of life and death in our lifetime. Literature thus serves to penetrate the sensorium of a specific age and society, while, at the same time, it probes the universal problem linked to the meaning of life and the role human beings play in the larger system of nature and history.

Melchor's work constitutes a multidirectional incursion into the social and political dynamics of our day, borne through a literary style, which, without having reached its highest point of aesthetic maturity, nonetheless displays an impressive array of poetic and ideological strategies. In some cases, her narrative methods have been described as hearkening back to the baroque tradition because of her exuberant use of language and the superabundance of details that come together to produce the effect of being saturated by and sutured to the worlds she creates.

In the Bakhtinian sense, the idea of a grotesque body that is tied to the surroundings and relationships associated with the experience of death, invokes a funereal vision of the carnivalesque, recalling modalities of the funereal Baroque, where decomposition (the dismemberment and corruption of a corpse) is presented as a pedagogical decorativism intended to recall the deceptiveness of appearances and the radical vulnerability of human beings. The carnivalesque manifests itself in the use and idea of masks and in the employment of inversions and unexpected associations. At the same time, Melchor's disjointed aesthetic draws on an ornamental hybridization and hyperbolics of details and concepts. The mix of idiolects and the use of a coarse vocabulary in her writing, augmented by mockery, insults, and other examples of the break with decorum, combines with her use of regionalisms and colloquial terms that insert the narrative into familiar but consequently even more intriguing contexts.

The body assumes the role of protagonist in transgressive scenes that erase the radical separation between the dominions of life and death, and of public and private. Melchor's fictional prose drips with sordidness, vulgarity and redundancy that function as stylistic elements that put the degraded quality of reality on display, presenting it as the excess or overflow of life beyond conventional limits. As Bakhtin has analyzed, the grotesque possesses a liberating quality because it provides a new perspective on mundane things and events allowing for a relativization of normality and a confrontation with shocking but expected elements of individual and collective existence. The grotesque is thus subversive in the sense that it displays a freeing of the instincts that occupy public spaces and make themselves visible and central, revindicating the position of marginal subjects or hidden aspects of humanity that are considered abnormal. Elements of the grotesque, the abject and the promiscuous that were historically explored in naturalist literature and more recently in radical forms of realism (dirty realism, poverty porn, etc.), discard the status quo and vindicate the primitive instincts that we associate with earlier stages of modernity or with the resistance to it, originating in social sectors outside of the capitalist mainstream and "high culture."

In *Powers of Perversion*, Julia Kristeva indicates that one of the qualities of the abject is its resistance to assimilation, which endows it with the power to dismantle subjectivity as well as the parameters that define the borders of the subject and the limits of its existential landscape. Abjection thus disarticulates, disassembles, deconstructs, and disturbs the individual, leaving it unhinged:

> There looms, within abjection, one of those violent, dark revolts of being, directed against a threat that seems to emanate from an exorbitant outside

or inside, ejected beyond the scope of the possible, the tolerable, the thinkable.... Unflaggingly, like an inescapable boomerang, a vortex of summons and repulsion places the one haunted by it literally beside himself.... The abject is not an ob-ject facing me, which I name or imagine. Nor is it an ob-jest, an otherness ceaselessly fleeing in a systematic quest of desire. What is abject is not my correlative, which, providing me with someone or something else as support, would allow me to be more or less detached and autonomous. The abject has only one quality of the object—that of being opposed to I.[6]

Abjection's disaggregating power penetrates the rough and attenuated territories of community networks that literature recodifies by appealing to the representation of the organic, the visceral, the triggering, and the licentious that dominant society has relegated to a position of invisibility and ineffability. These degraded human forms are expelled from the social body that has been domesticated by a civilizing normativity. Commenting on Kristeva's approach to the abject, Judith Butler indicates: "The 'abject' designates that which has been expelled from the body, discharged as excrement, literally rendered 'Other.'"[7] The subject's expulsion to society's margins that we see in Melchor's works, creates human conglomerates that are both spatial and relational and that function like negative assemblages in which forms of evil including modalities of death and its substitutes (the open wound, rape, dispossession, abuse, sacrifice, and victimization) concentrate. In the same movement, what is expelled is reduced to otherness and submerged into an irredeemable alterity.

In his analysis of the "powers of perversion" Martín Guerra Muente points out that "aquel que encarne la figura del otro será siempre un muerto en vida, o alguien que vive entre dos muertes" (those who embody the figure of the Other will always be the living dead, or someone who lives between two deaths).[8] This type of social horror, derived from radical exclusion, opens an abyss between this Otherness and the regulated space of sociability. In this sense, "lo abyecto es lo terrible que ya no está: los cadáveres amontonados, el hedor de la descomposición, lo no-humano, lo indefinible" (the abject is something terrible that is not there: piles of bodies, the stench of decomposition, the non-human, the undefinable).[9] The characters of *Falsa liebre*, as well as the setting created in *Temporada de huracanes*, exist in this zone of simultaneous indistinction and exceptional intensity. It is a world of lawless lands, anomalous and perturbing spaces, and radical otherness in which the submerged, margnalized, invisibilized, silenced and forgotten are given new life. What we identify as abject is, in fact, the return of the repressed:

Abjection is not only the form that it takes, or that was attributed to it, or that which wants to be withdrawn from circulation, but it is also the form that returns from that which wanted to be erased, a politics of restitution that protests the perverse and repressive power of the State . . . the horror always ends up emerging, whether as part of a visual merchandize or as the hideous unconscious that pursues us.[10]

Guerra Muente describes an aesthetics of abjection that recalls the ideas of the celebrated Brazilian director, Glauber Rocha, in his 1965 manifesto "Uma estética da fome" (An aesthetics of hunger).[11] In the manifesto, Glauber Rocha proposed an unhesitating display of violence as a way of challenging what Guerra Muente paraphrases as "el orden estético imperante promoviendo la circulación del horror com garantía subversive" (the prevailing aesthetic order promoting the circulation of horror with a subversive guarantee).[12] As Guerra Muente explains: "Si los poderes de la perversión querían obliterar el flujo de imágenes del horror el artista debía propiciar que éstas volvieran a entrar en circulación" (If the "powers of perversion" wanted to obliterate the flow of images of horror the artist should make sure they come back into circulation). This "ominous epistemology" consists of recognizing the body that has been expelled from the social order and from life, recognizing that it is impossible to reestablish the unity of a self that has been dismantled by systemic violence. In this sense, and following Guerra Muente's ideas, Melchor's work reveals the exploding of the representational field, from which "la legitimidad del orden simbólico y de sus lenguajes cerrados comienza a exponer sus cesuras" (the legitimacy of the symbolic order and its enclosed languages begin to reveal their incisions).[13] In addition, her work "propicia la re-circulación del cuerpo expulsado. No es, sin embargo, la imagen tópica del horror la que circula, sino una alteridad desbordada de fragmentos que inciden en ese estallido que deja la violencia" (fosters the re-circulation of the expelled body. It is not, however, the stereotyped image of horror that circulates, but rather an overwhelmed alterity made up of fragments that target the explosion violence has caused).[14]

(THANKFULLY) *THIS IS NOT MIAMI*

CHRONICLE, BORDER NARRATIVE, AND THE VILLA RICA OF LA VERA CRUZ

Impacted by the wounds of individual, collective and structural violence, Melchor's work incorporates spaces, idiolects, and subjectivities that come together to form a dense and grueling prose that critics quickly hailed as one of the finest examples of the most recent generation of Mexican writers. Her journey to Parnassus began with the writing of chronicles, a genre that was established in colonial times, purporting to offer an exhaustive and objective survey of lands, cultures, and customs. Assembling empirical elements and testimonial viewpoints, the colonial chronicle defined itself as a documentary device that used words to construct a referent perceived as otherwise unattainable. However, its claims to objectivity are clearly unsustainable since the chronicle's discourse reveals more about the subject who writes it than about the reality to which it refers in a mediated fashion. Beyond the momentary social instances that it uncovers, every chronicle in effect constitutes an aesthetic and ideological penetration into the popular imagination that the chronicler then uses, re-elaborates, interprets, and recycles, creating productive relationships between culture and politics, popular expressions and ideology, representation and power.

Deploying a written form that channels both the introduction of critical angles and the author's claims to detachment, from the outset the chronicle genre has placed the question of truth front and center. The exposition of descriptions, facts, and impressions and the use of a picturesque *costumbrismo* that is easily digestible by a variety of audiences only just covers the discourse's silences and hesitations. The chronicle is a selective genre because it focuses on carefully delimited parcels of society, selected from a vast context. It also represents a "border" discourse because it demarcates sociocultural territories, which it compares and appropriates in different ways. Connected to fictional narrative and to *testimonio*, the chronicle permits writers ample margin to make an overt display of their subjectivity, involving themselves in and hiding behind a documentary study of realities that generally pass unnoticed by the collective gaze. The chronicler rarely discloses his/her perspective on the selection of topics, the angles of observation, and the interest that guides them. In the proscenium, the rhetorical construction that evokes the referent is presented as an imaginary construction or rather a fictionalized product altered by the recorder's subjectivity.

Depending on the chronicler's objectives as well as his or her abilities, the discursive pragmatics come into focus close-up—the exercise of social critique, the romanticization of the popular, the idealization of identities, the pedagogical or moralizing intentions of the text, and the use of irony. The chronicle is, as we know, a flexible genre that often incorporates elements of the oral tradition (simple and colloquial language, social themes, concision, and a mixture of cultural topics) that appeal to a wide and heterogeneous public. In these types of texts, the reader generally seeks a gentle engagement with reality, facilitated by multiple forms of self-recognition or identification with spaces, situations, and characters. The chronicle's principal functions are to inform and entertain and to offer clues toward an interpretation of society as an intricate drama beset by power relations, myths, prejudices, and popular desires. In broad strokes, the chronicle mobilizes perceptions and knowledges, sheds new light on common experiences and familiarizes the reader with generally unknown, invisible, or unnoticed aspects of daily life.

With regard to the fields of history, sociology, journalism, *testimonio*, and literary fictions, the chronicle also represents "border writing" as in the hybrid forms that exemplify the "artículos de costumbres" (short literary sketches on customs, manners, or characters), as illustrated by Alfonso Reyes's Paris chronicles and José Joaquín Blanco's chronicles of the 1980s. Carlos Monsiváis's brilliant contributions to the genre crown a tradition of the most prolific and sharp observation and social critique in the Spanish language. Because of this legacy, the chronicle facilitates access to popular sensibility within the diversity of the Mexican tradition, as well as an appropriate way of penetrating Mexican cultural nationalism from the very beginnings of a literary career.[15]

In accordance with the genre's requirements, the texts that make up Fernanda Melchor's first publication *Aquí no es Miami* (2013) proclaim their desire to reclaim the local: knowledges, customs, forms of social (self-)recognition, values, and fantasies, all cover a wide array of themes that range from violence to UFOs, offering a gamut of representations that speak to the diverse and the contingent, the documentalist and the aesthetics of a syncretic regional and tropicalized culture.[16]

The cultural heritage we associate with the Villa Rica de la Vera Cruz, city of gold, also known as the "las Cuatro Veces Heroica Veracruz" (Four Times Heroic Veracruz) for its repeated resistance to invasions, goes back to the entry of Hernán Cortés into Mexico in 1519, which inaugurated one of the first and strongest settlements of the colonial world. The port of Veracruz was the first threshold crossed by the enslaved peoples who were brought to labor on the sugar plantations and cattle ranches or to be utilized as domestic servants or military troops. At the beginning of the seventeenth century, history also tells of a rebellion of runaway enslaved people ("cimarrones" or maroons) led by Gaspar Yanga (or Nyanga) who organized one of the first free towns in America. This would lead to the foundation of San Lorenzo de Los Negros, thus adding an element of early popular subversion and active sociocultural heterogeneity to modern Veracruz. Since the end of the twentieth century, the region's history has turned toward the actions of organized crime, particularly Los Zetas Cartel, who have been enthroned there since the 1990s.[17] Consequently, Veracruz has been subject to territorial struggles and criminal activities that have installed a climate of increasing incivility and violence that permeates all social, economic, and political levels of society.

Although the author recognizes the "carácter oblicuo del lenguaje" (language's oblique character), the prose of her chronicles and fictions at times betrays an over enthusiastic delight in the possibilities offered by semantic games, lexical abundance, hybrid speech patterns, and varied use of imagery that often imposes itself between text and reader.[18] However, the author usually succeeds in skillfully channeling the flow of signs and signifiers, relying on the twists and turns of language, peppered with short dialogs, captivating descriptions, and visualizations of modest lyricism.

Melchor acknowledges that her texts are constructions of language in which the border between reality and fiction tends to blur. Yet this does not diminish the claims to verisimilitude that underscores the chronicle's textuality. Far from disappearing to give way to textual "objectivity," the narrator's subjective perspective reclaims its role as the chronicle's principal tool. Interested above all in engaging the reader in the complicity of reading, the chronicler aesthetically and ideologically controls his/her version of reality with an iron fist, exposing or hiding the mediations that thematize it.

REGIONAL IDENTITIES: HETEROGENEITY AND CONSISTENCY

In the first pages of the book, Melchor promotes a conventional vision of the material and of the process of its depiction, evoking a world full of mainly urban tales that struggles to survive oblivion and where language acts as a tool to chisel something that eludes representation despite its connection to daily life.

> The book the reader holds in his/her hands was written in an attempt to tell stories in the most honest way possible: recognizing language's oblique character and making the most of it for the story's benefit. Who cares if we cannot "reproduce" reality with a tool that leaves our hands shredded; who cares that an image on our computers, however futile it may be, is worth a thousand words. Stories are born out of language and in it they attain their deepest sense, the sense that tape recorders and cameras cannot capture and in which we find the tribe's tangled voices and gestures.[19]

While avoiding clarifying the relationship between fictional production and authenticity and failing to address the consequences of the non-acceptance of language's obvious obliqueness, of note is the author's use of the paratext to explain the principles that gesture uncertainly toward the question of ethics. However, from her perspective, of most importance is the introduction of orality as a path toward the recuperation of the authenticity of the voice of the tribe—clichés resulting from the always-pointless exercise of having literature explain itself.

Written over a period of ten years and published in magazines or newspapers, many of the texts in *Aquí no es Miami* are republications and, in some cases, extended versions of earlier texts, apart from the previously unpublished "La vida no vale nada." Recognizing the genre's social and political context, Melchor details how she wrote the chronicles collected in *Aquí no es Miami* during "la calamitosa convergencia de los gobiernos de Fidel Herrera Beltrán como gobernador de Veracruz, y de Felipe Calderón Hinojosa como presidente de la República" (The calamitous convergence of the administrations of Fidel Herrera Beltrán as governor of the State of Veracruz and Felipe Calderón Hinojosa as President of Mexico).[20] Whether chronicles, stories, or journalistic pieces, the texts escape the classification of "realist fiction" since, as the author explains, "no hablo de lágrimas, hombres armados o niños heridos donde nunca los hubo" (There are no references to tears, armed men, or injured children where they didn't already exist).[21]

Melchor distinguishes explicitly between literature and life. For her, both novel and reportage can be considered as fiction "en el sentido de que son artificios y no pueden ser confundidos con la vida misma" (In the sense they are both constructs and can't be confused with real life).[22] Thus, Melchor emphasizes the *event* of the transformation levied on the protagonists. With this, she creates a point of departure that rejects any claim to impartiality with the texts collected in the book. She strives to deliberately capture the impact of the events on the imaginaries and sensibility of ordinary people, not to dispute "el valor de verdad" (the value of truth) of journalistic articles but "de tal forma que, por ejemplo, el texto que da nombre a este libro no cuenta solamente la historia de unos pobres diablos que confundieron a Veracruz con Miami, sino la de un muchacho que, una noche de invierno tropical, se topa por primera vez con el rostro de la brutalidad y la venganza" (In such a way that the text that gives the book its name, for example, doesn't just tell the story of some poor wretches who confused Veracruz with Miami but also of a young guy that, one tropical winter's night, encounters the face of brutality and vengeance for the first time).[23] In composing her discourse, the author defends the importance of direct experience, of the personal knowledge of protagonists who become informants and, on occasions, participate in the events. Furthermore, she claims that the reader will find neither a rejection of subjectivity in her text nor pure fiction or fantasy, but instead the traces that the events leave on the participants' affectivity and memory.

Aquí no es Miami presents itself as the other face of the USA's commercial iconicity. As a counterweight to the semiotics of the USA's cultural massification, the chronicles present the specific Afro-mestizo quality of the Veracruz region, in which we see the impact of Spanish colonizers mixed with the cultural traces left by the enslaved people for whom the city was one of the principal points of arrival. Veracruz was also the port of departure for the "Carreras de Indias" maritime operations that transported the riches of New Spain to the Iberian Peninsula, thus attracting pirates and corsairs to the port and neighboring islands. From these coordinates, the here and there that organizes the texts serves as an exercise of local recuperation that Melchor reaffirms with her valorizing of difference.

As the title of the book indicates, the theme of collective identities runs throughout the texts. The regions, and even specific places, challenge national identity as a discourse that forges and organizes through the State, its institutions, its cultural policies, education, celebrations, and emblems that exalt national culture as a totalizing homogeneous and hegemonic entity. In opposition to this ideological construction of the nation, *Aquí no es Miami* differentiates itself from the central discourses of Mexican identity that solidify and ossify the concept of the national by conceiving of social beings through leveling formulas. Melchor distances herself from typical urban experiences, principally those of the big cities, which obscure other forms of social existence with the devastating force of their diversity and urban acceleration.

Aquí no es Miami, instead, reaffirms the fluidity and diversity of interactions that are decentered from national identity and that are distanced from the identarian rigidity attributed to the USA, like the assimilation of the Mexican subject to the values and ways of being of the USA. The iconic city of Miami is frequently viewed from Mexico as the most representative space of transculturation and marketing, and as a place of artificiality and immediatism. Melchor's book offers a negative evocation of this city, naming it only to discard it. The texts' enunciative and representational position is framed as a between place, a crevice that reveals its specificities in a world marked by inequality, massification, and social injustice where Miami stands as a mythical version of American life and as the counterpart of Mexican culture and society, situated on very different social and economic foundations.

The idea of Mexico that flourishes in Melchor's book is defined in terms of the desire to vindicate textures of the real that have not yet been coopted by the market and mass culture but that are nonetheless filtered through community networks. Variety and the picturesque make up the principal elements of a reality that owes everything to the gaze that encounters it, when the fact begins to transform itself into a form of hallucination and the miracle inserts itself naturally into everyday life. In addition, however, Mexico, and in particular Veracruz, represent a space of social rawness that surpasses the limits of what is tolerable and that is expressed not only in scenes of politics and crime but also in scenes from daily life. In her desire to represent regional subjectivities, Melchor emphasizes the emotional perspectives, beliefs, values, and legends of everyday people, exposing the popular forms of their feelings, thoughts, and reactions to social phenomena and to the possibilities of their own imaginary worlds. The author recognizes that literature is a construct that, only in the most mediated of ways, channels the raw material that connects to reality. The words and images that memory furnishes, together with the mechanisms of fantasy, are the mediations that make "reality" an experience that can be assimilated into the collective imaginaries.

The term *Jarocha* references language and customs that indicate particularities of the Veracruz region and provide a way to unearth the port city's colonial origin and its constitutive roots along with elements that reference the region's unequal modernization. To this we can add the unsettling actions of drug trafficking, extractivist projects, and transnational companies. Beginning in the sixteenth century, the area's distinct history has marked regional identities along with the precarity and violence introduced by modernity.

The book portrays various identities. Port workers, tourists, common criminals, disorientated and naive youth, cartel assassins, regular people, children trapped in the web of collective deterioration all come together to form an intricate montage that, as the narrator points out, must be witnessed in all its aspects. Inequality, ambition, institutional abandonment, political decline, lack of perspectives, precarity, and violence all set the tone for a region that remains peripheral to the great economic and cultural circulations elsewhere, but that nonetheless has been activated as a nerve center of dynamics connected since colonial times to the activities of the port and its underlying cosmopolitan forces.

Present-day Veracruz is founded upon the immense common grave that the region primarily became following the ascent of Javier Duarte to state power at the end of 2010. Collective imaginaries became infused with a squalidness and gruesomeness that helps explain much of Fernanda Melchor's poetics, from the blistering force of her language to the creation of characters who have internalized society's deterioration only to then express it through real and symbolic violence. In the two novels that follow *Aquí no es Miami*, the struggle for survival opens into an atmosphere scorched by inhuman and erratic confrontations. The characters symbolize beings whose sensibilities have been left behind by the rigors of life, precarity, and social imbalance. They appear to lack sufficient rationality to process daily experiences and their frustrations lead them to an evil unleashing of limitless instincts and superstitions. Despite their psychological and emotional differences, all of the characters participate in the same traumatic, anguished and vulnerable substratum that challenges them but also implicates them in a shared destiny.

LIGHTS, FIRE, AND SHADOWS

Aquí no es Miami is divided into three sections ("Luces" / "Lights," "Fuegos" / "Fire," and "Sombras" / "Shadows") that bring together articles on different topics joined by a series of common axes around which plots, narrative procedures, and regional atmospheres are articulated. Melchor's bases her general approach to the different topics on an affective perspective that compiles reactions, beliefs, behaviors, and feelings whose principal characteristics offer a clear connection to Veracruz's social environment and the life of the port as a nucleus of intensity that shapes interrelations.

"Luces" features texts drawn from regional life. They present consequential tales that allow the reader to capture the contours of the popular imagination and the impact of external agents on the status quo and the customs of the inhabitants of Veracruz and its surrounding areas. Despite its diverse thematics, the five texts that make up the first part share what we might call the "spectacularization" of daily life. "Luces en el cielo" ("Lights in the Sky") provides a good example of the narrative angle that Melchor takes to demonstrate the credulity, the construction of a collective gaze, and the everyday subject's sublimations and projections as they interpret the arrival of flying saucers as a sign or, in other words, as the insertion of the fantastic into the texture of everyday reality. The lights in the sky turn out not to be an event connecting the earth with extraterrestrial beings but rather the lights of a small plane belonging to narcos that announces the transformation of the *jarocha* province into a drug marketplace. However, at the beginning of the 1990s, the dangerous Playa de Muerto, situated at the tip of Boca del Río, appears to local children as a type of fantastical backdrop that can be adapted to games inspired by the technological imagination they gleaned from TV and comics. To a child's mind dazzled by eclipses, mysterious adventures and the possibility of aliens on earth, and stimulated by the media who exploit the idea of "la oleada ovni en México" (the wave of UFOS in Mexico) it is more gratifying and easier to incorporate the idea of the arrival of intergalactic spaceships in which faraway beings travel "buscando un planeta más amable, otros mundos, otros hogares, nuevos amigos en galaxias distantes" (in search of a kinder planet, other worlds, other homes, new friends in faraway galaxies), than to try to understand the narco invasion with its attendant legacy of death and destruction.[24] As in her other texts, Melchor bases "Luces en el cielo" on the contrast between reality and belief and it sets the tone for what comes after—generally short accounts, forceful in nature and of controlled lyricism that recount an affecting and startling reality that she confronts literarily devoid of pretexts and mitigation.

"El cinturón del vicio" ("The Vice Belt") offers a vision of Veracruz in the 1970s from the perspective of El Ojón, an informant the narrator interviewed to obtain information on the topic. Fulfilling one of the chronicle genre's possible goals, this text includes a verbal picture of the port of Veracruz's in earlier times:

> Inhabited during the colonial period by freed people of African origin who erected their dwellings on the banks of the river Tenoya with wood from shipwrecked vessels, el Barrio (as it was simply called) was for many years the only home possible for the thousands of people who would arrive at the port fleeing the hunger and poverty of the rural areas to most often go on to swell the payrolls of the docks, of trade and of contraband.[25]

According to El Ojón, who became a stevedore when he was very young, the best way to survive was through the theft of merchandise of any type, big or small. He remembers, for example, someone stealing the *bacalao* he would roll up "en todo el cuerpo: en las pantorrillas, los muslos, el pecho, la espalda; hasta me hacía un pañal que me acomodaba debajo de las talegas, ¿no?" (all over my body: on my calves, thighs, chest, back, I would even make a diaper that I would put under my junk, right?).[26] This picaresque view of port life possesses a provincial naivety but at the same time we see a natural inclination toward transgression as a form of rebellion against the limitations of a life closed in upon itself.

None of the stories Melchor unearths in *Aquí no es Miami* can be truly understood without the attendant context of poverty, precariousness, and violence that has characterized the region throughout its history and that has only intensified since the arrival of drug trafficking in the region. "El callejón del vicio," for example, was a marginal and crime-ridden space but was also where people sought pleasure and a release from the tensions of exploitative labor practices, inequality, and the lack of a future. This lasted until the "restoration" of the Centro Histórico to make way for cafes with European-style terraces to attract tourists. Ojón's comments that "Quieren que el puerto se parezca a Miami" (They want the port to look like Miami) sums up working-class sentiments and highlights another of the book's organizing principles—a critique of the progress of Europeanized or Americanized modernization that destroys regional ways of life, imaginaries, and identities.[27] The text that gives the book its title unearths the story of some Dominican migrants who are caught by police as they approach the port in a small cargo ship: "unas 20 personas, al parecer de raza negra: mujeres y hombres esqueléticos que lloraban y se frotaban los brazos desnudos y que pronto desaparecieron en el interior de la furgoneta de Migración" (About twenty people, probably Black: skeletal men and women who were crying and rubbing their naked arms and who soon disappeared into the Immigration van).[28] However, those caught are not alone, and another nine who had hidden submerged in the water at the quay appear, pleading: "'¡Dinos que estamos en Miami, por favor!;'"(Please say this is Miami. Is this Miami?) to which the locals respond: "'¿Miami? ¡No mamen, están en Veracruz!'" (Miami? Are you fucking kidding? This is Veracruz).[29] The constant back and forth movement between the imaginaries inspired by the two cities reinforces the idea of them as poles of a transnational system of exchange and displacement. These dynamics channel the results of social inequality and the survival instincts of the dispossessed who see the US as the possibility for overcoming their life conditions and the inhabiting of a new reality.

The texts drawn from earlier newspaper articles also include the story of Evangelina Tejera who was crowned Carnival Queen in Veracruz in 1983. A few years later, under the influence of drugs and alcohol, she beat her two small children, two and three years old, to death. She later tried to burn them and then dismembered their bodies and buried them in large planters in her house. Although the contrast between her social triumph and her crime could easily be woven into an indictment of the excesses of sensationalist journalism or "yellow press," the focus of Melchor's story is problematic, to say the least. Reworking a newspaper article she wrote about the same case under the title of "La rubia que todos querían" (Everyone's favorite blonde), now with the new title of "Reina, esclava o mujer," ("Queen, Slave, Woman"), Melchor returns to this horrifying story to denounce the treatment Evangelina received at the hands of public opinion, characterizing it as an inquisitorial persecution. In an interview with Irma Gallo, Melchor claims:

> When news of Evangelina's crime got out, Veracruz's polite society turned into the Spanish Inquisition. Fernanda says that "She was out of her mind, they sent her to a psychiatrist but the journalists, society, everyone just wanted to punish her. The prevailing wisdom was: Evangelina Tejera's not crazy, she's a depraved woman who killed her kids because she's a terrible mother and needs to go to prison. . . . I didn't want to change the story, just the focus, because I started to think we should not just talk about what she did, her crime, her story, but also the world around her: in particular, the lynching she suffered at the hands of the media and the establishment.[30]

The chronicle incorporates multiple episodes connected to the murders, aspects of the trial, opinions and references to Evangelina's imprisonment, her affair with Óscar Sentíes Alfonsín (el Güero Valli), a Gulf Cartel member, as well as the now established presence of the Zetas in both Veracruz society as well as its prisons.

Drawing on a type of feminism worthy of a better cause, Melchor undertakes the rewriting of her original text to uncover this "linchamiento" (lynching). The author reveals the disquiet that "la contigüidad que existe entre la crónica de sociales y la nota roja" (the closeness between the society pages and the tabloids) has always provoked in her, not only because the two sections appear side by side in local newspapers but also because both social perspectives build their identity on the exceptional nature of their subjects, with which they construct their material and transform it into ideology by creating:

> opposing but nonetheless complementary archetypes, masks that dehumanize flesh and blood women and that serve as screens where a society that claims to be the sensual tropics but is instead deeply conservative, classist, and misogynist can project their desires, fears, and anxieties.[31]

Emerging from the sinister nature of the events, the links between the "nota roja" and the society pages resound in this text.

In her review of how the media mythologized Evangelina Tejeda's case, Melchor, in some ways, joins a chorus of voices without really distinguishing her own perspective. Her chronicle exposes different aspects of the events but does not distance itself sufficiently from a condemnation of the ex-beauty queen as she speculates about the possibility that the narcos killed the children. In my opinion, her effort is wasted and her feminism poorly channeled toward a case in which the murky facts provoke repulsion and repudiation.

Continuing her engagement with the "crónica roja," "Una cárcel de película" also centers on the spectacularization of poverty, drawing on the contrast between the sordid reality of the Allende prison from where inmates are relocated to other institutions, despite their families' horrified reactions, so a Mel Gibson project could be filmed there. Through the eyes of Rodrigo, who was sent to study the graffiti and other traces left there by the prisoners as proof of their presence, the reader learns of the process by which the inhumane and squalid prison is transformed into "una suerte de escenografía hiperrealista" (a type of hyperrealist stage) in order to provide the setting for the film.[32] Melchor's chronicle details how, at the same time in January 2010, the governor had declared that "bandas del crimen organizado se habían apropiado del penal Allende y que planeaban llevar a cabo un motín donde varios reos serían degollados y decapitados, a la usanza del grupo delictivo de Los Zetas" (criminal gangs had taken over the Allende prison and planned an uprising in which various prisoners would be decapitated Zeta style).[33]

In order to frame the destitution of prison life, Melchor fills her text with parallelisms and convergences between the prison's squalor and the intrusion of reality, which become indistinguishable from the film's manipulations and the staging it creates. This movement between appearance and reality is complemented by the corruption that swirls around the money paid for using the premises which, to the indignation of its inhabitants, never materializes in the payment promised to the extras for their services and whose reaction is to say "¡Chingas a tu madre, Mel! (Fuck you, Mel).[34] As we can see, the themes of society and politics, inequality, corruption, and their translation into the register of culture are Melchor's focus and will reappear in her later fiction.

The second section, entitled "Fuego," is made up of just two chronicles: "El corrido del quemado" ("Ballad of the Burned Man") on the lynching and burning to death of Rodolfo Soler, a.k.a. "the burned man of Tatahuicapa," and "La casa del Estero" ("The House on El Estero"), a relatively long and detailed account on the theme of youthful adventures, superstition, and drugs. In the first case, the rape and murder of Ana María Borromeo are avenged by her hometown who collectively decide to carry out justice for themselves, deploying a savagery comparable to the supposed murder: "que se le linche, que se le mate, que se le queme, para que no salga enseguida, para que no regrese a causar peores daños, si no, al rato, las hijas no van a poder andar solas, si no, va a regresar y va a seguir violando a las mujeres" (Let's lynch him, kill him, burn him so he can't escape and come back and cause more trouble, if we don't our daughters can never go out alone again, he'll come back and rape all the women).[35] The chronicle not only details the tension between the idea of justice and the lack of an institutionalized process able to guarantee legal solutions but also between orality and writing, assimilating the former to the will of an "ungovernable" town primarily owing to "la influencia de los caciques locales que desean que las regiones se independicen para controlarlas mejor y así enriquecerse" (influence of local caciques who want the regions to be independent so as to better control them and get rich).[36] The second tension stems from a corrupt system in which people have no faith. The narrator identifies this second tension as a principle of order, carrying out a journalistic investigation through which she tries to find proof ("el expediente, la autopsia, las fotos"; The file, the autopsy, the photographs) as well as the video published by the media where the "verdugos" (executioners) who carried out the accused's exemplary "castigo" (punishment).[37] Melchor's effective insertion of *corrido* verses that take up the events directly connects to popular sensibilities and to her particular way of understanding the relationship between an extra-legal crime and justice in a social system that has been transformed into a no-man's land and left to its own devices. The relationship between chaos and organized crime, the State's retreat in the face of the "caciques locales," and the predominance of an unbridled affectivity constitute the account's raw material, which the author maintains as the perspective of social critique that appears in the collection's other chronicles.

"La casa del estero," for its part, is one of the most ambitious pieces in *Aquí no es Miami* not only because its length allows Melchor to develop the plot in more detail but also because it deals with a more complex theme and gestures toward narrative spaces that productively articulate the story's nucleus. Divided into thirteen sections and running more than thirty-five pages, the narrative tells of a group of friends' youthful adventures as they explore a haunted house. Into this central event, Melchor weaves references to urban legends, superstition, and the topic of drugs. As a tale built around the atmosphere in which it occurs, the "Casa de estero" demonstrates an excellent command of narrative devices such as suspense and points of view, portraying the group's descent into a local hell where a subjective reality entraps them through a succession of rapid-fire actions. Legends of sadism and demonism incorporate local beliefs, exorcisms, shamanism, and spiritualist rituals. Nevertheless, dominating the narrative progression and the range of emotions that the horrific experience unleashes is the underlying love story between a young man who falls for the girl who listens to his story. She becomes entangled in a web of words and feelings that emerge from the story that she herself will later recount in a gesture toward autofiction.

Entitled "Sombra," the collection's third part presents five short chronicles developed around the theme of the presence of drugs in Veracruz. The arrival of crack and the subculture that grows up around it in the port and nearby areas controlled by the Zetas gives rise to "No se metan con mis muchachos" ("Don't Mess with My Boys"), whose central character, Lázaro Llinas Castro, was sentenced to thirty-two years in prison in 2009. This character acts as the nucleus of a small local constellation of minors, petty delinquents who seek to rise in the world of crime through drug trafficking. The character of Fito "ratero, asaltante y drogadicto" (thief, mugger, drug addict) is recruited into the narco world as Melchor relays in "Un buen elemento," finding himself from then on involved in crimes and undertakings that transform his life, providing him with ill-gotten money and subjecting him to a life of fear and marginalization.[38] In a complementary fashion, "Insomnio" (Insomnia) resurrects the theme of spaceships, as part of a character named Rita's dream that is interrupted by the sound of bullets outside of her house. The woman experiences feelings of persistent fear, underscoring the hyper-emotional atmosphere of a region subject to all types of social and political tensions and left by the State to fend for itself.

Almost at the end of the collection, the previously unpublished story "La vida no vale nada" ("Life's Not Worth a Thing") also investigates the era marked by Felipe Calderón's presidency and the local government of Fidel Herrera Beltrán. Melchor's attempts to explain and bring to life the historical circumstances she details speak to her desire to inscribe the chronicle, as is typical of the genre, in a context of recognizable and shared references.

"Veracruz se escribe con Zeta" ("Veracruz with a Zee for Zeta"), which has the subtitle "Estampas de la vida en el puerto en 2011" (Sketches of life in the port city in 2011) brings the book to a close. As in the "artículos de costumbres" or comedies of manners that resemble the chronicle, in *Aquí no es Miami* Melchor presents vignettes of life in Veracruz, configuring not only a nimble and nuanced narrative but also a grouping of informative pieces on the sensibilities that these circumstances create particularly for young people, who are in the process of defining their understandings of social belonging, behaviors, and values.

The last text closes this cycle gesturing to one of the defining factors of life in the port of Veracruz—the arrival and installation of the Zeta cartel in 2005 and the transformation that organized crime inflicts on all levels of life there. The narrator uses the second person voice to forge a rhetorical connection to anonymous, everyday individuals, both men and women, who have been involved in episodes connected to the narcos and who have witnessed different aspects of their operations. They carry these out with detachment, disregard for human life, pragmatism, and intransigence to demonstrate to the inhabitants of the *jarocha* region that narco power leaves no margin for disruption or disloyalty. Melchor portrays the Zetas as wielding a demonic and overwhelming force that is relentless in its desire to control the zone and exterminate all who stand in the way of their drug business. Again, the text is eloquent and is narrated rapidly and efficiently, intensely marked by emotions that exceed the boundaries of the individual. Overwhelming fear, anxiety, and feelings of guilt invade a society that witnesses the destruction of its community and familial networks by a systemic, necro power that subdues those in charge of maintaining order such as the police, the army, other State institutions and makes individuals defenseless in the face of forces they can barely comprehend.

The thematic interests and narrative mechanisms Melchor mobilized in *Aquí no es Miami* and *Falsa liebre* indicate an ambitious literary project, strongly situated in the author's experience as a journalist along with her profound knowledge of Veracruz's society. The narrators in *Aquí no es Miami*, like the ones she incorporates into her journalism, are involved in the very investigation of the events, and operate as a guiding conscience that orients the account from the perspective of order and community support. She undertakes an exposé not only of the events that have destroyed society but also interrogates the structural elements that have led to them, making a valuable aesthetic and ideological contribution. *Aquí no es Miami* reveals the particularisms that the narco-State wields in Latin America, exposing its poetics of evil, the construction of the narco-culture myth and the denunciation of a State that, either through involvement or neglect, is itself imbedded in the roots or in the branches of the phenomena that have brought Mexico to a severe state of civil deterioration.

"YOUTH, DIVINE TREASURE" IN *FALSA LIEBRE*

THE DEVASTATION OF SOCIETY

Fernanda Melchor's first long-form narrative is an exploration of the downtrodden elements of society in Veracruz that pre-dates the impact of drug trafficking on the city. *Falsa liebre* depicts a damaged affectivity in the portrait of four inhabitants of the port city's underworld. The novel penetrates the subjectivity of characters exhausted by their precarious surroundings and overwhelmed by systemic violence. The protagonists have interiorized these existential conditions, which they manifest in different ways through their behaviors and psychologies. Hatred, loyalty, fear, feelings of guilt and revenge create a sordid specter of affectivities whose cross currents form power relations that manifest themselves in all aspects of their interactions.

Published in 2013, *Falsa liebre* offers clear proof of Fernanda Melchor's experimentation with the creation of characters and situations that channel the death instincts that traverse Mexican literature like an underground river.[39] In her works, the death worlds move between erotic drives and a whirlwind of affect and desire in an indistinguishable flow that bear down on the thresholds of reality, making them retreat and dissolve. Death, and its stand-ins—perversion, violence, sin, and radical dread—form a platform upon which Melchor builds her narrative edifice. The necro-aesthetics that marks her writing are not, as could easily be believed, a cultural epiphenomenon designed to reproduce violence's paradoxical glamour and globalized despair, although it must be said that the work does fall inevitably into this orbit.

Through the narrative plot, the reader sees that the roots of the book's vision of the world are embedded in the longue durée of colonial devastation, in its modern and neoliberal reformulation. Echoes and continuations of the systems of colonial domination, reactivated by late capitalism's new forms of hegemony and exclusion, penetrate her work through multiple filters and mediations. Melchor's writing gives expression to lust, depravity, the distortion of family ties, raging differences between characters, social universes and situations, different forms of discrimination, aggression, and exclusion through a sharply-focused and at times extreme but still traditional realism that cannot be completely equated to either dirty realism's economic minimalism or to hyperrealism (where the author disappears so as to create a fictional reality that is a better likeness than a photograph). Instead, her texts incorporate traits of poverty porn that transform privation, marginality and its associated grotesque forms into a spectacle or a backdrop for actions and characters that illustrate and dramatize these conditions.[40]

With this aesthetic, the explicit and shocking scenes, language, and framing all emerge as obsessively obscene, exploiting the shock value and transgressive quality of the representations. The dense plot is replete with an abundant proliferation of visual elements that seem to exhaust the forms that the imagination gives to human degradation. With her skillful use of language, in which she employs words to support the signifier's uncertainty, Melchor tackles the overabundance of details and the use of grotesque scenes that reveal the emotional and human fracturing of subjects that reproduce and amplify their own wounds in each other. With an unrestrained vocabulary and an at times overwhelming use of local color, Melchor's narrative does not lay new ground here but instead confidently retreads the same ground's uneven surface.

Falsa liebre tells the story of four marginalized characters (Andrik, Zahir, Vinicio y Pachi) and the sadomasochistic relationships that consume them and with which they offset their absence of perspective and the weight of trauma and deprivation. This existence makes them extremely vulnerable and gradually leads them to self-destruction and withdrawal. Melchor has spoken in several interviews of her preference for masculine characters or at least of her interest, up until now, in an exploration of a sphere marked by traumatic configurations of masculinity, violence, sexual excesses, and also the hopelessness and impossibility of defining a productive societal role that exists at the margins of accepted forms.[41] *Falsa liebre*'s female characters (Pamela, Aurelia, Idalia, among others) occupy secondary, satellite roles and serve to support the male characters' resentful, acrimonious, and tormented identities. But they also bear a traumatic legacy that moves with them and shapes them:

> Aurelia hated her father: she described him as a miserable jealous old man to whom she had to lie to leave the house. Her mother was a ghost: she lived in another state with her new family, they only spoke once a year on Mother's Day and only because her dad would dial the number and hold the receiver up to her ear.[42]

The characters' tortured physicality brands them as "lived bodies," grotesquely marked by poverty, abuse, and social injustice.[43] The narration's decadence inevitably besieges the reader, who is buried under an avalanche of situations, images, gestures, words, actions, and thoughts that, like the tropical heat that surrounds them, presents suffocating and dead-end lives that unceremoniously exhibit the sacrifice of intimacy and the deterioration of the subjective world. Dirty clothes, trash, open wounds, and degrading and repellent physical acts come together to create a setting that is ripe for crime. The first time Pachi sees a naked female body it is that of an anonymous corpse, someone who had drowned and was slammed against the rocky coastline. On this occasion, "lo más impresionante fue el vistazo a su sexo" (the coolest thing was seeing her vagina).[44] From the outset of the novel, Melchor establishes the relationship between Eros/Thanatos, sustaining it throughout the narrative.

The characters of Andrik and Zahir, who consider themselves brothers as they grew up under the same roof, form a duo that symbolizes youth that has been both abandoned and abused by adults. The former, who is fourteen years old, is a weak and gaunt youth whose beauty paradoxically stems from his sickly and helpless appearance. Like others, he does sex work to survive, and he forms a relationship with an older man who simultaneously cares for him and abuses him. Embodiment in all its forms is the novel's main protagonist. It exists as evidence of alienation and pain, of ugliness and mistreatment, and of desire and subjugation. Alternatively, the body is the mechanism that, in a cyclical dynamic in which the wound is both origin and end, cause and consequence, operates as both victim and punisher.

In Melchor's work, and particularly in *Falsa liebre*, the masculine body is counter-normative and even contravenes gender stereotypes. Melchor references the transitional periods from infancy to adolescence and from youth to adulthood. In these stages, the body transforms and becomes alien to itself, thus representing another form of disassociation typical of Melchor's characters who exhibit traces of weakness, corruption, ugliness, indeterminacy, and deformity. In the case of Andrik, described as attractive in various ways, this signifies both misfortune and damnation as it transforms him into an object of desire contaminated by violence and degradation. Violence and homoeroticism unite Andrik and Zahir. Their lives exhibit intense levels of distress to the point where their aggressive impulses seem, at times, to be coping mechanisms. Their homoerotic quasi-incest (they are not biological brothers) connects them as two sides of an anomalous and afflicted coin, condemned to itself. The other two characters, Pachi and Vinicio, while not exempt from violence, are crushed by precarity and bad habits. They connect through drawing, which produces an alternative form of symbolic rapprochement and offsets affective voids and feelings of guilt and frustration.[45]

Illness is another signifier that displays its symbolism in the text, reinforcing humanity, as well as life's vulnerability and transitoriness. The text's desire for exhaustivity is perhaps overly evident as it tries to cover all bases and thus totalizes the collective and individual experiences of the microcosm it represents. At the same time, this display speaks to aspects of both the human and social condition including the instincts, needs, and reactions that have been set into motion by precarity and neglect. In its totality, the social body is contaminated and damaged from within, and its individual bodies agonizingly replicate these existential conditions. The characters' youth moreover suggests that their future is also under threat owing to the protracted nature of society's collective decadence.[46] Drugs, alcohol, machismo, perverse sexualities, lack of opportunity, a tendency toward crime and past traumas that project themselves in many directions—all seem to come together to trap the reader between an unsustainable social reality and a literary aesthetic whose best channel is an almost naturalistic literary realism where excess appears, at times, to be the only significant achievement. However, we find a measure of imaginative virtuosity in the creation of the narrative voice that shapes the novel's development, and which permits Melchor to bypass realist fiction's well-trodden ground.

A series of themes, also present in earlier eras but that have come to characterize Mexican society and culture in the new millennium, offer an easy contextualization for Melchor who, like other authors of her generation, attempts to poeticize the reality that emerges from late capitalism's regional labyrinths. Alongside its narrative tropicalism, Melchor's prose is also marked by State violence, the excesses of neoliberalism, the intensification of organized crime and socioeconomic inequality, creating a plot so crammed full that some critics have labelled it "baroque." If we choose to invoke the "Baroque," we should indicate, as per Bolívar Echeverría, that in *Temporada de huracanes* above all, Melchor's fiction expresses a contemporary baroque ethos: a symbolic form of resistance to capitalist modernity and the logic of capital accumulation, in which the surplus of the signifier arises from the ruins of the social.[47] As a symbolic recourse for the apprehension of the real, in her novels, Melchor uses language in a hyperbolic fashion not as a means of communication and expression but rather to mark reality's excess in the overrun of the models that crystalize and then succumb to modernity.[48] Evoking the funerary Baroque, along with heat, boredom, perversion, and linguistic adornment, inflamed degradation and sensuality come together in *Falsa liebre* to create a stifling and overwhelming atmosphere that punishes and suffocates the reader. Running parallel to life, an alternative order roams the text, its jagged breathing full of anxiety and fear, consuming its own reserves as it forges ahead. The stench of poverty combines the secretions of corpses with sweat brought on by nature that is as devastating as the State's silence. A spectral and invisible Power—minimal and fragmented—stalks the text and is disseminated to all corners of the social narrative. This systemic power, along with paradigms of gender, society (ineffective but nonetheless present), poverty, and feelings functions to both condemn and redeem.

As the principal platform upon which the action develops, the individual body—both singular and concrete—mixes with the notion of the social body. In both cases, they are formations—fragmented and dysfunctional organisms—barely holding together the precarious unity required for the continuation of life and intersubjective relationships. Race and gender, sexuality and desire, bodily and emotional primal needs, forms of resistance and domination, individual traits, tendencies, wrongdoings, and impulses wage war on the materiality of the body. From there, withdrawals, advances, alliances, and offensives are launched, and it is also from there that we notice the time-space impact, that those who enjoy continuity would call history and what *Falsa liebre*'s protagonists can only call existence. The doorway to Melchor's fiction is the representation of affective modes that express tormented and deficient ways of being and that offer an alternative form of cognition and integration in the world.

MAPPING SUBJECTIVITY

In "La producción de subjetividad del capitalismo mundial integrado," Félix Guattari indicates that, in the era of globalization, forms of "subjective integration" which are correlative to current capitalistic developments represent invisible processes that say more about the control of individuals than the production of subjectivity.[49] Understood in these terms, subjectivity surpasses the duality infra/superstructure and situates itself at a psychic and instinctual level that, although in the final instance refers to this duality, functions on an apparently autonomous plane. The semiotics of the city, social order, spatial distribution, class, race, and gender hierarchies all produce forms of existence and subjectivities that generate relationships of power and violence, affective systems, passions, tendencies, and behaviors. As Melchor shows in *Aquí no es Miami*, mass media creates a perceptive, emotional, and intellectual modeling that participates in the formation of subjectivities.

Deleuze refers to "desiring economies" that function at a molecular level and that appear at multiple levels that Guattari calls "ritornellos" or "little social rhythms," expressed in language, bodies, spatial usage, and relationships. "Existential territories" lead to identities or to forms of self-recognition and "microsocial practices" that connect the individual to the collective and crystallize them in aesthetic, moral, and conceptual paradigms. There is no doubt that Fernanda Melchor's characters illustrate forms of existence and social conscience that do not correspond to the dominant models that are accepted as representative of the values of "citizens" or belonging to capitalistic subjects or to the minorities that manage to integrate themselves into the regimes that are regulated through State apparatuses. These are figures and behaviors that find themselves at the margins of bourgeois society, nationalist rites, and the rules of urban life. They are also characters conceived of in terms of economic overdetermination, to which each responds in their own way. In each character the reader encounters variable behaviors and horizons, all connected to a limited and extra-institutional education and to the impact of precarity and violence.

In this sense, *Falsa liebre* functions as an overwhelming exposé that resists homogenization and presents a specific slice of Veracruz's society. The novel details individual stories with a litany-like redundancy in terms of gestures, actions, and desires depicting the characters within the closed circle of their interrelations and feelings. The recurrence of themes such as promiscuity, despair, isolation, and unease as well as the repetition of different forms of material and symbolic violence that simultaneously renders the characters both terrifying and pathetic, victimizers and victims of a system whose gears rotate their positions.

The power relations that are generated in the interactions between characters occur within a climate of widespread violence that nonetheless does not exclude tenderness, desire for love, and the need for redemption. However, these bonds clearly emit the idea of social and economic entrapment, as well as a lack of an emancipatory horizon. The existential space dominated by drugs and sex is a vexed location permeated by the idea of the simulacrum. Concealment, lies, furtiveness, double standards, immediatism, and refuge in appearances are just some of the paths traversed by *Falsa liebre*'s young characters.

In *Chaosmosis: An Ethico-aesthetic Paradigm*, Félix Guattari defines the subject as "the ensemble of conditions which render possible the emergence of individual and/ or collective instances as self-referential existential territories, adjacent, or in a delimiting relation, to an alterity that is itself subjective."[50] This implies, among other things, the continuance of an alienated state that begins with the alienation of the self and continues with the difficulty in seeing the Other in a more or less objective form devoid of the individual's needs vis-à-vis with whom they relate. The *self* projects onto the *Other* the need to identify an alter ego, an enemy, a victim, a model, a protector, or a reflection.

Conceived of as subjects who have been objectified by the relationships power imposes upon them, for the most part Melchor's characters only exercise agency within the domain of harm, as a contravention of norms including the value of life, as a violation of the space of the Other, and as a force of aggression, vengeance, or retribution. In these processes, bodies play an outsized role, as does language, since it presents itself as the most obvious space for the exercise of domination, subjugation, and punishment as well as submission, retreat of the subject, and instinctual freedom.

Interestingly, in her novels Melchor bypasses the city as a dynamic scenario of existential territorialization in favor of segmented social spaces riven with affective, social, and economic fissures. Urban space does not exist to support organicity or as a repository for institutional, human, or environmental resources. In the same way, we find no trace of a State that can operate as a supportive presence in daily life in any way. On the contrary, signs of intimidation or aggression on the part of the police appear frequently. The State maintains a spectral presence, as a latent form of intimidation or punishment, never as paternal protector, guarantor of rights, or architect of justice.

In the social and psychological subjective map, Melchor's work breaks with the family community network, traditions, religions, and institutions and eliminates all stable references that might be useful in supporting the development of individualities and collective identities. What remains is a desolate individual subjected to a present bereft of memory and future imagination. Each subjectivity drifts along exhibiting a specific form of connection to reality but also to social (self-)recognition. Each adheres to different regimes of truth and simulacrum, of power and of subjugation. These subjectivities are frozen with frustration and lack, and operate in a state of constant compensation, in search of vengeance and redemption and damaged by life. In Melchor's world, subjects lack the possibility of totalization and are immersed in a state of fragmentation and neglect. These characters are also exempt from discipline since they have exceeded these molds in multiple ways.

All this implies that the self-reflexive, affective, and Romantic subject who dedicates him/herself to finding utopia has been replaced by an individual who is dispersed into a series of erratic and ineffectual behaviors, guided by immediatism and the search for precarious and illusory forms of gratification. Melchor's characters are part of a dislocated, out of joint, disaggregated, and self-referential world. The question of the social is permeated by flows of energy, impulses, excess, absence, and silence. The characters' capacity for intimacy seems to have acquired strengths that act against the subject itself, where the death drive triumphs over life and objectification over humanity.

In Fernanda Melchor's world, the self-knowledge to which an individual can aspire is like a murky glass that only reveals blurred and indistinct images—prone to getting cloudy, splitting off, leaving only a residue of what it might have been. There is an inherent violence in the beings that carry out acts of aggression and self-harm, as if an eminently destructive force were working to erase the foundations of their personality and existence. The self is not the sum of its parts but rather a permanent subtraction and an interstice: the fissure that remains when the moral and affective body breaks down and the parts separate. The struggle is no longer between culture and nature but rather implies the breakdown of civilization and the dematerialization of a milieu rendered inhospitable as a living space.

The body persists as a site of need and desire and as a pretext for the convergence of multiple disjointed and disconnected narratives, and as a space to which the repressed always returns to re/present itself. The master/slave relationship appears in many guises in *Falsa liebre*: as a way of submitting the Other to sexuality and violence, as the prison of an Otherness whose very existence threatens the unity of the subject and as the only way in which the characters can establish interpersonal relationships. As per Lacan, the real is that which resists symbolization, what cannot be located nor explored because it lacks an assignable signifier. What the characters identify as the real is an amalgam of the symbolic and the imaginary. Melchor's characters live at a level whose meaning completely escapes them. The empirical dimension, the infinite fractioning of experience into microexistences that seem disconnected and that operate by accumulation trap individuals whose sense of belonging has been radically compromised by infantile trauma, frustrated attempts at socio-affective initiation, corrupt forms of sexuality, and their incapacity to generate systems of family and community support.

The mainly masculine characters take the reader deep into the dark corners of gender construction as a mechanism for the domestication of instincts and the institutionalization of interrelationship within civil society. Melchor's novels are an indictment of social control that exceeds modelization and disciplinary regimes. In the face of individual and collective trauma, what remains is an inevitable and disordered sentimentalization of relationships through gang associations, violence, same-sex relationships, and other bonds forged through perversion and degradation. Transgression does not operate as a productive form of rebellion but instead disorders social inflections.

Melchor presents stories about and interactions between her characters within an accumulative framework wherein she recovers the inner history of subjects who are lesser, marginalized, broken, and pathetic but who nonetheless display traces of sensitivity, yearning for love, despair, and pain that overcome their visceral encounters with others and with themselves. They are afflicted beings who demonstrate the negative of any scheme of social coexistence, the reality of degradation and the entrails of a system corroded by inefficiency and by material and symbolic violence. These characters are locked in a permanent struggle with gender paradigms. At every moment they challenge received ideas about virility and the values assigned to masculinity, such as the need to repress feelings and express one's will in an aggressive manner, conferring a dose of violence upon every action that hyperbolically reaffirms or compensates for the subject's essential weakness.

Women are a mystery to the characters as well as a constant source of frustration and resentment. Every woman embodies a present or absent maternal figure and, depending on the case, a repressor, an aggressor, a protector, or a mediator between the world and the child. All these functions frustrate the characters' traumatized sensibilities and push them toward actions that range from rape to murder. Desires and emotions are human feelings, understood from multiple positionalities and perspectives. With this focus on the creation of masculine characters, the author detaches herself from certain feminist ideas that assume a compartmentalized and endogamic sensibility, in which only a woman can truly represent feminine affect and psychology. This antiquated and restrictive vision ignores the fact that literature is a creative process whereby subjectivities, situations, and behaviors are invented, and which must remain faithful to an internal coherence, without necessarily correlating to reality. The consistency of the imagined world facilitates literature's "reality principle" and installs its own regime of truth. Avoiding the trap of cultural exoticization or *costumbrismo*, Melchor's novel draws on a social experience that allows her to imagine an excessive and hyperbolic world that takes the worst of reality and exhibits it through literature. In many ways, *Falsa liebre* confirms its place as an early work within the author's literary trajectory. In her later works Melchor will take this interest in exuberance to another level.

Regarding the representation of gender, it is worth remembering Pierre Bourdieu's reflections on the "masculine condition." For Bourdieu, "natural dispositions" have been incorporated into values and behaviors and thus into culture, as if they were necessary features of male socialization:

> being a man, in the sense of vir, implies an ought-to-be, a virtus, which imposes itself in the mode of self-evidence, the taken-for-granted. Like nobility, honour—which is inscribed in the body in the form of a set of seemingly natural dispositions, often visible in a particular way of sitting and

standing, a tilt of the head, a bearing, a gait, bound up with a way of thinking and acting, an ethos, a belief, etc. governs the man of honour, without the need for any external constraint.[51]

Melchor explores "the masculine condition" in detail in *Falsa liebre*, examining the expression of feelings and the conventions that impose repression and simulation of strength and psychological balance. She exposes the struggle between reason and affect as a distorted order that causes pain and frustration particularly in youth:

> Men don't cry and so Vinicio had learned to hold back his tears in front of his dad and then his teachers and the other kids. He couldn't stop his eyes from welling up, but he could keep them in his eyes, not let them fall, let them get sucked up into the eye tissue. The trick was to keep your eyes open, gaze straight ahead; not blink; not think about anything, especially not that; not think about the hurt, the meaning of the words. He would keep them in his throat and then swallow everything in big painful gulps that left his gut inflamed and his chest tight but his eyes dry and free of abject and cowardly tears.[52]

PERVERSION, EXCESS, AND GENDER

The topic of gender appears prominently in *Falsa liebre*, as the novel sets out to destabilize masculinity as an ideological formation within patriarchal society that is reaffirmed by sociocultural models of modernity. For the author, it appears that the representation of subjectivities is more important than facts or exterior circumstances. In this case, the novel deals with beings whose individuality has been fractured by political and economic determinants that also affect society (culture, the imaginary, the symbolic) in a mediated manner. Thus, the novel is—as *Temporada de huracanes* will also show in its own way—an eminently performative narrative, perhaps even contrived, focused on actions, short dialogs, rapid changes of scene, and forceful and repetitious descriptions of atmospheres, characters, and processes.

The novel begins with insults and abuse and ends with a murder, with a magnified domain of death functioning as a metaphor for a biopower threaded through social interactions, that, in a despicable and anonymous fashion, inevitably corrupt lives. As I have already indicated, *Falsa liebre*'s necro-aesthetic is grounded principally in excess and simulacra. Death and its stand-ins (violence, grief, humiliation, degradation, neglect) find neither defense nor relief in a world that closes in on the characters (as if it were a cell whose walls were shifting toward the center). Oppressive and implacable, the novel feeds on an abundance of malice and pessimism. The setting of the novel enhances this poetics of destruction, revisiting descriptions that emphasize the always latent presence of darkness, isolation and danger that are embedded within the landscape itself: "El mar cercano, en cambio, se confundía con la noche: una negrura sin horizonte (The nearby ocean, on the other hand, blended into the night, creating an endless blackness), and

> The streets were weirdly empty, even though it wasn't late; even the shops were closed and no one was around to show him how to get to the avenue with the broken traffic lights, the way back to the man's house. The sky was totally black; the storm arrived a few minutes later.[53]

Pachi dreams about submerged monsters: "El mar apestaba a peces muertos; no lo había notado antes, quizás debido al viento. El fondo del agua estaba sembrado de bultos inflados que reventaban bajo sus pies, trozos de hueso y espinas que le herían las plantas desnudas" (The ocean stank of dead fish; he hadn't noticed before, maybe it was the wind. The seabed was littered with bloated shapes that burst under his feet, slivers of bone and spines that cut his naked feet).[54] Vinicio appears in the dream too:

> The monsters surrounded him; now he could see that none of them had eyes; only some slits above their jaws . . . he felt teeth sinking into his shoulder, his neck. Vincio was on the ground, a few feet away. The monsters were eviscerating him but he didn't make a sound, just stared at Pachi.[55]

And the dream repeats itself in his memory: "Aún podía recordar partes del sueño: el mar inmóvil como una laguna oscura, los escombros del puerto devastado, los monstruos y los hoyos rojos de sus caras y aquella terrible sensación de no poder moverse más que en cámara lenta" (Even now he could recall parts of the dream; the ocean as still as a dark lake, the port reduced to ruins, the monsters with their red orifices and that terrible feeling of moving in slow motion).[56] But Vinicio not only has to fight off his dreams and his memories but also his father's ghost, who torments his mother. It then comes for him. And he must battle the delirium caused by illness:

> The fever laid waste to him and turned the blood in his head into molten lead and the pain was excruciating. Then came the tremors and finally the

paralysis. He knew then he was going to die, that he had died, that he was no longer lying on the bed in his room but instead on the hard floor, under the starry sky. He was dead and could no longer feel anything, the only thing left of him were his bones scattered by animals. And just when he was about to disappear, when he no longer knew who he was, who he had been, he heard his dad's voice, from very far away, as if it were a gust of wind.[57]

Vinicio derives no comfort or support from his mother's presence or support, since, among other things: "El olor a hembra sudorosa de su madre le molestaba" (He was disgusted by the stench of female sweat his mother gave off).[58]

The schematic representation of gender, the stereotypes and the identities that are displayed throughout *Falsa liebre*'s sordid setting exposes, above all, the impact of inequality on individual and collective subjectivities regarding their relationship to masculinity as well as women's roles in both the domestic and public spheres. At an embodied level, all the characters lead a miserable existence that has been corroded by despair, systemic violence, and precarity. On the body, subjectivity shows the corrosion of certainty and of the values that impact the relationship between subjects and their bodies and with the bodies that surround them, transformed into all that the subject lacks, and all that torments it. All the male characters are disoriented individuals, lacking in purpose and concrete support systems (family, community, religion, politics). These abandoned subjects inhabit a peripheral and economically depressed region that has been particularly hit by social inequities.

In the construction of identity, the question of gender is one of the most crucial pillars since it functions as a point of departure for the articulation of relationships of control and pleasure, of affective production and sexual reproduction, interrelationships, and self-recognition, of physicality and thought.[59] Melchor foregrounds an unending series of imbalances that affects these relationships and that cannot be separated from the regional infrastructure and the class stratification that gives them meaning. As scholars of masculinity have demonstrated, in order not to essentialize this form of subjectification nor reduce it to a series of stereotypical traits, a complex series of factors that render each behavior masculine or masculinist must be analyzed. In her studies on masculinities, Raewyn Connell explains:

> Because gender is a way of structuring social practice in general, not a special type of practice, it is unavoidably involved with other social structures.

It is now common to say that gender "intersects"—better, interacts—with race and class. We might add that it constantly interacts with nationality or position in the world order.[60]

Poverty leads to sex work, in which power relations are intensified and made more perverse since sexual behaviors now involve one's public image as well as the dimension of the private, the affective, the intellectual, and the instinctive. Moreover, far from liberating, the deviation from the norm that is experienced as exploitation, humiliation, and suffering serves to disfigure the subject to itself. Counter-normative behaviors attempt to transgress limits that would not be trespassed under different circumstances, and jeopardize physical integrity, dignity, and physical and affective balance. In the novel, the physical is constantly (con)fused with the affective, the contingent with the permanent, and the transitional with the enduring.

To avoid reducing *Falsa liebre*'s complex scenarios to contextual determinism, I am not applying here what Terry Eagleton has called "the community-worker theory of morality" since we must recognize that the novel, with its repetitive litany of poverty and deprivation, tells us something additional about the topic of evil, in an ethical and philosophical sense.[61] The problem is that evil constitutes an attractive and profound poetics and requires a transcendent projection (but not necessarily a religious or moral one) that challenges empiricism and gestures toward a more distant and, in its own way, utopian horizon so that evil does not exhaust itself in its own onanistic dynamics. Eagleton explains:

> You can believe in evil without supposing that it is supernatural in origin. . . . Evil as I see it is indeed metaphysical in the sense that it takes up an attitude toward being as such, not just toward this or that bit of it. Fundamentally, it wants to annihilate the lot of it. But this is not to suggest it is fundamentally supernatural, or that it lacks all human causality.

The novel never reaches these heights since, from the beginning, it demonstrates signs of drowning in its own essence. Rather than controlling and ordering its murky narrative material, *Falsa liebre* seems itself to be subjugated to the pathos of a world that is caught up in its own vertiginous and incessant movements. Aesthetically, the novel presents itself in incremental repetitions that excruciatingly and insatiably accumulate as the narrative progresses. In fact, *Falsa liebre* could have been a twenty-page short story, or could have gone on for two hundred pages more, like the intensification of a foreseeable process whose teleology is always an aborted arrival. As Eagleton points out, in an era in which we have moved from the soul to the psyche or perhaps better still, from theology to psychoanalysis, Melchor's novel appears as a staging of the drives that make up the subconscious of a damaged and self-contained world that is on a path of self-destruction. Bereft of State, God, family, and community, *Falsa liebre*'s characters are pariahs in their own land, nomads trapped in a claustrophobic environment.

To analyze the question of gender and sexuality in *Falsa liebre* we must recognize that most of the characters are very young, almost adolescents, just beginning their foray into adulthood, so that their sexual and social behaviors stem from psychologies that are still developing. The characters vacillate between what they are and what they seem, between how they feel and how they want to be perceived, and between what they desire and what they need. Melchor's descriptions of them correlate to their behaviors and relate to the settings and circumstances that surround the action, in an overpowering search for aesthetic coherence that while being one of the novel's positive attributes inevitably ends up overwhelming the reader. The novel's psychological and social determinism weighs the character down as a literary construction. The characters' own appearance suggests that they are trapped in a one-way street, although the author tries to nuance the situation in different ways.

Melchor describes Andrik as follows: "Tenía una cara de bruto labrada en carne prieta y una bocaza fruncida en un eterno gesto de rencor. Parecía un adulto, sobre todo cuando callaba; solo la risa y la voz delataban su juventud. Ni él sabía bien qué edad tenía; se calculaba a sí mismo dieciséis años" (He was an idiot carved out of black stone with a giant permanently sneering piehole. He looked like an adult, especially when he shut his mouth; only his laugh and his voice gave his age away. He had no clue how old he was; he thought maybe around sixteen).[62] This undefined quality is emblematic of the character who is both youth and adult, of uncertain age, tender and hard, downtrodden by life. His desire to be loved repeats itself insistently throughout the text, revealing him as a defenseless, sensitive, solitary and highly vulnerable boy.

> [Vincio] wanted to sketch Pachi but he needed to distract him first. The best way was to get him to tell a story, draw him into describing some exploit or other. Then, and only then would Pachi drift off into a fictional world and let someone draw him, photograph him or even make faces at him because he wouldn't realize, lost in his own web of lies (because all his stories were about things he'd heard, and he'd always exaggerate) and then Vinicio could

sit back and watch him and then translate the shape of his face and body on to the page without Pachi mocking him or storming out of the room.[63]

We see this too in his response to his father:

> He scrutinized his father's face: his dark skin, stick straight hair jet black hair, slicked back with some special pomade he'd buy in one of the drugstores in the town center. He looked at his own childish face: his ruddy cheeks, his white eyebrows and lashes, this mop of dark blonde hair; his pale blue eyes. "Just like him" thought Vincio bitterly. Identical.[64]

The images of fathers, mothers, aunts, brothers, or those who play similar roles in the novel, reveal the characters' emotional dependence. They are both cruel and affectionate, marked by horrific experiences and consequential actions in this early stage of their development. All of this creates a suffocating and intensely emotional atmosphere that at times is contained but at others explodes into fragments that wound and extend the pain throughout the whole radius of the novel's social relations.

At the end of the novel, and after a series of crimes that close the cycle, the murder of Idalia by Zahir seems more like the profaning of a dead body than the demise of a living one. The memory of Andrik's sweetness converges with the attack's brutality that frees in the woman "algo pútrido en su interior, algo fétido y deforme como tejido cicatrizado" (Something putrid and fetid inside, warped like scar tissue).[65]

The recollections that accompany Zahir's punches reveal the writer's imaginative power as she provides a paragraph deserving of a place in a horror anthology and begs the question as to whether the novel is anything more than an intense language experiment and an inflammatory exercise to test the reader's tolerance when faced with the horror of everyday life.

TEMPORADA DE HURACANES OR THE WHIRLWIND OF LANGUAGE

Heralding an indisputable milestone in the quality of Melchor's work, *Temporada de huracanes* employs the same mechanisms as the previous novel: the use of character types that contribute to the construction of a narrative as well as the invoking of symbolic capital that is both settled and pre-established. Adolescents, sex workers, marginal subjects dominated by poverty, lust, violence, and promiscuity move through a world of excess and delirium redeemed by the language in which it is narrated. However, the development of the text endows these characters with density and differentiation within the numerous common denominators that identify them. Melchor exposes these fictious beings' vulnerability as well as the way in which passion, misfortune, and despair seep through the deep fissures of their subjectivity.

By means of a luscious and "arborescent" codification, Melchor's use of language reclaims the folds and labyrinths of everyday experiences that are inseparable from the subjectivities that animate them and transform them into narrative. The novel opens with a gang of kids and the body of a dead witch. From the outset, the discovery of a body points to a world turned upside down, that begins with the end of a life.[66] At stake, then, is what provoked the murder, what we discover and what is hidden because of it, what unfolds or is buried in the intricacies of society. Even before they are fully fleshed out, innocence, evil and death, or perhaps, origin, magic and the macabre all bring an emotional and symbolic charge that sets the production of signifiers into definitive motion. Beginning with a death and the surrender of the body/object allows for the mobilization of a series of impulses and energies that engender various constellations of meaning: life transforms into evocation and lends itself to different variations, selections of materials, and imaginary accessories that allow for its vicarious reconstruction.

Temporada de huracanes' structural key draws on the relational networks that inscribe beings, events, and spaces into an intersubjective productivity in which actions and emotions can only be understood through association and entanglement. In this sense, the initial death that serves as the trigger for the processes of generation and symbolic transformation provides a necro-aesthetic framework that defines the novel's principal axis. In terms of death's generative quality, Walter Benjamin says:

> With the vitiation of their use value, the alienated things are hollowed out and, as ciphers, they draw in meanings. Subjectivity takes possession of them insofar as it invests them with intentions of desire and fear. And insofar as defunct things stand in as images of subjective intentions, these latter present themselves as immemorial and eternal. Dialectical images are constellated between alienated things and incoming and disappearing meaning, are instantiated in a moment of indifference between death and meaning.[67]

The tales emerge from the corpse like "lines of flight" that pursue the novel's poetic reason: the expression of what I have called elsewhere "la verdad de los cuerpos" (the truth of bodies) or that which bodies hide (emotions, thoughts intuitions, organic functioning, illness, trauma, and knowledge) and that they reveal not only in the cutoff point where the body finds itself in extreme situations (through sex, violence, sacrifice, and pain) but also in death itself as an instance of when the body carries away its own "truth," acceding to a truth beyond life.[68]

In *Temporada de huracanes* the exacerbating presence of uncontrolled bodies culminates in the present/absent figure of la Bruja/the Witch, the symbol of forbidden knowledge: premodern, contrafactual, counter-normative, meta-rational, post-human. These prefixes signal an alternative space that exceeds representability, as indicated by the novel's language-tsunami. The novel is an attempt to make the photographic negative intelligible and, in this sense, to reveal the flipside of reality, the constitutive outside/exterior that circumscribes the known world, making it what it is. Thus, the playing with time dramatized in the novel transforms the narrative present into a multifaceted exploration of the past, in a game of illuminations and discontinuities that represents one of the text's greatest achievements.

To cite Benjamin again:

> It is not that what is past casts its light on what is present, or what is present its light on what is past, image is that wherein what has been comes together in a flash with the now to form a constellation. In other words, image is dialectics at a standstill. For while the relation of the present to the past is a purely temporal, continuous one, the relation of what-has-been to the now is dialectical: is not progression but image, suddenly emergent.[69]

Temporada de huracanes is a constellation, in the Benjaminian sense, like a system that organizes elements according to a semantic nucleus by way of the narrative composition. We glimpse figures, designs, and chains of meanings in the narrative discourse via the association between these elements. The system does not outline the singularity of its constitutive elements but instead gives them meaning and transforms them into spectacle by organizing the fragment into potential images that speak to our sensibility and cognition.

In this well-crafted novel, Melchor manipulates and unravels a plot that both approaches and moves away, constructs and deconstructs objects and proceedings, while language overwhelms the text. Some critics have claimed that Melchor employs aspects of the detective novel in the development of *Temporada de huracanes*. For me, this classification is unnecessary and, in any case, only applies to some of its more generic traits. Melchor's novel is different in that it is a syncretic product, the possible chronicle of an imaginary world, and the displacement of a social system onto a seductive but immeasurable aesthetic and ideological system. At the center of this necro-aesthetic, death functions as an irresistible nucleus that attracts signifiers through an internal force that magnetically accumulates them. This produces a magical effect on reality, where outlandish elements metaphorize the necropolitical excess that informs society. The discovery of the body thus serves as a pretext that initiates the proliferation of stories. The novel situates itself in the undifferentiated moment referenced by Benjamin between death and the signifier.

"Blood sells" and violence ensures intensity and creates expectations, even more so when it is framed as tragedy. In an almost semiotic manner, Melchor has no difficulty in making language fit the unfolding of events, although at times the proliferation of signs seems to separate them from the process of producing meaning. Language serves to populate the world, dispersing connotations in the text that becomes a way of allowing the fictional universe to support itself and shine forth. Another of the novel's great achievements is the contrast it displays between the hurricane force of the language and the novel's organization at the level of storytelling in which, deep inside the plot, reason prevails. In the novel's eight sections, Melchor uses the characters' material and or symbolic presence to organize the plot. "Real" beings within the fictional universe, but also spectral and intangible, the characters come and go as if carried by a wind whose origin is not natural but instead comes from within a social milieu that Melchor's text symbolizes until it becomes viscously transparent and impregnated with the unmistakable stench of death. The necro-aesthetic serves as a drive that finds its motion in neglected and marginal bodies who, beyond the fictional realm, are merely statistics. In addition, the novel draws on familiar references: the oil company, police corruption, domestic violence, drug trafficking, sexual perversion, and machismo. All of these are beads of a familiar rosary that constantly disperse and then join back together. Beyond the question of plot and the solving of the crime, the novel features the sumptuous effects of language that from the beginning make readers wonder what the purpose of this enunciative excess might be, and toward what final goal the pages are directed.

With another title, the book would wield less impact. This reference to nature's destructive cycles speaks to the familiarization of violence connected to everyday life that lays waste to it and breaks into pieces on a regular basis, to the point where we anticipate its arrival. The cycles of life and death that the novel references are not however, climactic, but rather ideological. They are a form of false consciousness that translate terms like witchcraft, bad luck, predestination, custom, inevitability, fatality, and destiny or, in other words the relapses that go hand in hand with poverty in a world controlled, as far back as memory goes, by inequality and impunity. Plunder (ill-gotten gains), defenselessness, and precariousness are part of a social, political, and economic cyclone that affect the low-income sectors that populate Melchor's narrative. But this narrative perspective gestures toward the way these circumstances filter into collective imaginaries and ruminates on how legends and myths are built around questions that involve power, in all its varieties, as a way of negotiating or defending oneself against what is perceived as its inevitable return.

Organized into blocks of text with little punctuation and very few paragraph separations, the body of the novel distributes the narrative function among different voices who fall under the organizing perspective of the principal narrator. This structure filters content, selects and articulates different discursive strands with an accumulative and progressive logic that gradually leads to the crux of the story—the solving of the crime. Each chapter centers on one of the characters—Luismi, Munra, Chabela, Norma and Brando—and their lives and interactions with an array of secondary figures. The perspectives vary throughout, endowing the text with diversity and complexity. Despite the novel's compositional fragmentation, Melchor's totalizing language lends it unity.

The author moves ably from the rocky path of contingency to systemic structures that she evokes through their effects, traversing a fictional terrain that represents the power relations that underlie the narrative's imaginary sociality from the microphysics of minimal actions. From the vantage point of a fractured community, Melchor explores communality's intricacies and underworld.

Via movements that are skillfully devoid of artifice, the author attempts to give profound meaning to the afflictions of characters who only achieve relevance through death. An implicit and diffuse oscillation between micro and macro structures infuses all aspects of the story. The overarching story accrues the sense of an illustration of how the values and strategies of domination impact life. The implicit presence of narco violence, transnational companies, and extractivism all make discreet appearances in the text. Social inequality has been ossified in a social manifestation scarred by a history of real and symbolic structural violence that is indistinguishable from daily life.

The novel is fundamentally performative and features theatricalized actions that are orchestrated as if in a film script. These actions are directly rooted in popular culture (legends and superstitions, Luis Miguel's music as an identifying element, the conduct of la Bruja who moves through the narrative almost like a literary device) and the language itself is like a permanent and overwhelming fluttering of signs and sounds. When the reader of *Temporada de huracanes* starts to fear a return to magical realism, the author's depiction of la Bruja imposes calm. The author uses this to bring density to the plot, inserting the triviality of the death into another space, where it essentially belongs. This space lies beyond reason and spells, curses, and charms, thus framing the idea of life as hallucination or punishment. The bewitched space occupied by la Bruja's story and persona, is one of exception and counter-normativity where excess and transgression reign. These conditions allow Melchor to re-tell reality, or to approach reality like a story. La Bruja is the eye of the hurricane around whom characters and anecdotes turn like satellites. Alongside the narrator's lengthy interventions, her character channels ideas and images and symbols that invoke a collective unconscious. According to Carl Jung, this collective consciousness is a place where archetypes—supposedly universal forms that distill psychological meanings, functions, and preexisting qualities—converge. For him, the collective unconscious represents a psychic supraindividual and transhistorical system that filters through the subject's experience allowing it to metaphorically express fears, ideas and desires that do not clearly or distinctly reach the level of personal consciousness. Dreams, experiences, and fantasies reactivate these mytho-poetic forms that both precede and transcend the subject and that interact with both the individual conscious and unconscious.

The development of the different characters' stories is empirical in nature. In each story, there is a proliferation of events, anecdotes, circumstances, and subjectivities that emerge from a tumultuous context marked by multiple absences: community structure, the family as the facilitating nucleus of social life, the State, and its institutions, and alternatives to the lifestyles that have trapped the characters. Mechanisms of domination dating from the colonial era have infused affective networks, psychology, and community values where survival is the daily goal.

THE PROBLEM WITH TRUTH

Following the discursive strategy analyzed by Mikhail Bakhtin, *Temporada de huracanes* possesses a polyphonic organization in which the tension between discursive fragmentation (of points of view, voices, and experiences) and totalizing impulses stands out. The narration constantly makes and unmakes itself; versions and visions of reality come together and move apart and reshuffle on the unstable basis of comments, rumors, gossip, and opinions, invoking what Bakhtin called carnivalesque discourse. Opposed to rigidity and the centralization of more stable constructions articulated by the narrator's monologic figure, this type of discursivity calls into question the problematic of truth.

This choreographing undermines the possibility of a unique and dominant version. Instead, the dialogism opens a range of possibilities that illuminate a fragment of the world from different perspectives as they unfurl. This mechanism—that goes beyond the limits of relativism—is not purely stylistic but is also a cognitive positioning with respect to the nature of the real and resists systematization by one sole consciousness. The chapters articulate perspectives elaborated from different enunciative positions, giving the novel an open and prismatic character.

For Bakhtin, truth cannot be separated from the subject that perceives it. The differentiation would result in "disembodied truth," "no-man's thoughts." He instead believes in the embodiment of ideas and utterances and of the intrinsic relationship between language and subjectivity. This plurality of versions gestures to individual differences and to the relativism of evil, in that each person constructs their own point of observation and of resistance. In the novel, each version stems from the subject's life experience and from their own singular experience of the event and, in other words, how each person was first interpellated by the blazing figure of la Bruja.

The novel searches, then, for *the truth of the body*. In this sense, it explores the value that each character is assigned at a sensory, cognitive, and emotional level, and according to the capacity for belief, skepticism, submission, and resistance that each one exercised in their relationship with her. Only the careful integration of the different independent versions can create a kaleidoscopic rapprochement with the truth, which can be understood as an unknown entity around which the narration revolves. But even such a rapprochement would be always relative or unstable. It is, then, a collectivized interpretative process that dialectically consolidates and then separates from its center in a movement that tends erratically toward a final, but also relative, synthesis.

The theme of truth is inseparable from the conflicts of guilt and redemption that feature in *Temporada de huracanes*. The plurality of stories gestures toward the attribution of blame, the search for its location—whether individual, social, or epistemic—and for a subject that can expiate it on behalf of the entire community, whose members have participated in the process of demonizing la Bruja and (even before) in her emergence as a cultural epiphenomenon created by poverty and marginalization. Each story moves the mechanisms of language in an attempt to generate coherence, which ensures nothing more than the logical cohesion of the different plots. The theme of blame hovers over Melchor's text, like a question mark suspended over individuals as well as over the macrostructures of power.

In other cases, a lack of definition represents the unambiguous sign of civil society's decline. The fixity and firm boundaries invoked by a given name are instead destroyed by the linguistic avalanche and lost in the fragmentation and cumulative nature of the social:

> They called her The Witch, the same as her mother; the Young Witch when she'd first started trading in curses and cures, and then, when she wound up alone, the year of the landslide, simply the Witch. If she'd had another name scrawled on some timeworn, worm-eaten piece of paper, buried at the back of one of those wardrobes that the old crone crammed full of plastic bags and filthy rags, locks of hair, bones, rotten leftovers, if at some point she'd been given a name and surname like everyone else in town, well, no one had ever known it, not even the women who visited the house each Friday had ever heard her called otherwise. She'd always been you, retard, or you, asshole, or you, devil child, if ever the Witch wanted her to come, or to be quiet, or even just to sit still under the table so she could listen to the women's maudlin pleas.[70]

Dispersed between worms and waste, as if already dwelling in the land of the dead, the possible name is part of a dark and depressing landscape in which individuality is cast in a time without names. Her name is replaced by nicknames and insults, which are used to make la Bruja invisible as a person, to be rendered a thing, an outcast, a shadow of herself. The variations of her name serve to dehumanize her, and, at some level, make her superhuman or infrahuman depending on the focus. Moreover, it is obvious that la Bruja's lack of a name inserts her clearly into the category of an archetype, linking her to the universal line of witches from where she comes.[71] She will become the result of the accumulation of her actions, destined to foresee or change reality, to manipulate it with witchcraft or influence it to eliminate illness or lack of affection, interpret dreams or wield an evil influence. A sorceress thus plays the therapeutic role of physical and spiritual healing albeit one that can quickly transform into punishment, vengeance, or curses or secret forms of revenge to satisfy the wishes of victims abandoned by legal and social justice. As a mediating or interstitial character, the witch is literally situated beyond good and evil, in a zone of moral undifferentiation that brings her closer to sin, which she understands as an organic and natural part of reality. Her own experience prepares her to inhabit a border zone, to always dwell in the margins of society. At the novel's outset, Melchor explains: "no se espantaba al parecer de nada, si hasta decían que había matado a su marido" (Nothing seemed to shock her, and frankly, what would you expect from a woman they say killed her own husband).[72]

As in *Falsa liebre*, in *Temporada de huracanes* bodies bear witness to tormented lives that find themselves at bursting point. Any emerging vitality is always self-destructive, aggravated, and counter-productive and shows evidence of death's constant progress through the social and organic collective. Bodies are thus physical, psychological, and emotional repositories that put the narrative machine and its assembled parts into operation. In *Temporada de huracanes*, the question of the body is essential because it serves to anchor a narrative that, as in the words that constitute it, possesses an amalgamating and tempestuous quality.

Melchor's work with language is intense, rich, and chiseled but it is not innovative. Many of her approaches invoke the techniques of Modernist authors that were reworked in the novels of the Boom, as well as stream of consciousness narration and some of the techniques of the *nouveau roman*. However, Melchor's appropriation of these methods makes us believe they are original narrative strategies, tightly connected to the narrative action. Colloquialisms, multiple registers, saturation of details, and a "horror of silence" that invokes baroque decorativism all represent audible indications of subjectivities in action that plunge us into linguistic accumulation which the long narrative paragraphs wield as a theatrical artifice for the reader. More than an evocation of baroque discourse, for other critics Melchor's book summons traces of the gothic and more specifically of "the southern gothic" represented no less than by authors of the quality of William Faulkner, Flannery O'Connor, and Cormac McCarthy, some of whom Melchor has acknowledged as influences. In *Temporada de huracanes*, the stifling heat, the use of stream of consciousness, of marginalized characters and the grotesque has been seen in relation to the aesthetic of these authors.[73]

Language's opacity is relative in this novel. The discourse calls attention to itself but is also limited by zones of cloudy transparency behind which we can glimpse the subjectivities of peripheral characters, destroyed by life, and inseparable from their surroundings. As if looking through a dirty window, the reader finds La Matosa's reality evasive. Indeed, continuous recurrences of "the same thing" and persistent insertions of "something different" alternate in Melchor's prose fiction, populating the imagined world with a mix of consciousness and visions that, owing to their fragmentation and exuberance, surpass any objective version of events. At stake here is the liquid way in which words and meanings circulate through the text and the form assumed by the semantic density of the discourses that are always ready to dissolve or hybridize in a tense and carnivalesque struggle over visions/versions.

However, as the author explains in an interview, the space and time of the novel corresponds to concrete coordinates that fuel the fictional machine. The very idea of the town where the novel is set emerges from the figurative process that shapes an imagined site that the plot depends on for its surroundings. It is, moreover, a fantasy that adjusts to both regional possibilities and the characters' subjective needs.

As Melchor clarifies:

> La Matosa does not exist as a town as such. There was a place of that name, it was a community on the banks of Lake Alvarado (Veracruz state), but it died when they built the Punta Tiburón development (apartments, marina, and golf course.... For me, La Matosa is that Veracruz jungle where there are no trees, just pure grass, grass, grass, green, green, that grows and grows, and you must just keep cutting it. You almost have to cut it down as you walk along, but it grows back behind you, and you can't see anything because it is so tall and as isolated as fuck... that that was the image that I had had of that town. But it doesn't exist.[74]

In the same interview and commenting on the time of year of the novel's setting, Melchor explains that "la novela transcurre durante los últimos días de abril y acaba cuando empieza la temporada de huracanes, que en el Pacífico es en mayo" (the novel takes place during the end of April and ends when hurricane season begins which in the Pacific is in May) which gives verisimilitude to the fictional world, if not "truth."[75]

More complex is the way subjectivities are created along with the coordination of characters and events, feelings, and desires, considering the novel's principal movement which is the gravitational pull toward la Bruja—the text's vital center—as the eye of the hurricane and point of intensification of the stories that converge in her. Luismi's gayness, the sexual desire that Brando feels for him, the description of both of their sexual proclivities, Norma's abortion, Chabela's supposedly contagious disease, the contempt constantly directed toward Yesenia, the propensity for drugs, promiscuity, and the characters' violence pervade the narration and suggest a world in which marginalization, poverty, and moral decadence are inextricably connected.

In these terms, the function of la Bruja—just like her power as an archetype—is to expose the sins of those around her, making sure they reveal themselves in all their splendor until they are extinguished. In this sense her death reestablishes the order of the simulacrum and the mask, transforming the entire narrative into a theatricalization that, as in Greek tragedy (albeit with tones informed by modernity), situates itself so as to provoke both *sympathy and terror* in the reader and a compassion for the characters' fate along with a fear that such a destiny might befall them. However, in the novel this exemplary value is not directed toward catharsis nor toward the rectifying of collective behavior but instead toward bringing awareness to the structural, political, economic, and social determinants that produce these types of subjectivities.

La Bruja's gender is essential to how Melchor approaches the question of truth. She is presented as both man and woman, or rather as a man presenting as a woman who does not set out to trick people but instead covers and disguises her body, revealing it as a simulacrum or as an artifice of a truth that is not only hidden but not relevant in terms of the effects of her gender performance. Melchor admits that it was her editor, Martín Solares, who convinced her to call the character la Bruja, so that she would better conform to the archetype. However, it was her reading of Vladimir Propp's classic book *Morphology of the Folktale* that introduced her to the idea that "uno de los atributos de las brujas es la capacidad de transformarse en varón; además, el poder de una bruja la masculiniza ante la sociedad. La bruja en una comunidad es la que tiene el poder, por lo tanto, se parece a un hombre" (one of the hallmarks of a witch is her ability to transform into a man; in addition, a witch's power masculinizes her in the eyes of society. A witch is the one in a community who has power and therefore seems like a man).[76] Although the quality Propp describes is a familiar one, Melchor's second statement is debatable since witches retain the feminine qualities that are necessary for them to carry out their principal functions—the disruption of the social order by means of a self-awarded and unnatural power. According to conventional wisdom, if a woman exercises an unquestionable social and countercultural power, it will markedly and unnaturally alter power relations. In the novel, The Witch's supernatural accoutrements consist of the preparation of potions and in her understanding of and influence over affairs of the heart. She complements these tools with her cunning and her propensity for spreading rumors, which all feed into the stereotype of the woman/witch, emphasizing that her power comes not from physical force or any type of "natural" authority but from resourcefulness, a spirit of betrayal, hypocrisy, and simulation.

In addition, as she explains, through her use of the grotesque Melchor attempts to differentiate the representation of evil as expressed in *Falsa liebre*:

> I began to create the Witch as male, but it seemed very like the situation in *Falsa liebre* and I did not want to repeat it (the story of a man that falls in love with a boy and threatens to kill him). During this time, I had also read a book (she doesn't remember the name) about how crime is spoken about from the perspective of gender in criminology. Of how violence in society is normally perpetrated by men, and above all, violence against women. And I said to myself, why don't you talk about—since now feminicide is mentioned so much—why not convert the brujo into a woman.... But when the character became a woman there was something in the mystery that didn't quite work, it seemed vague. And suddenly it hit me. I know. Let's play with the idea that she's woman and in the end the original story will come out. Deep down, this is a gay love affair.[77]

Making the critic's job perhaps too easy, the author explains these compositional options as the result of adapting the material she was narrating while differentiating between her two novels, and opportunely inserting *Temporada de huracanes* into the wave of attention being paid to gender violence and particularly to feminicide. In this novel, through the development of a personal poetics that fits successfully into the market, we see how she is particularly attuned to its vagaries. Along with these considerations, Melchor has evaluated the logic of the character, pointing out the familial determinism that makes la Bruja heir to her mother's nature and victim of the latter's own frustrations. Thus, constructed as clearly human, the character is over-controlled and vulnerable:

> She's a human being who comes to the world with a mother obviously traumatized by the violence she received and thus is bereft of options: the witch is a witch because her mother was a witch, no one asked her if she wanted to be one, and she also had no choice as to whether she wants to present as a girl or not. Let's just say that the witch-mother hated men so much that she prevented her son from being one and that's why she treated him like that.[78]

The violence enshrined in both the system and in daily life serves as the factor from which, in the final instance, all the existential conditions in the fictional world derive, and which itself is a product of colonial violence. La Bruja picks the plants that grow on the hill:

> Among the old ruins that, according to those suits from the government, were the ancient tombs of men who'd once lived up there, the first dwellers, even before the Spaniards who, from their boats, took one look at all that land spread out before them and said finders keepers, this land belongs to us and the Kingdom of Castile, and the ancients, the few who were left, had to run for the hills and they lost everything, right down to the stones of their temples.[79]

This genealogy of violence exposes the installation of power regimes that dislocate interhuman relationships and demonize subalternized spaces through the force of different sectors and processes that have been transmitted over centuries as a way of annihilating the value of life and consolidating disrupted forms of coexistence and subjectivity. Without negating the influence of the Zetas or the effects of PRI's disastrous administration in the Veracruz region since 2010, we can identify La Matosa as anomalous world, permeated by corruption, instincts, immediacy and contingency, marked by individual and collective trauma, without utopia or God, equality or progress.

But if la Bruja is the product of historical and biological heredity, she is also the product of nature, since her emergence as such occurs upon the death of her mother:

> as the hurricane hit the coast with bitter, thunderous force, and day after day rumbling storm clouds pumped the sky with water, inundating the fields and rotting everything, drowning the animals that, blindsided by the gale and the thunder, couldn't escape their pens in time; drowning even some children, the ones no one scooped up quickly enough when the hillside broke away and came crashing down in a tumult of rocks and uprooted oak trees and a black sludge that swamped everything in its path, eventually spilling out onto the coast but only after having converted two thirds of the town into a graveyard.[80]

Finally, reality itself—or at least the version that appears in the sensationalist pages of the *nota roja*—turns up a reference to an article about a real crime committed nearby in the sugarcane-growing area of Cardel, where it was reported that a local shaman was killed by his lover. This event, in the author's ambit, demonstrates the conditions of possibility of a situation that has been mythicized in the popular imagination as the embodiment of ordinary people's perverse powers or a fictionalizing of the real.[81]

When a character is described as a witch, truth breaks into fragments since it belongs to another logic, outside of the working of mythical discourse. The Witch's deceptiveness is obvious, but the myth and the phenomenon of belief surpass the senses, and affect (fear, passion, the desire for vengeance, the survival instinct) presents a different and powerful form of the real. For example, we see this play out in the character of Munra:

> And up until that point nobody had told him that the Witch they all went on about was in fact a man, a fellow of about forty, forty-five back then, dressed in black clothing, in ladies clothing, and with long, black painted nails: gruesome. And even though he had something, a sort of veil, covering his face, you only had to hear his voice and see his hands to know he was a homosexual.[82]

Munra moves through the witch's depressing and foul-smelling milieu as if descending into hell: "todo lleno de mugre y la cocina apestosa a comida descompuesta y la pared del otro lado, la que daba al pasillo, estaba cubierta de imágenes pornográficas y rayones con pintura de lata y unos signos cabalísticos" (crap spread all over the place and the kitchen stinking of rotten food, and the opposite wall, the one that led out into the hallway, plastered in scratched out pornographic images and spray paint and some mysterious symbols saying who knows what).[83] But in effect, we are witnessing the emergence of his knowledge and understanding of the real.

In Melchor's work the assimilation of homosexuality, promiscuity, violence, esotericism, and pornography is obviously extremely problematic. Following the path she first trod in *Falsa liebre*, we sense that she finds it difficult to inscribe these types of stories—and other possible kinds—in settings less laden with shock value. The theme of "forbidden love"—that Melchor admits is one of her favorites—is buried in the novels under the tangled mess of settings and atmospheres.[84] In these narratives, the delight in lurid details and events diminishes the characters' force, as if a hurricane had destroyed the stories, leaving only the debris of a world that becomes visible after its destruction.

The truth about la Bruja, then, stems from this convergence of factors that explain the appearance of evil, not just as individual propension or superhuman (supernatural) compulsion, but rather as a constellation of causes and effects that allow for the emergence of depravity as an event, or as an exceptional occurrence that changes the course of time and of lives. After the first introductory paragraph and the second dedicated to the story of las Brujas—mother and daughter—the rest of the chapters focus on different characters and incorporate their stories into that of la Bruja and her murder. "La Lagarta" Yesenia's story, and the beginning of Luismi's in chapter 3, followed by the relationship between Munra, Chabela, Luismi, Norma and a version of the murder (chapter 4); the arrival of Norma in La Matosa, her relationship with Luismi and her abortion (chapter 5) that will set la Bruja's murder in motion; the character of Brando and his sexual connection with Luismi and the occurrence of the crime make up chapter 6. In the next, the novel offers a brief recap of different versions and recounts the events that follow la Bruja's death. Finally, in chapter 8, the novel focuses on el Abuelo/the Grandfather and on the dignified burial he gives la Bruja's remains.

The thematic options and the evolution of the plot turn on a handful of definitive topics: the question of gender and forbidden love, eroticism in all its manifestations, vengeance, and death. Finally, Norma's abortion, performed by la Bruja, sets off Luismi's reaction, bringing to light the question of women's bodily autonomy, masculine (macho) imaginaries regarding female subjectivity and mutually supportive alliances between women. To this abject setting, Melchor adds prejudice, ideology, and myth, transforming La Matosa into a repository of perversion and chaos where passions and desires circulate like subterranean rivers, submerging the lives that move through an area covered in vermin and waste.

In its search for truth, the novel traverses a maze of oversaturated and unrelenting language. Like the floodgates of a collective unconscious that have been opened to inundate the microhistory of the inhabitants of a town in Veracruz that represents the underworld of postcolonial society, the distinct versions of the facts weaken the imaginaries and articulating signs and transform reality into a kaleidoscope turned by guilty fingers. The central thread that the novel unwinds to uncover the truth about the crime has led some critics, as I've already mentioned, to focus on the novel's detective-story-like structure. In the novel, "shifting suspicion" is employed throughout all the chapters, allowing for the development of alternative interactions, accounts, and frame stories. As in all novels that contain a crime and a mysterious perpetrator, the crime must stand out against a principle of order, or at least differentiate itself within this context, to define the limits of the event and point toward the reestablishment of the status quo. In the case of *Temporada de huracanes*, the title warns of an atmospheric and natural disruption that will envelop and overwhelm the subjects. However, since the fictional world is an anomalous totality that is penetrated by a propensity for corruption and illegality, the creation of la Bruja as the nucleus of intensification allows the author both to intensify these topics and to situate the drama, placing the killing at the climatic center of the story, even in the lust-filled universe of La Matosa. Each chapter focuses on and then discards the characters as potential authors of the crime, although the novel maintains ambiguity with a skillful deployment of perspectives and subjectivism. Thus, la Bruja's world occupies a preeminent place in the narrative universe, although she is already dead as the novel opens and her evil surroundings are relegated to a memory that functions as reminder and referent.

THE BLACK HOLE OF LA BRUJA

A black hole is a point to which all other elements feel drawn to and that, once penetrated, cannot be abandoned. Magic can transform aspects that escape rational consciousness, regulations, socialization, normativity, and logic into reality. For the same reason, it erases limits and destabilizes categories. Ambiguity, the unspoken, polyvalence, perspectivism, relativity, and simulacrum are all qualities that approximate the working of magic, which establishes an environment where contradiction is embraced, and negativity prospers.

In *Temporada de huracanes*, la Bruja is not one but two, *she is who she was* and all those who were before her. In the novel, she gives rise to a specific narrative place within the saturated and sutured general fictional economy. As in *Macbeth*, la Bruja is pluralized, disseminating evil and allowing it to unfold its different facets throughout the text in a polyphony that seems independent of the character's singularity. Representing the exogenous, witchcraft is made up of anomalous elements that make the social conflict stranger and more dynamic. Witchcraft poisons relationships between the characters, by incorporating unusual mechanisms and supernatural powers that bring previously buried aspects of the characters to the surface. At the same time, witchcraft can ally itself with the causes of weak characters with exceptional needs for whom la Bruja feels sympathy. In my view, determining the existence of witchcraft is less important than an examination of the project to which it applies its powers and the effects it achieves in its attempts to derail prevailing legal models.

Contrasting with the modern surroundings within which Melchor anachronistically inscribes them, sorcery and superstition enjoy a catalytic, primitive, and enigmatic power that creates dramatic and/or parodic tensions. Witches usually embody evil, but in *Temporada de huracanes* evil both precedes and constitutes society. La Matosa is built upon the graves of the dead, in a land destroyed by hurricanes and earthquakes, the activities of colonialism and organized crime, police corruption and the dealings of transnational and extractivist companies, the complicity of the State and the acquiescence of its followers.

Perceived as the possessor of allure and demonic knowledge, la Bruja is believed to possess the ability to radically disrupt the social order and "colonize" it with her weirdness and her magical powers. No one knows la Bruja's origins, which imbues her with a malignant and intriguing exoticism as well as an anomalous and savage seductive capacity to subvert order. The biographical details we possess do nothing to undermine her mysterious origins or her significance. Although la Bruja is a product of La Matosa's society, her not entirely unpredictable evolution (her avatar and her becoming) places her in the realm of the diabolical.

Following her death, she maintains a social and affective function that reverberates rather than simply persists. A character without a name, her insertion in the world arises from precarity and from a constant struggle for survival. Living among trash, her world appears like a stain on reality: "había que ver como vivía en un cuchitril lleno de cachivaches y cajas de cartón ya podrido y bolsas de basura llenas de papeles y trapos y rafia y olotes y bolas de pelo caspiento y de polvo y cartones de leche y botellas de plástico vacías, pura pinche basura, puras pinches porquerías que los abusadores aquellos pisoteaban y rompían" (you only had to see how she lived, in a pigsty literally brimming with trash and moldy cardboard boxes, trash bags full of papers and old rags and raffia and corncobs and flaky hairballs and dust and empty milk cartons and plastic bottles; crap, nothing but craps, which those thugs trampled on or smashed up).[85]

Her lack is not only material but affective. A black hole, la Bruja attracts and consumes all the emotions that surround her with a diabolic voraciousness. A ghostly presence, la Bruja's absent/present image is the anomaly that colonizes and corrupts the life of the community when irrationality and disorder are installed as social and affective connectors. Dead or alive, her image represents the residual essence of an irreducible Otherness. In spectral terms, la Bruja is almost completely disembodied and is, above all, an idea and a function: "una mujer muy alta y muy flaca, el manojo de llaves tintineando entre sus manos de palmas pálidas como cangrejos lunares que por momentos asomaban por las mangas negras de aquella túnica que parecía flotar en la oscuridad" (a very tall, scraggy woman, a set of keys jangling in her big hands like pale palm leaves, like lunar crabs poking out from the black sleeves of that tunic that seemed, in the darkness, to hover above the ground).[86]

At times she is depicted as a powerful and grotesque vision of intense clichés and indisputable marks of violence: "la Bruja se asomaba, vestida con su túnica negra, y el velo torcido que a la luz del día, en la cocina revuelta, con el caldero volcado y el piso mugroso y salpicado de sangre seca, no bastaba para disimular los moretones que le inflaban los párpados, las costras que partían la boca y las cejas tupidas" (the Witch appeared, dressed in her black tunic and that crooked veil, which even in the full light of day—in that bomb site of a kitchen with the kettle tipped on its side and the grimy, blood-spattered floor—couldn't hide the swollen bruising on her eyelids, the scabs where her lip and bushy eyebrows had split).[87]

As if straight from the pages of a children's story, Melchor reworks the stereotype of the witch in over-literal and predictable ways. During her sexual encounter with Luismi, la Bruja's actions are more expressively eloquent than her appearance. Her body is presented as a hole in time, which becomes flesh only during the sex act. Her bodily surface bears witness to a grotesque sensuality and exhibits traces of her occasional lovers. Filth and promiscuity act as indications of her impending death, until she is buried in the dirt of the town where the bodies of her ancestors are interred. La Bruja is uniquely and metonymically instinctual: "una boca que era también como una sombra que aparecía y desaparecía detrás de la tela áspera y mugrienta que le cubría la cabeza y que apenas se levantaba lo necesario cuando hacía falta pero que nunca desvelaba por completo" (A mouth that was also like a shadow, poking in and out from behind the scratchy, grubby fabric that veiled her face—she only ever lifted it when strictly necessary—and even then only a fraction, never fully revealing herself).[88]

Venerated as an anti-Virgin or as the image of the Santa Muerte, the sexual availability of la Bruja's body convenes lines of men and women, who make pilgrimages to her house in search of relief, exoticism, and money (all possible forms of salvation). They create an evil constellation around la Bruja, where reality is more diabolical than it is mythical. Women come to la Bruja in search of help in coping with different forms of masculine abuse caused by their marginalized and objectified position in society that makes them agree to vile acts of physical exploitation. They come to heal wounds or withstand sexual abuse and unwanted pregnancies—often the products of multiple rapes or incest—or emotional and physical turmoil. In all cases, la Bruja provides many different services from the sexual services she herself fulfills, to healing, the dispensing of herbs and potions, acting as counsellor and fortune teller, and assisting those who need some kind of small miracle to deal with the pressures of daily life.

In her Otherness, la Bruja embodies base instincts, habits, the hangover of the organic, spiritual, individual, and community degradation that, in the postcolonial microcosm of La Matosa, express the deep crisis that has invaded a social universe that has been transfigured by a linguistic elaboration that appears interminable. However, what else can be found in the character of la Bruja beyond her capacity to embody an immense emotional energy which, building on both her life and her death, produces a proliferation of actions and stories that circulate through the text with a hurricane-like force? One of the ways we can interpret Melchor's text is as a modern-day witch hunt that engenders forms of persecution and demonization that seem obsolete but that underlie contemporary mechanisms of power, such as the many anonymous, unpunished, and never-documented crimes against women in many different cultures.

In the preface to *On Evil*, Terry Eagleton develops the idea that the witches are the true protagonists of *Macbeth*. As he explains, the three—as exiled and border characters—have cut all ties with the masculine-dominated social order and seek only to unsettle it. The three women "signify a realm of non-meaning and of poetic wordplay on the edges of orthodox society."[89] Through the effects they achieve with their tricks—double meanings, mockery, and riddles—the witches move in a space of undifferentiation and mystery, a construction of image and language that creates, according to Eagleton, "the play's unconscious, the place where language slithers and tangles," continuing:

> In their presence, clear definitions dissolve and oppositions are inverted: fair is foul, and foul is fair, nothing is but what is not. The three weird sisters are androgynous (they are bearded women) and both singular and plural (three in one). As such they strike at the route of all social and sexual stability. They are radical separatists who scorn male power, laying bare the hollow sound and fury at its heart. They are devotees of a female cult whose words and bodies mock rigorous boundaries and make sport of fixed identities.[90]

With this description of the character and function of the witches in Shakespeare's Scotland, Eagleton introduces a series of elements that gets at the very essence of the concept of magic which, as it references a mythical paradigm, can be applied to the case of Melchor's witch. In *Temporada de huracanes*, the character of la Bruja who, as I have said is dead at the novel's outset, is characterized through undefinition (she's both man and woman) and plurality (la Bruja Chica, la Bruja Vieja). Also, la Bruja represents the oscillation between good and evil, traversing these territories, depending on the case, with notable adaptability. Above all, and as in the case of Macbeth's "protagonists," her purpose is to dismantle a precarious and tension filled order through the radicalization of actions into which different characters from the novel plunge, carrying out potentialities, tendencies, and deviations that exist in a constant state of latency and that contain both their flow and overflow. La Bruja is thus a nucleus that generates meanings including the unsayable. She is a self-referential, iconic and polysemic character.

Along with his characterization of the witches in *Macbeth*, Eagleton adds the fact that their acts are not planned and appear to be directed at no end in particular: "They are sorceresses, not strategists."[91] They move in accordance with a cyclical time, something we also see with la Bruja in *Temporada de huracanes*, whose life is recounted after she is dead. Using her mysterious origins, sex, purpose, and character, her function is to contaminate and colonize the present. In so doing, la Bruja succeeds in destabilizing identities and interrelations, demonizing a world that is already primed for self-destruction and that is situated upon the rot of mass graves, impunity, and crime.

For Eagleton, Macbeth's witches represent "the hollow sound and fury at the heart of male power."[92] The figure of la Bruja in *Temporada de huracanes* embodies this condition and serves as the dumping ground for the collapse of meaning and the activation of signs of dissolution. She is both supernatural and not and exists both inside and outside of nature, culture, and history. Although she can trace her genealogy and mark out the material conditions of her existence, hers is nonetheless an uncertain condition and a form of exceptionality that consists of erasing normality and replacing it with a conglomeration of functions, behaviors, insinuations, and possibilities that expand the realm of lust and crime while at the same time depletesfundamental areas of life.

La Bruja is like a magnet because she represents a plural space: of debauchery and relief, of freedom and rebellion. But she is also associated with the important material and symbolic element of hidden treasure that increases her air of mystery and sparks ambition that adds to the lure of criminal activity. Eros and Thanatos come together in a lawless space devoid of any moral judgement that might regulate behavior. Are her artefacts, potions, and talismans truly sinister paraphernalia or perhaps simply a glut of debris made glorious through myth? La Bruja deploys a carnivalesque and demonic alter ego in which the order of the universe is inverted and transgression overflows like an intense and erratic hurricane. Drugs stimulate effects in those who frequent the house, and delirium mixes with desire and dreams with nightmares, until la Bruja reveals her gender identity and her true sex, disguises herself as the Other, and challenges reality with her appearance.

As a chaos agent, la Bruja possesses all beings who approach her. They are debased to the point of madness, sunk into a performance in which all dissemble, all play act, and all reproduce themselves like lines of flight directed toward a symbolic territory from which there is no return. The novel moves relentlessly upward, and violence and promiscuity run wild. The characters project impossible and improbable identities, staking a claim for virility that disappears into thin air, progressing through the narrative because of fabrications, tricks, and schemes that lead nowhere. Everything capitalist modernity has succeeded in burying or concealing makes a comeback, demolishing civil and moral barriers and a rampant and voracious unconscious rises to the surface of the ego.

PATRIARCHY AND WITCHCRAFT

It is impossible, of course, to separate the question of gender from the treatment of witches, sorceresses, and soothsayers etc. throughout history. The social and political approximation of these subcultural practices (minoritized and subjugated to dominant society) moves from the conceptualization of occult practices to different forms of social marginalization, demonizing, persecution, punishment (including torture, attacks within the community, inquisitorial persecution, burning at the stake and other forms). Such processes were utilized to control and eventually eliminate belief in the practices of witchcraft and their occurrence within the community and demonstrate a wide array of hyperbolic reactions to forms of knowledge and control (violation, manipulation, transgression) of social norms from countercultural and, ultimately, counterhegemonic perspectives.

As a challenge to instrumental reason, that is, to scientific logic (drawing on causality, experimentalism, and logic) redefined by illuminism, the connection magic/gender emerges as the tip of a much bigger iceberg, submerged but solidly founded on the bases of Western society. In a challenge to religious doctrine and ecclesiastical power, magic has served for centuries as the flip side of the desire for humanistic totalization and as a defense of the values of subjugated sectors of the population. Religious and political thought has always displaced any impulse to the margins of society that is not sanctioned by official culture nor representative of the elite interests enshrined in educational institutions and social regulation at all levels. Moreover, we must also consider the relationship between countercultural thought and economics.

Silvia Federici's work on witches and witch hunts in the sixteenth and seventeenth centuries emphasizes the relationship that exists between witches and the enclosure of communal lands, which produced an itinerant population of beggars and vagabonds in Europe who, in turn, threatened capitalism's social and economic order. Materially and symbolically, women's bodies are crucial in these processes since, because of their role at the center of communitarian organization, the State imposes control upon them. The State effectively appropriates sexuality and women's reproductive capacity, exploiting their vulnerability and condemning actions that supposedly exceed the moral and religious tolerance of the age. Poverty and the rupture of communal bonds promote practices that are considered dangerous, transgressive, and iniquitous such as the seeking of alms, prostitution, folk healing, and female communal support.

In *Caliban and the Witch* and *Witches, Witch Hunting and Women*, Silvia Federici affirms the importance of a return to witch-hunting in the era of globalization, a period in which we are revisiting forms of the primitive accumulation of capital, as some critics have pointed out.[93] As in the case of witches and witch hunting, Federici believes that women's bodies have been exploited by power as well as by mechanisms put in place by religion and even tourism at different historical moments. As part of the process of the *commercialization* of human relationships, witch hunting was commodified by presenting witches as undesirable—albeit picturesque—personages, opposed to the system and thus expendable. This commodification thus promoted another way to degrade women and their forms of socialization and symbolic productivity in addition to the subalternization they received politically, culturally, and economically. In this regard, the witch's world is reduced in all senses to an enclosed, regulated, typical and peripheral space that engenders social recognition.[94] The witch's marginalization underscores the centrality of practical male rationality and the qualities attributed to men, excluding intuition, affectivity, and subjective digressions toward socially non-productive zones (in the context of capital accumulation).

Since the Age of Antiquity, patriarchal control of the State and the family reduces and overdetermines the space designated for feminine action. In addition, the systematic destruction of the environment alienates women from contact with nature, imposing forms of knowledge reserved only for society's masculine elite. According to Federici, together with the destruction of Indigenous peoples and enslaved Africans, witch hunts served as one of the paths that led to modern capitalism in the New World. Women saw their communities dismantled and privatized and mounted a resistance that was continually interpreted as a pact with the devil.[95] The rise of the medical profession and the expansion of philosophical and scientific thinking about the body transformed remedies—including midwifery, the work of healers with poor families, and the use of medicinal herbs—into primitive tendencies and later into markers of underdevelopment that were linked to social phenomena viewed as clear paths toward social disintegration including homelessness, violence, and illiteracy.

As Federici indicates in *Caliban and the Witch*, the poverty of so-called witches and their peasant origins were omnipresent in the sixteenth and seventeenth centuries' trial proceedings against these women. Far from passive victims, this indicates that they instead actively and ingeniously resisted social exclusion, hence their fame as aggressive and resentful subjects who rejected their marginalization and sought ways to impose their knowledge to foster solidarity in hostile surroundings.

> Witches' magic power endowed them with authority and inspired fear and respect within the community and therefore must be destroyed: "This is one reason why women became the primary targets in the capitalist attempt to construct a more mechanized conception of the world. The "rationalization" of the natural world—the precondition for a more regimented work discipline and for the scientific revolution—passed through the destruction of the "witch."[96]

Melchor assimilates the cultural charge that the figure of the witch embodies in all its facets into *Temporada de huracanes*, where the character exhibits an extraordinary power within the community. The money that la Bruja has supposedly hidden and that serves as the alleged motive for the murder indicates the relationship between women and capital and the association of the latter with the demonic that leads to perdition and death. Sexuality as well as both real and symbolic capital, together with their strategies of social control (evil deeds, tricks, potions) comprise the fundamental axis of the character in whom damaging and devastating affective forces are concentrated. As Federici explains "Female sexuality has historically represented a social danger, a threat to the discipline of work, a power over others, and an obstacle to the maintenance of social hierarchies and class relations."[97] We see this reflected in Melchor's novel, where la Bruja irradiates a sexual power (libidinal reproduction) over everything that penetrates the symbolic realm. The system of social relationships surrounding la Bruja is, ultimately, a tangled web of micro powers that she deploys upon having concentrated all the contradictions and drives of her social space into her iconic figure. The demonizing of the social relationships within her milieu as well as her life and death are the focus that lights the literary fuse.

As a witch, la Bruja finds herself at the nucleus of a fluctuating and peculiar female sisterhood from where she draws in the sex workers and abused wives or other women who come in search of help with their problems of love, sex, violence etc. La Bruja pays them specific attention, revealing a special understanding of their conflicts and sorrows. In some of the novel's best pages, Melchor describes the grotesque crowd of people that the iconic figure of the Witch attracts: lecherous men looking for sex, drugs, and transgressive acts to get rid of frustrations and traumas and release their instincts and women who embody a wide range of misfortune, promiscuity, and pain:

> They would beg for her help, to cook up one of her concoctions, the stuff that the women in town harped on about: potions to pin down the men, to really knock them off their feet, and indeed potions to ward the bastards off for good; potions that wiped their own memories or that directed every drop of their destructive potential into the seed that those bastards had left in the women's bellies before scuttling back to their trucks; or those other tinctures, stronger still, which they say could purge hearts of the fatuous allure of suicide.[98]

Potions to counteract machismo, patriarchal authoritarianism, and gender privileges, concoctions to control abuse and overcome despair, herbs to protect against the results of unsafe sex and rape, secret biopowers that, under the name of occultism, reach out a helping hand to women during times of femicide and of increased systemic violence are all some of The Witch's "sins." She exists only because the popular imagination needs her existence: a cesspool where deviance, aggression, urgency, transgression and suffering dwell: "Fueron ellas las únicas, en suma, a las que la Bruja decidió ayudar y, cosa rara, sin cobrarles un solo peso, lo cual era bueno porque la mayor parte de las chicas de la carretera con dificultad comían una vez al día y muchas no eran dueñas ni de la toalla con la que se limpiaban" (Those girls from the highway, not the meddlesome old bags in town, were the only ones the Witch chose to help for free, without charging a peso, which was just as well because most of them could barely own enough to eat once a day, and plenty of then didn't own as much as the towels they used to wipe away the bodily fluids of the men who screwed them).[99]

Only the women seek to bury her body after her death, viewing her as the wretched image of their shared destiny: "si ella en el fondo era bien buena y siempre las estaba ayudando y no les cobraba nada ni les pedía nada a cambio más que un poquito de compañía; por eso fue que se animaron, entre todas las chicas de la carretera y una que otra que trabajaba en las cantinas de Villa, a juntar aquel dinerito para darle un entierro digno al pobre cuerpo podrido de la Bruja" (because deep down she was a good egg always helping them out and she never charged them or asked for more than a bit of company; and that's why they—the girls from the highway and the odd stray from the cantinas in Villa—decided to do a little collection, raise enough to give the putrid body of the Witch a worthy burial).[100]

The theme of the corpse that appears at the beginning of the narrative is still relevant at the end of the novel, although rumor has it that la Bruja never actually died but instead turned into a lizard, rabbit, or giant bird—animals are often witches' avatars—who circles over the demonic reality that swarms the land. The belief in her hidden riches remains and the townspeople enter her intimate and diabolic space with sticks and shovels, digging holes and searching for hidden doors and secret chambers. We can link the material value of this supposed treasure to la Bruja's own symbolic value, that is, to the social capital she has accrued as counselor, soothsayer, and healer.

Toward the end of the novel, the attempt to commemorate la Bruja's body comes up against the ministerial bureaucracy, which requires documents to demonstrate kinship in order to release the remains to the women who claim them in a gesture of support. But the women lack the money and the necessary administrative knowledge to secure her body. A lack of money is always associated with the figure of witches who are paradigmatic women in terms of their marginal status and counter normative resources. The sequence money/power/body/name is connected to the relationship between the individual and the State and its institutions: formalized, conventional, and regulated by bureaucratic, economic, and dehumanized criteria informed by biopolitics.

The question of names is repeated throughout the novel, associated with the question of identity and forms of social (self-)recognition. As already mentioned, and following Derrida, the given name is a mechanism that can be decodified within a certain sphere of knowledge and social action, since it only possesses meaning within a particular sphere of social knowledge and action or within a system of relations. The lack or suppression of a given name indicates social alienation and, more specifically, the absence of a protective mask since without a name we are reduced to what we do, and our actions and image replace our naming identity. In this sense, la Bruja has no way out—*she is what she is* and *what she does*, as well as how the Other sees her. She has lost her name and lost herself.[101]

BETWEEN PRIVATE AND PUBLIC LIFE: SECRETS AND GOSSIP

Orality plays an important role in the novel, setting the tone for a narrative style in which one dominant voice builds the story as a series of connected events. Orality also acts as the organizing principle for the versions of multiple characters who contribute information to the general archive of happenings in La Matosa. In its principal form orality functions as a mediating and interstitial mechanism between the private sphere and public life that gradually sheds light on la Bruja's murder. Like in any crime thriller, a key element is determining the identity of the perpetrator and their motive and means of carrying out the homicide. But in *Temporada de huracanes*, the task excludes law enforcement. Instead, the novel's plot is designed as a popular fable, while at the same time it develops aspects of the lives of its characters and their singular stories of misfortune and exclusion.

A prominent element in *Temporada de huracanes* is the use of gossip as a form of aesthetic and ideological productivity that leads to the incessant generation of opinions, ideas, possibilities, alternatives, visions, and versions of reality.[102] Gossip acts as a polyphonic tool and as a de-institutionalized communicative option that operates outside of the protocols of writing and orality (in the cases when the latter is formalized as a discursive transmission such as myth, legend, song etc.). In this way, gossip can be understood as a particular form of orality that generally includes false information that, deliberately or not, distorts, deforms, ignores, or misinterprets the truth. In this case, gossip encompasses both the original narrator's version as well as that of other incidental narrators and centralizes the verbal flow and the writing that shapes it into a text. Gossip includes descriptive elements and random facts about the history of and happenings in the region. In some cases, more than slander, the focus is on the oral transmission of information as, for example, when Melchor invokes the "deslave del año setenta y ocho" (landslide of '78) when an exceptionally strong hurricane buried three quarters of the town, turning it into an enormous cemetery where the Old Witch is buried.[103]

An element that underscores the idea of the novel as a conjunction of gossip, rumor, and calumnies is the language itself not only in terms of lexical and syntactical style but also in its devastating, intensifying and very visual rhythmic build up. It mirrors the dynamics of speech that have been accelerated by passion and by the proliferation of elements embedded in the narrative flow. Based on speech and on the interactions between two or more speakers, orality is by nature spontaneous, immediate, and ephemeral. The use of language in speech is informal and generally employs redundancies, filler words, interruptions, the use of idiolects, colloquial forms, and frequent reliance on gestures (extraverbal signs). Gossip and rumors include unsubstantiated information, which is generally the product of popular exchanges that circulates by word of mouth. Rumor is vaguer than gossip and generally has less personal impact. Gossip is usually accompanied by judgment over the behavior of others and can sometimes reach the level of slander. Rumor is usually less concrete and less directly connected to the speaker (rumors about politics, economic situations, or even about people are communicated much less trenchantly than scandal or scuttlebutt).

Rumors and gossip replace any possibility of sharing objective and trustworthy information for la Bruja's social circle and the population of La Matosa in general. The oral nature of gossip forms a web that traps the inhabitants along with those targeted. However, gossip can also be thought of as a recourse of the disenfranchised and a form of action that shields itself with anonymity. Nevertheless, it is more frequently associated with betrayal, lies, or at least with the unseemly divulging of facts that will often roil the social atmosphere and foster enmities and rancor. At the same time, gossip is a means of transmitting information about daily life in the town. La Bruja's existence as well as her habits are talked about and popularized by information transmitted by word-of-mouth.[104] Her supposed sexual habits reveal her preferences but also their transactional nature: she not only sells sex, but she also buys it, acting also as a loan shark. This places her at the center of a small domestic economy in which the logic of capitalism adapts to the covert forms developed by marginalized subjects. While still youthful and bearing the name of the Young Witch, she demonstrates a better understanding of the market than her mother. Attentive to her competitor (Señor de Palogacho) who seemed more effective than the Old Witch, she announces to her:

> that starting now, prices would reflect the complexity of the request, the ways and means that the mother would have to employ and the kind of magic required to pull off the job, because it was hardly the same thing to cure their piles as to make a man fall at their knees, or say, to make contact with their dead mother to find out if she'd forgiven them for having neglected the old bitch when she was alive, right?[105]

Diversifying the merchandise requires defining the charges since word of mouth is the only way they attract the clients they need to survive. Other forms of orality are found in the consultations that the Witch carries out, along with the confession she makes with Father Castro, who tries to stop his flock from resorting to witchcraft. Together with the spontaneous publicity la Bruja's clients give her, negative and mocking rumors about her also circulate around La Matosa.[106]

To this we can add other oral forms of communication like messages, indirect dialogue, songs, disputes etc., devised as part of the big discursive puzzle that makes up the novel. All of this leads to the understanding that *Temporada de huracanes* moves in a between-space where popular societal forms, which are both dispersed and lifeless, recognize their marginality and develop strategies to counteract its effects. But these popular societal forms, as the narrative demonstrates, are intimately impacted by social conflict. Far from acting as a collective character, La Matosa is instead a hive of intense energy and carnivalesque relationships paradoxically attenuated by sexual desire.

In her book *Gossip*, Patricia Meyer Spacks points out that both gossip and the novel are positioned between the individual and society, between public and private spheres.[107] In this sense, she explains, "Gossip occurs at the same intersection, serving social purposes, defining social opinion, embodying social power (the power of opinion), but issuing from individual mouths and tracing psychic agendas as well."[108] She further details that, to some degree, gossip is "the world's talk" since information arrives channeled through various consciences. For Meyer Spacks, gossip invents its own territory and is a self-contained oral artefact that concocts possibilities based on appearances or that are the product of pure speculation. Trivialization, hyperbole, frivolity, deliberate falsification, mean-spirited interpretation, and violation of privacy are all generally associated with gossip, and all contribute to its devaluing. Meyer Spacks, however, also offers numerous arguments that point to some of gossip's positive aspects such as the strengthening of community bonds, the definition of intimacy as it pertains to the collective, the handling of silence that surrounds verbal interchanges and of the dynamics between discretion and revelation. For the author, the dynamics of the production and reception of gossip are like surreptitiously reading a novel: the flow of language and silence, the inscription of reality into fiction, the entertainment value, the intensity of information, and the expectation of new communicative situations.

The previous analysis implies that gossip cannot exist without secrets. A secret is, then, the mechanism that underlies gossip and that threatens to uncover it. Gossip can, however, suggest a secret that does not exist, but that appears to be present within the mysteries of social action. *Temporada de huracanes* constantly plays with the question of truth and with the hidden existence of situations, actions, and feelings that resist discovery. The story is replete with furtive situations and characters that lead mysterious and turbulent lives, which come to the surface like social explosions only to bury themselves again deep in the community. As one of the driving forces of many different literary genres throughout history, secrets play with reason and affect and implicate memory, intuition, and imagination. Secrets require that we pay attention to appearances that run parallel to consciousness beneath which lie mechanisms that may surface and manifest themselves openly or through signs that we must decipher. All the novel's action occurs around the murder of la Bruja at the beginning, with suspicion falling on all the characters, each of whom hides their participation in events for their own reasons and sometimes from themselves. Gossip is fueled by a substrate that is rich and viscous in suggestions and dissimulations. Each chapter explores a different character's secrets, or a few characters who are tightly connected and whose connections to the facts are partially revealed. But the secret is also embedded in the text's nerve center, in the very figure of la Bruja who embodies it. So, occultism—the science of the occult, of mystery and of what is deemed to be forbidden and diabolic—is the element that moves the fictional mechanisms. In this sense, La Matosa is the quintessential unspeakable place, and la Bruja the figure that embodies a penetration that is concealed by realities that are hidden from public view. But if la Bruja was the center of simulation and collective farce in life, her death will also be the consequence of these practices that threaten to leave her murder unpunished forever.

As an aesthetic, the Baroque perfected the hall of mirrors to demonstrate how to encase secrecy and play with the tension between appearance and reality and form and content. In its own register, gothic horror exacerbated the question of deformation to transform monstrosity into something chilling in which the extra-human makes an appearance, proliferating in hidden places that obscure the secret depths of the unconscious and allegorize fears and anxieties. In both cases, decorativism serves to dramatize secrets and conceal their outlines. In the case of the grotesque, promiscuity, organic interiority, bodily humors, decomposing flesh, and repulsive acts appear at the forefront to stimulate rejection of vice, deviance, and abnormality. In a selective manner, *Temporada de huracanes* incorporates elements of these aesthetics to represent the secret of its alienation and violence. In this sense, La Matosa is the perfect setting, the scene of the crime from which the process of criminal/police "excavation" occurs, as if exploring a common grave.

Gossip is the element that unexpectedly mediates between truth and lies and between cover-up and revelation. In chapter 5 of *Witches, Witch Hunting, and Women*, Silvia Federici analyzes how gossip has traditionally been interpreted as a discordant element that supposedly destroys female sociability. In this sense, it can be understood as a discursive aberration and as a perversion of the norms of social conduct. Federici challenges this interpretation, underlining how gossip has functioned historically as an element of social cohesion, complicity, and differentiation for female society, above all in traditional and under-resourced communities. In this context, it represents a form of power that bisects both the private as well as the public spheres, connecting them in unexpected and variable ways. For patriarchal society, this asset appears to threaten not only the social order but also masculine hegemony and the rationalist, utilitarian, and theological views that characterizes it. In this sense, gossip represents a crucial component for the study of gender relations and female subaltern subjectivity, what Josefina Ludmer calls "tretas del débil" (tricks of the weak), which are used to consolidate networks of female community, creating alliances, and strengthening alternative positions to those that dominate society.[109] Because of its inorganic and spontaneous workings, gossip constitutes a type of social energy that becomes powerful in its own right and that possesses its own form of circulation and social energy. Its dissemination at the level of the lower classes forms part of what Marianne Hester calls "the feminization of poverty."[110]

As Edgardo Cozarinsky explains, gossip is simply the word-of-mouth transmission of a story that is modified each time it is told. It represents both difference and repetition. Its unstable and transitory nature is part of the dramatization of rumor and represents the staging of a subjectivity that weaves a web that covers various possible forms that advance and recede, tangle and untangle in a dynamic that draws in others as accomplices and actors into the same masquerade. As he goes on to say, the question of truth is practically unsustainable given its contextual and interpretative boundlessness: "La 'verdad', que tanta dignidad confiere a la historia, es apenas la ausencia de contradicción entre las versiones recibidas de un hecho; pero ningún hecho es inmune a la interpretación, ni puede eludir su carácter de función, cuyo valor se modifica según el contexto histórico de cada nueva lectura" (The question of "truth" that has conferred so much dignity upon history is just the absence of contradiction between different versions of a fact. However, no fact is immune to interpretation, nor can it escape its functional character in which its value shifts according to the historical context of each reading).[111]

Emerging from lower-class enclaves, as in the case of *Temporada de huracanes*, gossip provides a channel for worldviews and knowledge that has been sidelined from educated wisdom in the form of analyses and expressions that are considered more trustworthy and where the information resembles the interpretative patterns that filter, organize, and order facts. The rumors, desires, emotions, and fantasies create a hybridity that "besmirches" discourse and renders it disposable. As a practice linked to female forms of socialization, this semantic contamination characterizes the speakers' surroundings and their public persona. The person who generates or transmits gossip absorbs the untrustworthy and minor quality of their declaration. It is precisely this feminine space, devalued by patriarchal, utilitarian, and homogenizing society, to which Melchor gives voice, as if in an orchestrated version of what Rancière would call the "distribution of the sensible" to characters whose backstories and lifestyles shape their worldview since, as Marx would have it, their "social being determines their consciousness."[112]

Although male characters engage in gossip in the novel, the circulation of rumors and instability of discourse is primarily attributed to women, who in this case occupy a "contaminated" and "bewitched" social space: "It is women who 'gossip,' presumably having nothing better to do and having less access to real knowledge and information and a structural inability to construct factually based, rational discourses. Thus, gossip is an integral part of the devaluation of women's personality and work, especially domestic work, reputedly the ideal terrain on which this practice flourishes."[113] Women also assume the crucial function of producing and preserving memory. They feel responsible for keeping the voices of both the distant and the recent past alive and for transmitting them from generation to generation to contribute to the preservation of collective identity and community cohesion. Melchor develops this idea in the way she orchestrates voices, affect, and stories to make the construction of orality a central part in the creation of the fictional world of the novel.

According to Federici, we are currently witnessing an escalation of violence against women that can be attributed to the power of globalized capital that seeks to recolonize the world through the reappropriation of natural resources and human labor. Federici posits that this proposition can only be achieved through attacking women since it is they who are responsible for the reproduction of communities, the care of the land, and the resistance to the exploitation of resources and the dissolution of families. The production of new forms of appropriation (redistribution of lands, natural resources, and imaginaries) through strategies directed at privatization, ecological devastation and deregulated labor, violence against women, and real and symbolic "witch hunts" send a message to both communities and the world concerning new forms of hegemony and marginalization that are in accord with globalizing designs. According to the author, in this context:

> The attack on women comes above all from capital's need to destroy what it cannot control and degrade what it most needs for its reproduction.... Witch-hunting in all its different forms is also a powerful means to destroy

communal relations, injecting the suspicion that underneath the neighbor, the friend, the lover, hides another person, lusting for power, sex, wealth, or simply wanting to commit evil deeds.[114]

It is significant that *Temporada de huracanes* is able to articulate these concerns in its presentation of a hyper-emotional, excessive, lugubrious, and forceful world which is simultaneously residual and productive and where evil is not primarily concentrated in the figures of the narcos, or in extractivism or in contemporary forms of primitive accumulation, privatization and the exploitation of labor (all of which lurk in the novel's background) but rather in the scams of a super-sexualized woman who is herself the product of systemic violence and who tries to control the status quo through the magic of radical transgression and difference.

In his study of the body through the lens of gossip and abjection in Melchor's novel, Marcos Eduardo Ávalos Reyes identifies the latter as one of the three elements together with filth and corpses that lead to the creation of a "texto putrefacto en el que tanto los personajes como las formas narrativas edifican una poética de lo abyecto" (a putrefying text in which both the characters and the narrative forms construct a poetics of abjection).[115] He explains that several critics agree that "la narración como fosa donde, entre más excavas, más voces se hacen presentes" (the narrative is like a grave where the more you dig the more voices you uncover).[116] As he astutely notes, gossip creates the sensation of a rotating and plural narrator, a voice that proliferates like a malignant cell that invades the body of the text.[117] The course of the novel dismantles the narrative structure, leaving in its place large dialogues made up of details, descriptions, fragments, snippets of stories, inferences in search of a subject, subjects in search of connections, collusions, betrayals, and pleasures that threaten the literary, cognitive, and epistemological totalization and instead allow it to split into infinite paths toward meaning. The kingdom of difference attacks the unified body of modernity's meaning and its dregs corrode history's living organism, displaying its remains as if the gaze of Benjamin's angel spied the ruins of the present while turning toward the past. The constant revisiting of baroque poetics during modernity has been characterized by this virulence as if it were a mechanism for witnessing the chaotic multiplicity of The One who, plagued by colonial ghosts, shatters in postcolonial society. Contradictions such as love and sacrifice, torture and desire, magic, and reason, good and evil, community cohesion and individual disaggregation, identity and difference coexist in society both complementing and resisting each other.

Gossip constantly reappropriates meaning and recycles popular imaginaries. As an alternative to lettered discourse, and lacking in the fixity and authority of writing, gossip liberates the collective unconsciousness and the imagination that traverses everyday life. But gossip is not unique, and there are other similar but equally unstable similar forms in which a relationship to truth is also negotiated, albeit in a different way. Testimonial literature, for example, possesses the same directionality since it presents itself as a faithful account of a witness who establishes a point of view from which an event draws meaning and public recognition. This narrative material makes up the chapters that gives voice to characters with very different stories and psychologies such as Yesenia, Norma, Brando, and Luismi. They frequently bear witness to events in which they participated or witnessed, and they inject their impressions, assessments, lies, assumptions, and distortions into the narrative. Because gossip says more about the person who gossips rather than the person who is gossiped about, the advantage it possesses in the novel is its ability to offer information indirectly and cryptically about the characters' desires, fears, and frustrations that bring to light things that would otherwise remain buried.

The decoding that can be done of the characters' stories in *Temporada de huracanes* resembles the interpretation of nightmares or access to the mental state of a hypnotized subject. This entrancing effect, also an attribute of the Baroque, succeeds in using the decorativism of language or images to *derealize*. In this sense, language is exceptionally opaque since it reveals nothing. Instead, like a dirty window, it calls attention to itself, hiding what it's supposed to reveal.

Reinforcing the novel's oral tendency, chapter 7 comprises four long paragraphs that all begin with the expression "Dicen que" that situates the story in an ambiguous and uncertain space. This aspect recalls the famous beginning of Jorge Luis Borges's short story "La intrusa" which begins: "Dicen (lo cual es improbable) que la historia fue referida por Eduardo" (People say [but this is unlikely] that the story was first told by Eduardo), and where the narration resides in an uncertain zone between oral discourse and the writing that retrieves and reworks it.[118] Melchor constantly underscores the importance of orality in her work and her anti-academic style comes across as having been directly informed by everyday imaginaries and speech. In other words, it stands as an enunciative form that is always subordinated to the subtexts that precede it.

The litany-like effect of the repetition of "dicen que" (they say) serves to emphasize the content but also to highlight the idea of a floating narration that is possible, probable, and plausible but not necessarily true. This is orality's fluctuation, the discourse of a world that is not the literary, an unfixed discourse that is nonetheless richly immediate although perceived by some to be more primitive and ephemeral than the written word. But what we find in *Temporada de huracanes* is a "secondary orality," embedded in the writing and absorbed and coopted by the literary discourse. With this litany Melchor unearths La Matosa's fictional imaginary, its provincial character, its alienation, its existence at the margins of official culture where it dwells in the territory of belief, superstition, and experience. This "secondary orality" poses a cognitive question but also represents an exercise of memory on the part of the narrator involved in the act of narrating "from within" the collective imagination:

> They say she never really died, because witches don't go without a fight. They say that, at the last minute, just before those kids stabbed her, she transformed into something else; a lizard or a rabbit. . . . They say there was no shortage of people who entered that house looking for the treasure after her death. . . . They say the place the hot, that it won't be long before they send in the marines to restore order in the region. They say the heat's driven the locals crazy . . . and that the hurricane season's coming hard, that it must be bad vibes. . . . They say that's why the women are on edge, especially in La Matosa. That's what the women in town say: there is no treasure in there, no gold or silver or diamonds or anything more than a searing pain that refuses to go away.[119]

In the chapter's last lines, the reader discovers that the women, with their marginal and residual voices, have created the rumors and premonitions and spread them freely and anonymously through the fictional world. Hearsay, rumor, and gossip form a cohesive substance that surrounds the community and that precariously but clearly unites it in a feeling of grief for the primal and suffering part of all those who die with la Bruja rather than for her herself. The narrator's words shape the chaos found in the literary hurricane that the writing captures.

Regarding the relationship between irrationality and literature, Italo Calvino suggests: "It is probably not pushing things too far to connect the functions of shamanism and witchcraft documented in ethnology and folklore with the catalogue of images contained in literature. On the contrary, I think that the deepest rationality behind every literary operation has to be sought out in the anthropological needs to which it corresponds."[120] In this vein, Melchor's work embodies literature's inherent ability to bewitch, conjure up fear, and reveal content that instrumental reason suppresses and denies.

(ANTI)MODERNITY AND COMMUNITY IN LA MATOSA

In conclusion, I'd like to emphasize two aspects of Melchor's work that I have implicitly emphasized throughout this study. The first is connected to Melchor's critique of modernity. From the perspective of language, *Temporada de huracanes* makes a claim against modernity's exclusions and inequalities that are implemented not only in peripheral spaces but also in hybrid societies marked by conflict between globalization and regionalism, between tradition and progress, and colonialism and postcolonialism. Although this position might seem to be connected to binaries such as center/periphery, at the same time it introduces polarities that have not yet been discarded in favor of new conceptualizations more suited for our globalized times. In this case, these binaries serve to highlight socioeconomic, political, and cultural antagonisms that are, to a large degree, unreconcilable, especially if we consider the weakened and corrosive condition of the still persistent State and its institutions in social development at both the national and transnational level. Binaries such as north/south, capital/province, city/countryside, along with antagonisms pertaining to class, race, and gender, still serve as support for a nuanced analysis of social conflict and for understanding the fluidity of our postmodern and postcolonial society.

In this sense, *Temporada de huracanes* is illustrative of the type of sociocultural upheaval that is directly connected to manifestations of a virulently nihilistic society in search of other forms of social consciousness, such as necropolitical experiences and a collective engagement with death and systemic violence. The baroque language, the privileging of orality, the employment of profane language and shocking scenes, the creation of marginalized characters, the appeal to simulacrum, deception, deceptive appearances and perspectivism all serve to upset the modern bourgeois order in both its liberal and conservative manifestations and impugn in and of themselves the hegemony of high culture (although it could be argued that the novel qua novel plays a double and duplicitous game in this regard). To understand the storylines that Melchor develops, we clearly cannot bypass the social historical context of Veracruz and its region, its colonial antecedents as well as its recently burgeoning economic productivity of the last few decades, due to oil field exploration.

Both central and neighboring areas of the port city of Veracruz have suffered the onslaught of cosmopolitanism and neoliberalism as well as of external imaginaries resulting from political and economic dependency and the penetration of European and Anglo-Saxon models into traditional societies. In addition, we must also consider the toll of drug trafficking, extractivism, corruption, and other forms of organized crime that, with the tacit agreement or, in many cases, outright complicity of the State and economies and culture of the region and the rest of Latin America, have devastated both Mexico as well as Latin America as a whole. Precarity, insecurity and State abdication have thus impacted society and the ensuing social corrosion provides undeniable evidence of the breakdown of the social pact and the gutting of its corresponding political life. Modernity's strategies are superimposed upon traditional subject matter, ancestral customs, and atavistic rites and repress and consign everyday traditions to the grave, shattering the delicate surface of the collective sensorium.

Following the text's allegorical focus, this content finds an escape valve in la Bruja's occult surroundings that facilitates the emergence of the repressed and bears witness to its erotic and thanatotic force. The latter expresses itself as a carnivalesque dynamic of disguises, simulacra, and inversions of the unstable social order. Using literature to assume a prominent role in society, the axiological pillars upholding the status quo are shaken by the snarled and heaving mass of instincts and drives that overtake its libidinal positionality. The lettered ritual of the poetics of textuality reveals how abjection functions as a societal blight with its own aesthetic and countercultural energy. Modernity's failed promises collapse under the re-enchantment of the world, roiling enlightened rationality, the myth of progress and social order, the ideologemes of citizenship and the social pact, and replacing them with a world rooted in mass graves, decapitations, land grabs, and biopolitical manipulation.

The text's marked negativity lends itself to a less idiosyncratic and more technical interpretation than the novel suggests on a first reading, revealing that the novel represents the negative (in photographic terms) of what Bolívar Echeverría calls "capitalist modernity" (to differentiate it from other possible ways of bringing the modern project to fruition).[121] Some critics have identified what they believe to be a symbolic concession to brightness in the character of el Abuelo, who speaks to the dead, seeing him as a possible way out of the hole in which society finds itself. Rather than viewing this little light as a ray of hope, we should see it as the glimpse of a train that is barreling down the track at top speed.

The second aspect worth highlighting in *Temporada de huracanes* is Melchor's treatment of the concept of community that, from Max Weber on, has been the focus of studies in sociology and politics. The question of community has caught the attention of contemporary society's philosophical thought, particularly after the Cold War, given the readjustments in power relations at the international level, changes to the nation-State, as well as migrations and other social and political phenomena.[122]

Using the concept developed by Leela Gandhi in her book *Affective Communities: Anticolonial Thought, Fin-de-Siècle Radicalism, and the Politics of Friendship*, we see that, despite this charge of negative energy, the social space created in *Temporada de huracanes* around the figure of la Bruja provides an environment of compensatory and affective solidarity in which feelings, emotions, passions, and desires are expressed and even heightened, creating a microclimate that counteracts the experience of exclusion and social alienation felt by the inhabitants of La Matosa.[123] The "affective community" that arises and develops in the novel absorbs individualities that, at the same time, express themselves and dissolve into a form of deranged freedom that corresponds to the dismantling of the social fabric.

Together with promiscuity and perversion, a ludic debauchery unfolds around the figure of la Bruja in which demonism, vulnerability, solidarity, and aggression combine giving rise to emotional tensions and relational complexities that intensify and culminate in murder. In fact, the murder is the only moment capable of absorbing the narrative crescendo. To sexuality's force, Melchor adds the myth of the hidden treasure (perhaps they are two sides of the same coin), thus articulating complementary forms of symbolic capital whose value resides in their potentiality: what sex can release and what money can buy. This virtuality, in other words the promise of a potential existence, is one of the elements that brings the anomalous community of La Matosa together and allows it to flourish in the intense spaces created by the failure of the social contract.

In Veracruz, "the affective community" arises in an autonomous and self-contained space, disassociated from dominant norms. As Jean-Luc Nancy indicates, the community must exist in counterpoint to the discourse around work, understood as necessary productivity, to create its own terms of reference, define its spatial coordinates, its use of time and the nature of its connections.[124] Neither productive (in the work sense) nor reproductive (in the procreative sense) la Bruja's affective community features characteristics that distinguish it and alienate it from dominant social norms. At the community's center, its productivity stems from unceasing libidinal flows that replace the values of a modernity that has cast aside the social excess its projects of progress and citizenship have failed to absorb with debauchery, clandestine practices and alliances based on concealment and complicity. This community's habitus locates itself in the promiscuous cave, the garbage dump, swampland and underbrush, backwoods, grime, detritus, human cracks and fissures, herbs, and potions—in other words, in witchcraft—which itself can be seen as the epicenter of marginality in which modernity yields and instinct rules.

At the beginning of *The Inoperative Community*, Nancy explains that the most powerful evidence of the contemporary world is the dissolution or dislocation of community since, along with the myth of democracy and communism, it no longer provides a possible alternative. The crises of these categories begs the question about the origins and constitutive elements of community and its regulatory and organizational social function. According to Nancy, at modernity's beginnings, the notion of individuality was fundamental for the articulation of totality and for sustaining questions of collective identity as principles of cohesion and social organization. The problem was always how to institutionally reconcile the conflicts that existed at society's heart or how to manage the relationship between homogeneity/heterogeneity and identity/alterity as well as the plurality of projects at the center of society with the principal problem stemming from the activation of mutually incompatible individualities and the use of State violence as a form of social regulation.

According to Carlos Roa Hewstone and Vania Albornoz, at the end of the Cold War, with the elimination of the East/West binary, the need to "desplazar la noción misma de frontera" (displace the very notion of border) and rethink dualities such as identity/Otherness and friend/enemy in the face of the challenges of globalization and the emergence of new forms of hegemony and marginality arose.[125] Beginning in the 1980s, the dynamics of migration also destabilized the relationship between inside and outside, exposing a world of real and symbolic borders that are both mobile and internalized as well as boundaries that are displaced to the nation's furthest limits (the use of transnational customs systems for example).

All this radically transforms the theme of community and reinforces the mythical notion of democratic space, suggesting that the latter is the only political sphere that can fulfill the promise of well-being and justice. Democracy has been reinforced as a myth that is based on self-anointed values that transform the conception of community into a simulacrum that is disconnected from ideas of the nation, State, country, or national identity. As Nancy explains, the individual is itself a mythical invention, and not the reverse. For the French philosopher, in contemporary society we cannot now speak of communal existence but rather of a "being-in-common." The community as we know it has become a non-operational form as such, desired in the abstract, never fulfilled, absent, and constantly imagined and sought after. In other words, it has become a form of utopia that is simultaneously old and new.[126]

Against the tradition of liberal thought that sees community as a limitation that excludes Otherness, Nancy postulates community as an open and inclusive category that emphasizes being-in-common or being-with (others) and co-existence and intersubjective relationships.[127] The world of la Bruja is undoubtedly a dislocated and agitated space. But at the same time, it functions according to its own "logic," as space of solidarity that welcomes and rejects sex workers, drifters, abused women, young men frenziedly exploring their sexuality and machismo—all of whom are trying their best to hide their traumas, weaknesses, frustrations, and pain. Obviously, none of this serves to glorify or obscure the inherent perversity of this "affective community" founded on the basis of pathology, derangement, and deviation. It does underscore, however, its role as an alternative landscape to productivist, alienating and exclusionary principles of modernity that base themselves on the marginalization of the many and the privileging of the few. Nor does this imply an emergent social or political conscience that could orient itself toward an emancipatory horizon since the condition of being subjects of La Matosa's characters has been made impossible by the deterioration of interpersonal connections and the systemic violence that controls them.[128]

Within this context, la Bruja occupies a corporeal place and a visceral site, both viscous and foul-smelling, where life is degraded like a death drive, a destructive hurricane, an implosion, or contagion. For the same reason, and as in *Falsa liebre*, it is also a highly emotionalized space, radically queer, anti-conventional, experimental and also solitary and dispersed where difference flourishes and despair wears its heart on its sleeve. The nuclear community that surrounds la Bruja evokes Nancy's idea that the social community can only emerge from a space that is neither regulated nor pragmatic. Communitarianism instead alludes to a way of experimenting with society, in accordance with what Blanchot calls the "unworking" of what work entails, an unfolding of the self and of the collective that eludes the disciplining of labor.[129] In this social experimentation, time and action are interrupted and fragmented to give way to an anti-productivist *jouissance* that, in *Temporada de huracanes*, is both self-destructive and evil.

CHAPTER 3
Valeria Luiselli
The Unbearable Lightness of Being

Displacements, *Dispositifs*, and Gestures

Papeles falsos: The Exoskeleton and the Seeing Eye
    The Map and the Hole
    Liminality and Name Dropping

Los ingrávidos: Owen and I (or Vice Versa?)
    The Metaphyiscs of Presence and the Absence of the Self
    Mobility and Fixity
    Fabricating the Model: Translation and Simulacrum

The Irritating *Historia de mis dientes*
    Collectionism and the Aura of the Object
    The Auction House as Negotiation of Meaning

Los niños perdidos (un ensayo en cuarenta preguntas)
    The Migrant's Via Crucis and the Theater of Belonging
    Microhistory and Literature

Lost Children Archive
    Word and Silence; Body and Specter
    Experience, Archive, and Narration
    Border Semiotics and Autofiction
    Luiselli's Use of Children
    Elegaic Discourse

Born in 1983 and resident in the US, Valeria Luiselli has become one of the most successful voices of the most recent generation of Mexican writers. One of the central traits of her work is her transnational perspective, gesturing toward the negotiation of the distance that separates her US-produced work from Mexican national culture, much of which takes center stage in her writing. The vast repertoire of Mexican literature appears in Luiselli's texts, filtered through a sensibility marked by multicultural experiences, questions of gender, and a clear connection to a large corpus of writers, works, and cultural spaces of modernity that she reactivates in her narrative.

The stories of the travels that shaped her childhood as the daughter of a diplomat, which she continues to reference as an adult, locate her in different contexts (Costa Rica, South Korea, South Africa, France, New York). She integrates this element, indicative of a social privilege inaccessible to most of her contemporaries, into her public image. To some degree, her multicultural experience contributes to an explanation of a certain disconnect between her aesthetic project and Mexican national culture and, on the flip side, to the greater success her work has garnered in international arenas that are more receptive of her way of dialoguing with both literary tradition and the social problems of her time. More so than is the case of other Mexican writers, she clearly inscribes her work in a convergence zone of different interpretive communities, each with disparate expectations and reading experiences.

In effect, the recognition Luiselli's work has garnered in Europe, North America, and some Latin American countries provides evidence of the swift and positive incorporation of her literary production into both imaginaries and cultural markets. Through her journalistic work in *Letras libres*, the *New York Times*, and *El País*, as well as in literary journals from different countries, Luiselli has made a name for herself in many different spaces thanks to a nimble prose that is capable of sustaining dialogue at different cultural levels.[1] Viewed as one of the writers who has contributed to a renewal of Latin American literature, Luiselli's texts engage with the Western canon, particularly that of Mexico, through the implementation of a varied register of compositional and representational techniques and strategies.

Continuously evoked and summoned in her writing, Mexico's literary and cultural history acquires renewed verve. In her fluid and accessible prose, high-culture references co-exist comfortably with the domestic sphere, the passage of urban life, and a creative output that persistently returns to the imaginaries of modernity. The inconsistent forms and levels of incorporation and distancing between these domains, the opportune and fleeting affective approaches to themes, the insistent intellectual characteristic of her topics, and the levity of her involvement in the problems that her fiction sets out are all perhaps the traits that have most clearly distinguished her work up until now. What follows represents my attempt to capture some of the lines along which she has taken her poetics.

DISPLACEMENTS, *DISPOSITIFS*, GESTURES

In a perhaps overly deliberate attempt to create a literary terrain that clearly and distinctly diverges from a Mexican literary canon attached to more traditional forms, (auto)biographical elements switch from one text to another, from one register to the next, surpassing the borders of fiction and testimonial literature, connecting visual images and sound recordings to the phonic and semantic texture of the word, and linking photography to textuality. However, Luiselli's membership of what Ángel Rama dubbed the "ciudad letrada" or "lettered city" seems to be one of her work's most obvious hallmarks.[2]

In effect, Luiselli has carefully laid out the scope of her work through its interaction with tradition and with certain omnipresent themes such as border/migration and gender. The latter topics are a constant presence in literature written in the US and also feature prominently in contemporary Mexican writing. In her work, biofiction, intertextuality, genre hybridity, the combination of symbolic registers, the fictionalization of historical personages, shifting narrators, the incorporation of fantasy elements, road literature, documentalism, and pastiche all co-exist and confer variety upon a world that conceives of itself as decentered and nomadic but is nonetheless in persistent search of a center.

Although none of the aforementioned concepts are new, their insistent presence transforms them into *dispostifs* or apparatuses, that is, into organizing elements for the power of the text, which is presented as a heterogeneous set of implements and implementations that belong both to the realm of *the said* as well as *the unsaid*.[3] These discursive practices—in general, the use of apparatuses—point to a willingness to open the text to other forms of rationality and link it to nondiscursive forms of semiotic behavior. In Luiselli's case, for example, these variants point to her repeated forays into urban space as well as her mobilization of cultural domains (museums, cemeteries, the canonical register of high culture within literature, music, paintings). These practices gesture to a search for new forms of meaning and intelligibility and imply the exhaustion of both knowledge and forms of representation and interpretation that no longer channel content that supposedly exceeds traditional models. As a network that produces meaning, the *dispositif* (in this case, the appeal to a cross-media set of procedures, strategies, and leitmotifs) indicates a highly relational dialogue that is essential for the production of meaning. In the different sections of this study, I will investigate the significance that this discursive dynamic acquires and its repercussions for the generation of meaning.

In addition to the elements mentioned earlier, Luiselli's work orients itself toward thematic and compositional directions that clearly dialogue with some of the paths followed by Mexican literature's wide and varied production. Present in many of Luiselli's texts—even in those that are clearly the most fictionalized—is an interest in the *crónica*, or chronicle, that forms a key part of Mexican literature. Themes such as identity, belonging, real and symbolic borders, urban space, childhood, citizenship, and travel come together to form an evident thematic and ideological nucleus in her work. The problem of the self, self-recognition, and personal genealogy all make up facets of an image that is permanently undone and redone and that, from the perspective of gender, sexuality, rationality, and social interactions, unfolds and refolds itself.

The chronicle's style lends itself not only to multiple incursions into the surrounding world—extending in Luiselli's case to different latitudes—but also to channeling comments and impressions (subjective, ideological, affective) that highlight the world from where the story comes. Luiselli's penchant for the essay demonstrates her interest in the presentation of ideas and perspectives that allow her to influence public opinion and insert herself into cultural spaces. This trait will also emerge in an intellectualized narrative that she clearly inscribes within a transnational dimension.

In interviews, essays, and news stories, she has supplied a large number of comments that offer useful clues for reading her work, and that can be interpreted as a desire to control the production/reception cycle and put a personal and definitive stamp on the way her work enters the cultural marketplace. The facts of her personal narrative that circulate in the media and constitute the projection of the author's poetic self come together to construct a prismatic image of elements of class and gender in which aspects such as cosmopolitanism, multiculturalism, intellectualism, postnationalism, maternity, access to material resources, cult of personality, referentialism, a fondness for citation, observation from a distance, and the desire to put a personal seal on the literary space into which she ventures all stand out.

In *Volver a la modernidad: Genealogías de la literatura mexicana de fin de siglo*, Oswaldo Zavala captures best the emergence of Valeria Luiselli's creative and professional image, analyzing her exploration within the framework of neoliberal politics, explaining:

> Lusielli's work normalizes the coordinates of neoliberalism to the point where they disappear precisely because no traces remain of the now redundant national paradigm, ... which not only delocalizes the author but also allows her to inhabit in a legitimate way new spaces of cultural meaning beyond the geopolitical Mexican setting. Her work is built on a deliberate connection between references to high culture and the author's own life situated in a single postnational plane where Mexico City comfortably disappears into the folds of transnational globalization.[4]

Lusielli's work undergoes multiple displacements in a variety of ways. The author's own transnational and multicultural biography displaces her from Mexican national culture, distancing her and providing a contrast to her contemporaries' regional, provincial, or urban rootedness. Her work also undergoes a displacement from genre, which she manipulates on specific occasions to anchor her transgressive manner, along with a displacement from aesthetic styles (such as fantasy literature, realism, memoir, testimonialism, etc.) that she evokes only as brief stops on a journey to elsewhere. Displacement also occurs from high culture to which she constantly returns only to then performatively move away in an occasional and provisional manner. Finally, Luiselli's work is displaced from meaning itself, from her own writing toward the immense repertoire she evokes and assembles in her texts, since their meaning is only generated thanks to the distinguished grouping of allusion, quotations, borrowing, and recycling that form part of her fictional plots.

Paradoxically, the continuous displacement to the margins transforms this repertoire into the focal point of the text. In this sense, Luiselli's work can be considered an example of diasporic literature (an example of what I've called elsewhere "nomadic literature"), which we can define above all by its flight, its performative disregard for all kinds of rootedness, and its search for an outlying place from where to observe the real and symbolic movements of subjects that express diverse forms of voluntary or forced sedentism in ideological territories, registers, and positionings.

What I am calling here "the dynamics of the gesture" consumes a large part of the creative energy of Luiselli's poetics. Displacements, journeys, fragmentarism, spectralization, the theatricalization of the generational gesture, and the continual appeal to high-culture references and themes that connect to questions of the transnational all reveal not only the strong biographical charge that informs her methodology—and that always seem to be evoking her cosmopolitan life, which was connected to her father's diplomatic career and then her own life choices—but also the persistent metaphorizations that inspire her real and symbolic nomadic condition.

Her adoption, conscious or not, of the ideologeme of world literature connects her to postmodern (although not new) forms of the understanding of undoubtedly prestigious intellectual and creative work, from both the period of what Bolívar Echeverría calls "capitalist modernity" and of today.[5] Such a positioning allows her to withdraw selectively from national conflicts and limitations, screening some out and implying not a renunciation of this repository of themes, traditions, and connections, but instead an efficient connection between the elements selected from both this cultural archive and from the international marketplace. These elements are particularly receptive when they are exported from the periphery and are imbued with a controlled counterhegemonic, suggestive, and exotic character with respect to the centers of late capitalism. Here I am not describing a flat version of the concept of locus of enunciation but instead, on the contrary, a locus that is more ideological than geocultural, aesthetic more than biographical, liminal, beyond consciousness and premeditation, although the terms here in counterpoint maintain an indisputably fluid and permanent feedback loop.

PAPELES FALSOS: THE EXOSKELETON AND THE SEEING EYE

As the first of Valeria Luiselli's works, *Papeles falsos* puts a series of thematic and stylistic patterns into place that she will develop in subsequent publications.[6] The text is organized around the topic of displacement, specifically here around a foray through urban landscapes that have put some critics in mind of Benjamin's flâneur.[7] A journey always allows for a varied array of impressions regarding the space that is being traversed. It comments, offers observations, and makes associations that are then organized in the style of a chronicle, complemented by digressions, ideas, and annotations that connect urban space with other cultural registers and the contemporary sensorium. The model of the chronicle is highly familiar, and as we know, offers more information about the author's gaze than the reality that it observes. Heterogeneity, inequality, continuities, and contrasts converge under the chronicler's eye, and all serve to underscore modernity's scopic system according to which the visualization of progress deems the city the main landscape for promoting and exhibiting the burgeoning marketplace and the bourgeois subject that fuels it.

THE MAP AND THE HOLE

The self-celebration of the poetic "I" is at center of this book that, in this sense, seems to have been written in another era when self-reflection constituted a way of being in a stratified universe and where the world operated as a subjective mirror. The cartographic theme that appears in one way or another in the author's subsequent works, here functions as a means of articulating the book's spatiotemporal coordinates. As in a stage set, this cartographic projection theatricalizes the vicissitudes and transformations of real and imaginary characters since the urban setting presents itself as a blank page upon which pathways of bodily or intellectual movement, affective comings and goings, journeys through time, and exercises of historical memory can be traced. The observing eye is always above and outside, offering the illusion of an aerial viewpoint that controls the represented universe and freely comes and goes from the world that contains us all. The entry point to the New York cartography on display in *Papeles falsos* is both horizontal and vertical in the same way in which an aerial map offers an image that captures the idea that the observer is above the observed, encompassing and overtaking. From the outset, in the map spread out before us we perceive that "el silencio y quietud del territorio abstracto" (the silence and quietude of a spatial abstraction) puts pressure on the imagination since "sólo sobre una superficie estática y sin tiempo puede andar la mente a sus anchas" (only on a static timeless surface can the mind roam freely).[8] In a world bereft of drama, thought wanders without restraint or purpose, in an exploration of space as freedom or as tabula rasa that we can fill with our own reflection. The map serves both as spatial projection and a representation *of a place in time*. Or, as critics of cartography have pointed out, every map signals a place in history. *A place, in history*. In this case, the map indicates the place occupied by the self in its own story as well as the meaning that this positionality is allotted in the History of us all. Nostalgia, happiness, seclusion, memory, all swirl around the self that reflects on the meaning and pathways of its own sensibility, as if writing were a boomerang that leaves the subject and then returns to it after having flown over the reality of others.

Maps are thus the platform upon which we trace the movement of the subject, who traverses it, reworks it, and rearticulates it according to its own interests and experiences. Cartographic fixity provides a contrast to subjective mobility.[9] Movement and thought run parallel to the urban asphalt, to the horizontal nature of a land drained of water and flooded with human waste. With its teeming labyrinths, its acceleration, and its joyous contemporaneity, Mexico City nonetheless reveals a savage inequality and systemic violence that coexist with the devastating force of folk art and the elitism of "high culture." Unfathomable at its own level, Mexico City becomes more accessible and even representable at a distance, where it seems to dissipate: "Desde arriba, el mundo es inmenso pero asequible, como si fuera un mapa de sí mismo, una analogía más liviana y más fácil de aprehender" (Viewed from above, that world is immense but attainable, as if it were a map of itself, a lighter and more easily apprehended analogy).[10] And a few pages later: "desde la ventanilla de un avión, la ciudad de México es caso comprensible, como una representación sencilla de sí misma, a escala de la imaginación humana" (And on a clear day the city [Mexico City] is almost comprehensible—a simpler representation of itself, to the scale of the human imagination).[11]

A space of dramatic contrasts and impossible to conceal social and political conflicts, Luiselli views the megalopolis as a stage design of exotic overtones that allows the stroller, in Néstor García Canclini's words, "entrar y salir de la modernidad" (to enter and leave modernity) as if it were a revolving door.[12] The elite's nomadic tourism, radically different from the working classes, is not, however, simply a pleasurable, constant, and voluntary mobility. It also represents an epistemological uprooting that is both distanced and relativistic, a form of the social self and a way of understanding identity, the nation, and the essentialisms that nourish the official version of history and the present in Mexico. Luiselli's narrative gesture reveals itself in contrast to the idea of Mexican-ness as a static space linked to national stereotypes by substituting it for the myth of cosmopolitanism (an illusion fed by the author's own transnational experience) that is equally ideological and inflected by stereotypes of worldliness, belonging to multiple spaces and none, and an idealized rootlessness operating as a synonym of freedom.

Ideas of autonomy and free will run through the texts, defining the parameters of a subjectivity supposedly liberated from conventions and from geocultural limits. Material distance, the literary canon, New York bohemia watered down for family life, all are mediations that separate the narrator's subjectivity from internal tensions that in Luiselli's works manifest themselves in different forms, employing other devices of discursive intercalation.

References to cartography are a constant in Luiselli's work and are organized around the topic of movement and associated motifs such as getting lost in the city; territoriality; belonging and its deconstruction into various forms such as debris, vacant lots, between-spaces, ghostly forms or individuals; and spectrality in general as a way of being with the real/reality.

Evocation is also a way of addressing the question of the residual: what remains of former presences and what memory can bring to the present. In *Papeles falsos*, the evocation of the Russian poet Joseph Brodsky (1940–1996), winner of the 1987 Nobel Prize in Literature, contrasts with the anonymous graves in "Mancha de agua" ("Flying Home") and also, in a further exploration of the theme of spatiality "La habitación y media de Joseph Brodsky" ("Joseph Brodsky's Room and a Half"). In the Venetian cemetery of San Michele, Luiselli locates Brodsky's grave, a space that, imagining it as if seen from an aerial view, she compares with "un enorme libro de tapas duras" (a huge hardcover book) in which the words are "esqueletos en descomposición" (decomposing skeletons).[13]

Beginning with its title, *Papeles falsos* reveals four characteristics of Luiselli's writing: *fragmentation, banalization, referentialism*, and the *simulacrum*.[14] As regards the first, we see the *segmentation* of physical and narrative space in the description of walks, notes, references, quotations, and impressions that the author articulates in her books as a summation of elements that form variable groups whose primary function is to situate, at the center of this assemblage, the subjectivity that is established as a character of its own story (or, alternatively, a trans-textual character created by the writer). Secondly, *banalization* is a method that Luiselli uses as a way of self-assessing her texts, in a rhetorical gesture of false modesty. Neither articles, dispatches, studies, or chronicles, her "papeles" or "papers" attempt to communicate spontaneity, a lack of solemnity in engaging with the literary, indifference toward the process of professionalization, as well as novelty and insouciance. Formal fragmentation collides with the totalizing impulse that appears as a nostalgic undertone in her writing. We see this impulse in her desire to write herself into the historical and cultural continuity of the Western canon, not only in terms of Mexican literature, but also into the best cultural tradition modernity has to offer. To achieve this objective, her principal strategy is the obviously unilateral bond she creates with authors who are not only prestigious but are also praised for their intellectual qualities and who seem to be the (imaginary) *ideal readers* of her fiction.

Similarly, the constant referentialism in her texts reveals a process of appropriation and recycling of heterogeneous sources that create a network of connections that supposedly lend prestige to the author/reader/consumer of high culture, creating a proliferation of sources which seem indispensable to Luiselli's writing. This galaxy of readings, urban references, and ways of approaching the cultural product are simultaneously celebrated and banalized, as way of imprinting a casual tone, of insouciant familiarity, regarding the material being used, which could be classified as either primary or secondary depending on how we interpret the author's relationship to the texts. What has been called "the art of quotation" consists precisely in the configuration of a context (perhaps metafictional) that surrounds, protects, and authorizes the narrative voice inscribing it into a controlled universe (a bubble) that connects her virtually to her surroundings, isolating her from its harshness and upheavals.

Finally, the theme of the simulacrum surfaces everywhere. It will be central in her next novel, *Los ingrávidos*, but also appears in *Papeles falsos*.[15] Falsity functions as the flip side to legitimacy and truth. Beginning with the title of the work, the idea of falsity underpins the deliberate rejection of any regime of truth, not just because the book's fragments belong to the world of fiction, imagination, or fantasy but also because "falsity" is put in the service of forging an alternative path: the production of versions of the real that cannot be confronted with anything except themselves. The theme of the simulacrum is connected to the fabrication of gadgets, artefacts, or figurations that, preserving a close relationship with what is represented, nonetheless exceeds its limits.

Regarded as one of postmodernity's key devices, the simulacrum—which emerged in response to the exhaustion of the original's auratic value and then as a reaction to the devaluing of the copy—brings an element of mimicry and sarcasm to the poetics of reproducibility. The replica succeeds in overtaking its model, adding a dose of parodic intentionality and an epistemic proposition that primary reality lacks. The book's final essay, entitled "Papeles falsos: La enfermedad de la ciudadanía," (Permanent residence: The disease of citizenship), offers one of the clearest examples of how this operates in Luiselli's work.[16] Here, the narrator explains how, having falsely claimed to be the mistress of an Italian friend, she obtains a residency permit in Venice that allows her to access free medical care. If we understand "papeles falsos" (fake papers) in its obvious meaning as the securing of rights associated with citizenship, the theme connects us to the drama of so-called "illegal" immigration that has caused and continues to cause persecutions that often end in death for those who are unsuccessful in deploying the same tactics Luiselli celebrates in her book as a trivial and ingenious gesture.

Along these lines, we come directly to the heart of the question of class that reveals an immense rift between the narrator's social standing and that of her Mexican compatriots in their multiple mobilizations across borders that, for them, are less friendly and less porous than those crossed by tourists or by those who know how to bend the rules. The difference between transnationalism for pleasure and that which is brought on by situations of precarity and violence, among others, allows us to reevaluate the meaning of literature and the possible forms of the reception of the literary text in a country such as Mexico that constitutes one of the most pivotal centers of migratory struggles and significant abuse of human rights. Similar reflections present themselves in the face of Luiselli's romanticization of *relingos*, interstitial spaces or vacant lots, and where the dynamics of urbanization seem to have been suspended and, in many cases, are occupied by unhoused people, "residual," "disposable" or "supernumerary" beings. Luiselli imagines these areas as ideal spaces to be filled with words, images, and cultural references.

Acknowledging the intricacies that always accompany the processes of metaphorization, and the transfer of content drawn from "reality" to literature, our current horizon of social experience seems to have reduced the space hitherto consecrated to poetic license, and simultaneously widened the margins of an absent but always necessary social conscience. When is a metaphor interpreted too literally? Beyond its poetic value, should we just accept that it lacks meaning? Can the phantom of literature take the "desert of the real" by storm or should this vast empty space (*relingo*) be filled with other content?

In this regard, in *Simulacra and Simulacrum* Jean Baudrillard uses Jorge Luis Borges's famous text "Del rigor en la ciencia," itself a rewriting of Lewis Carroll's reflections on cartography, to introduce the topic:

> If once we were able to view the Borges fable in which the cartographers of the Empire draw up a map so detailed that it ends up covering the territory exactly (the decline of the Empire witnesses the fraying of this map, little by little, and its fall into ruins, though some shreds are still discernible in the deserts—the metaphysical beauty of this ruined abstraction testifying to a pride equal to the Empire and rotting like a carcass, returning to the substance of the soil, a bit as the double ends by being confused with the real

through aging)—as the most beautiful allegory of simulation, this fable has now come full circle for us, and possesses nothing but the discrete charm of second-order simulacra.[17]

For Baudrillard, the simulacrum points to a hyperreality that reflects the weakening of the certainties Borges foresaw and that Lyotard demonstrated, and to the liquidation of meaning of the categories of modernity (nation, identity, belong, consensus, totality, utopia). This hyperreality underscores this emptiness's conspicuous existence, in which the frayed threads of the social fabric reveal that residue, fragmentation, dispersion, and discontinuity constitute the keys of a present in which what remains is only simulacra and the aesthetic anguish of a lost totality:

> Abstraction today is no longer that of the map, the double, the mirror or the concept. Simulation is no longer that of a territory, a referential being or a substance. It is the generation by models of a real without origin or reality: a hyperreal. The territory no longer precedes the map, nor survives it. Henceforth, it is the map that precedes the territory—precession of simulacra—it is the map that engenders the territory and if we were to revive the fable today, it would be the territory whose shreds are slowly rotting across the map. It is the real, and not the map, whose vestiges subsist here and there, in the deserts which are no longer those of the Empire, but our own. The desert of the real itself.[18]

LIMINALITY AND NAME DROPPING

Regarding the narrator's construction as a passer-by, as discussed by several critics, Patrick O'Connor opportunely mentions that great protagonist of modernity, the flâneur, as a figure of double consciousness with respect to the marketplace. The flâneur locates him/herself within the paradise of commodities as a possible consumer (at least as a visual or virtual consumer) when he/she is in fact searching for a buyer in this space of exchange, appropriation, and profit. As Benjamin explains, "In the flâneur, the intelligentsia sets foot in the marketplace—ostensibly to look around but in truth to find a buyer."[19] The substantial difference between the cultural context of modernity, described by Benjamin, and modernism as a cultural and aesthetic movement wielding a profound influence over Western literature is that, as Oswaldo Zavala correctly points out, between then and now, neoliberal transformations have radically changed the literary world.

The scope of Luiselli's engagement with modernism glosses over such differences, creating an artificial continuity between moments that are very different in terms of development and the commodification of the symbolic product. Although Luiselli attempts to create distance via a demystifying attitude channeled through irony and the irreverent use of canonical names and personalities with which she justifies her appropriation of a prestigious corpus (that cannot however be assimilated to contemporary conditions), her literary project's approximation to and identification with a prestigious part of Western cultural history persists.

The theme of insertion in the market connects, in turn, to her use of referentialism, which can be understood as the dominant gesture of creating a constant support network of names, works, texts and other types of literary references to stimulate her prose and to foster superficial associations between other authors' ideas and her own writing. Without resulting in intertexuality, this tiresomely persistent gesture in Luiselli's writing provides evidence of intellectual insecurity. In this sense, this method constitutes the *exoskeleton* of her writing: an exterior framework that undergirds it, begging the question as to what would happen if this exterior reinforcement, from which the author deploys her digressive and impressionistic repertoire, were dismantled. Perhaps we can think of this device as a "servo-armature," which copies the natural support structure of an arthropod using robotization or other technological applications. And perhaps the techniques Luiselli employs to build both her poetic I and her literary expressions resemble this type of prothesis that, in a crustacean, helps with its fossilization. However, seen within these parameters and for a reader who tolerates or even welcomes referentialism, Luiselli's prose can be viewed as nimble and fluid, albeit undoubtedly repetitive and inconsistent.

Despite the name-dropping that characterizes this book—and in general all of Luiselli's work—she fails to mention, for example, Ángel Rama's now classic work *La ciudad letrada*, which discusses the institutionalization of culture in Latin America from colonial times to the twentieth century.[20] In my opinion, the most obvious explanation for this absence is that she concentrates her intellectual nomadism on highlighting all the authors revered by the intellectual class, those who captured the imagination of the lettered elite, not because of their critical profile, but rather because of their creative and innovative insertion in certain areas of transnational cultural history. Secondly, Luiselli tacitly puts herself forward as an exponent of postmodern culture, someone who gestures toward modernity with an affected and cavalier nostalgia for certain acclaimed traditions that are sometimes obscured in contemporary culture. The author/character in her texts believes and disbelieves, fragments, and totalizes, assembles and disassembles, celebrates and trivializes. It is exactly in the between-space of these operations where we see flourish this double consciousness of "global Mexican," mother and intellectual, wife and lover, immersed and distracted that we find at the center of all her texts. Benjamin, Brodsky, Stravinsky, Visconti, Pound, Pessoa, Le Corbusier, Steiner, Cioran are all safe bets to "adorn" Luiselli's texts.

In *Papeles falsos*, the different settings (Mexico City, New York City, Venice) follow one after another and, within them, the journeys illustrate the persistence of certain spaces that underscore the idea of a slightly eccentric and uncommon subjectivity. What the author herself calls "turismo necrológico" (necro-intellectual tourism) takes the author through cemeteries where, just as in the city, circuitous paths lead her to unintended places.[21] The view from above, that brings the aerial map into being, metaphorizes real or desired exteriority or what we might call the strategic point of view from where the observer's vision is total, or at least panoramic, without being seen to belong to the observed world. The same thing occurs in cemeteries, museums and, according to Luiselli, on bike rides where the person becomes invisible, and their uninvolved observations possess only a fleeting presence.

Additional evidence of Luiselli's hallmark modernist affectation is provided by her interest in ghosts, books displayed as an indication of individual identity, aestheticism, and the search for a reader connected to the fictional world, as well as the centrality of a gaze that constructs both the object and the subject that projects it from different planes. The cemetery is like a book and language is a territory that is both rich and arid. Opinions on both language and literature reproduce these ideas in formulaic and quotable phrases, using cliches that rob the prose of its density: "aprender un idioma es un primer destierro, exilio involuntario y mudo hacia el interior de esa nada en el corazón de todo lo que nombramos.... Aprender a hablar es darse cuenta, poco a poco, de que no podemos decir nada sobre nada" (learning a language is a first banishment, an involuntary, silent exile to the interior of that nothing in the heart of everything that we name.... Learning to speak is realizing, little by little, that we can say nothing about anything).[22] Rereading is to revisit an appropriated and lost urban space: "Volver a un libro se parece a volver a las ciudades que creímos nuestras, pero que en realidad hemos y nos han olvidado" (Going back to a book is like returning to the cities we believe to be our own, but which, in reality, we've forgotten and been forgotten by).[23] Infused with an unquestionably romantic air, the mythification of literature, the weightlessness of the world, these clichés speak to a young writer in thrall to her own charms.

In their marked preference for interstices and between spaces, these works are defined by their liminality. Situated between life and death, the cemetery and the ghost locate Luiselli's writing in places that are marked by limits or borders in the same way that her literary references promote the appropriation of elements of modernity. Oswaldo Zavala sees the latter as "una subversión calculada de ese legado, el deseo no siempre exitoso de reformularlo, el ansia inaplazable de su dispersión" (a calculated subversion of this legacy, the not always successful desire to reformulate it, an urgent need to disperse it).[24] Throughout his study, Zavala increasingly adds complexity to his perspective on the meaning of this strategy, seeing it as a reworking of cosmopolitanism "en tensión con la conceptualización de una literatura nacional ante la circulación transnacional" (in tension with the conceptualization of a national literature in the face of transnational circulation), and a phenomenon that "implica múltiples dinámicas en el campo literario" (puts into play multiple dynamics in the literary sphere).[25] The return to modern writers as listed by Zavala (Jorge Volpi, Pedro Ángel Palou, Roberto Bolaño, Juan Villoro, Daniel Sada, and Cristina Rivera Garza) occurs differently in each case, although taken all together they represent a gesture that Zavala correctly refuses to deem a simple form of cosmopolitanism—pointing out that, in his opinion, it is more a question of "el calculado intento de apertura del campo literario como práctica recurrente entre los escritores de clase media alta que comenzaron a publicar en México desde finales de 1990 con las mismas ansias de globalización que estimuló la implementación del Tratado de Libre Comercio en 1994.[26] In the case of Luiselli, however, as Zavala explains, her neoliberal perspective wields the most profound impact on both her rereading of modernity and her aesthetic and ideological genealogies.

Bringing together similar texts like those in *Papeles falsos*, the book *Where You Are: A Collection of Maps that Will Leave You Feeling Completely Lost* published by a group of authors including Luiselli, also brings together a heterogeneous collection of articles, photographs, and aerial maps that present a simplified and panoramic view of a specific location.[27] In this regard, María Paz Oliver explains:

> This type of map functions as an indication of surveillance and control vis-à-vis the notebook that accompanies the photograph and as a way of regulating and normalizing the space and the way in which they occupy it. The clash between the freedom of daily writing inspired by walking through New York and the objective spirit of the photographic map resituates the narra-

tive in another perspective and rereads the emotivity of these texts from an eye mediated by street view technology.[28]

The narrator's excursions through the cities she mentions are marked in many ways by gender: the parks she goes to with her children and the photographs that accompany some of the texts. We also see this in the attachment she feels for certain stereotypes that are traditionally associated with femininity: daydreaming, digression, gratuitous movements and exchanges, and volubility. While dilettantism and nomadism are not exclusive to the female subject, they indicate a deviation from professionalism and can be assimilated to the idea that culture is, for women, a decorative quality.

LOS INGRÁVIDOS: OWEN AND I (OR VICE VERSA?)

One of the ways Luiselli defines literature is via a comparison with the technique of the construction worker who builds a building by filling in cracks and holes, trying to join fragments in a constant totalizing drive that the author identifies with the goals of literature. Construction/deconstruction is thus present in *Los ingrávidos* as a persistent dynamic that is employed in creative formulas and recipes. As she says in the novel: "Nunca meter más de la cuenta, nunca estofar, nunca amueblar ni adornar. Abrir puertas, ventanas. Levantar muros y después tirarlos" (Never . . . to put in more than is necessary, never overlay, never furnish or adorn. Open doors, windows. Raise walls and demolish them).[29] Another metaphor she uses is that of fabric and, by extension, rags: "el tejido de [la] realidad inmediata se desgasta y quiebra" (the mesh of her immediate reality wears thin and breaks).[30] Both similes are clichés used in the (self-)critique of creative work that transforms the word into a brick for building or a thread to weave words and sounds, creating the texture that can be called style or discursive strategies. In this regard, if *Los ingrávidos* were a building it would be rickety and buffeted by the weather, with staircases that lead nowhere, windows that open onto a wall and narrow, poorly lit dead-end hallways. If it were fabric, it would be loosely woven and colorful, an immaterial garment designed for a non-existent body.

A narration with two voices, *Los ingrávidos* alternates two points of view, two timeframes, and two cultural spaces. These oscillations correspond to a key moment in modernity and, of course, postmodernity, following the First World War and the years preceding the financial crash of 1929. Through numerous frame stories, the anecdotic space produces multiple segments and episodes that bring a dynamism to the narration alongside a profusion of characters and events. Intertextuality complements these internal movements filtering texts from one author to another and from one period to another since the author views literature's canonical repertoire as a stream that resists temporal sites, textual limits, and concepts of authorship.[31] Literature is a world apart, self-contained and endogamic, which you can inhabit while dispensing with an exterior world that is, in any case, assimilable to fictional terms.

This invention overcomes (or encases and coopts) the real, and the very act of storytelling, of "making" literature, becomes more important than the content of the narration. Conceived as a combination of fabrication and daydream, literary creation serves as a romanticized and exceptional activity that gives meaning to life and creates its own rules. Words fill the gaps, imaginatively challenging meaning so that instability takes up residence in the very heart of the fictional world affecting the relationship between truth and fiction, origin, and simulacrum all of which become interchangeable, confusing their limits. This loss of consciousness is *Los ingrávidos* essential trait, since the world and its characters grow progressively fainter throughout the novel as if they were walking toward their own ghost.

THE METAPHYSICS OF PRESENCE AND THE ABSENCE OF THE SELF

The question of presence is a constant in Luiselli's narrative and serves as a way of approaching the relationship between reality and appearance, truth, and fiction, original and simulacrum. Her different works are variations on this theme, engaging with the relationship between author, narrator, and protagonist all of which are figures that overlap, superimpose, and interact. The unfurling of different narrative planes and varied forms of the relationship between the image and the surrounding world, indicates a desire to break with narrative linearity and unity, and relativize realist versions while imposing elements that have been transfigured and displaced from this orbit and this level. Between the plane of "the real" and that of "the imagined," between presence and absence, the figure of the poetic "I" centralizes the narrative development, placing itself like the dispositive that mediates between both levels and that, in turn, is made up of alloying elements from different domains. The poetic "I" is the narrative center of intensification from which meaning is generated.

If we have already noted the tendency toward the creation of a poetic "I" that voraciously occupies literary ground in *Papeles falsos*, in *Los ingrávidos* we see the creation of space from where the narrator's protagonism can be expanded and multiplied and that inserts different elements and devices for the exaltation of this centrality within the first-person fiction. Oswaldo Zavala has remarked on the process of re-signifying of modernity in the narrative of the last few decades, in which a type of "cosmopolitanism for export" is deployed, revisiting the tradition only to reappropriate it on its own terms. At the same time, this gesture of reappropriation creates a common platform from which the texts of the authors Zavala analyzes are themselves inscribed within a canonical register of well-earned recognition. According to Zavala: "Luiselli muestra el éxito de esta recodificación de la ciudad letrada con *Los ingrávidos*, celebratoria de un regreso de la alta cultura, el refinamiento global y la aventura de la clase alta en un momento irremediablemente despolitizado y post-nacional de nuestro presente neoliberal" (With *Los ingrávidos*, Luiselli demonstrates the success of this recodifying of the lettered city, celebrating a return to high culture, global refinement and the adventures of the upper classes in a desperately depoliticized and post-national moment of our neoliberal present).[32]

The novel is organized along the topics of lightness and ensuing notions of immateriality, disappearance, and spectrality in which, according to the author, the characters gradually dissolve until they are mere voices, or sounds and audio traces of a presence that is no longer there. As we know, the representation of dematerialization leads to a reflection on time as continuity, duration, and the capturing of meaning of a passing moment that we identify with the idea of the present, or the notion of *presence*, or of being in the *now* of perception. Without directly engaging with these themes that have gripped philosophy from Aristotle to Heidegger and that assume another angle with Derrida, the idea of the ghost encompasses notions of evanescence, fleetingness of meaning, relativization and the primacy of the presence of the self over its absence, thus putting forth the type of binary system (good/evil, up/down, man/woman) that dooms the philosopher of deconstruction. From this perspective, Luiselli's novel proposes a vindication of the self in its absence and the impossibility of opposing presence to absence, body to phantasm, with weightlessness as the quality that encompasses all in a timeless duration that represents the continuous presence, or perhaps the absence of the present.

Luiselli's text, however, cannot be viewed in anyway as philosophical but rather as the fruit of the exercise of a poetics of dematerialization that begins with *Papeles falsos* and progresses interruptedly to *Lost Children Archive* and, drawing on a rich literary tradition, explores forms of fusion and dissemination of presence within absence, voice within echo, death within life and vice versa. In effect, the space where the living and the dead coexist, an oft visited place in Mexican literature, albeit in this case marked by a certain cheerful triviality, contributes to the creation of an atmosphere replete with emotional elements, intuitions, and rationalization that rapidly fuel the narrative space, its plots, and symbolic deployments, in which presences and absences, bodies and spirits, sounds and echoes, share coordinates.

But Luiselli's world is not Rulfo's Comala, and her characters never reach the intriguing and evasive heights of, for example, Carlos Fuentes's *Aura*. There is no tragedy or mystery in *Los ingrávidos*, no social or political agenda, no questioning of past or present, no austere exercise of literature, like the aforementioned examples, where fictional components move and connect like the workings of a clock. Instead, in Luiselli's novel we find a celebration of the encounter with the shadows of the past in which a dialogue of equals is made possible, not to demystify the lettered city, but rather to incorporate it in a less solemn light and perhaps from a condescending angle. *Los ingrávidos* does not offer a fictional prose laden with the rigors of history but is instead a fragmentary and joyful reconstruction of the past in which, as the book's title suggests, characters and plot share an ability to float in a space of freedom and imagination.

As the connection between the spheres of life and death, past and present, presence and absence, the figure of Gilberto Owen (1904–1952), celebrated member of the modernist literary group the Contemporáneos plays a connective, interstitial but not secondary role.[33] Luiselli installs the author of the 1928 *Novela como nube* in her prose with all his references and connotations: his zeal for innovation, his experimentalism, his struggle against traditional poetic models, his shuffling between literary genres, his essential ambiguity as we see in the texts he dedicates to Tomás Segovia, his strange linking of the personal and the cultural, and his interest in the intangible and the transcendent. From this brief account, we can perceive the pivotal nature here of the Contemporáneos's transnationalizing mission that, without falling into the trap of an atemporal universality, succeeds in imprinting Mexican literature with a new feeling that while not cosmopolitan is certainly worldly. Despite the din of recent revolutions (Mexico, Russia) and war and hints of what is to come (the Spanish Civil War) this group's work allows us to hear that era's voice of Mexico as an aesthetic and ideological summons that, faithful to the group's name, searches out forms for inhabiting its present moment and defining its goals, challenges, and principal pathways. Well-known in Mexico, Gilberto Owen is a representative figure, whom the author connects to her own literary project (principally carried out outside of Mexico) in a risky exercise of borrowed prestige that invites the reader to read her work along certain continuities, as if literary roots were joined together under the earth, nourishing their fruits.

Los ingrávidos strings together moments in the life of a writer and an editor who, like the author herself, lives and works in New York City. The interactions between the protagonist and the ghostly world that lives alongside her define the plot's center, in which Gilberto Owen, about whom the protagonist is writing a book, takes center stage. The story is organized around the concept of the two writers' parallel lives from youth to adulthood, in which episodes of a personal and professional nature alternate. As the novel progresses, the writers begin to lose materiality, presence, and "weight"; their ghosts begin to coexist with their life in the present, creating a narrative space in which the lack of differentiation between life and death and truth and simulacrum is foregrounded. The narrator sees Owen's ghost on the subway and at home and her son gives him the name "Consincara" (Sometimes Without) incorporating the character's intrinsic ambiguity into his name. We also see the relative nature of limits of the truth or falseness of the details of the narrator's own novel, about which her husband questions her, trying to discover if it can be interpreted autobiographically. The author tries to fill the holes in her life with literature, reinforcing the protagonist's dilettantism and in line with her bohemian life, her attempt to aestheticize the real, and the way in which the life of literature, along with its ghosts, permeates everyday life. At the same time as the narrative voices of Owen and other writers intermingle, the real stories filter into the main narrative and plot details are attributed to the real characters who assemble in the book.

For some critics, Owen's dematerialization emerges from an anecdote found in his correspondence, in which he explains that, during the years he lived in New York, he would weigh himself after riding the subway, realizing that he got thinner with every journey. The circumstances of the character's physical fading, about which the author writes, are paradoxical to say the least. It appears she were attempting to verbally materialize an existence that loses physicality and concreteness, thus creating a substitute reality that highlights the individual whose organic base evaporates, consolidating the poetic "I" that sustains it. What is clear is that Owen's dematerialization starts with the isolation the narrator causes when she removes him from his own historical context and places him in her own depoliticized milieu. As Oswaldo Zavala explains:

> Owen's historical context is essentially erased as is that of the female narrator. In its place we find only contemporary New York City, inhabited by

ironic artists, uninterested in politics, distracted by personal questions and lacking in interest beyond their own intellectual project and immediate surroundings. Owen's ghost is without a past: he only belongs to the narrator's present.[34]

The displacements I have identified in Luiselli's work can be viewed through her patent and constant use of the previously mentioned simulacrum, or rather, in the introduction of a model that she assembles only to break (the wall that is built only to be destroyed, to which the author refers). The novel's structure reveals the framework underpinning the textual project, transforming the scaffolding (to continue with the building metaphor) into a visible and prominent part of the final construct.

Postmodern in its detotalizing directionality, Luiselli employs this device throughout all her works, evoking what Sylvia Molloy calls the "politics of the pose," with which phrase she characterizes certain inflections of fin-de-siècle Hispanic American works.[35] Molloy's context is clearly different than the present moment but, for our purposes here, what is interesting is the deconstructive value that she identifies in the pose in light of the reading produced by *modernismo*. She explains that such an appeal to cultural theatricalization of certain attitudes or positionalities can exercise a "destabilizing energy" that converts them into "un gesto político" (a political gesture). But another possibility is also present: that the *gesture* maintains itself only as simulation or subterfuge and that it exhausts itself in its superficial demonstration, as a sign of its *era*.

In the same text, Sylvia Molloy also refers to spectrality, reminding us of Rubén Darío's comments on the work of Lautréamont, in which he evokes the recommendation from the Kabbalah "No hay que jugar al espectro, porque se llega a serlo." According to Molloy, although in its deepest sense this suggestion "estaría advirtiendo sobre los peligros de un afantasmamiento, una desrealización, un volverse no-tangible o no-visible," Darío seems to call attention "sobre el efecto contrario, es decir, sobre el hecho de que la espectralización resulta en un exceso de visibilidad, de presencia."[36]

Liliana Muñoz has explained that the narrator in *Los ingrávidos* uses literature as an escape valve from an overwhelming family situation, displacing personal energy toward fantasy to the point where the ghost of Gilberto Owen takes over reality:

> *Los ingrávidos* is a novel about two characters who become blurry to the point of becoming ghosts of themselves in different realms of time and space. The narrator writes from her current life. She cannot breathe. She has a child,

a baby, and a meddling husband. Writing is her escape valve. During nights of insomnia, she writes long paragraphs about another life, a life that is not her own, while Gilberto Owen's ghost starts to fill the spaces she has left empty.[37]

As a character in the novel, Owen is presented as a defeated individual who, at the end of his life, is blind, alone, and aged. He takes refuge in a fictional relationship with Federico García Lorca and in unproductive love letters written to Clementina Otero. Above all, the character of Owen imbues Lusielli's narrative with the aura of the era and a strong tie to modernity as a space of cultural richness, Europeanism, and the process of literary institutionalization in Mexican national culture. Owen, and the evocation of the Contemporáneos in general, serves as a reference to a powerhouse of prestige and an air of transnationalism to which Luiselli's work tacitly offers itself as an heir.

MOBILITY AND FIXITY

Luiselli's texts generally oscillate between the poles of reinforcement and instability. The "female condition" was conceived of by dominant Western European discourses as a series of entrenched identities connected to matrimony, maternity, and domestic life. All of these are spaces that have been historically opening to multiple forms of female inclusion and the adapting of sociocultural norms that restricted women's participation in the public sphere (professional, intellectual, creative, etc.). Both instances appear in Luiselli's texts, with a particular emphasis on matrimony and maternity, albeit carried out self-reflexively and in a desultory fashion. The constant mention of children and domestic/couple dynamics fixes an image that, in the rest of the plot, is weighed against the protagonist's insertion into situations of imaginative display, intellectual quests, and insistent demonstrations of sensibility and erudition. Luiselli revisits all these narrative spaces in her different novels, and they play a clear role in *Los ingrávidos*. In this novel, the intense dynamics of life in New York are gradually colonized by an imagination that evokes the image of Owen as the object of desire and as the figure who represents a cultural space capable of challenging US culture's pragmatism and the impositions of domestic life in daily routines. His ghostly "presence" symbolically reduces the distance between Philadelphia/New York and Mexico, between the heart of capitalist modernity and peripheral modernity, between the Harlem Renaissance and the present moment.[38]

The narrator splits her creative activity, combining her previous life as an editor in New York City with the reconstruction that the narrator Gilberto Owen carries out at the end of his life in his fifties looking back on his youth thirty years earlier. Two alternative and intertwined textualities co-exist in which autobiography and fictionalization create a hybrid and ambiguous literary product that encompasses reality and fantasy without establishing clear limits between each domain. The narrator is working on another novel entitled *Filadelfia* (Philadelphia), thus inscribing one text into another.

The character of Owen runs into the narrator twice in New York: once in a museum and once on the subway although the second "meeting" is more of a parallel encounter in which the two figures cross paths on trains that circle in opposite directions. The vision the narrator has of superimposed faces metaphorizes the novel's dual composition and illustrates the idea of the ghost as a dematerialized, weightless "existence" that serves as counterpoint to life like a type of alter ego that stalks the poetic "I." Other coincidences in which both narrators experience identical situations on different planes reinforce this idea.[39] In my reading, these displacements of the poetic "I" correspond to the marked individuation that Luiselli's texts develop in all possible forms, searching for ways to reproduce the poetic "I," duplicating it in other figures, through the presence of the ghost, by way of superimposing images on faces, by creating continuity between the names that the narrator uses with her children, appropriating the name Owen gave his cats etc. As Licata explains, the categories of "original" and "double" vary and oscillate from one narrator to another and from one character to another, increasing the idea of weightlessness, of the specific weight of each person and of the whole world that seems to float in narrative space.[40] Identity/otherness come together fluidly, strengthening the construction of fiction as an self-sufficient and self-contained bubble along with the romantic vision of the writer as a creator of worlds in which the poetic "I" resounds like an echo and in which the voice and its exacerbated sensibility are reproduced.

In *Los ingrávidos*, the narrator finds her daily life in Mexico overwhelming, since her obligations as wife and mother leave her little time for creative work. At multiple times she expands on the challenges she is forced to confront owing to the lack of space and time to pursue her literary works. For Nicolás Licata, all this leaves its mark on the narrative:

> In *Los ingrávidos*, the doubling and spectralization of the narrator-protagonist echo and reflect the mishaps of her life as a mother as her bodily frontiers become fluid and her poetic "I" appears symbolically divided between past

and present, work and the care of her children, between her personal life and her maternal responsibilities.[41]

The relationship intensifies because of multiple references to pregnancy, lactation etc., as if the author were providing useful clues not only for reading her texts but for appreciating them, indirectly suggesting mitigating circumstances in the face of the novel's potential weaknesses. Interpreting the hermeneutic value that these indications might possess, it is worth noting that a "gravid" (heavy) woman is synonymous with a pregnant woman in the way that the world of the "weightless" would be all those who do not experience it, especially men, for obvious reasons. Or perhaps the novel's title is an expression of nostalgia for the lack of anchoring and fixity that the "feminine condition" produces and because of the freedom the title could impart. Fortunately, Licata addresses this interpretation with restraint, directing it toward the question of the double and seeing "un yo corporalmente escindido en sí mismo, como si se tratara de dos personajes distintos o como si fuera solamente ahora el fantasma de la que era antes de convertirse en madre" (a poetic "I" whose body is split into two, as if it were two different people or as if were only now the ghost of what she was earlier before she became a mother) in the narration.[42]

Together with these metaphors of fixity, of the existential place that it occupies and the root and derivations of individuality, *Los ingrávidos* is based on the notion of ideas of mobility and displacement as practices that literally and symbolically constitute "flight lines" from certainty and the space-time of the present subject. Possessing a prominent role in the novel (and featuring, significantly, on the cover of the Sexto Piso edition) the subway is also an overly evident metaphor for life and time, offering a perspective on life. Deep underground, dirty, dark, impossible to appropriate, the subway train's route is in and of itself irrelevant. Each station can be substituted for another that will be left behind without a trace.[43] Space and time fuse in a continuous, obsessive movement through a darkness above which the world always exists for others. The passengers meet up during the journey, not at its end, and are together but incommunicado, each one lost in their own thoughts. The train also metaphorizes intermediate states, between-spaces inhabited by ambiguous beings or experiences that belong to two different levels of reality.

In his correspondence with Clementina Otero and with other Mexican friends, Gilberto Owen makes explicit reference to the subway, pointing out the fact, then repeated in Luiselli's novel, that it was built in 1904 the same year he was born: "El metro, sus múltiples paradas, sus averías, sus aceleraciones repentinas, sus zonas oscuras, podría funcionar como esquema del tiempo de esa otra novela" (the subway, its multiple stops, its breakdowns, its sudden accelerations, its dark zones, could function as the space-time scheme for this other novel).[44] His 1928 trip to New York was Owen's first experience of a big city and confusion and rejection came together, enriching his poetic sensibility. From the beginning he proclaims his intention to compose a "plegaría en el subway" (subway prayer) that he'll later refer to as "retrato del subway" (subway portrait) and finally "autorretrato del subway" (subway self-portrait). As Anthony Stanton reminds us in his study of Owen's poetic creations on this favorite topic of modernity, where technology challenges traditional ways of understanding space and time, Owen remarks that people become savages in the subway stations. As Stanton explains, "Así invoca [Owen] un tema central de los contemporáneos, el del dinamismo del viaje exterior y su relación con la inmovilidad del viaje interior o lo que el mismo Villaurrutia llamaba, con una frase de Paul Morand, el viaje alrededor de la alcoba" (Thus Owen invokes one of the Contemporáneos's central themes, that of the exterior journey's dynamism and its relationship to the interior journey's immobility or what Villarrutia himself called, in turn referencing Paul Morand's phrase, the journey around the bedroom).[45] And in a letter to Celestino Gorostiza, Owens indicates: "A New York se la empieza a ver desde el subway. Acaba allí la perspectiva plana, horizontal. Empieza un paisaje de bulto ahí, con la doble profundidad, o eso que llaman cuarta dimensión del tiempo" (He begins to see New York from the subway. There, the flat and horizontal perspective ends. From there the bulky landscape begins, doubly deep, or what they call the fourth dimension of time).[46]

The lyric impulse that the experience of the New York subway awakens in the Sinaolan poet begins to materialize in two short, interconnected poems that first appear in the Contemporáneos group's eponoymous literary magazine *Contemporáneos* and then in Owen's book *Línea* (1930).[47] The first poem, "Perfil," presents the subway via metaphors: first as a flute and then as a stone thrown from David's catapult: impulse, trajectory, and directionality. The subway's depths are dream-like, replete with feelings and desires. In "Vuelo," the second of the two interconnected poems, Owen uses the subway to conjure up the idea of birds and bullets, a rapid displacement in space and time, doing so with a lyrical diction that is more hermetically sealed than the previous poem, communicating a high level of dynamism as well as the aura of mystery that technology held for the avantgarde poets.

Interestingly, Luiselli appropriates these elements for her novel as part of a poetics that illustrates a modern sensibility. Her engagement with the

Contemporáneos is not limited to names and topics but instead evinces a perspective on *modernity* as a new *sensorium* that leads to a *derealization of the real*, to its progressive dematerialization in an alienated world that offers itself even more rigorously to the foreigner who finds himself/herself immersed in a "theater of belonging."

Appearing frequently in Luiselli's literature, in these types of situations the figure of the ghost represents the "between-space," conceived of as an adjacent area where duplicity predominates, where we can be in two places at one time but in none, where we occupy a third hybridized and essentially impure locale. The nature of this space participates simultaneously as the presence/absence of life and death. We see a similar duality in the figure of the child, an id(entity) that exists between the non-being before life and the future being. Up to a point, a similar ambiguity exists in literature, textuality (thought, sensibility) that is defined between individual creation and the text's public circulation, or in the case of the archive, a dipositive between past and presence, experience, and discourse. In all these cases, Lusielli dramatizes the distance between two points revealing an energy that flows and crystallizes in intermediate, temporal, and experimental states that prevent polarization.

In *Los ingrávidos* the narrator is not the only one who possesses the capacity to perceive the presence of the ghost and interact with it, incorporating it into her life and that of her family. There is also the character of White, the editor, who sees his dead wife in a tree outside his house.[48] While they are both on a platform waiting for the subway, in a highly virtual moment, White tells the narrator:

> In that very station, the poet Ezra Pound had seen his friend Henri Gaudier-Brzeska, who had been killed in a trench in Neuville-Saint-Vaast a few months before. Pound was waiting on the platform, leaning against a pillar, when the train first pulled in. The doors of the carriage opened and he saw the face of his friend.[49]

The subway's approach always seems to precipitate the arrival of the ghost, along with dematerialization and confession. The ghosts or specters of the dead constantly reappear, as visions, dreams, conversation topics, references, etc. projecting themselves toward a plane of imagined relationships between characters, whether contemporaries or not.

> I closed my eyes for a moment. When I opened them, I saw William Carlos Williams beside me, wearing enormous glasses, inspecting the vagina of a

miniature women lying on a napkin on the bar; there was the poet Zvorsky sitting at a table, conducting an imaginary orchestra; Ezra Pound hanging in a cage at the counter of the counter and García Lorca tossing him peanuts, which he accepted gleefully.[50]

For its part, the imaginary relationship between Owen and García Lorca takes up a few pages of the novel. The Spanish poet, who is referred to in one part as "el maricón," is described in the following terms:

> He was a plump, pampered little Spaniard, with a tight little ass, who virtuously complained about the bohemian life in the big city; doves and swarms of coins, buildings under perpetual construction, vomiting multitudes, alienation, and solitude. The problem with Federico's poems was that they all ended up being Federiquized.[51]

The narrator describes her life in New York as a trompe-l'oeil.[52] Subjectivism is the text's dominant perspective, imprinting itself on thoughts, perceptions, and interpretations of the real. The inexpressible ambiguity of interiority is the only certainty and language the only (slippery) tool for its communication. Other surrounding elements confirm the weightlessness of the world and of the beings that inhabit it. Cats, blindness, lies, the bohemian life, the very act of writing as a form of insurmountable incompleteness, Owen's weight loss as a progressive dematerialization; all these forms present a metaphor of the real and reinforce the sensation of the constant lurking of the spectral, which expresses the deterioration of time and space and generalized existential dissolution and dispersion. The passage from life to death and the persistence of the shadow of the self after the existential disappearance are concentrated in Owen's dried up plant. Retrieved from the Mexican writer's previous century's cosmopolitan modernity, the plant (albeit in a constant state of deterioration) sustains a material link between two asynchronous realities, connecting the two writers within the space of fiction and desire.

In a world imagined as constantly disappearing, fiction unchains the characters' realities. After reading Owen's work, the narrator feels that this moment marks the beginning of her existence: "como habitada por otra posible vida que no era la mía, pero que bastaba imaginar para abandonarme en ella por complete (as if inhabited by another possible life that wasn't mine, but one which, simply by the use of imagination, I could give myself up to completely).[53] Or, as she says later in the novel, "La narradora descubre que mientras hilvana un relato, el tejido de su realidad inmediata se desgasta y quiebra. La fibra de la ficción empieza a modificar la realidad y no viceversa, como debiera ser" (The narrator discovers that while she is stringing together the tale, the mesh of her immediate reality wears thin and breaks. The fiber of fiction begins to modify reality and not vice versa, as it should be).[54]

The gradual loss of limits announces the beginning of the end:

> But the day those things began to arrive—the blindness, the cats, the ghosts, the pieces of furniture, and dozens of books I hadn't bought, and of course, later on, the flies and the cockroaches—I knew it was the beginning of the end. Not mine, but the end of something I had identified with so closely that it would soon do away with me too.[55]

Appearances/disappearances expose inconsistency in the objective world that, in an inverse journey from fiction to life itself, changes the solidity of the real. Mobility begins to take root, and fixity dissolves in the face of the force of imagined universes that destabilize it.

It is impossible to ignore the ideological implications of the dissolving of the real along with the desire to belong to a decadent space that has been displaced from culture. The constant high culture references in Luiselli's work are perhaps its most striking and eloquent displacement since they presuppose a journey through symbolic spaces whose value has already been enshrined. According to Oswaldo Zavala, this form of *flânerie* in Luiselli is:

> a way of organically integrating the neoliberal present of Western culture. It is, in sum, a way of being recognized by neoliberal culture and not a form of protest against it. With her novel *Los ingrávidos*, Luiselli refines her inscription into this literary genealogy in order to establish with greater clarity her belonging into a global cultural order, that is, her decisive integration into the Mexican and US literary field as an organic intellectual of neoliberal capitalist modernity.[56]

Along with these elements of ideological inscription, themes of gender and race also appear in Luiselli's work. Together with the question of class the topic of how she positions herself vis a vis both Mexican and US society deserves a separate study. References to race appear in the text, configuring a space of thought and social conscience that does not reject the use of stereotypes but instead uses them for their comic value. In fact, they serve as ready-made expressions of a mentality that still resonates in different levels of society and that can be useful precisely in terms of their shock value and irreverence.[57]

FABRICATING THE MODEL: TRANSLATION AND SIMULACRUM

The mediating function that I've been discussing here finds one of its principal expressions in the figure of Gilberto Owen as the transmitter of avant-garde aesthetics during the Harlem Renaissance or, in other words, as a bicultural operator that favors the appropriation of the inter-war poetics in the US via the elaboration that these movements received in the work of Mexican artists and writers, particularly in Owen's own. As a way of conceptualizing and representing a work sunk in a post-war crisis, transfixed by diasporas, economic debacles, and political convulsions, avant-garde movements represent one of the strongest arguments against the traditional definition of art and its social and political function. Despite its members' multiple aesthetics, as a group the Contemporáneos tried to forge a common space for poetic language, capable of expanding the lyrical horizons of Mexican literature, liberating what appeared as an excessive inculcation of the nation's problematics in its post-revolutionary period. For its part, in the Harlem Renaissance African American culture emerges into the public sphere as an expression of sensibilities that have been displaced from contemporary culture. In the 1920s and 30s, the otherness of this sector's artistic expression colonized social space by way of an aesthetics that inserts the strength of new subjects into an exhausted Western society heading toward one of modern capitalism's biggest crises.

For the Contemporáneos, the reaction against the idea of communicative transparency in language and literary form emphasizes poetic language as textual opacity, or as a texture that calls attention to itself through the density of images and convergence of meanings. The decomposition of the objective world, the insertion of supra-real images that are both playful and dreamlike into poetic contexts as well as sensory alteration, provides a rich and frequently metaphorical repository that opens multiple levels of aesthetic exploration. Poetic art is resignified as a space of liberation and vindication of levels that have been rendered invisible by modernizing projects and eclipsed by the rhetoric of nationalism. Beyond an explicit or tacit dialogue with national literary tradition, the Contemporáneos aesthetic project launches itself onto a worldly cultural space, redefining the function of the symbolic product.

Owen's work exemplifies and transmits many of the lines of this poetic production, relying on a considerable cultural referentialism that Luiselli incorporates into her own work, appropriating the poet's methods with a high degree of affectation. From her Mexican model, the author of *Los ingrávidos* also appropriates esoterism and the tendency to modify biographical information that, once fictionalized, transforms the poetic "I" into a space of experimentation and self-construction that celebrates its centrality and polyvalence. Both the use of metaphors that extend throughout the text offering clues to the understanding of the figurative world, as well as the persistence of auto-fiction, acquire renewed energy in Luiselli's work, thus establishing concrete and traceable ties to Gilberto Owen.

A series of clues appears in the text that Luiselli dedicates to Owen in *Letras Libres* (and that I will gloss in what follows) and are then incorporated into *Los ingrávidos*. In this article, Luiselli recuperates Tomás Segovia's phrase, in which he describes Owen's work as "transmutación poética de la materia biográfica" (poetic transmutation of biographical material), which is something that could also be said of Luiselli's work that, in this aspect, follows the same path.[58] Luiselli's *ars poetica* assimilates Owen's compositional desideratum in the way she presents her literary network, demonstrating "la preferencia por una escritura ajena al tiempo. No una que fuera intemporal sino una que, en el interior del relato, estuviera libre del corsé de la trama cronológica" (a preference for writing that is indifferent to time. Not one that is eternal but that in the story's inner workings is free of the straitjacket of chronological plot).[59] It is a textuality that "despliega un conjunto de eventos simultáneos—un mito, un sueño, una vivencia íntima, un evento concreto—en un mismo espacio narrativo" (displays a handful of simultaneous events—a myth, a dream, an intimate experience, a concrete evento—in a single narrative space).[60] A simultaneity of narrative lines, heterogeneity of registers and combination of experiences, happenings and oneiric events indicate relevant aspects in *Los ingrávidos* and later on, in *Lost Children Archive*. But what most seduces Luiselli in the figure and work of the mythical *contemporáneo* poet is his "lenta y paciente" (slow and patient) gaze with which he soars from his surroundings toward a hyperreality that only a few can perceive.[61] As Owen points out in *Novela como nube*, he held fast to a renunciation of "los datos exactos del mundo, por buscar los datos del trasmundo" (this world's exact facts, to instead search for the facts of the underworld).[62] In this way, like an impatient and creative photographer, Owen produces a "retrato desenfocado del objeto, y un retrato fiel de la mirada que lo tomó" (an unfocused portrait of the object and a faithful portrait of the gaze that took it).[63] Again, the centrality of the creator is undeniable. Everything comes back to the eye that sees, its positionality, its sharpness, and selectivity that separate it from a conventional perspective and allows it to capture, via the biased gaze, everything that the in between-place, and the interstice contains.

> The strength of Owen's gaze lies in his capacity to see between things. Owen fails to see the successive moments that make up a scene focusing instead on those brief spaces between one moment and another; that's where he trains his eye.... This, in a word, could be understood as a particular intelligence to understand distances.... Owen sees from an intermediate space.[64]

Finally, Luiselli finds in Owen the same fascination with the authorial voice that orients her own writing:

> It's not a discovery nor my own paranoia: we live in a time obsessed with the author's voice. A writer dedicates all his efforts to searching for his/her own voice—whatever that might be—as if one day it might be actually found somewhere. Why didn't Owen devote himself to his gaze in the same way? It's accepted, moreover, that the writer's voice should be untroubled, cultivated, ironic, perhaps a touch cynical and definitely agreeable. Referring to Owen, Segovia writes that feelings are not really valued in our day and age. Nothing could be truer. And Owen undoubtedly turned off some readers for whom emotion equaled affectation and vulgarity.[65]

In this way, and in an inverse and simultaneous process, Luiselli dedicates a large part of the novel to building a model that she will follow in her own poetics: as the narrator displays her actions, the paradigmatic figure is adapted (in the selection of certain traits, in certain emphasis and omissions) to the requirements of the novel. Owen's figure forms a point of intensity that activates an imagination that manifests itself in many ways: as hallucination, as desire, as simulation, as untruth, and as a proposal for situations (meetings, relationships) that never happened nor could happen. The novel unfolds as a space of desire and as a fabricator of unrealities that stand in for the real world.

Toward the end of the first third of the novel the narrator introduces the lie that triggers the situation with the editor, White, whom she wants to convince that Owen is the new Bolaño, uniting the two myths of modernity and postmodernity:

> I told him that, in the small, disorganized library of Columbia University's Casa Hispánica, I had found an original, badly typed and barely typed, in which there were a series of annotated translations of poems by Owen. The

translations were almost certainly by Zvorsky, I said. They're signed JZ&GO. It was the most unlikely of all possible lies about Owen and White never believed it, but he decided to go along with me. I promised to bring him my own literal transcriptions of the text.[66]

The fake translation attributed to Louis Zukofsky (Joshua Zvorsky in *Faces in the Crowd*), founder of the Objectivist group of poets who were followers of Modernism and influenced by Ezra Pound and William Carlos Williams, ended up being published and the fraud revealed which led to the narrator losing her job and returning to Mexico. But more importantly the fraud gives rise to a web of improbable encounters between characters like Federico García Lorca, José Limón, and others. This imaginary plot underscores the projection of a transnationalized literary modernity, in a dialogue of equals with the great names of inter-war poetry.

A series of bohemian and picturesque secondary characters form a cohort that reinforces the narrator's positioning as a free-spirited, erratic, and fanciful woman who roams through cemeteries, parks, and rooftops—between spaces that symbolize transitoriness and evanescence in which the narrator "vivía en un estado perpetuo de comunión con los muertos" (was living in a perpetual state of communion with the dead).[67] Moby, Dakota, Pajarote enter and leave the narrative space, hovering like a group of shadowy presences that move the plot along. Each one is the protagonist of an erratic and fantastical existence that converges on the narrator's life. The character of Moby presents a variation on the theme of the simulacrum, in his dedication to the faking of "falsos libros viejos que él mismo fabricaba en una imprenta casera" (old books that he himself produced on a homemade printing press).[68] In addition: "reimprimía ejemplares únicos de clásicos estadounidenses en formatos igualmente únicos. Tenía un ejemplar ilustrado de *Leaves of Grass*, un manuscrito a lápiz de *Walden* y una versión grabada en cinta de los ensayos de Ralph Waldo Emerson leídos por su abuela polaca (He [also] reprinted unique copies of American classics in equally unique formats. He had an illustrated copy of *Leaves of Grass*, a manuscript of *Walden* he'd written out in pencil, and an audiotape of the essays of Ralph Waldo Emerson written by his Polish grandmother).[69]

The alteration of reality becomes a way of life for the "los ingrávidos" (the weightless ones), a way of eluding the limits of daily life and opening the floodgates to an imagination capable of colonizing the world. The narrator acknowledges: "En esa etapa me dio por mentir. Mentía cada vez más, hasta en situaciones que en definitiva no lo ameritaban. Supongo que esa es la lógica de la mentira: un día pones la primera piedra y al día siguiente tienes que poner dos" (During that period I took to telling lies. I lied more and more often, even in situations that didn't merit it. I suppose that's the logic of lies: one day you lay the first stone and the next you have to lay two).[70] Within this context of levity and fraud, literature circulates like a symbolic product that animates the snobbery of a lightweight society represented as joyful, carefree, and eccentric.

Language provides lies with their chief negotiating area with the real and literature their most legitimate and auratic form of social realization. The theme of original language and translation positions another relational level between texts and their "real" signifiers. The prominence of the market and the importance of inserting its symbolic product therein are part of a reality that authors have interiorized, developing different strategies to prepare their texts for translation and circulation in the global market. Their translatable quality becomes an important part of the process of textual construction in terms of lexical, thematic, and compositional selection. Therefore, literary translation (linguistic, cultural, ideological) has become a fundamental part of analyzing the social functioning of texts, and, in addition, their internal construction or adaptability for a diversity of publics and expectations.

In *Born Translated: The Contemporary Novel in an Age of World Literature*, Rebecca Walkowitz identifies the fundamental aspect pertaining to contemporary literature as a marketable product: its ability to function in different languages and attract and interpellate diverse publics that possess clearly differentiated horizons of expectations.[71] Ilse Logie has taken up this theme in Luiselli, of whom some of her texts can be said to be "born translated" in the words of Walkowitz.[72] First published in English and then in Spanish, some of the Mexican writer's works contain elements that could be considered in and of themselves as part of the repertory of the adaptation of the literary artefact for the global market. Distinctive among the resources she employs are her use of intercultural dialogue, inter- or transnational narrative spaces, references that speak to interiorization in several languages, a restriction on localist references, an appeal to universal topics, the use of a standardized language—albeit one that makes use of terms or concepts that add a certain "picturesque" quality ("relingos" or empty spaces, for example)—the multisite location of plots, and the development of characters whose origin and nature function in different contexts etc. Although many of these traits exist in a variety of different texts from different periods, what distinguishes them as aspects of "born translated" literature is their seeming deliberate and conscious interaction with the actual process of production. In these terms, Walkowitz recognizes that some literary texts are directed at varied audiences and participate in different "literary cultures."⁷³ These diverse cultural registers do not necessarily flow seamlessly one into the other, resulting, in some cases, in the untranslatability of certain content, in the retreat of the signifier, and in the incommensurability of the Other that, like a specter, floats outside of time.

Applying Walkowitz's theory, Logie believes *Los ingrávidos* (translated into English as *Faces in the Crowd* from a poem by Ezra Pound) to be an example of the type of writing that reveals the mechanisms at work in the production and translation of a text. The global reception of this type of work can be explained in great part by the fact it projects the author's transnational capital in addition to the "el gesto cosmopolita a través del cual conectan referencias culturales que a primera vista parecen lejanas e incompatibles" (the cosmopolitan gesture through which they connect cultural references that at first seem distant and incompatible).⁷⁴ According to Logie, the first key aspect is "la tensión entre lo local y lo mundial, con lo cual (los autores) logran expandir la noción de literatura latinoamericana, al tiempo que subvierten ese mismo ecosistema global del que forman parte" (the tension between the local and the global, with which [authors] expand the notion of Latin American literature while subverting the very global ecosystem of which they form a part).⁷⁵ The second key aspect can be found in the reference to avant-garde literatures as models that destabilize the traditional conception of the literary by appropriating previous writings or using apocryphal materials etc. It in this sense we should understand Luiselli's rejection of the "translator's invisibility" and the auratic (or "sagrado" [sacred] according to Lorie) value attributed to the original, in service of what could be called a "creative translation" in which the translator modifies or embellishes the original text. More than the transference from one linguistic code to another, the translator's work consists of shaping the text's accessibility as a commodifiable object, adaptable to diverse publics.⁷⁶

Apart from the components inherent to the composition of a literary text that participates in its global reception, we see Luiselli's recognition of translation's creative importance at various levels in her work. Firstly, her involvement in the actual process of translation and the freedom she gives her translators, principally Christina MacSweeney to whom she gave such a free rein that the translator made modifications and additions to the translation of *La historia de mis dientes* (*The Story of My Teeth*).⁷⁷ In addition, Luiselli's Italian translator, Elsa Tramontin, made suggestions that, when incorporated to the original version of *Los ingrávidos* produced a modified text that is now used as the source text by other translators.⁷⁸ Further, Luiselli integrates translation's problematics into the text, reflecting the cultural specificity of Latin American literature and aspects of bilingualism.[79] Logie concludes that "*Los ingrávidos* presenta una estructura de quiasmo: el texto posee aquella misma traducibilidad que pone en tela de juicio. Se caracteriza por una tensión entre su ansia de plasmar un modus operandi multilingüe, que a fin de cuentas constituye la matriz de su pensamiento y de su afecto, y la necesidad de escribir en una sola lengua para poder publicar."[80]

THE IRRITATING *HISTORIA DE MIS DIENTES*

In a hybrid narrative, incorporating visual materials and essay fragments, a Mexican auctioneer tells his story. While the protagonist reveals the events of his picaresque life, an obscure writer pens the auctioneer's (auto)biography, giving rise to a reflection on literary writing, and creating a parallelism in which the symbolic product, like every other object that's offered for sale, attempts to appeal to a competitive, voluble, and fetishistic market. For a more traditional Mexican public, equating literature to merchandise and affirming the superiority of culture's commercialized relationships might have seemed a provocation that too overtly attacks the elitist notion of a culture as spiritual expression, a representation of values, aestheticism, and distraction from everyday challenges. But it is also possible that, above and beyond this discrepancy, this desire to defy conventions, seek originality and experiment with its readers' horizons of expectations, has undermined the book's reception in some circles. Viewed as just chit chat (Roberto Pliego), as an installation and as an example of "humor bobalicón" (dumb humor) (Christopher Domínguez Michael), the text tries to impress the reader with formal stylistic and thematic innovation in a decentered and deliberately fragmented plot, like pieces of a kaleidoscope.[81] From the outset, the protagonist Gustavo Sánchez Sánchez's name embodies redundancy which is then reaffirmed by the alliteration and allusion to the space of automized rapid transit in his nickname "Carretera" (Highway). As a parodic project about literary creation and the construction of communicative spaces, the novel possesses a caricature-like style where narrative fragmentation is extreme and genre classification dissolves into pastiche and experimentation.

In this book, little-appreciated by Mexican critics, the reader is also left feeling impatient and disconnected from the twists and turns of multiple textualities and textures. In my opinion the adverse reaction toward Luiselli's text goes beyond mere impatience with experimentation or the questioning of conventional rules of literary composition and is instead connected to its achievements and not its goals. Immersed in a complex and problematic reality, the Mexican reader is trained in literatures that, for the most part, maintain tight bonds with a cultural experience that, even when involved in sophisticated representational mediations, continues to dialogue with the historical contexts of its past and present. This does not imply that Mexican literary production is always engaged with a discernable representation of events, but the symbolic space of national culture still operates, even in its flight lines, as the primary ambit that few authors can or wish to evade. Strongly marked by a historicist perspective, the horizon of expectations bends toward the conception of literature as a construction by which ideological questions, political tensions, and displacements that go from the real to the imaginary are elaborated in a rich and ample spectrum of proposals and accomplishments. Mexico's socio-cultural, historical, and anthropological density has fertilized an immense territory that, since its colonial origins, has disseminated the real via the imaginary and the material via the symbolic, without allowing parody, satire, sarcasm, or various hybrid forms of the simulacrum to impede the projection of literature as a form of symbolic intervention in the collective imaginary. To my view, these are some of the lines through which the skein of the reception of Mexican literature might be unwound in contemporary Mexico, while still maintaining a connection to some of the latest trends in literary representation as demonstrated in many of the works published in the last few decades.

Rooted in exaggeration and extravagance, hyperbole is the most frequent device in Luiselli's novel. Traces of camp peek out from under an aesthetic of bad taste and irony that artistically positions itself as a counterpoint to the values of beauty and sophistication cultivated and enshrined by modernism. After all, transforming false teeth into an aesthetic and nail clippings into a fetish for collectors can only be a gesture of rebellion—or a theatricalization of that position—against bourgeois taste.

In "Notes on Camp," Susan Sontag characterizes camp's "sensibility" as a form of artificial aestheticism that is frivolous and naively pretentious, playful, performative, disproportionate, depoliticized, and based on excess and the shock value of its aesthetic intentions.[82] In any case, in Luiselli's novel, this aspect—one of several that make up the book—is particularly significant since it offers a clue about the text's poetic synthesis and about the aesthetic perspective that informs it.

COLLECTIONISM AND THE AURA OF THE OBJECT

Divided into six parts, *La historia de mis dientes* is organized into sections whose titles announce their relationship with the central text and their connection to the thematic nucleus in a book that is designed as collage or perhaps pastiche.⁸³ Order and chaos appear from the outset like poles that tighten the book's writing. The different parts into which *La historia de mis dientes* are organized as books with roman numerals, and entitled "Hiperbólicas" (The hyperbolics), "Parabólicas" (The parabolics), "Circulares" (The circulars), "Alegóricas" (The allegorics), "Elípticas" (The elliptics), and "Cronológicas" (The chronologics).

"Hiperbólicas" presents elements of a "autobiografía dental" (dental autobiography) of the character, who from his early childhood, has been obsessed with the idea of changing his teeth, along with an interest in collecting things (his first item being the fingernails his father bit off and spat out in his bedroom). Now an adult, the character's vocation crystallizes in his profession as "el mejor cantador de subastas del mundo" (the best auctioneer in the world) according to his own judgement. His acquisition of "la sagrada dentadura de la mismísima Marilyn Monroe" (the sacred teeth of none other than Marilyn Monroe) for his collection, and the eventual replacement of his own teeth with those of the famed actress, transform the character himself into a collage in which the false teeth, especially because of their provenance, define his entire identity.⁸⁴

Chapters II, III, and IV refer to the different methods used in the auctions to place items and provoke the buyer's interest. The "Parabólicas" that take place in chapter II reveal the characteristics of famous people's teeth (Plato, St. Augustine, Petrarch, Montaigne, Rousseau, Virginia Woolf, Vila-Matas, among others), giving another turn of the screw to the referentialism that Luiselli employs profusely in other works. The last set of teeth to be sold in the auction in the church belongs to Carretera, who inscribes himself into the long sequence of famous people. In his case, the sale of the auratic object, Marilyn Monroe's teeth, bought by Ratzinger, the auctioneer's son, implies the surrender of the body, which is placed against the material and symbolic element that defines it. By means of a strange metonymical situation, Carretera reduces his perpetual object of desire to himself. In Book III, Carretera "seguro de haber ingresado al infierno" (certain of having gone to hell) discovers his teeth are missing, and have been stolen.⁸⁵ In the next section, Roberto Bálser, Beto, appears, introducing himself as "escritor y guía de turistas" (writer and . . . tour guide) again placing creative work in conjunction with more practical and utilitarian functions.⁸⁶ Carretera principally charges him with drafting his biography: "[n]ecesito que escribas mi historia, la historia de mis dientes. Yo te la cuento, tú la escribes, luego la publicas en un periódico para que el mundo sepa de mí. Y ya (I need you to write my story, the story of my teeth. I tell it to you, you just write it. We sell millions and I get my teeth fixed for good. When I die, you write about that too).⁸⁷ In addition, he commissions him to make a catalogue of his collections. Reduced to the category of scribe, Bálser subsumes his creativity into more pedestrian task, although finally he becomes the novel's second narrator. In chapter V, he reveals that the previous sections form part of the (auto)biography he's writing at Carretera's request, upon which he becomes his alter ego.

A hyperbolic and boundless narrative, like the personality of the character it describes, Bálser's (auto)biographical text fulfills its patron's commission, with whom he is linked in an "una amistad a primera vista" (a friendship at first sight) cultivated over a long period of time.⁸⁸

> Highway was one of those vast, eternal spirits. His presence was at times menacing—not because he was a real threat to anyone, but because, in comparison with his ferocious freedom, all the parameters we normally use to measure our actions seem trivial.⁸⁹

The arrival of Bálser puts the theme of authorship into question, since in real life the (auto)biography seems like another's discourse superimposed on the narrative "I" (supposedly protagonist and author of the narration), which violates the principle of this scriptural form. The reader has received the story of Carretera's life as if he himself had told it, when in reality Bálser is responsible for putting together the text, its tone, selection, and plot outlines. The relationship between the characters begins when Carretera is already deteriorating, despite which he convinces Bálser to "escribir [su] autobiografía dental a cambio de asilo" (In exchange for my work as a transcriber, Highway not only gave me board and lodging, but also an education).⁹⁰ He goes on to offer further details:

> When I first knew Highway, he was sick and weak. Whenever he saw his reflection in a mirror, he would say that he looked like a backyard hen and then cluck at himself. Indeed, the little hair that he had was permanently sticking up heavenward; he had scrawny, veined legs, and a rounded, bulging belly. He had lost his beloved false teeth, so that such an ordinary thing as speaking was, if not impossible, a constant battle against humiliation.⁹¹

Bálser's narrative, subject to the patronage of his protector Carretera, is a nonsensical recounting of the most esoteric aspects of the auctioneer's many lives, of his likes, misfortunes, and anecdotes all of which involve characters with famous names (Lina Meruane, Julián Herbert among others). More interesting than his adventures is the description of the "método alegórico" (allegoric method) with which Carretera explains the strategy he invented to promote the items in the auction house.[92] This is consistent with the acknowledgment that:

> it is not objects that are sold (during the allegoric auctions), but the stories that give them value and meaning. The allegorics were, according to Highway, postcapitalist, radical recycling auctions that would save the world from its existential condition as the garbage can of history.[93]

This operation constitutes a new form of fetishization in which, in lieu of valuing an object's aura, its unique and unrepeatable character, we instead value its commodification that, despite its condition as simulacrum, allows us to commercialize it.

The substitution of merchandize for discourse, or the object itself for a statement of its symbolic value, gestures toward a dematerialization that passes through a process of "reciclaje radical" (radical recycling) and ends up turning the object into a residual element ("basura" or garbage) that speaks to the instance of the association of capitalism with the accumulation and fetishization of merchandise. In other words, faced with the decadence of the capitalist world, the materiality of merchandise persists only as excrescence, but discourse (literature?) can imbue this waste with meaning via nostalgia. Stories, not objects, are what sells, and the buyer's competitiveness is oriented toward the affective value of loss and the valorizing of grief which are an effect of language.

In Book V, Luiselli incorporates a long parade of names of well-known writers to whom the author assigns jobs and functions. The auctioning of their stories, that serves to put the allegorical method into practice, invokes the names of Alan Pauls, the retired seamstress Margo Glantz and her son Primo Levi, the not quite young lady Valeria Luiselli, the Captain of Alfa patrol, Yuri Herrera, Tito Livio, Rubén Gallo, Verónica Gerber, Mario Bellatín, Mario Levrero, Heriberto Yépez, Álvaro Enrigue, Guadalupe Nettel, and Guillermo Fadanelli among others. Exhausting, inconsequential and predictable, in the final part entitled "Paseo circular," the list is followed by a series of photographs accompanied by inscriptions that perhaps some critics will understand.

The critical exploration of the function of language and discourse undertaken by Luiselli in her previous book comes into sharper focus in this novel about the life and work of the auctioneer, with its focus on the pragmatic performance of language customary in this profession. In this discursive style, repetition, insistence, monotony along with the development of ample verbal energy rooted in the superfluous all stand out. The auctioneer's voice and diction create a hypnotic effect along with an extreme focus on the audience, encouraging the potential buyer to secure the collectibles and to impose their will on other clients. The points of contact between the auctioneer's platform and the pulpit from which a priest emits a sermon or mass demystifies the solemnity of official and institutional discourses, revealing their pragmatic orientation as well as the process of auratic commodification which is being offered from the stage (collectibles, salvation, ideology). In this way, language is revealed as a malleable and corruptible object, subject to manipulation and decline.

In *The System of Objects*, Jean Baudrillard analyzes the theme of collecting that experts in psychoanalysis, art history and anthropology have also examined. As a never-ending pursuit, this practice (passion, hobby, professional interest) has been viewed as a compensatory act and as a libidinal transference connected to feelings of lack and loss, fetishism, drive satisfaction, and egocentrism. For collectors, their vital impulse centers on acquiring the "missing" object and on the possession of that which completes or crowns a series and thus gives meaning to life itself. Closer to obsession than pastime, collecting only has meaning when the object forms part of a series. The question of belonging strengthens it and gives it value: "And just one object no longer suffices; the fulfillment of the project of possession always means a succession or even a complete series of objects."[94] Baudrillard writes:

> This is what we might call the symbolism of the object, in the etymological sense (cf. Greek sumballein, to put together) in accordance with which a chain of signifiers may be summed up in just one of its terms. The object is the symbol, not of some external agency or value but first and foremost of the whole series of objects of which it is the (final) term. (This in addition to symbolizing the person whose object it is).[95]

As a passion, the art of collecting allows for the investing of almost uncontrollable emotional energy, through which insatiability whose emotional and psychological origins are channeled and become less visible. This feeling crystallizes in the identification of subject and object which can be seen clearly in the character of Carretera who, living in a mental state of mythification, cannot conceive of himself as separate from Marilyn Monroe's teeth. As Baudrillard explains,

> Objects in this sense have another aspect which is intimately bound up with the subject—no longer simply material bodies offering a certain resistance,

they become mental precincts over which I hold sway, they become things of which I am the meaning, they become my property and my passion.⁹⁶

A dynamic is thus created between subject and object:

> For what you really collect is always yourself. This makes it easier to understand the structure of the system of possession: any collection comprises a succession of items, but the last in the set is the person of the collector. Reciprocally, the person of the collector is constituted as such only if it replaces each item in the collection in turn.⁹⁷

Carretera's absurd fixation on Marilyn Monroe's teeth gives him existential support with which the object appears to radiate a symbolic content that gradually takes over his life. Thus, the character experiences separation anxiety from the object and the fear of the self-destruction that loss might cause. The fact that dispossession occurs through the involvement of his son lends the situation greater poignancy along with a psychological and emotional charge. In his pursuit of the object and the discourses that enshrine it, Carretera is always in search of himself. The implanting of Marilyn's teeth into his mouth clearly represents the fusion of subject/object and hybridizes the character from the point of view of class, race and gender (we should remember that his father described himself at birth as "prieto como el petróleo" (dark as the inside of a needle).⁹⁸

In the figure of Carretera the collector, every part of his hypertrophied and, in this sense, anomalous poetic "I" returns to this "I" because, as Baudrillard says, "what you really collect is always yourself."⁹⁹ Each object is a part of him and every famous name with which the object is associated acts as a worn-out fragment of someone else's prestige that sticks to his skin in a process that recalls the interminable referentialism that characterizes Luiselli's work. In Carretera, the question of names finds another explanation here since it feeds into the origin myth and the desire for authenticity that he, as a good auctioneer, has learned to value and use in selling his articles. As Baudrillard points out, the object is important for the collector not only for what it is but also for what it has been, thus imbuing each article with an element of authenticity that stimulates the desire to possess it.¹⁰⁰ Thus, the collector and the auction mutually determine each other through the mediation of language. The auctioneer's rhetoric offers information about the object's previous life, of which the present thing is only its trace. The object thus enters what Baudrillard calls the "'spoken' system of objects" whereby, through the discourse that connects and empowers them, objects generate behaviors, reactions, and relationships between individuals.[101] In the case of Carretera, however, the discourse of legitimization and authentication is a simulacrum that serves to increase the character's pathos and levity (depending on the sensibility of the reader). As Baudrillard explains, indicating his skepticism with respect to the attainment of "authenticity": "it is a cultural irony—but an economic fact—that this thirst for 'authenticity' can now be slaked only by forgery."[102]

The auction house itself is "a fact of language" in which, as John L. Austin would have it, the auctioneer "does things with language." Language expresses itself via its performative function, based on actions or changes that occur in reality, dramatizing the negotiation around value and the meaning of the object as the trace of something superior and intangible. Baudrillard recognizes that there could be something sublime in this insatiable search that goes beyond all functionality: "The collector's sublimity, then, derives not from the nature of the objects he collects (which will vary according to his age, profession and social milieu) but from his fanaticism."[103] Every collection seeks completeness, although it is obvious that this is out of reach. Together with the possession of the thing there is an appropriation of cultural memory since "The past in its entirety has been pressed into the service of consumption."[104] In this sense, collecting proposes a different relationship with the object and modifies its relationship with the medium that contains it:

Our ordinary environment is always ambiguous: functionality is always collapsing into subjectivity and possession is constantly getting tangled with utility as part of the ever disappointed effort to achieve a total integration. Collecting, however, offers a model here: through collecting, the passionate pursuit of possession is transformed into poetry, into a triumphant unconscious discourse.[105]

Collecting saves Carretera from himself, although it also exposes his weaknesses and extravagance:

> The collector is never an utterly hopeless fanatic, precisely because he collects objects that in some way always prevent him from regressing into the ultimate abstraction of a delusional state, but at the same time the discourse he thus creates can never—for the very same reason—get beyond a certain poverty and infantilism. Collecting is always a limited, repetitive process, and the very material objects with which it is concerned are too concrete and too discontinuous ever to be articulated as a true dialectical structure. So if non collectors are indeed "nothing but morons," collectors, for their part, invariably have something impoverished and inhuman about them.[106]

The same applies to the collection of names that form the repertoire of a character who paradoxically uses them in his search for authenticity.

In *La historia de mis dientes*, the attempt to craft an ironic narrative that goes against popular conceptions of the novel, literary language, and narrative composition seems from the outset to be an overly deliberate idea that never clearly establishes a contract with the reader but instead bombards him or her with visual elements, anecdotes, humor, questioning of biographical discourse, ruptures, and pastiche in a sort of chaotic accumulation that serves to exasperate rather than interest. Illustrations (by Daniela Franco), phrases taken from fortune cookies, weird titles, outlandish aspects, photographs, and internet images all come together to form a sometimes-irritating potpourri designed to define an extravagant character who moves through marginal spaces and executes random tasks that some critics have likened to the picaro's improvised and criminal trajectory.

Demonstrating an overly obvious desire for singularity and debunking of the literary canon and "high" culture in general in which the author nonetheless strives to organically insert herself, *La historia de mis dientes* reveals these goals through the intentional way the text was produced. Employees of the Jumex factory, whose art gallery underwrote the writing of the novel, participated in its composition, thus situating the genesis of the text in an unusual space of creative populism that does not seem to have had the desired effect on the reception of the finished product. A group of workers at the factory received installments of Luiselli's work that they then critiqued via MP3 recordings, creating an inter-media circulation of literary textuality that was used to break down the creative process and attempt a collectivized intellectual project.

Contrasts present another relevant element for evaluating the text. These appear at different levels: between the character's humble milieu and the star-studded prestigious names that fuel the text; between writing and orality; between the character names drawn from the universal cultural (primarily Latin American) realm and the jobs they do in the novel; between the type of literature that *La historia de mis dientes* sets out to be and is and the dramatic quality of Mexico's current political and social context. In effect, Luiselli's novel is a ludic text that affirms the idea of literature as entertainment although parody could always be employed in the service of deeper reflections on the parodied materials. However, the narration's anecdotical and trivial emphasis reaffirms what Fredric Jameson said about the weakening of parody in postmodernity, where its ideological and even self-critical value tends to be diluted.[107]

In effect, in his analysis of parody and pastiche as ideological devices, Jameson refers to what he terms "blank parody," which is a critical emptying of this procedure and its replacement with pastiche. He explains that pastiche, like parody, starts out as an imitation of a peculiar style, but it is a neutral practice of mimicry in which the satirical impulse has been "amputated."[108] For Jameson, this weakening responds to the deterioration of the aesthetics of Modernism, in which each of the movement's great authors (Faulkner, Lawrence, Stevens, etc.) possessed their own unique and inimitable style. Postmodernism can only be compared to this aesthetics through its stylistic codes. The cannibalization of these styles is revealed through random and inconsequential stylistic allusions, which result in the proliferation of the "neo."[109] According to Jameson, in this usage of pastiche we lose the connection with history, which transforms into a simulacrum, leaving us submerged in a world of mere "texts" as if the past were nothing more than a repository of genres, styles, and codes to be used as symbolic goods.[110] These reflections on the transformation of parody into pastiche can be usefully adapted to what Luiselli is doing in that the lightness of the appropriative gesture is clearly visible: the referentialism and fictionalization of characters from Modernism who are incorporated into her text without this technique yielding anything more than the "rhetoric of citation." This intensifies the novel's digressive quality to the point where its metatextuality seems more central and interesting than the text itself.

Incorporating ideas from Graziela Speranza's *Atlas portátil de América Latina. Arte y ficciones errantes*, Lorena Amaro Castro sums up the crossings that bisect the novel:

> In this sense, *La historia de mis dientes* is a nomadic form, like those that Speranza describes: an aesthetic at a crossroads, a crossing between diverse geographies (from the office of the author "Luiselli" in New York to her collaborators who read her in a marginal neighborhood in Mexico City, or from this neighborhood's streets to the great avenues and destroyed monuments of European history) and also between artistic and literary genres (the autobiography that becomes a biography, the picaresque, the short biographies the accompany the auction, photographs of a "tourist" itinerary, an artistic catalogue).[111]

The novel's polysemy and multiplicity of voices are not problematic. On the contrary, these are among its most effective techniques because of the possibility they offer to pluralize perspectives, styles, languages, and contexts. But far from resulting in a questioning of totality, or a critique of the authoritarianism of the narrative voice and authorial activity, or the situatedness of the text's meaning, this polysemy and multiplicity of voices disperses in the proliferation of operations, vignettes and materials that cluster around an inconsequential tale.

The novel's reception was far more enthusiastic outside of Mexico, particularly in the US where the reader engaged with the text as a cultural artefact, preferring in many cases works detached from the social problematics of Latin American countries, and which communicate the idea of literature as a space of convergence in which the aesthetic value, experimentalism, and/or reverie are devices for the filtering of political content. In the case of this novel, the translation to English by Christina MacSweeney not only delivers a cultural and linguistic transfer of the original but also channels a text modified by the translator herself for the Anglo-Saxon reader. In effect, MacSweeney changes the names of characters and modifies events along with composing a chapter in which the life of the protagonist is "contextualized," with mentions of the expropriation of oil in Mexico along with trivial facts included to provide ironic contrast. This intervention problematizes the theme of authorship by disassembling the genre's predictable protocols, replacing them with an almost erratic textuality. Both texts, in Spanish and English, constitute variations of the story, adapted for the publics for which they are intended. The English translation cuts the number of images by half and changes their accompanying annotations. Literary textuality is negotiated through attention to the market and the plurality of publics for which it is intended.

The text's ironic aspects are thus situated in both formal questions (compositional, lexical etc.) as well as questions of content. The irony establishes itself thematically in the singular materiality that provokes the protagonist's interest: his collectibles, the courses he takes, the names of the people who surround him including his wives, whose quirks add humor and whimsy to the text. But the meta-textual elements that are found in the margins of the central narrative also incorporate images, explanations of these, aphorisms, drawings, headings, etc. that serve to frame the text in the fragmentary, heterogeneous register of "radical recycling" that organizes it.

Regarding the use of names of famous writers that appear as a way of propping up the introduction of fictious stories in which their imagined identities intervene, Amaro Castro has explained that the list of names in Book II that provides information about one of Carretera's most important auctions is not in fact arbitrary but instead incorporates names of authors who belong to a specific tradition. While Plato, Augustine of Hippo, Petrarch, Montaigne, and Rousseau are all precursors of the genre of biography, Chesterton, Virginia Woolf, Borges and Vila-Matas all interweave their own lives with literary creation, in other words auto-fiction. In this sense, according to Amaro Castro "[e]l libro de Luiselli parece poner en jaque, particularmente, la idea de tradición literaria, no solo desacralizando la definición de lo autobiográfico y lo biográfico, sino también apropiándose de la historia de un pícaro contemporáneo" (Luiselli's book seems to particularly question the concept of literary tradition, not only demystifying how we define biography and autobiography but also appropriating the story of a contemporary pícaro).[112] Following Amaro Castro's reading, Luiselli's perspective "permite identificar el texto como una "fábula biográfica" que muestra la vida "ejemplar" de un insólito y chapucero self-made-man, en mucho cercano a la figura de un narrador contemporáneo" (allows us to classify the text as a "biographical fable" that reveals the "exemplary" life of a peculiar and amateurish self-made man, who in many ways approximates the figure of a contemporary narrator).[113] But to arrive at this conclusion, Amaro Castro should have isolated this list of authors from the novel's overall process of referentialism and "name dropping" that persists throughout all of Luiselli's work and does not uphold an interpretation connected to author theory but instead, in my opinion, speaks more to the cultural gesture of self-inscription as well as irony and iconoclasm toward tradition. Amaro Castro does affirm that while "a veces es posible hallar un sentido, . . . en otros momentos del libro predominan el chiste, la impostura y el sinsentido; el uso disparatado del nombre no parece tener un significado profundo, oculto y unívoco tras su uso" (at times it is posible to find meaning . . . at other times in the book jokes, artificiality and nonsense prevail; the ludicrous use of names does not seem to possess a deeper, hidden and unambiguous meaning behind it).[114] I agree.

THE AUCTION HOUSE AS NEGOTIATION OF MEANING

As we know, every object has a value that is relative to the way it inserts itself in the market, both in material as well as symbolic terms. The auction theatricalizes the relationship between supply and demand, creating a competitive dynamic around the object to which different potential buyers can attribute value, depending on the estimate of its utility and the positioning of each regarding the object. Use value and exchange value are articulated or confront one another, transforming each element into merchandise that constantly redefines its price. In this realm, negotiation consists of a semiotic exchange in which language functions as a dipositive of acquisitional power and of the constant reassigning of value within a variable context determined by acceleration and the persistence of discourse. In this sense, Marco Ramírez Rojas has suggested that *La historia de mis dientes* is a ludic reflection on transnational processes and the assigning of value with regards to literary discourse.[115] Luiselli's novel begins by offering one of the least prestigious corporal elements as the heart of the story. Since antiquity, eyes and then hearing are the most recognizable centers of human physicality, but teeth refer not only to a part of the body that possesses limited poetic resonance but that is also, in this case, a prosthetic substitution. The dentures that the character Sánchez Sánchez, or "Carretera" collects, replace his own teeth, thus placing the narrative in an absurd and risible plane of comedic significance. This protagonist, a working-class man from one of the marginal and most dangerous neighborhoods in Mexico City, is obsessed with collecting. He began his hobby as a child when he started to collect and treasure his father's fingernails. He becomes obsessed with other objects (straws, rubber bands, paperclips) during distinct phases of his life, in the same way that he compulsively takes personal enrichment classes that cover a wide spectrum of topics, from first aid to dance and auctioneering. He marries a woman whom he met in dance class and together they have a child from whom he grows apart until he meets him again during an auction, years later. He marries again and dedicates himself to collecting the false teeth of famous people, with Marilyn Monroe's dentures being his prized possession, which he adapts for his own use. In the auction Carretera holds in the Santa Apolonia church he reencounters his son who kidnaps him; he also loses Marilyn's teeth. There he meets Roberto Bálser and together they undertake to recover this and other possessions. Bálser agrees to write his biography and ends up drafting the book's final chapter.

During "Carretera's" activities, language is not a trustworthy instrument. He uses it to sell strange objects about which he strives to pique people's curiosity and desire to possess them. The rhetorical devices he puts into practice (circularity, ellipsis, parabola, hyperbole, and allegory) are referenced with ironically technical names that present a ridiculous contrast with the objects and the procedures that the auctioneer's language channels in a farcical theatricalization for his public. He possesses an irritating, utilitarian, and obsessive orality, designed to bestow value on garbage. Residue and relic become confused, installing a relativism that touches languages.

Carretera's own story features the description of a fictional character as told by another character in a narrative unfurling that illustrates the relationship between literary production and the selling of a story, between commercialization and consumption. A mechanism inherent to poetic and fictional production that postmodernity has brought to light, literature's commodification within the preeminence of the market also existed in earlier historical periods in less visible and accepted forms that were normalized as part of the history of Western culture. Writing acknowledges itself as recycling, as a material that constructs, deconstructs, and reconstructs at different moments in the cycle of production, publication, and dissemination of the product. Ramírez Rojas believes this process to be a reconfiguration of the literary "archive" since Luiselli reuses stories, biographies, songs and internet materials in a new context.[116] The perspective shaped by commercialization and by the cultural politics of neoliberalism is offset with a vision of art and literature as auratic processes and products, derived from individualities marked by the gift of symbolic representation who are bearers of transcendent messages and that were popular and still are today in Mexico and in Latin America in general.[117]

Hyperbole is one of Luiselli's chief techniques. According to "Carretera," he is the best auctioneer in the world. Opinions, evaluations, estimates, prices etc. all possess a subjective force that imposes itself as objective fact, although the simulacrum and the effect of the rhetoric of persuasion and seduction of the listener possess only a limited impact. Language modifies reality, imprinting an aura of prestige that results in profit. The "truth value" of discourse does not count since everything depends on the way words are manipulated to convince potential buyers, creating competition to artificially elevate the price of the item whose value comes from people's desire. The reader thus participates in a particular form of production of commercial fetishization, since the set of teeth according to "Carretera" will bestow the original owner's gifts on the purchaser (Plato, St. Augustine, Rousseau, Woolf, Borges, Vila-Matas, among others).[118] In this way, the auction creates a farcical and irreverent circulation not only of intimate objects and body parts of famous people, but also of their intellectual attributes that have been magically transferred through teeth that are perceived as transmitters of cultural memory, thus demonstrating the allegorical and mediatized nature of commercial value. All stories affirm their value when materialized through commercial pricing. Do we, therefore, measure art by its marketable value?

Since value is arbitrarily consigned, ephemeral, and completely subjective, everything is potentially valuable and collectable. Preparing for a great auction, he points to the emptiness and the things he does not possess. Among the objects that are not in his warehouse—which supposedly contains collections of all types of things—he describes "colecciones de dientes, mapas antiguos, partes de coches, muñecas rusas, periódicos en todos los idiomas imaginables, monedas viejas, uñas, bicicletas, timbres, puertas, ligas, suéteres, piedras, máquinas de coser" (collections of teeth of course, but also antique maps, car parts, Russian dolls, newspapers in every imaginable language, old coins, nails, bicycles, bells, doors, belts, sweaters, stones, sewing machines).[119]

But the empty shelves display only a space of desire, where the mental image of possible objects gestures toward a not yet fully realized form of existence. Ramírez Rojas opportunely reminds us of the archive's spectral quality—neither visible nor invisible—as defined by Derrida.[120] Seen from the perspective of the archive, all collections are a nostalgic expression of totality, a project that is necessarily unfinished and unfinishable that carries a great symbolic and affective charge.

But if the novel revolves around the topic of collecting, the work's actual composition echoes this gesture by encompassing, as I pointed out earlier, contrasting if not opposing aspects related to the language and the cultural forms represented in the narrative. The sequence of names of acclaimed representatives of Western literature and philosophy, constitutes an attempt of parodic appropriation that inscribes the author's name within an advantageous company of a wide corpus, indicating a desire to belong to this intellectual Parnassus in which, at least at the level of names, the narrator appears to move alongside her peers. The familiarity she demonstrates with these authors, whom she casually references using nicknames, diminutives, first names etc. and whose names she uses for secondary characters in the frame narratives, is part of a process of appropriation that, without traveling the risky pathways of parricide or without subjecting herself to the "anxiety of influence," elaborates an ironic distance that seems to indicate simultaneously vanquishing and reinforcing the aura. The appropriation of the name but not the cultural person or the work itself of these authors creates an emptying that dilutes a text that in any case remains circumscribed within a symbolic field that is open to wide public who are generally unfamiliar with high culture.

In this sense, from the outset, *La historia de mis dientes* cultivates a populist tone that tries to demystify literary creation and convert it into a collective operation in which the Jumex employees participate directly as the first recipients and critics of the text about which they recommend modifications and plot ideas that, according to Luiselli, were incorporated into the final version, bringing into the writing the language of orality. The minoritized figure of "Carretera" and the peripheral neighborhood of Ecatepec where he resided also add a populist tone to the work, which flirts with some of the canonical registers of Western literature such as popular culture, camp, photography, the world of the spectacle and the contributions of Google maps, making the reader undergo a type of marathon destined to put his/her resistance to the test and perhaps reinforce postmodern arguments against literature.

The extravagant nature of *La historia de mis dientes* is not limited to the above. Among other things, this work suffers from excess. It presents a saturated textuality that does not know when to draw the line and, at the end of the novel, uses the phrase all auctioneers employ to bring the auction to an end for both readers and critics "¿Quién da más?" to which, undoubtedly, we will not lack for answers.[121]

LOS NIÑOS PERDIDOS (UN ENSAYO EN CUARENTA PREGUNTAS)

THE MIGRANT'S VIA CRUCIS AND THE THEATER OF BELONGING

Los niños perdidos (un ensayo en cuarenta preguntas) presents itself as essay but, in fact, possesses a hybrid quality that is more sociological than literary and is framed around the official questionnaires that are given to minor children, mainly from the Northern Triangle countries of Central America (Guatemala, El Salvador, and Honduras as well as Mexico) who enter the US without documents.[122] In the text, Valeria Luiselli aims to expose the situation endured by this specific and particularly vulnerable sector of the migratory movement. The essay, published in English as *Tell Me How It Ends: An Essay in Forty Questions* won the American Book Award in recognition of the importance of its theme and the originality of its engagement with it.[123] The essay draws on the experience of the narrator as a volunteer interpreter in New York City Family Court, which reviews the potential legal immigration status and the circumstances of arrival into the US of unaccompanied minors. If refused admission, these children are to be deported to their country of origin. The text combines the actual content of official questioning with a description of the institutional setting where these proceedings take place, the work of lawyers and other officials, and the participation of the children and their relatives who are residents in the US. At the same time Luiselli, identified with the narrator, reveals aspects of her personal life and her own experiences before she herself secured residency in the US. Again, the method followed is the identification of the narrator with a bigger group that offers her legitimacy through inclusion.

The theme gives rise to a series of aspects that connect to the question of migration: the twists and turns of the law and its applications in Mexico as well as in the US; the different anti-immigration policies that have been applied to stem the flow of people from the south; the victimization of economically vulnerable populations who risk their lives in search of a dignified means of survival, fleeing systemic violence and daily violence, as well as precarity, scarcity of resources, and lack of employment opportunities. Maps, descriptions, reports on migrant deaths, multiple stories of routes followed by people as they abandon their countries of origin as well as the obstacles they encounter and the abuse they suffer all come together to form a narrative that finds its unity in the figure of the narrator who organizes the different elements from a position of empathy, invested in the situation of migrants, particularly children, who travel alone and who represent one of the most desperate and dramatic aspects of this transnational situation.

At the same time as the text sheds light upon situations of lack, State negligence, organized crime, and the collapse of civil society in the countries south of the Rio Grande, it also informs us of the equally reprehensible political and cultural violence in the US where migrant children and adults are subject to discrimination, persecution, and different kinds of abuse. References to forms of resistance and solidarity appear, like the work of Las Patronas in Veracruz who help migrants who travel on top of the carriages of cargo trains, and the organization Hermanos del Camino led by Father Alejandro Solalinde who also helps migrants who pass through those areas. However, the book makes clear that, while these actions bring comfort, they are not sufficient to address the scope of the problem.

> If anything, they are fleeting glimpses of hope in the dark and raucous nightmare where the metal wheels of La Bestia continually screech and howl. . . . The country (Mexico) is now a limbo for migrants, an enormous and terrifying customs office staffed as often by white-collar criminals as it is by criminals with guns and pickup trucks.[124]

The children are reluctant to talk about their lives and family situations and when they do, they feel intimidated, embarrassed, stumbling over their usage of an alien language since theirs is transformed into a subaltern tongue that needs to be mediated and interpreted before being entered into the official record. As Luiselli explains in the text: "El problema es que las historias de los niños siempre llegan como revueltas, llenas de interferencia, casi tartamudeadas. Son historias de vidas tan devastadas y rotas, que a veces resulta imposible imponerles un orden narrativo" (The children's stories are always shuffled, stuttered, always shattered beyond the repair of a narrative order. The problem with trying to tell their story is that it has no beginning, no middle and no end).[125]

The migrants face threats at the hands of drug cartels and gangs such as Mara Salvatrucha and Barrio 18 as well as the coyotes they hire to guide them in their border crossings and connected journeys. They are also exposed to other forms of common crime and abuse at the hands of delinquents and border officials, police, and the army. This is a sketch of some of the most salient lines of a complex and variable mobilization that has given rise to a plethora of conflicting theories. These situations are also impacted by the circulation of stereotypes that are intended to dissuade migrants from embarking on their journey. Alongside regional differences and a constantly changing and unstable situation subject to pressure from a diverse range of interest groups, the children emerge as a constant sector, almost like a collective character that, despite the atomization that they represent and the differences in personal origins and situations, are the object of a necropolitics that the author describes as "una grieta, una fisura, la larga cicatriz continental."[126]

> The roots and reach of the current situation branch out across hemispheres and form a global network whose size and real reach can't even imagine. It's urgent that we begin talking about the drug war as a hemispheric war, at least—one that begins in the Great Lakes of the northern United States and ends in the mountains of Celaque in southern Honduras. . . . The children who cross Mexico and arrive at the US border are not "immigrants," not "illegals," not merely "undocumented minors." Those children are refugees of war and, as such, they should all have the right to asylum.[127]

Using the same ideological construct of "barbarism" that Yuri Herrera employs in *Señales que precederán al fin del mundo*, Luiselli demonstrates how the child migrants are classified as "los bárbaros del sur" (the southern barbarians), in contrast to the "we" who live in the "el civilizado norte" (the northern civilization), in accordance with the stereotypes that appear in the press, official discourse and transnational imaginaries:[128]

> Official accounts in the United States—what circulates in the newspaper or on the radio, the message from Washington, and public opinion in general—almost always locate the dividing line between "civilization" and "barbarity" just below the Río Grande.[129]

In his prologue to *Los niños perdidos*, Jon Lee Anderson highlights the opportune nature of the topic and the close connection between race and migration. While the latter is not an aspect that Luiselli explicitly develops in the book, it nonetheless underlies the whole issue:

In this hallucinatory global political climate, in which bigoted notions about national identity, sect, and race have reared their heads to a degree not seen in many decades, Trump's statements gained him a sizeable American following. It is distressingly clear that the fears and hatreds he has unleased . . . will not be easily put to rest.[130]

As a potential instance for an articulation of the social and the political, community is another important topic that appears in *Los niños perdidos*. In the reactions and forms of community organization, the author sees a possible practical response to the migration question, offering as an example the actions proposed by her students (giving English lessons, creating radio programs and opportunities for team sports as well as offering advice on civil rights and responsibilities).[131]

In *Los niños perdidos*, Luiselli pays special attention to the question of the children's integration in and adaptation to a new social milieu once they have been inserted into their new reality either as residents or with temporary permits. "The great theater of belonging" is the fiction American society imposes daily to accept the inclusion of the Other, but also implies what can be lost in the adoption of new ways of life:

> No matter the cost. No matter the cost of the rent, and milk, and cigarettes. The humiliations, the daily battles. You will give everything. You will convince yourself that it is only a matter of time before you can be yourself again, in America, despite the added layers of its otherness already so adhered to your skin. But perhaps you will never want to be your former self again.[132]

The display of sensibility, the theme of return and the way it transforms individuals again recalls the fiction of Yuri Herrera who, with the character of the protagonist's brother in *Señales que precederán al fin del mundo* expresses the drama of the situation remain/return, confronting the reader with the complexity of the topic and the costs of border crossing. More impactful in my opinion than any documentary engagement with the topic, Herrera's fiction possesses the virtue of transferring the locus of enunciation to a third space that mediates between reality and the simple creation of purely imagined situations. In this contaminated and hybrid between-space, the author deploys a range of possibilities without the narrator's consciousness explicitly interfering with the process of novelistic reception. The contract between reader and writer that *Señales que precederán al fin del mundo* establishes is different since the narrator's individuality gives free rein to the book's characters, as if they were masters of their own domain. The value of Luiselli's text is more direct and makes room for the editor or interpreter to interject themselves into the textual scenario as a mediating figure whose conscience communicates the message of the text. This process, while not completely alien to fiction, makes its appearance wrapped in the aesthetics of re/presentation. *Testimonio*, chronicle, and even essay can lay claim to "truth" that fiction cannot, since its principal function is to interpret and translate the source material into the symbolic realm.

At the end of the essay, the author claims that the stories she narrates are true, although she has modified the children's names and identifying information to protect the integrity of their court cases. Alongside reemphasizing the authenticity of the facts and situations included in the text, she explains how she has incorporated statistics, journalistic articles, reports, and information communicated by lawyers and social workers etc. These explanations reference the names of the people and the documents she consulted proving that, at the time of the text's publication, such information was in wide circulation within academia and the media (although for the reader of Luiselli's work these facts and the circumstances of the migrants'—particularly the children—were less familiar). Further, it is obvious that Luiselli makes use of the symbolic capital she has garnered as a well-known writer to emphasize the social and political importance of the processes that require, as she herself points out, the engagement of the community.

Luiselli's efforts to identify the narrator with the object of study and to build a public image in which daily domestic matters of a personal nature enter into the topic under consideration are obvious. The accumulation of unnecessary references to her niece, who works alongside her as a court interpreter, as well as to her daughter's questions about the fate of the highly expendable child migrants, constitute an attempt to bring the social problem closer to home, and implicate the author of this essay in the topic. This leads to an identification with the reading public around the topic of transnationalization, which holds great sway at the grassroots level and is undoubtedly an important and constantly debated social question. This in turn brings us to the concept of "differential inclusion," or what we might call the selective procedures that have always been at play on the US–Mexico border as a way of filtering individuals according to US labor needs, diplomatic privileges and other considerations that view poor and particularly unproductive migrants as a residual and disposable sector of the immigrant community.

MICROHISTORY AND LITERATURE

Los niños perdidos could be seen as an example of an against the grain reading of official discourses. This tactic has been deployed on occasions, albeit without much of a theoretical framework, by different subaltern orientations in a variety of critical contexts. It involves the recuperation of voices, events, circumstances, processes, and social and political agents who, for varied reasons, have remained at the margins of dominant historical narratives. Minimized or invisiblized by official or prevailing narratives, such aspects of the development of historical and social struggles tend to disappear under the weight of the archive that is administered by cultural and political powers in accordance with their interests and perspectives. These kinds of counter-readings begin by investigating the discourse along with the documents that sustain it. Above all, in this process, the main interpretive focus rests on the place occupied by vanquished or economically, politically, culturally, or socially disadvantaged sectors, in order to recover alternative narratives that would otherwise remain lost to history. A form of cultural resistance or historical memory, this type of reading also represents an attempt to vindicate the positionality and circumstances of the Other (the dispossessed, vanquished, devalued, the protagonist of minor histories or infrapolitical processes unrecognized by official history, as if they had occurred under the radar of traditional historiography).

Childhood represents a particularly vulnerable and unseen sector of society that seems incapable of developing its own agency, existing in a situation of subordination that leads it to cede its rights to its progenitors, or to those who function as assigned guardians. In the case of the migrant, various levels of subalternity are layered upon each other and combine to create the dramatic figure of the *child migrant*, above all minors who suffer the violent and risky aftermath of deterritorialization. In this sense, the child migrant is, in a way, an excessive figure, laden with meaning, since it acquires diverse levels of significance that appeal to various societal domains such as psychology, law, politics, culture, or other converging cultural and economic perspectives.

For this reason, the representation of childhood implies specific aesthetic and ideological challenges among which we find discursive heterogeneity with respect to the world that is being described. This social sector is always studied from *outside* or from *above* by narrators or researchers who are not part of the universe of childhood but instead see it as a discursive object to be interpreted—translating or speculating about children's thoughts, needs, desires, and emotionality.

In *Los niños perdidos*, the narrator and interpreter of the children's world, seeks to give voice to the voiceless in a rational, discursive, coherent, and conventional manner and relay the messages that will render their circumstances and interior lives intelligible. This act of ventriloquism highlights not only the subaltern nature of childhood but also the diversity of languages used to engage with it. In Luiselli's text, the child represents the center of a Babel-like exchange that uses different codes and registers: English, Spanish, "standard" Spanish as well as working-class variants and dialects, regionalisms and slang, administrative and day-to-day language, adults' idiomatic speech, and the still-forming language of children. In the case of the child migrants, low levels of education and the intimidating and tense situation of the interviews also make communication more challenging.

Loosely following the order of the official questionnaires, Luiselli's text is fragmentary and marked by several interpolated stories that lend verisimilitude to the narration and include episodes relayed by the children during questioning, as well as references to exchanges between the narrator and other family members (her niece who works with her as a court interpreter, her daughter). Emotional but not excessively sentimental, the writing in *Los niños perdidos* is serious and clear and demonstrates a desire to communicate the author's engagement with the topic and its protagonists.

The against the grain reading of *Los niños perdidos* combines essay-like traits with those of a report and a chronicle. Objectivity, incorporated via facts, responses to the questions and information about the meaning of the process and its implementation (institutional space, figures who channel the legal process, interactions, etc.) is also contingent on a subjective perspective that editorially interprets and modifies, as in testimonial literature, the raw material. In this way, the reader encounters an interpellative writing that does not disguise its bias nor its attempt to denounce a dramatically relevant social problem whose details are unknown to much of the public.

The other important aspect in the text is its adherence to microhistory, a style that took off in the 1970s.[133] As a reaction to the all-encompassing and homogenizing nature of grand historical narratives that claim to cover a wide range of processes and that above all highlight the story of the victors and the dominant ideological perspective, microhistory focuses more on small units of communal action, case studies, individuals or discrete experiences that prioritize persons or groups as well as actions, circumstances and representative situations. Connected to cultural history, the reconstruction of daily life and the experience of specific spaces and subjects that in other ways would not be considered part of general cultural, economic, or political development, microhistory digs into "minor" events that complicate (interrupt, interpellate) large-scale historical narratives. Marginalized subjects (Indigenous peoples, sexual minorities, exploited peasants, guerrillas), peripheral spaces (convents, asylums, prisons) disadvantaged individuals (disabled, children, the elderly, unhoused people etc.) thus encounter a space in which an era's big problems and questions crystallize in a concrete and eloquent way. Through this method of reading history, discursive forms as well as silences and restraint, writing as well as orality, institutional forms as well as domestic ones, symbolic and material aspects are all open to interpretation. For this reason, the "editorial" perspective of the interpreter who selects these materials is fundamental. In *Los niños perdidos*, Luiselli expresses this idea in the following terms:

> And perhaps the only way to grant any justice—were that even possible—is by hearing and recording those stories over and over again so that they come back, always, to haunt and shame us. Because being aware of what is happening in our era and choosing to do nothing about it has become unacceptable. Because we cannot allow ourselves to go on normalizing horror and violence. Because we can all be held accountable if something happens under our noses and we don't dare even look.[134]

Luiselli appears to use all these micro-historical elements in *Los niños perdidos* in which the textual interactions between questionnaire and interrogation, the replies obtained and the interpretation of them allow us to connect and problematize the relationship between high culture and popular culture, between migratory policy and concrete situations or, in other words, counterpose law and life, regulations and experiences and power and vulnerability.

Far from allowing the preeminence of the "minor" stories of the migrant children to displace the narrator's individuality, *Los niños perdidos* not only highlights but also complements, to a large degree, the writer's public image as someone engaged with the realities of her historical moment, an attitude that prevails among Latin American authors. The continuity she creates between her own children and the migrant children also reinforces the identification between the narrator and the actual author. The text affirms the idea that the author's principal contribution is to provide knowledge of the facts and thus contribute to creating a social conscience: "Contar historias no sirve de nada, no arregla vidas rotas. Pero es una forma de entender lo impensable"

(Telling stories doesn't solve anything, doesn't reassemble broken lives. But perhaps it is a way of understanding the unthinkable).¹³⁵

At the same time, many of the micro stories that she analyzes will remain buried in the archive's static record, and the "cases" found there need a voice to project them out into the world. Literature, especially that of a testimonial nature, encompasses writing's "mission" to speak for the Other, for those without a voice, thus creating a complex ventriloquism that channels the exteriority of the editor, or compiler or interpreter of testimonials toward the interiority of the enunciation:

> The girls were so young and even if they had a story that secured legal intervention in their favor, they didn't know the words necessary to tell it. For children of that age, telling a story—in a second language, translated to a third—a round and convincing story that successfully inserts them into legal proceedings working up to their defense is impossible.¹³⁶

Language is, in and of itself, a territory, one's own or someone else's that must be crossed so that existence can be recognized in its alternatives and in its dramas, and so that discourse can effectively activate mechanisms that can guarantee the rights of human beings. *Los niños perdidos* serves as a pre-text for the literariness that will become more prominent in *Lost Children Archive* and as an embryonic form of the fictionalization that two years later will provide the raw material for the novel that incorporates the question of migration as one of its lines of argument.

The question of truth competes in both books with that of verisimilitude. As in any testimonial text, mediation is central, whether in personalized forms that are part of the situations represented in the book (interviewers, relatives, transcribers) or in the procedures that are used to channel the material the children provide. Between their utterances and the text itself, filtering elements deliver the reactions the migrant children's experiences provoke in the translator, whose subjectivation finds expression, for example, in the superimposing of the translator's "I" upon the "I" that produces the enunciation, or in a back and forth that makes the children's words float between their emission, reception by the translator and (second hand) reception by the reader. As the narrator of *Los niños perdidos* acknowledges:

> During the interviews, I sometimes note the children's answers in the first person and sometimes in the third. I crossed the border by foot. She swam across the river. He comes from San Pedro Sula. She comes from Tegucigalpa. She comes from Guatemala City. He has not ever met his father. Yes I have met

my mother. But she doesn't remember the last time she saw her. He doesn't know if she abandoned him.[137]

In ethnographic discourse, contact between the expert and the realities and subjects under examination modifies the object of analysis. The children and situations connected to the questionnaires are altered and perhaps fictionalized in some ways (by the narrator filling in gaps in the information with conjectures or attributing a meaning to them, emotionalizing them, identifying the children who are interviewed with her own, or including the migrant children in the pre-text for a literary discourse that will become a novel). The critical, essayistic, and testimonial discourse—to a degree that that is difficult to gauge and unnoticed by the reader—turns the raw material into literature. Without losing force, this material remains trapped in a limbo where reality becomes part of the world being represented, subject to the mechanisms of symbolic production.

Much of the information Lusielli included in her 2016 book was already circulating by then in the large body of work on migration, border studies, scholarship on deportation, studies on traditional and modern technologies for border control, persecution of undocumented people, and other similar situations. Testimonial-type studies such as US anthropologist Jason de León's *The Land of Open Graves: Living and Dying on the Migrant Trail* (with photographs by Michael Wells) offer an enormous quantity of details on the dramatic crossings of Mexico's northern border and the tragic end that many migrants meet on US soil.[138] Novels and chronicles, testimonials and narratives, microhistories and documentary texts have all invaded the cultural market and proliferated at both the academic and journalistic level. In this way, concrete information on methods, conditions, routes, and reprisals connected to the question of migration as it appears in *Los niños perdidos* is not new, although it might have been for Luiselli's readers, especially those that know her through her fiction. However, her focus on children who make the journey alone from the direct perspective of having worked with them provides a different facet of the maternity that the author has incorporated into her public person along with the enunciative voice that is operational in her fictional works, adding an emotional and empathetic charge to the real horror that underlies the story.

Among the themes that Luiselli's book brings up are the situations of violence and vulnerability that the migrant children are escaping. She expands on the conditions they encounter when they arrive in the US not only from the point of view of migrant persecution and legal impediments but also regarding the discrimination and danger they experience in the poor neighborhoods where they end up that are not so different from the ones they left behind. She also includes references to the stereotypes that describe the children as "una plaga bíblica" (a biblical plague) that has come to lay waste to the American Eden and describes the different journeys they take from their homes during which they undergo a myriad of obstacles and almost unimaginable situations.[139] Among the most extreme is the journey aboard "la Bestia" (The Beast), a train that migrants board secretly, traveling on the roof, from where they often fall when the train moves. There they often suffer abuse at the hands of coyotes or gang members who prey on the most vulnerable. In addition, the governments of the USA and/or Mexico implement bilateral or unilateral plans to detect and prosecute migrants and deport them, etc. These include the Mexican government's Programa Frontera Sur (Southern Border Program), which aims to prevent the transmigration of Central Americans through Mexico. Some of the measures included in this plan include, for example,

> Drones, security cameras and control centers in strategic locations (trains, tunnels, bridges, railway crossings, and city centers); fences and floodlights in the rail yards; private security teams and geolocation technology in trains; alarm systems and motion detectors on the tracks; and last but not least, the notorious Grupos Beta, which, under the guise of a humanitarian aid organization, locates and then reports migrants to immigration officials who can then "secure" them—a Mexican euphemism for "capture and deport." Programa Frontera Sur is the Mexican government's new augmented-reality videogame: the player who hunts down the most migrants wins.[140]

With its accessible structure, its factual but simultaneously subjective tone (the narrator/author's identification with the topic), *Los Niños Perdidos* has reached a wide public, above all in the US. In my opinion, far from helping the cause, the (over)utilization of the same topic in her next work, the novel *Lost Children Archive* undermines the position of the author by allowing a theme, whose dramatic quality and particular protagonists lends itself to *testimonio*, melodrama, fictionalization and other registers—albeit not at the same time nor for the same purpose—to redundantly permeate first one text and then another.

LOST CHILDREN ARCHIVE

Possessing greater narrative consistency than Luiselli's earlier texts, *Lost Children Archive* incorporates lessons from previous works. The author engages with literary devices and discursive threads that reveal a more ambitious and complex project, gesturing toward a public with more diverse interests. With my previously expressed reservations in mind, the novel attempts to articulate various lines of argument or, more precisely, various mechanisms that guide the narration.

Originally published in English with the title of *Lost Children Archive*, the text possesses a palimpsestic structure that accumulates levels of meaning, narrative strata and perspectives, resulting in a novelistic constellation that veers off in different directions, unravelling various interior stories that emerge as the characters move through space and time.[141] Both the themes of the novel and the literary devices used by the author form the poetic foundations of a literary project of obvious historical relevance. Employing an accessible and fluid prose that is in dialogue with her other works, Luiselli efficiently configures an interpretation of perspectives, changing scenarios, a plurality of voices, and the progression of the plot. *Lost Children Archive* constructs a discursive space that comprises other books and stories. In this sense, the novel serves as a matrix text within which she reworks her previous book, *Los niños perdidos (un ensayo en cuarenta preguntas)*. In addition, Luiselli inserts another text within the pages of *Lost Children Archive*: the *Elegies for Lost Children* by the fictitious author Ella Camposanto. Similarly, *Lost Children Archive* constitutes a journey through space and time that contains other journeys within it—both real and fictitious—like those in the audiobooks of William Golding's *Lord of the Flies* and Cormac McCarthy's *The Road* that tell of children who have survived the apocalypse and that the family listen to in the car.[142] Also forming part of the family's listening material during their road trip is David Bowie's song "Space Oddity," which tells the story of an interplanetary journey. This technique metaphorizes the vision of the novel and, perhaps the story itself, and serves as a master narrative that contains infinite stories, visions/versions within itself that problematize the knowledge, representation, and interpretation of the events, exhibiting the folds and refolds of a multiple and never-ending temporality. In the plurality of experience, simultaneous stories compete for visibility, creating reciprocal meaning between themselves. In a variety of registers, we see relationships between power and knowledge that activate languages and memories and open themselves to the heterogeneous and never-ending production of meaning.

Both essay and denunciation, fiction and chronicle, testimonial and literary creation combine in a text where the subjective interacts with the facts recorded by empirical observation and bibliographical information. Memories from other books, erudite references, interior monologue, continual discourse, fragmentation, and intercalation of visual and auditory materials such as radio news bulletins and songs, etc., appeal to the process of pastiche employed less effectively in the author's previous works. In addition, the novel also includes contrapuntal chronologies that act like polyphonous lines in search of a center. In this way, past and present, the ephemeral and the transcendent, the local/quotidian, the longue durée of history, and the cycles of life and death overlap. *Lost Children Archive* serves, then, as a narrative constellation that revolves around the paradigm of mobility through the real and imaginary territories of a modernity that sits atop the outrages of colonialism. This process introduces the dynamics between the imposing civilizing ethos of Western cultures, which requires the annihilation of otherness, a binary notion that will be at the center of *Lost Children Archive*. Following a path Luiselli established in *Los niños perdidos*, the novel's plot is oriented toward a reconstruction of the traces left by lives excluded from US territories through the mobilization of the soundscape as the auditory archive of the eradication of North American Indigenous peoples and of the human groups who are currently being obliterated through anti-migratory practices.

This focus on the auditory is part of a trend that cultural criticism has used to recover traces of life under threat from environmental problems or in sociopolitical situations that disconnect the subject from the world that surrounds him or her. In this regard, sound has been studied in situations of extermination, imprisonment, voluntary isolation, captivity etc. that acknowledge the importance of the auditory as a way of engaging with one's surroundings. When vision is impeded, sound becomes the chief element for understanding the ambient conditions in which the subject finds him or herself, facilitating spatial and temporal orientation and stimulating forms of both resisting and memorizing the experience. Pierre Schaeffer's book, *Traité des objets musicaux* is a pioneering study in the reconceptualization of the auditory beyond traditional musical forms.[143] Expanding the repertoire of significant sounds to incorporate urban, industrial, and ecological noises or those associated with transportation or the workplace, Schaeffer, recognized as one of the creators of concrete music, modifies the study of auditory art through new aesthetic paradigms that allow for a different and more complete approximation toward the real. Sound is thus understood not only as an element of cognitive value but also as an essential instrument for emotional expression and for communication between living beings as well as for understanding interactions between human beings and nature, and with the world of objects. As José Luis Carles has pointed out:

We need to recover and reclaim the importance of sound in everyday life as a form of sensory communication and for the transmission of emotion. The concept of acoustic ecology rests on the relationship people hold with their acoustic surroundings, examining, for example, if such a relationship is balanced or not or whether it facilitates the integration of the individual within the community or if it is something alien and unsustainable.[144]

Acoustic ecology allows us to also approximate the phenomenon of energy transfer and to emphasize aspects of our surroundings that would otherwise remain unnoticed:

> With its great capacity for evocation, sound definitively acquires a value that goes beyond the concrete characteristics of the moment and through its power it can remind us of other situations. By way of sonic indexes that traditional acoustics has studied in almost physical ways—sonic levels, frequencies, spectrums—sound reveals new dimensions of itself that can activate long forgotten moments and experiences and "transport" us to other situations. Sound helps to "recreate" place that determines how the subject evaluates space and how it prepares to act.[145]

Lost Children Archive is situated within this interdisciplinary current, drawing on cultural anthropology, ecology, and epistemology.

WORD AND SILENCE; BODY AND SPECTER

Structurally, Luiselli lays out *Lost Children Archive* like a travel narrative, with the kinetic element as organizing principle. Alongside spatial transference we also find movements through time that converge and accompany the journey, identifying its purposes and connecting the different narrative axis between themselves. Faithful to its objective of fictionalizing material that has been previously presented to the public in the form of testimonial, *Lost Children Archive* combines elements of reality with the imagination, interweaving culture histories of the US past with moments connected to the question of migration, particularly to the Mexican and Central American diaspora of children dispersed in the desert in search of ways to cross the border. In this way, the journey also references an intellectual pilgrimage that leads to a cultural recovery, documentation, and recording of episodes both past and present involving subaltern sectors understood as precariously situated and vulnerable groups who find themselves subject to harsh treatment by dominant power structures. In addition, spatial displacement is a movement from life to death. The family unit in the novel leaves behind the daily routine of their upper middle-class life to travel to the spaces connected to the dispossession and disappearance of different human groups—some lost in the past, others in the present—and who search fruitlessly for a space of shelter and survival.

The novel can also be read as a journey toward childhood, understood in general terms, as the moment of historical initiation, carried out, in this case, by a couple and their two children who embark on a road trip from New York to Arizona. The adults are working on different projects that nonetheless have points in common since they are both researching themes that combine ethnographic, historical, social, and political aspects. The man wishes to document and record echoes of the last Apache to inhabit the US, before settlers exterminated them. He is interested in the Native tribe as representatives of an early stage of national development and for their resistance to the invasions of their lands and the destruction of their way of life. For her part, the woman is seeking to obtain information about the children who cross the border with Mexico alone in search of the American dream, often without documentation or accompanying adults. In both cases and at different moments in the history of colonialism and exclusion that goes to the present day, human beings are victims of the imposition of the US's political and military superiority.

Children (the couple's own, migrant children, Apache children, imaginary lost children, those who appear in the story within the story) all possess a growing importance in the novel, occupying a narrative space Luiselli has been developing since the publication of her previous book. The narrator's two children absorb the stories the parents tell them, integrating them into their own universe. Finally, the children become temporarily lost in the desert, becoming fleeting members of the cohort of anonymous children who constitute their mother's object of study. For their part, the migrant children reactivate the usurpation of Mexican territories, foregrounding the theme of migrant expulsion from lands that belonged to Mexico before the US appropriated them. In this sense, this is a journey to the past with children as the paradoxical protagonists of a future that has been frustrated by State violence.

The desert space can only be partially mapped and escapes the control and the representation of locations and distances, transforming it into an empty labyrinth in which obstacles are invisible and cardinal points are confused. It appears as an infinite and immaterial space; more category than a habitat where humans might dwell. Thus, the desert's secrets can only be revealed through residual elements: echoes, memories, ghosts of the past, traces, silences. The couple remains outside of the world they explore and the landscape they traverse. Their incursion into the desert's silences is an intellectual intervention into an alien sociocultural space marked by exceptionalism. Operating within the logic of capitalism their explorations have a paradigmatic value. Both the Native population of the past and the migrant children of the present constitute objectives that represent both cultural difference and the asymmetric social order, vis-à-vis dominant power structures. The couple situates itself between the State and the victimized sectors, taking on the familiar characteristics of intellectual mediators. Located beyond the world they analyze, along with observing their objects they also try to rescue them. In this case, the couple use ethnographic methods to disseminate knowledge about specific cases, collecting and developing information from the surrounding areas. The epistemological privilege of the dominant culture examines the dominated cultures in an attempt to understand their logics and symbols, superimposing upon them their own categories, concepts, and paradigms.

As I explained earlier, in *Lost Children Archive* the emphasis on the auditory indicates a displacement from a scopic regime, characteristic of modernity, to the world of sound. This movement implies the unearthing of the importance of the ear, preeminent in medieval times, as the most faithful way of understanding a world that is deceptive to the eye. Following Kant, we understand the necessary alliance between sensory and rational aspects as a basis for acquiring the knowledge and interpreting the real to better understand the world. The project of capturing sound and echoes of a distant past also unearths the idea of the phantasmagoric, since acoustic resonances represent immaterial traces of a long-lost human presence that surrounds the spaces of a nation founded on genocide and territorial dispossession. The ear's preeminence also manifests itself in connection with disappearance or situations in which the body has been removed from the field of vision and only shows itself through movement or other bodily signals (the sound of breathing, for example). The apparently empty desert space becomes a place of memory in which the couple attempt to track down a shared but hidden past. The search for a residual sound from this period is a way of investigating, remembering, and (re)cognition that seeks to recover the past to read it against the grain of historical narratives. Revealing it implies modifying the historical and cultural archive upon which the modern nation was founded.

The theme of language as a producer of subjects is exemplified in the characters of the children who have developed an intermittently multicultural form of speech that introduces other logics and other forms of knowing and interpreting the world. They move between speech and language, making use of words and sounds as if they were an intersubjective key that offered access to an intuitive appropriation of the world. But the theme of language also figures in the adult characters who superimpose sound registers—whose semantic content must be intuited and imagined and whose semiotic sense unfolds in counterpoint to the silence and reticence of the desert—upon the codes of different languages. The world only makes sense of experience linguistically and thus we see the desire to capture sounds and record them to appropriate in some way the ghostly sense of a previous existence. This information can be eventually transformed into a truth regime that converts the meaning into something capable of circulating and upholding knowledge since, as Agamben points out, "Language appears as the place where experience must become truth."[146] However, citing Émile Benveniste, he recognizes the presence of a mediating space between language and discourse: "what separates discourse from language and at what point can we say that language becomes discourse?"[147]

An eloquent and dramatic silence that communicates the grief and anger that words cannot express serves as the flipside to sound, like the female protagonist's recordings in *Lost Children Archive* during a protest in support of disappeared migrants. Some content exceeds language's communicative capacity and can only be expressed through the absence of words. But the real drama also appears as a simulacrum in the narrator's children's theatricalizations. Appropriating the situations in their own way, they turn them into play, or myth and eventually into a tool for learning. For his part, the male character's project to capture the echoes of the Apache moves between language and discourse, sign and signifier, semiotics, and semantics, reminding us that while language references signs, discourse articulates meaning. As Agamben, again citing Benveniste says, "Taken in itself, the sign is pure correspondence with itself, and pure difference in relation to any other sign. . . . It exists when it is recognized as a signifier by all the members of the linguistic community. . . . With the semantic, we enter into the specific mode of signification engendered by DISCOURSE."[148]

The position that emerges from the language of the Other and that finds a parallel in the narrator's children's language acquisition and the absence of the migrant children is interestingly located in the desert, which serves as a metaphor of emptiness and the retreat of meaning. The boxes that the family members take with them on their journey serve as receptacles of virtual content and tabula rasa in which they collect their impressions and experiences, serving as a metaphor for knowledge and the gradual formation of a cultural heritage that is incorporated into everyday life, where it becomes impossible to distinguish the degrees and forms of subjectification, deformations of memory, and the trace of forgetting. The man, for example, seeks to collect the signs of the Apache's cultural history along with their tragic demise, but not necessarily their meaning. Instead, in the boxes we find desire, a civilizing fissure, cultural and linguistic difference, class difference, a difference that is both "imperialist" and "disciplined" (in the sense of being subject to the compartmentalized and regulated disciplines of knowledge) of the Other who is on the outside looking in. The man's ethnographic gaze simultaneously constructs and renders the Other invisible, by filling up his/her emptiness with words and representational models that emerge from the linguistic repertoire of the victor/colonizer.

The act of auditory experimentation involves digging into Apache history, viewed as the problematic infancy of an imperial citizenry that devastated Native cultures to establish its own regime of truth. It represents the search for what Lacan calls "the elided signifier" and which has exceeded the chain of meanings and must be retrieved from its unconscious existence. At the journey's heart we find the transformation of sign to meaning, the route of the semiotic and the semantic. To do so, the original must be recovered; in this sense, childhood enacts a key role owing to its foundational character and its vital potentiality:

> In this sense, to experience necessarily means to re-accede to infancy as history's transcendental place of origin. The enigma which infancy ushered in for man can be dissolved only in history, just as experience, being infancy and human place of origin, is something he is always in the act of falling from, into language and into speech. History, therefore, cannot be the continuous progress of speaking humanity through linear time, but in its essence is hiatus, discontinuity, *epochē*. That which has its place of origin in infancy must keep on travelling toward and through infancy.... The semantic order corresponds to the world of enunciation and the universe of discourse.... The semiotic marks a property of language, the semantic results from the speaker's enactment of language.[149]

Once again citing Benveniste, Agamben explains, "We can transpose the semantics of one language into that of another, "salva veritate"; this is the potential for translation. But we cannot transpose the semiotics of one language into that of another; this is the non-potential for translation. This is where the difference between semiotic and semantic lies."[150]

The use of given names represents another fundamental aspect of the use of language and the relationship between signifier/signified. In the novel, the characters have nicknames rather than names, or are identified generically ("the boy," "the girl"). The nicknames change as the characters become involved in the narratives linked to the couple's research. These represent forms of identification that, depersonalizing the character, incorporate him or her into the fictional plot, rendering each an imagined substitute for the original people.

Nicknames and or pseudonyms such as Ella Camposanto function as reproductions of the narrator who, while avoiding the creation of a real character who might compete with her, assumes various positions within the narrative. The narrator changes the children's names, and they take on new nicknames that connect them to the Apache and signal their gradual disconnection from their roots and their increasing identification with the imagined world by way of constant references to their parents who continue to immerse them in a captivating unreality. After becoming separated from their parents, the children's journey to Echo Canyon turns them into ghosts, like echoes resounding within the immense desert. David Bowie's song "Space Oddity"—inspired by Stanley Kubrick's 1968 film *2001: A Space Odyssey*—references Major Tom who chooses to drift off into Space after cutting off communication with Earth. The reference reinforces the idea of radical displacement, the spectrality of individual materiality, and the persistence of echoes. The scene where a priest carries out a ritual of commemoration and homage to the lost migrants provides another facet of names and naming, presenting a scene of ceremonial silence during which the names of the disappeared are read out, like an invocation. The use of names here is infused with an almost magical sense, nominally unearthing a symbolic presence that is unattainable in its materiality.

The exterminated Apache and the disappeared migrants are connected through their position as victims of an implacable system that exterminates them in the service of defending territories privatized by nationalism and unlimited expansionism. The adoption of similar names to those used in the Native world creates an artificial correlation with the world the novel invokes. The children's language constantly interrupts the couple's discourse, adding a twist to the use of terms and to the meaning assigned to them, a technique Luiselli has used in her previous works. As the narrator says in the novel, perhaps as a way of legitimizing the repetition of this technique, "Children's words, in some ways, are the escape route out of family dramas, taking us to their strangely luminous underworld, safe from our middle-class catastrophes."[151] The speakers' interpolations imbue the narrative with an interior rhythm, which becomes a type of detour or predictable counterpoint, a two-way street that leads nowhere.

The theme of language is essential for understanding the limits of communication and to illustrate the unsayable nature of the intermediate zones between cultures and border areas, which *Lost Children Archive* promotes both symbolically and materially. The inclusion of a quotation from Gloria Anzaldúa guides this approach, summing up the evanescent territory of something that no longer exists or has been redrawn by national borders until it disappears: "A borderland is a vague and undetermined place created by the emotional residue of an unnatural boundary. It is in a constant state of transition. The prohibited and forbidden are its inhabitants."[152]

Along with the section headings and the names Luiselli cites in diverse ways throughout the text, she also inserts lists of the contents of the boxes or the couple's notebooks throughout, creating the opportunity to reference names that again bolster and lend prestige to the couple's project. In effect, *Lost Children Archive* forms intertextual relationships with a series of works ranging from Ezra Pound's "Canto 1" or Book XI of Homer's *Odyssey* to Conrad's *The Heart of Darkness*, T. S. Eliot's *The Wasteland*, Rainer Maria Rilke's *Duino Elegies* and Whitman's *Leaves of Grass*. These canonical texts represent real or imaginary shifts to hidden worlds that facilitate journeys in knowledge and sensibility, situating the human being in transcendental situations or feelings linked to life and death, finitude, temporality, and the human condition (power, victimization, loss, etc.). Quotations from or references to other authors (Augusto Monterroso, Jerzy Andrzejewski, Nathalie Léger, Galway Kinnell, Carson McCullers, Susan Sontag, Jack Kerouac, William Golding, Franz Kafka, and Anne Carson) also form a repertoire that repeats the referentialist gesture of Luiselli's other works, inscribing her text in a prestigious tradition, positioning it as part of this same poetic catalogue or "archive." An obligatory reference to Juan Rulfo's *Pedro Páramo* and, in a different vein, the fictional allusion to Sergio Pitol, who Luiselli credits with the translation of Ella Camposanto's work, constitute her homage to certain landmarks of Mexico's literary history and Western culture.

EXPERIENCE, ARCHIVE, AND NARRATION

The novel raises the question of the dialectic between experience and discourse. For Walter Benjamin, the war, advances in technology, and the rupture of collective imaginaries came together in the first decades of the twentieth century to produce the degradation of experience. He describes humanity's experiential crisis and the effect it has on the individual as if "something that seemed inalienable to us, the securest among our possessions, were taken from us: the ability to exchange experiences."[153] In his article "Experience and Poverty" Benjamin distinguishes between *Erlebnis* and *Erfahrung*, that is, between immediate experience and cultural and historical experience, with the latter being produced via memory.[154] The latter requires an elaboration of perception and empirical fact and not the reception of the effects of events or processes. Experience requires action over knowledge, a deep and interpretive incorporation of lived experience within intersubjective space. In other words, language provides the necessary mediation for empirical elements and cognition of the real to manifest themselves discursively and thus becoming visible to reason.

Nowadays, experience does not often appear directly and spontaneously but instead must be deliberately reclaimed, buried as it is among the debris of the accelerated progress of social and economic processes. For Benjamin, the experience of modernity was intimately tied to travel and exploration, or to discovery. More than knowledge, experience is the incorporation of occurrences into the self's very structure, which is in turn interpellated by the event.

In *Infancy and History*, Agamben takes up Benjamin's reflections, agreeing that, in a world saturated by daily events, experience as such is disappearing: "Modern man arrives home at night wearied by a jumble of events but however entertaining or tedious, unusual or commonplace, harrowing or pleasurable they are, none of them will have become experience."[155] According to Agamben, experience translates more easily into authority than into discourse, into the accumulation of knowledge verified by experience and that rationally interpellates the subject that interprets it. He cites the following ideas from Francis Bacon:

> There remains but mere experience, which when it offers itself is called chance; when it is sought after, experiment. But this kind of experience is nothing but a loose faggot, and mere groping in the dark, as men at night try all means of discovering the right road, whilst it would be better and more prudent either to wait for day or procure a light and then proceed. On the contrary the real order of experience begins by setting up a light, and then shows the road by it, commencing with a regulated and digested, not a misplaced and vague course of experiment, and thence deducing axioms, and from these axioms new experiments.[156]

Lost Children Archive also demonstrates its experimental character thematically in its desire to not only evoke but also *convoke* the real or ghostly presence of those whom history has rendered invisible. The couple want to highlight latent aspects of a history that has been suppressed to allow the modern project to acquire verisimilitude and space like a lineal and evolutionary process whose social cost is concealed. From this perspective, Luiselli's novel rests on the idea of written invention as a type of survey, actualization, and incorporation of historical experience. Embedded in the US desert, the couple embark on a mission of recovery that precedes the act of narration. In both cases, the construction of an archive is presented as essential for laying the foundations for the later stage of interpretation and critical evaluation.

The archive permits a systematization that, in turn, facilitates the generation of knowledge or the correction of previous versions of events and processes, etc. In this sense, it represents a space of knowledge and power in which empirical "evidence" is recorded for further interpretation. In *Archive Fever*'s psychoanalytical framework, Derrida underscores the theme of origins as a key point of this type of recording, as research into the emergence of subjectivities, practices, events, and processes, and of the circumstances that surround them.[157] This aspect manifests itself in *Lost Children Archive*'s parallel—and eventually convergent—projects. Both the Apache and the migrant children hearken back to a past in which US expansionism deprived the original inhabitants (both Mexicans and Apache) of their land in such a way that exploring these origins modifies the interpretation of history and the supremacist concept that undergirds it. According to Freud, memories are indelible, even those that are buried, as demonstrated by how our unconscious functions as a repository of repressed and forgotten elements that come to the surface, albeit metaphorically. As Derrida points out, in its Greek etymological origins, archive means a house, a domicile, an address.[158] As repository of knowledge and place that allows for hermeneutical exercise, the archive guards the proof of hidden truths, or discourse that lays claim to truth. In *Lost Children Archive*, the boxes are the virtual dwellings of possible knowledges; each one has its own: a place of individualized memory that aspires to reach the public and society.

The relationship between experience and discourse as well as the question of the archive have received widespread critical attention since both address operations that underpin scientific methodologies as well as a large part of humanistic inquiry that takes the analysis of cultural development and practices as its object of study. Freud apprised us of the imprecise nature of the archive and its connections to questions of origin, memory, repression, and transference. Following this line of thought, in *Lost Children Archive*, as in previous texts, Luiselli explores the themes of absences, echoes or specters of that which returns to remind us of its departure or materializes to affirm its disappearance. The novel articulates Freud's identification of the archive's characteristics, as a record that collects and represses, highlights and invisiblizes, relegates and recovers. The construction of the archive is thus a fluid and progressive process. While, akin to other records, the archive seems to communicate the fixity and institutionalization of memory, in reality it assumes an incessant dynamic since all new materials it incorporates flow over the previous collection, accentuating and relativizing them in a constant reconfiguration of materials and meanings.

The construction of the archive implies an engagement with the power relations and symbolic associations that such a record maintains as the apparatus that institutionalizes memory and assigns positions to subjects and subjectivities, submitting them to a selective and hierarchical ordering. Every archive contains a possible confrontation with both dominant narratives and institutionalized narratives of the past. The journey toward a modification of official history that the family undertakes in *Lost Children Archive* gestures to an intent to rewrite the US's origin story, to reread that which the gaze cannot recover from the perspective of sound and from the sign. Along these lines, it's clear that every archive, including the auditory archive, is built upon the nostalgia for materiality, for physical, evidence-based, and lasting elements of significant events, situations, actions, and occurrences.

The novel addresses the theme of memory, or rather, time as a continuum, and of the traces through which this project we can be recovered, read, and constructed. As Borges explains in "Funes, el memorioso" (Funes, the memorious), memory is not merely an accumulation of elements but rather the infinite disorder of countless possibilities.[159] As already discussed, the archive organizes the relationship between power and knowledge, as per Foucault, as well as the individual's connection to his/her *origin* and the concept of *mandate*, as emphasized by both Freud and Derrida. For the latter, the archive's principal function is to record or, in other words, assemble all elements into a corpus, thus creating a synchronic and unified system. Every archive, then, gestures toward "la exterioridad que enmarca y valida la narración del pasado" (the exteriority that defines and validates the narration of the past).[160]

In *Lost Children Archive*, Luiselli makes frequent allusions to the records that make up the cultural archive: recordings, photographs, books, interviews, notes, clippings, music scores, radio news programs, all of which provide multiple opportunities to document the past as well as the present. This positions the couple as typical members of the middle-class intelligentsia who, in a rather pretentious and at times elitist gesture, assign themselves the mission of preserving historical legacies and of re-signifying them, unleashing a wave of emotion regarding the historical loss of both the Native Americans and the migrant children (which are, of course, legitimate causes that have been silenced by dominant discourses). Gesturing toward the future, their son also participates in this accumulation of facts with his Polaroids, which sometimes turn out completely white as if the image did not want to be taken or as if it had been replaced by its ghostly double. The shared quest brings the different members of the group together but also distinguishes them from each other. In the case of the couple, and despite their commonalities, this intensifies the weakening of their bond that had begun before the journey began.

BORDER SEMIOTICS AND AUTOFICTION

The border deploys a hybrid semiosis in which sadness and saturation, abandonment, and chaotic accumulation alternate. The border activates a conglomeration of images, sounds, tastes, producing multiple meanings which reveal a multicultural dimension. The communication network of border zones is complex since it encompasses different manifestations of signs, linguistics, performance, and perceptions that come together to form an intricate network of relationships in which bodies must learn to move. The migrant's body always appears "out of place," accused at times of contravening health regulations or living in unsuitable places that have contaminated them, transforming them into a potential carrier of disease that threatens to infect society. The social meaning of these denigrating and stereotypical attributions is obvious. From the dominant perspective, the migrant is an excessive and suspicious body who destabilizes order and who, through their appearance, attitudes, and civil status, reveals a lack of integration within the nation-State and represents a threat to society. In addition, migration puts new categories and concepts into circulation that derive meaning from the border's unstable and labyrinthine context but that operate within the adopted society, comparing the bodies deemed to be "exogenous" to those that possess national identities. Notions like "foreigner," "stranger," and "recent arrival" are all some of the names directed toward the Other, whether they be legal or undocumented migrants, refugees, or asylum seekers, creating situations that indicate need, exteriority, and vulnerability.

In this sense, migration appears as a transitional, transnational, translocalized, transregional, and transitory instance. The "trans" prefix indicates the migrant's mobile and provisional condition, in a perpetual movement from here-to-there that alters both temporality and the notion of individual space and existence. Subjectivity—the body, sensory and intellectual cognition, affect, beliefs, sociality (family, community belonging) memory and imagination—forms part of the movement and the victimization inflicted upon the undocumented migrant and are the platforms which facilitate the crossing and the subject's installation in new existential territories.

Critics have also analyzed the body as a border, as the limit between interiority and exteriority, between the being and the world. As we know, the border's polyvalent nature includes many meanings that gesture to its condition as boundary (margin, edge, verge, delimitation, perimeter) that can be applied to different situations that define the tense encounter between real or symbolic territories. As "living space," the body receives and emits signals from an environment which is both *given* and subjectively constructed as well as shaped by social relationships. The body as border gestures to the delimitation inside/outside, I/them, self/other as well as to the flows that connect these domains in a complex and unstable fashion. The concepts of Otherness and alterity are configured via this understanding of the border as a way of ordering identity within an imaginary space. As the zone where representations are produced, the body is considered a crucial point for encounters, convergences, shocks, alliances, continuities, and disparities. It stands symbolically as the semiotic example of both union and separation in areas such as sexuality, violence, solidarity, and community formation.

In an interview with Carlos Puig, Luiselli speaks of the concept of foreignness in *Lost Children Archive* in the following terms:

> It's not a novel about my life, but rather about being alien ... the narrator sees the world as horrific and abandoned at times, and as a world that behaves with brutality toward asylum seekers ... we're facing a migration crisis and the reality of this US/Mexico border, that in some ways is the dark heart of the US.[161]

The border, with its repertoire of persecution, detention, and deportation, transforms the novel into a testimonial and a denunciation, where lived experience and the narrative that represents it become indistinguishable. According to Luiselli, in the novel experience and fiction meld together through writing that she classifies as "ficción documental" (documentary fiction).

> It's impossible for me to separate lived experience from the internal experience of a book. The two things are always enriching each other. After we

read some books, we don't always see the world in the same way.... It's a fictitious division. This is how I think, and I shape my books in this way, they are spaces that are formed by total experience.[162]

This unwillingness to distinguish between experience and culture, between experience and content attained through reading, speaks to an intellectualism that, in general, informs Luiselli's narrative, revealing an intense desire for controlling how reader and critics interpret her texts:

> In other words, references to sources—textual, musical, visual, or audiovisual—were not conceived of as marginalia or as adornments to the story but function instead as interlineal markers that indicate the polyphonic conversation the book maintains with these other works.... I'm not interested in intertexuality as an explanatory or performative gesture but instead as a compositional method or procedure.[163]

Alongside the author's own comments on the roles she intentionally assigns different elements as well as the impulses that shape her creative action, critical interpretation illuminates questions of style, emotional effects, thematic selection, narrative strategies, technical devices etc. that the author herself does not perceive. One of the questions critics have highlighted is the relationship between experience and language and lived experience and fictional rewriting that appears in her work.

Critics have also invoked the concept of autofiction to refer to the frequent inclusion of biographical elements within the fictional world in Luiselli's narrative. The concept of "ficción documental" (documentary fiction) has much in common with autofiction although the latter expression puts a greater emphasis on the recreation of life events as the basis for the creative process. Luiselli's attempt to fuse events and particular elements of her family life with her fictional characters. She gives her characters the names of her family members or reveals, in other ways, her identification with them, displaying her persistent interest in creating a text that involves a real person, whose life becomes apparent through her texts as well as in interviews and newspaper articles. In Luiselli's novels this compositional aspect superimposes itself on the characters and the storylines, creating a salient trait inherent to her work. Her insistence on these stylistic elements, akin to her constant deployment of cultural references, emphasizes her desire to construct a public persona that at times occupies more space than her characters as if the literary world were an echo chamber for the self or a space inextricably intertwined with the author.

Situated between autobiography and novelistic narration, autofiction is an ambiguous subgenre that consolidates the centrality of the author, exalting him or her through imaginary elements that complement true facts. The fusion of these two levels renders them indistinguishable. Autofiction's primary device is the use of the distance between the figure of the author, narrator, and character in which the topic of naming is central since it is used to define identities and connections between the figures that populate the literary construct and biographical elements. In Luiselli's work, the elimination of names and their replacement with fluctuating nicknames destabilizes possible identifications merged into one character, such as the case of the mother, narrator, character, and person, suggesting that one of the objectives of the plot is to fulfill the technical demands of the ongoing self-portrait that emerges as the journey and action advance and develop.

As Paul de Man indicates, autobiography involves the creation of a figural reading and understanding of the text. For de Man, the "autobiographical moment" occurs when two subjects align during the act of reading, in an act of mutual determination.[164] Such an identification possesses as many similarities as differences, creating a specular structure in which the author becomes the subject of his or her own understanding. In autofiction, the author fictionalizes life itself to a greater or lesser degree, combining true as well as fictional elements. According to Phillipe Lejeune, in autobiography identity is not only representational and cognitive but also contractual, connected to the speech through which the writer invokes the "I" as he/she develops the subject who represents him/her (summed up by Lejeune's use of the phrase "je est un autre").[165] The name that appears on the cover of an autobiography is not the real name of the subject who is an object of his/her own discourse, but instead the signature that underpins the "autobiographical pact" without offering an epistemological guarantee of any kind. In other words, nothing guarantees the truth that the subject claims for the character he/she has constructed to represent the "I."

Neither the subject nor the life narrated by the autobiography really "exist" beyond the story, instead they are produced through the narration that makes them intelligible and confers sense upon them via language. It is not the case, then, that the life precedes the narration as if it were an original, but that it is instead inseparable from the story that narrates it. Autofiction's connection to real life is much looser than autobiography since the pact with the reader allows fictionalization or the deliberate alteration of the facts and of memory a priori.

In speaking of the "politics of self-representation" Leigh Gilmore addresses the themes of the fictionalization of the "I," and of the true/

false nature of the autobiographical construct, above all in the case of women who, as subjects marginalized by patriarchy, were forced to cultivate "minor" literary genres (letters, intimate diaries, confessions, epistolary novels) as a form of social (self-)recognition.[166] Fragmentary, interrupted, and discontinuous writing was associated for a long time with subjective marginalization as the channeling of a segmented social experience subject to masculine authority. Autobiography then resignified itself as a literary form that defies the positionality of gender. Luiselli's work centralizes and vindicates the female position as the nucleus of a vast system of highbrow referentialism and as the principal subjectivity for the construction of the fictional world.

The couple's ten-year-old son narrates the second part of the novel, but his narration exists in name only since his voice is channeled through the narrator who identifies herself as his mother. This results in a controlled and relative narrative displacement of limited literary efficacy. Some readers and critics found this device to be unconvincing, since Luiselli puts words and ideas into the mouth of this improvised narrator that do not correspond to someone his age, removing verisimilitude and autonomy from the voice. For one critic, this narrator is a means to an end for Luiselli: "In the end, *Lost Children Archive* runs out of steam and has to change tack, switching perspective to the narrator's stepson as he plans to run away, as if becoming a lost child himself might make him more interesting to his mother."[167]

In its narrative techniques, *Lost Children Archive* also dramatizes the problem of the limit and semiotics of the border since the story occurs in compositionally marginal zones relative to the spaces of reality and fiction, the narrative voices, and the question of presence. The processes of dematerialization (the characters' gradual dissipation through their echoes and absences, the importance of silence as an encoded form of communication and emotional and cognitive expression, the choice of peripheral spaces such as the desert, the margins of dominant "civilization," the imaginary zone, the constant digressions etc.) for their part create a liminal narrative space that is situated in an unstable "between space" that hastens toward its own vanishing point.

LUISELLI'S USE OF CHILDREN

The constant insertion of children and their voices into Luiselli's literary prose produces various effects, the most obvious being the sustaining of autofiction, the inclusion of a variety of narrative tones, the lightening of the narrative, and the introduction of ludic references. On the one hand, the narrative use of children confirms the author's engagement with gender. The novel presents maternity as something that not only does not hinder intellectual labor but also lends it nuance and emphasis. This in turn affirms not only the place of class—from where literature is deployed—but also the intellectual, educational, and social location of the family unit characterized as something close-knit but flexible as befits educated and progressive people unencumbered by financial worries. Children represent a malleable form of Otherness that, without undermining the family's character, accompanies it, reproducing its fundamental principles and performing interventions that incorporate humorous elements, emotionality, and diverse viewpoints. Such effects are produced within the manageable margins of the centrality of the dominant vision, embodied in the figure of the mother. The subjective orbit connected to intimacy and privacy is thus illuminated by other logics: childish intuition, fantasy, arbitrary or paradoxical associations that integrate spontaneous, oneiric, and ludic elements that give way to explications and reactions by the adults and intercalate practical details from daily life and the interaction with the real world. In Luiselli's work the action within the children's world always acts as a counterpoint and contributes to integrating different—albeit assimilable to the parents' world—spatio-temporal levels into the narrative. The children move on alternative planes with different purposes than the adults. Although supervised, they freely and erratically occupy and traverse the open space of the home or the city. Surveilled and chastised, they embody a peculiar form of subalternity, of randomly unfolding and potential agency.

Incorporating aspects of the visual, the intriguing, the direct and fragmentary, as a character the figure of the child also connotes inconstancy, variety, unpredictability, vulnerability, and charm. Departing from the principle of simultaneity and digression that the adults eliminate in favor of linearity and purpose, the child moves through time unencumbered by limits and unconcerned with the notion of order. The child's movement within urban, domestic, public, and natural spaces simulates the flow of free writing that draws routes, designs stations, and areas of rest, play and instant gratification. In this way, Luiselli assembles a parallel cartography that at times converges with the central threads of the story that the adults narrate, instilling a prismatic and polyvalent dimension into the text.

In this sense, the figure of the child in Luiselli's work goes beyond a merely auxiliary function and instead delineates an itinerary that intensifies the fiction's experimental character, as if alternatives to the text were being produced by chance, replete with volubility and inconstancy. The children are frequently inserted into the narrative in ways that are brief, intriguing, and usually of little substance so that their appearances offer moments of reprieve from the dramatic tension of the novel (although drama is not the novel's key register) and maintain the simultaneously developing narrative axes. In addition, in *Lost Children Archive* the children move from the margin to the center, taking on an increasingly visible leading role. In terms of composition, inserting the children intensifies the fragmentation of the narrative, amplifying the segmentation of discourse and disrupting the continuity of situations and plot development. Paradoxically, at the same time the characters of the children also serve as connective threads that string the narrative together and reinforce it. Thus, the center/margin dynamic becomes fluid, subject to the construction and deconstruction of elements and narrative nuclei.

In Luiselli's work, the child characters bring orality and the processes of language acquisition into focus. Situated between two cultures and various languages, exposed to accents, lexicons, and diverse syntactical constructions, the children's speech in *Lost Children Archive*, along with their drawings, gestures, and behaviors, emphasizes the interstitial function of these types of characters who, for the most part, occupy a spatial and affective between-space that gradually takes distance from the adult world. As they move between reality and daydream, history and fiction, and memory and performance, the children are also mediators between cultures, timeframes, and existential territories.

In terms of questions of gender, the role of the children in Luiselli's work clearly forms part of the overall assemblage of her literary project where the different parts come together to reinforce the centrality of the "I" and the coexistence and interrelationship between the domains of writing and maternity that replicate subjectivity in a variety of registers, mutually complementing and sustaining each other. The narrative "I" projects and extends itself through the children who expand their parents' space in concentric circles.

Lost Children Archive exemplifies Pierre Bourdieu's theorizing on how the family primarily functions as a site for the exchange of symbolic capital, with each member of the nuclear family supporting the role of the other members, underscoring the meaning assigned to each as well as the relational ties that bind them.[168] In this sense, the father is merely a formal and predictable figure, lacking a well-developed identity that would allow him to compete with his wife (despite his study of the Apache, which, often occasions, obscures the parallel project of the missing children). His objectives, personality, and contributions are relative, stereotypical, limited, and clearly intended as a symmetrical reproduction of the mother's. From a sensory and spatial point of view, the children in the novel give rise to multiple perspectives. They move between furniture, in corners, under the beds and the tables, playing with discarded items, insects, and parts of objects, deconstructing the material world, and replacing it with their imaginative and syncretic cosmovision, replete with the force of magic and dreams. Their universe is overwhelmingly synesthetic, labile, and kinetic.

From the perspective of the sociology of the family and following the theories of Bourdieu, James S. Coleman indicates that when children are subjected to constant mobility, they experience a great disruption in their social capital and as a result, more closely engage with the family group.[169] In the novel, the two children undergo constant displacements in space and time but also in terms of cultural experiences that incorporate other present-day dimensions and the very texture of the real. The family group thus functions as a controlled and organic nucleus that mimics the organization of the modern nation, centralized in the figure of the State/father that imposes progress at the collective level. In line with this role, the State surveils and dispenses in accordance with republicanism's paternalistic ideas. Citizens, on the other hand, serve as outgrowths of institutionalized and hierarchical power, connected to it in a regulated fashion mediated by institutions.

The nuclear family in *Lost Children Archive* is not integrated in any lasting way with the community and instead functions as a self-contained and self-sufficient bubble that progressively disintegrates as the journey goes on, as if the friction between past and present were eroding its interpersonal ties. Due to its intrinsically transnational nomadism, the family searches for roots in which they reveal nostalgia for a community to give meaning to the search for the Apache past and the missing children. These searches channel the nomadic instinct along with the seduction of the figure of the specter or the shadow of the past that dominates Luiselli's work, and the communitarian flight lines that disperse as they move toward the margins of nation and history.

The couple tries a variety of ways to channel their social capital, through notions of civic engagement that include the desire for political participation through culture and the early social education of their children who they expose to complex and challenging situations that put pressure on their sensibility and rationality. Social justice is an essential element in the novel, privileging a culturalist perspective that emphasizes the importance of behavior and spontaneous forms of communitarian organization. These pathways are offered as possible solutions to resolve or at least ameliorate social drama. Thus, a faith in networks of social cooperation that emphasizes horizontal relationships and ways of being and the possibility of thus mobilizing mechanisms and forces for the improvement of disadvantaged sectors of society. Removed from the economism that verticalizes social relationships, this perspective horizontalizes the analysis and comprehension of social conflict, particularly regarding social justice, focusing on it as if it were a primarily cultural phenomenon, and placing responsibility upon societal resources, the individual or community.

As the couple traverse the desert landscape in search of traces of past and present, their divergent interests and concerns fracture their relationship. The impact of the migratory crisis absorbs the mother, making her children feel secondary, and the father dedicates himself to telling them stories about Geronimo (1829–1909), the mythical Apache military leader and traditional healer. His interest in the struggle and resistance of the Chiricahuas, whom he considers "the last free peoples on the entire American continent" also draw him away from his wife's interests, producing a gradual distancing between them.[170]

The narrator also reflects explicitly on ethical and practical questions regarding the composition of the text as well as the social and political incorporation of the archives the couple is producing:

> How can a radio documentary be useful in helping more undocumented children find asylum? . . . Maybe it is better to keep the children's stories as far away from the media as possible, anyway, because the media the more susceptible it is to becoming politicized, and in these times, a politicized issue is no longer a matter that urgently calls for committed debate in the public arena, but rather a bargaining chip that parties use frivolously in order to move their own agendas forward.[171]

The political and ethical concern these quotes express helps to elucidate the positioning of this type of intellectual engagement rooted in the good intentions and social sensibility that conceives of political and economic problems in overwhelmingly cultural and activist terms. While demonstrating a degree of professionalization, the man and the woman nonetheless behave like amateurs or dilettantes in the face of undoubtedly interesting topics, with which they engage diffusely and moderately progressively but without any clear idea of what to do with their findings. The journey seems like a way of channeling the breakup of the couple who tentatively and unsuccessfully attempt to reconcile, their failure impacting the whole family.

The wife's project is both more concrete and more unfocused than her husband's and undergoes various reformulations as the journey advances. When they begin to read the *Elegies*, the narrator feels as though all her doubts and difficulties regarding defining and implementing her work only deepen. She realizes the magnitude of her undertaking and the truly elusive nature of her object of study:

> There is this one certainty. It arrives like a blow to my face as we speed along an empty highway into Texas. The story I have to record is not the story of children who arrive, those who finally make it to their destinations and can tell their own story.... I am still not sure how I'll do it, but the story I need to tell is the one of the children who are missing, those whose voices can no longer be heard because they are, possibly, forever lost.[172]

In the face of the dispersion and dematerialization of her research, the narrator repositions herself as the quest's true goal, an object both closer and more concrete and that resides in an interiority that unceasingly projects itself outward, transferring her own uncertainty and the fragmentation of her private world on to an object of desire:

> Perhaps ... I'm also chasing ghosts and echoes. Except mine are not in the history books, and not in cemeteries. Where are they—the lost children? And where are Manuela's two girls? I don't know, but I do know; if I'm going to find anything, anyone, if I'm going to tell their story, I need to start looking somewhere else.[173]

Distanced from its objectives, the quest becomes subjective and dispersed, loses its teleology, recentering itself in an "I" in search of an echo chamber and a world to give meaning to a scattered existence. At this point, the search for sounds has become a form of therapy, and the reader feels overwhelmed by the romanticization of the void as a form of intellectual solipsism that, without tarnishing the real social drama it employs as a pretext, is then cannibalized by the interior world.

ELEGAIC DISCOURSE

The question articulated by Luiselli's daughter throughout *Los niños perdidos* "¿cómo termina la historia de los niños perdidos?" also functions as a leitmotif in *Lost Children Archive*. The lack of answer in both these works indicates the inconclusive nature of diasporic movements and their projection toward an indefinite and inconclusive space and time. The inclusion of children serves only to accentuate these movements' dramatic character. Framed by this question, the narrative of *Lost Children Archive* is organized as a discourse that registers the perspective of an imminent ending that, while unknown, is feared and imagined, positioning the action at the edge of an abyss that the reader is drawn to as the action progresses. As in the case of the disappearance of the Apache, to hear the lost children one must listen to the murmur of the land to capture what might have been the soundscape of these human beings before they disappeared into the space of silence and oblivion. All the elements and operations including ghosts, echoes, the recording of auditory traces, nomadism, the diverse forms of deterritorialization, the flight of children, migrants lost in the desert, and the couple's unraveling relationship signal an atmosphere of residue and grief and a lament for all that has been lost to time.

Elegiac discourse is a limit-discourse that only makes sense in the context of impending death or an irreparable loss (exile, disappearance, for example). A song of grief and lament, elegy can include eulogies as well as reflections on immortality, time, and spirituality. It represents a final intent to capture the vestiges of what will rapidly become absence and oblivion. *Lost Children Archive's* elegiac orientation, connected to the topics of echoes and ghosts that can be seen in Luiselli's previous work, operates both in the main body of the novel as well as in the many embedded stories within. Dematerialization is a constant presence through which the narration directs itself toward the collection of intangible traces, and the seventeen embedded "elegies" both document and thematize this process.

As an embedded text within the narrative's frame story, for which *Los niños perdidos (un ensayo en cuarenta preguntas)* serves as paratext, the fictitious book *Elegies for Lost Children* written by Ella Camposanto (a name formed from the third person singular pronoun in Spanish and by a synonym of "cementerio" [cemetery] in this language), is incorporated into the larger narrative via the mother reading excerpts from it to the children during the journey through the Arizonan desert. With writing and orality thus combined, the fragmentary text thus marks out the encroachment of limits, recuperating distant scenes of other diasporic children left to fend for themselves that form part of a larger narrative that *Lost Children Archive* brings back to life in a new context. The narrator explains that Camposanto's work is loosely based on the historical Children's Crusade, which involved tens of thousands of children who traveled alone across, and probably beyond, Europe, and which took place in the year 1212 (though historians disagree about most of this crusade's fundamental details). In Camposanto's version, the "crusade" takes place in what seems like a not-so-distant future in a region that can possibly be mapped back to North Africa, the Middle East, and southern Europe, or to Central and North America (the children ride atop "gondolas" for example, a word used in Central America to refer to the wagons or cars of trains.[174] Although the initial reference to the train directly evokes the journeys migrants, including children, undertake clinging to the roof of the freight cars of "La Bestia" from Central America to Mexico, Camposanto's text hearkens back to other contexts and historical moments, thus universalizing the experience of a children's diaspora as something that recurs at different times throughout history.

In the novel, Lusielli constantly reflects or reproduces one narrative element in another. The dangerous journey on the roof of the train will appear at different moments in the elegies. In addition, the reference to the train is repeated in the inclusion of the photograph of the enslaved children who are transported on The Orphan Train (included in the unnumbered Box 5 section in *Lost Children Archive*), as well as the mobilization of the imprisoned Apache who are transported to Florida as detailed in the photograph from the tenth of September, 1886 (also included in the unnumbered Box 5 section in *Lost Children Archive*). The persistent reproduction of this element, along with other leitmotifs (like echoes, ghosts, maps, names, childhood as a narrative space etc.) introduces a predictable rhythm into the novelist discourse, which appears to weaken as it progresses, relying more and more on the children as a locus of enunciation and generator of narrative action.

One of the narrative axes is the concept of disappearance as a form of dematerialization, absence, and silence and Luiselli repeats it in the incorporation of the children of Manuela, a migrant whose daughters vanish on an airplane journey from New Mexico to Arizona, with no explanation given.[175] The migrant children lost in the desert, the Apache children, the children of the couple who are on their trail, and the multiple references incorporated into Camposanto's elegies push down too often on the same emotional and compositional narrative spring, transmitting a sense of argumentative exhaustion and unnecessary drawing out of the story whose principal points were more than sufficiently laid out in the first half of the novel. The children's language, ideas, and the emotional charge of their actions and their mimicking of the lost children to get their parents' attention is a redundant addition that, predictably, can only lead to a happy reunion in Echo Park, a symbolic space that ties up the plot's loose ends, like the returning voice of an echo that, like a boomerang, comes back to the place from where it started.

If the relationship the novel suggests between the children and the parents often appears like an example of postmodern childrearing based on the latter's level of involvement in the intellectual guidance of the former and by the intensity of the exchanges on topics that generally pertain only to children themselves, the novel's structure also pays homage to this desire for innovation, with its challenging of linear and unifying models through digressions, switching between narrators, the insertion of visual materials etc. already established by Modernist authors. The reader will be familiar with the characteristics of this modus operandi: fragmentation, pastiche, run on sentences bereft of punctuation in a stream of consciousness style, multiple and shifting narrators, multimedia insertions etc. The mix of writing and photography, the fluctuation between dialogues, thoughts, essayistic reflections, the use of audiobooks, music and other forms of communication and entertainment, Polaroids etc., serves to diversify the textual discourse, imbuing it with elements of orality or visual materials that lend the novel a hybrid and open-ended quality.

The segments that make up the "Elegies for Lost Children" center the question of migration in different historical and geo-cultural contexts connected to questions of precarity and violence. Hunger and war, for example, have grave emotional repercussions, and offer a wide panorama of context that nonetheless consistently focuses on deterritorialization as a contemporary social, political, and economic phenomenon. The transformations inflicted upon the human body offer evidence of the regulatory politics of life and death and the right to territoriality, applying different forms of exclusion, persecution, and extermination that have children as their most potent objectives. Mixing poetry and drama, lyricism and biographical references and locating itself between particularism and transcendentalism, the genre of elegy expresses our universal grief at the loss, denunciation, and condemnation of biopower that implements the expulsion of certain subjects in the name of the dominant order. The Other is expelled to form part of an alterity conceived of as impossible to assimilate to the id/entity of the "I" that controls space and time, the right to exist and to mobility, to survival and belonging within a society and a culture that guarantees the right to life.

It could be said that Lusielli's novel is in and of itself an elegy in the sense that it is located in a space of disappearance, pursuing the traces of Natives exterminated in the nineteenth century and migrants victimized in the present, although the excessive focus on the figure and mind of the narrator and her nuclear family relativizes the migration question to the point that it becomes a pre-text that competes with the elimination of the Apache and the family's own circumstances that anchor the plot, emphasizing the relativism of the different narrative axes.

The route the family follows on the trail of the last stages of Apache resistance leads them to Geronimo's tomb and his protracted resistance against the US Army. The father revisits Native American history along with their customs and struggles, framed within stories intended to entertain and educate his son and daughter who fictionalize them, incorporating them within their imagination as if they were children's stories. It is obvious that the novel's set up, the intercalation of the narrative axes, points of view and reflections are given priority, cannibalizing the narrative threads centered on disappearances and echoes of immensely significant biopolitical significance. In other words, the novel is explicitly based on two situations of undeniable social importance that imply serious debates on topics of citizenship, power, territoriality, State violence, human rights, the individual's drives (emotional and intellectual) as well as the family's, all of which strengthen and intensify the novel's autofictional nature, tipping its balance toward authorial centrality and subordinating the novel's themes to it.

The search for the lost children in the desert generates other losses, new traces, new disappearances, as if a death machine had been put into motion, transforming genocide into the social cost of capital reproduction and territorial accumulation. Seduced by the elegiac pathos that courses through US history and guided by a historicist tendency that exhausts itself in the collecting and ordering of facts and in their aesthetic repercussions as well as in their values as raw material to be reworked as literature or soundscapes, the intellectual couple of *Lost Children Archive* registers and assemble these events, translating them into discourse and archive, elements that the intellectual middle classes celebrate as a formal recognition of loss and, perhaps, of guilt.

Notes

INTRODUCTION

1. Mabel Moraña, *Arguedas / Vargas Llosa: Dilemas y ensamblajes* (Madrid: Iberoamericana Editorial Vervuert, 2013).
2. Roland Barthes, *The Semiotic Challenge*, trans. Richard Howard (Berkeley: University of California Press, 1994).
3. Osvaldo Zavala, *Volver a la modernidad: Genealogías de la literatura mexicana de fin de siglo* (Valencia, Spain: Albatros, 2017).
4. Sayak Valencia, *Capitalismo Gore: Control económico, violencia y narcopoder* (Barcelona: Melusina, 2010).
5. See for example Rossana Reguillo, "Precariedad(es): Necropolítica y máquinas de guerra," in *Precariedades, exclusiones y emergencias: Necropolítica y sociedad civil en América Latina*, ed. Mabel Moraña, 53–73 (Mexico City: Gedisa, 2017); and José Manuel Valenzuela Arce, *Jefe de jefes: Corridos y narcocultura en México* (Mexico City: Plaza y Janés, 2002).

CHAPTER 1

1. In 2003, Yuri Herrera received the Premio Binacional de Novela Joven Frontera de Palabras for *Trabajos del reino*, which led the following year to the novel's publication by Tierra Adentro (Conaculta) and served as an official recognition of his talents. The same novel was awarded the Otras Voces, Otros Ámbitos prize for the best novel published in Spain in 2008. His second novel, *Señales que precederán al fin del mundo*, was a finalist in the Rómulo Gallegos literary competition. In 2016, along with his translator Lisa Dillman, he won an award for the English version of the novel. The same year the Academy of Arts in Berlin awarded him the Anna Seghers Prize for the works he had published to date. Regarding the prizes and national recognition Herrera has received, Juan Rogelio Rosado Marrera references the debate between

Rafael Lemus and Eduardo Antonio Parra concerning the characteristics and specificity of literature from Northern Mexico and its use of a *costumbrista* aesthetic to commercially exploit the theme of drug trafficking, "domesticating" its principal traits and transforming it into a populist and popularized product. See Juan Rogelio Rosado Marrero, "La consagración y el reposicionamiento de un escritor fronterizo: El fenómeno del mercado editorial en la obra de Yuri Herrera," *Iberoamericana* 18, no. 68 (2018): 187–200. Valeria Lusielli has also joined this debate with her 2012 comments on Mexican literature's preference for alienation and violence. Qtd. in Rosado Marrero, "La consagración," 191. According to Parra, this literature leverages the treatment of violence not as a theme but rather as an unavoidable context. Rosado Marrero, "La consagración," 192–94.
2. As José Manuel Valenzuela points out, it is worth remembering here the importance of collective imaginaries as shared representations of social content and meanings, and he refers to Durkheim's observation in *The Elementary Forms of the Religious Life* on the relationship between the individual and the collective. Valenzuela, *Jefe de jefes*, 24.
3. Yuri Herrera and Humberto Aguirre, *¡Éste es mi nahual!* (Pachuca, Mexico: Consejo Estatal para la Cultura y las Artes, 2007).
4. Ésta es la historia de Lucio, un niño al que le gustaban las historietas, la salsa picosa y correr como si volara. Lucio no tenía muchas preocupaciones, hasta el día en que, por andar distraído, se perdió en la ciudad. Entonces, para encontrar su camino a casa, tuvo que buscar a un ser fantástico que lo ayudara. Así comenzó una aventura en la que descubrió una nueva manera de ver el mundo. Yuri Herrera and Humberto Aguirre, *¡Éste es mi nahual!*
5. Yuri Herrera and Patricio Betteo, illustrator, *Los ojos de Lía* (Mexico City: Sexto Piso, 2012).
6. Christian Sperling, "Apuntes para un mundo feliz: La violencia como experiencia en *Los ojos de Lía*," *Tema y variaciones de literatura*, 41 (2013): 141–54.
7. Sperling, "Apuntes para un mundo feliz," 148.
8. Sperling, "Apuntes para un mundo feliz," 149.
9. Sperling, "Apuntes para un mundo feliz," 142–43.
10. Sperling, "Apuntes para un final feliz," 152.
11. Yuri Herrera, *Talud* (Mexico City: Literal Publishing, 2016).
12. Ivonne Sánchez Becerril discusses Herrera's stories in "Como una cosa ajena: Sobre un talud de cuentos de Yuri Herrera," SENALC, April 1, 2018, https://www.senalc.com/2018/04/01/como-una-cosa-ajena-sobre-un-talud-de-cuentos-de-yuri-herrera, and in further detail in "No por taparse los ojos las cosas desaparecen: La obra cuentística de Yuri Herrera," in *De la alegoría a la palabra: El reino de Yuri Herrera*, ed. Ivonne Sánchez Becerril, 107–37 (Mexico City: Facultad de Filosofía y Letras, UNAM).
13. Herrera, *Talud*, 31.
14. Herrera, *Talud*, 31.

15. Herrera, *Talud*, 15.
16. Herrera, *Talud*, 15.
17. Herrera, *Talud*, 50.
18. Herrera, *Talud*, 183.
19. es, en primer lugar, una manifestación de escepticismo frente a la manera en que entendemos las reglas, el lenguaje, nuestras emociones; es un ejercicio de crítica y es un juego que pone en tela de juicio cómo entendemos eso que llaman normalidad (social, lingüística, sexual, etc.). En ese sentido, de lo que se trata es de no sólo mirar críticamente eso de lo que nos estamos burlando o con lo que estamos jugando, sino de hacer esa investigación en nosotros mismos, averiguar qué solemnidades nos habitan y utilizarlas como materia para el juego. Carmen de Eusebio, "Entrevista: Yuri Herrera," *Cuadernos Hispanoamericanos*, no. 839-840 (May–June 2020): 158–65, https://cuadernoshispanoamericanos.com/yuri-herrera.
20. imaginar es romper con un cierto orden, el de las cosas ajenas, y concebir un orden propio; imaginar es conciliar el mundo con nuestros deseos y con nuestros miedos; imaginar es la íntima declaración de soberanía que todos podemos hacer sobre el universo. Eso que llamamos realidad no es un objeto imperturbable, sino la materia que moldeamos con la imaginación. Cada lugar en el mundo está esperando que le demos, una y otra vez, nuevos nombres, como corresponde a nuevos seres humanos. Herrera, *Talud*, 4.
21. de Eusebio, "Entrevista: Yuri Herrera."
22. Yuri Herrera, *Diez planetas* (Cáceres, Spain: Editorial Periférica, 2019); Yuri Herrera, *Ten Planets*, trans. Lisa Dillman (Minneapolis, MN: Graywolf Press, 2023).
23. de Eusebio, "Entrevista: Yuri Herrera."
24. For a study of the monstrous and its development within the literary canon as well as its political, anthropological and philosophical implications, see Mabel Moraña, *El monstruo como máquina de guerra* (Madrid: Iberoamericana Editorial Vervuert, 2017).
25. Translator's note: Translations of titles of the short stories in *Ten Planets* come from Lisa Dillman's translation. Translations of the text are mine.
26. Yuri Herrera, *Señales que precederán al fin del mundo* (Madrid: Editorial Periférica, 2010).
27. El perfume de un amante, la raspadura de sus zapatos, la peste de su deseo por otra persona; la bilis derramada tras un expolio, la densidad del encierro en un cofre, los cambios del paisaje en la ruta para esconder el cofre, la piedra húmeda bajo la que fue olvidado. Por más que la cosa se aleje o que uno se aleje del lugar, la nariz se engancha y conserva su rastro como si fuera una coordenada. Herrera, *Diez planetas*, 26.
28. In this regard see my essay on Borges's short story: Mabel Moraña, "Borges y yo: Primera reflexión sobre 'El etnógrafo,'" in *Heterotropías: Narrativas de identidad y alteridad latinoamericanas*, ed. Carlos A Jáuregui and Juan

Pablo Dabove, 263–86 (Pittsburgh, PA: Instituto International de Literatura Iberoamericana, 2003).
29. Herrera, "La consolidación anímica," *Diez planetas*, 41–43.
30. Herrera, *Diez planetas*, 64.
31. Herrera, *Diez planetas*, 112.
32. Herrera, *Diez planetas*, 82.
33. Herrera, *Diez planetas*, 84.
34. Lo más fácil es decir que alguien actúa simplemente porque lo han herido o porque lo han llamado, pero entonces un personaje no es sino el ruido que produce una cosa al ser tocada, y eso qué. Tu personaje, en cambio, edifica sus propios motivos. Como cuando Sancho le dice que por qué quiere hacer locuras, si a él Dulcinea no le ha dado causa para estar celoso, y Don Quijote dice "ésa es la fineza de mi negocio; que volverse loco un caballero andante con causa, ni grado, ni gracias: el toque está en desatinar sin ocasión y dar a entender a mi dama que, si en seco hago esto, ¿qué hiciera en mojado?" Herrera, *Diez planetas*, 86.
35. Herrera, *Diez planetas*, 89.
36. Herrera, *Diez planetas*, 29.
37. Darko Suvin, *Metamorphoses of Science Fiction* (New Haven, CT: Yale University Press, 1979).
38. Carl Freedman, *Critical Theory and Science Fiction* (Middletown, CT: Wesleyan University Press, 2000).
39. In this regard see Eric D. Smith, "Introduction: The Desire Called Postcolonial Science Fiction," in *Globalization, Utopia, and Postcolonial Science Fiction* (London: Palgrave Macmillan, 2012, 1–19); Suvin, *Metamorphoses*; and Freedman, *Critical Theory*.
40. Suvin, *Metamorphoses*, 9.
41. Smith, "Introduction," 4.
42. Smith, "Introduction," 7.
43. Yolanda Molina-Gavilán, "Ciencia ficción en español: Una mitología moderna ante el cambio," *Journal of the Fantastic in the Arts* 14, no. 2 (Summer 2003): 283–85.
44. Yuri Herrera, *El incendio de la mina El Bordo* (Madrid: Editorial Periférica, 2018).
45. Herrera, *El incendio*, 9; Herrera, *A Silent Fury: The El Bordo Mine Fire*, trans. Lisa Dillman (Sheffield, UK: And Other Stories, 2020), 10.
46. Yuri Herrera, "Los demonios de la mímesis: Textualidad de una tragedia en el México posrevolucionario" (PhD diss., University of California, Berkeley, 2009).
47. Rodolfo Benavides, *El doble nueve* (written in 1949, Mexico City: Ediciones Mexicanos Unidos, 1971).
48. *El doble nueve* es una novela de hombres. Hombres malvados, los gringos; hombres derrotados, los mineros; hombres despreciables, los funcionarios

públicos. Salvo una excepción, las mujeres aparecen como telón de fondo, apenas delineadas, producidas en serie; no hay mayor interés por su individualidad pues su papel en la novela—aun el de la que sí es protagonista—está claramente establecido: son símbolo de pureza y apoyo emocional, elemento necesario para la reproducción de la vida social del hombre; y son, claro está, objeto de deseo y origen de los conflictos. Herrera, "Los demonios de la mímesis," 89.

49. Herrera, *El incendio*, 12; *A Silent Fury*, 11.
50. Herrera, *El incendio*, 12; *A Silent Fury*, 11.
51. Herrera, *El incendio*, 16; *A Silent Fury*, 18.
52. Herrera, *El incendio*, 18; *A Silent Fury*, 19.
53. Herrera, *El incendio*, 20; *A Silent Fury*, 21.
54. En la foto se ve a los siete sobrevivientes, descalzos, impolutamente vestidos de blanco, con las manos sobre las piernas, salvo uno de ellos, que recarga su brazo derecho sobre el hombro de un compañero. Todos están afeitados o tienen el bigote limpiamente recortado y miran a la cámara. No parecen haber salido del infierno: la semana de inanición bajo tierra no se refleja en sus miradas ni en sus cuerpos, salvo uno de ellos, el primero de izquierda a derecha, en quien puede advertirse una furia silenciosa: aprieta los labios, enarca las cejas. Pero, como se ha dicho, nadie registró lo que pensaba o sentía en ese momento. Herrera, *El incendio*, 45–46; *A Silent Fury*, 45.
55. Herrera, *El incendio*, 50; *A Silent Fury*, 50.
56. Herrera, *El incendio*, 55; *A Silent Fury*, 56.
57. The court clerks are translators of voice: they listen to citizens unqualified to enter into dialogue with the law and transform their voices—unique, unpolished—into a neutral universal voice that fits the legal codes used in proceedings. Herrera, *El incendio*, 63; *A Silent Fury*, 61.
58. Herrera, *El incendio*, 71; *A Silent Fury*, 67.
59. Herrera, *El incendio*, 67; *A Silent Fury*, 71.
60. Herrera, *El incendio*, 77; *A Silent Fury*, 73.
61. Herrera, *El incendio*, 93; *A Silent Fury*, 97
62. Herrera, *El incendio*, 95; *A Silent Fury*, 99
63. This well-known phrase (First as tragedy, then as farce) comes from Marx's *Eighteenth Brumaire of Louis Bonaparte* (New York: International Publishers Co, 1994) although he attributes it to Hegel without quoting the source, which has never been identified. He implies that this historical repetition allows the people to distance themselves from heroism and from memorable acts and internalize historical development with a certain dose of humor and irony. Marx's uses the notion of farce (as I do here in this book) to allude to a type of theatrical work in which the characters behave in a strange and over the top fashion but nonetheless with believable if always exaggerated reactions. This is a popular genre that arises after moralizing and religious theatre reached its peak with the public who seek out lighter fare. Farce tends to channel social

critique and the situations it presents are consequently true to life, allowing for a deep understanding of the problems being referenced. The word farce comes from the Latin word *farcire* (to fill). Farces were used, in fact, as brief comic interludes during traditional dramas. The genre includes comic, grotesque, and ridiculous elements, crude language, and situations full of mischief; the plots lay out complicated circumstances. Characters' defects or peculiarities are openly exhibited as well as situations in which they follow their instincts. There is a liberatory feeling to this comic form that releases tensions and always ends in an open and upbeat fashion. Yuri Herrera, *Trabajos del reino* (Mexico City: Consejo Nacional para la Cultura y las Artes de México, 2004). It was translated into English by Lisa Dillman as *Kingdom Cons* (Sheffield, UK: And Other Stories, 2017).

64. Likewise, in his thesis on the use of stereotypes in narcoculture, Jesús Ángel González explores the heroic construction of the narco/drug trafficker, following what Joseph Campbell outlines in *The Hero with a Thousand Faces*. He explains that "el narco se convierte en héroe porque pelea en contra del sistema institucionalizado por la hegemonía del estado mexicano al mismo tiempo que contribuye a corromper las leyes. Entonces, este personaje es un ser complejo que es visto de manera negativa por la aristocracia mexicana y de forma positiva por el estrato social medio y el sector compuesto por los de abajo" (The narco becomes a hero because he's fighting against the Mexican State's institutionalized hegemony at the same time as he contributes to corrupting laws. This character is thus a complex being who's viewed negatively by the Mexican aristocracy but positively by those in the middle and those at the bottom). In the realm of narcofolklore, the figure of Jesús Malverde exemplifies the social rebellion against *porfirismo* and the *caciquismo* of the beginning of the twentieth century. This character embodies marginality and banditry as well as solidarity with the dispossessed. Thus, the negative impact of Malverde's association with the world of drugs is neutralized, functioning instead as a compensatory force for the State's weakness and deviations. Jesús Ángel González, "El arquetipo del narco mexicano en la novela, el cine, y la música" (PhD diss., University of North Texas, 2014), 18.

65. David Thelen, "Mexico's Cultural Landscapes: A Conversation with Carlos Monsiváis," *Journal of American History* 86, no. 2 (1999): 613–22.

66. Thelen, "Mexico's Cultural Landscapes," 621.

67. In reference to narcoculture in Sinaloa, Jorge Alan Sánchez Godoy has pointed out that it contains deep-seated values connected to bravery, loyalty, protection, vengeance, hospitality, generosity, and nobility all of which serve as mechanisms of internal regulation and creates behavioral models (80). Jorge Alan Sánchez Godoy, "Procesos de institucionalización de la narcocultura en Sinaloa," *Frontera norte* 21, no. 41 (2009): 77–103.

68. La narcocultura ha logrado permear en gran medida la sociedad con sus hábitos y valorizaciones, deslegitimando las instituciones sociales anteriores a su

aparición. Por tanto, esta manifestación representa un conglomerado significativo mucho más extenso que el que aseguran algunos investigadores del tema, que no sólo incluye a un sector mafioso que resiste bajo las trincheras de una "subcultura," sino amalgama una multiplicidad de actores y expresiones que se (re)construyen, reproducen y legitiman, día con día, en esta construcción imaginaria de raíces eminentemente campiranas. Sánchez Godoy, "Procesos de institucionalización," 99.

69. Valenzuela has ironically identified a narco-Victorian style or "art-narcó" in reference to the style of dress and decoration preferred by narcos. "Narco" taste is generally ostentatious and eclectic, and includes baroque, classic, and orientalist elements, etc., often in curious combinations (conversation with Moraña).

70. Hablar del narcorcorrido es considerar, también una constante evolución. En un principio, los narcocorridos tenían una fuerte relación (aunque un tanto transfigurada) con el arquetipo del bandolero y héroe popular regional (como se ve en las figuras de Heraclio Bernal y Jesús Malverde). Estos figuraban como una forma de resistencia al poder del Estado y exaltaban su representación de valiente burlador de la autoridad y habilidoso transgresor de la ley; sin embargo, el tema del contrabando de drogas aparecía de manera indirecta. Es a partir de los ochenta cuando "se desvanece por completo en los corridos de los narcotraficantes el sociograma del valiente para dar lugar a la tematización directa del contrabando de narcóticos" (Héau y Giménez 651). De esta manera, el narcocorrido sinaloense elimina toda connotación social, política y diluye su vinculación con el pueblo y con la tradición épica, para enfrascarse en la nueva empresa, ahora, hedonista, utilitarista e individualista. Sánchez Godoy, "Procesos de institucionalización," 97. Godoy cites Catherine Héau Lambert and Gilberto Giménez "La representación social de la violencia en la trova popular mexicana." *Revista Mexicana de Sociología* 66, no. 4 (2004): 651.

71. Yuri Herrera, "Semántica de luminol," *Revista Dossier*, vol. 20, Mar. 2013, https://revistadossier.udp.cl/dossier/semantica-del-luminol.

72. Yuri Herrera, "Semántica de luminol."

73. Yuri Herrera, "Semántica de luminol."

74. Yuri Herrera, "Semántica de luminol."

75. Cited by Herrera in "Semántica del luminol." Vullamy's original article is entitled "Ciudad Juarez Is All Our Futures: This Is the Inevitable War of Capitalism Gone Mad," *Guardian*, June 20, 2011, https://www.theguardian.com/commentisfree/2011/jun/20/war-capitalism-mexico-drug-cartels.

76. On this topic, see Liliana Colanzi "En la frontera: Una conversación con el escritor mexicano Yuri Herrera," *Americas Quarterly*, February 5, 2010, https://www.americasquarterly.org/blog/en-la-frontera-una-conversacion-con-el-escritor-mexicano-yuri-herrera.

77. Herrera, *Trabajos del reino*, 18.

78. Herrera, *Trabajos del reino*, 13; *Kingdom Cons*, 10.

79. Sánchez Godoy, "Procesos de institucionalización," 93.

80. Sánchez Godoy, "Procesos de institucionalización," 95.
81. Herrera, *Trabajos del reino*, 23; *Kingdom Cons*, 17.
82. La única vez que Lobo fue al cine vio una película donde aparecía otro hombre así: fuerte, suntuoso, con poder sobre las cosas del mundo. Era un rey, y a su alrededor todo cobraba sentido. Los hombres luchaban por él, las mujeres parían para él, él protegía y regalaba, y cada cual, en el reino, tenía por su gracia un lugar preciso. Pero los que acompañaban a este Rey no eran simples vasallos. Eran la Corte. Herrera, *Trabajos del reino*, 23; *Kingdom Cons*, 7–8.
83. Herrera, *Trabajos del reino*, 13; *Kingdom Cons*, 10.
84. He never took notice of the calendar. It seemed absurd because all days were alike: do the rounds of the tables, offer songs, hold out your hand, fill your pockets with change. . . . Endings and eccentricities were the most notable why to order time. That was how he spent it. Herrera, *Trabajos del reino*, 17; *Kingdom Cons*, 15.
85. Herrera, *Trabajos del reino*, 17; *Kingdom Cons*, 15.
86. Gente de todas partes, de cada lugar del mundo conocido, gente de más allá del desierto. Había, verdad de Dios, hasta algunos que habían visto el mar. Y mujeres que andaban como leopardos, hombres de guerra gigantescos y condecorados de cicatrices en el rostro, había indios y negros, hasta un enano vio. . . . Escuchó de cordilleras, de selvas, de golfos, de montañas, en sonsonetes que nunca había oído: yes como shes, palabras sin eses, y unos que subían y bajaban el tono como si viajaran en cada oración. Herrera, *Trabajos del reino*, 19–20; *Kingdom Cons*, 14.
87. Herrera, *Trabajos del reino*, 19; *Kingdom Cons*, 15.
88. Carlos Monsiváis, "Reír llorando: Notas sobre la cultura popular urbana," in *Política cultural del Estado mexicano*, ed. Moisés Ladrón de Guevara (Mexico City: Centro de Estudios Educativos, 1983), 56, quoted in Valenzuela, *Jefe de jefes*, 33.
89. In reference to narcoculture's mechanisms of legitimation, Sánchez Godoy references the following: "extensión de los hábitos e instituciones sociales del campo a la ciudad; transición de una identidad de resistencia (subcultura) a una legitimadora (narcocultura); uso constante de violencia simbólica y/o física; la narcolimosna a particulares y organizaciones civiles; dominación de tipo carismática con la reencarnación del narcotraficante en el nuevo bandolero social; edificación de un narcoestado, una narcoeconomía, y una narcosociedad, etcétera" (the transference of rural social customs and institutions to the city; the transition from an identity of resistance [subculture] to a legitimizing one [narcoculture]; the constant use of symbolic and physical violence; the extension of narco-charity to individuals and civic organizations; charismatic domination as the narco is transformed into the new social bandit; the construction of the narco-State, a narco-economy and a narco-society, etc.). Sánchez Godoy, "Procesos de institucionalización," 92n38.
90. Sánchez Godoy, "Procesos de institucionalización," 85–86.

91. For the same reason, critics have spoken about the archetypal nature of Herrera's characters. Serrato Córdova, "Arquetipos de la narcocultura en *Trabajos del reino* de Yuri Herrera," in *Nada es lo que parece: Estudios sobre la novela mexicana 2000–2009*, ed. Miguel G. Rodríguez Lozano, 69–82 (Mexico City: UNAM, 2013), 76. This nature allows for the reader to "verse involucrado dentro de una realidad alejada de los principios morales y de los constructos ideológicos que ha creado el Estado como una medida de restricción en contra de las manifestaciones locales de la 'narcocultura'" (feel involved in a reality distance from moral principles and ideological constructs that the State has created as a way of restricting local manifestations of narcoculture). Rosado Marrero, "La consagración," 189–90.
92. Carlos Ávila, "La utilidad de la sangre: En diálogo con *Trabajos del reino*, de Yuri Herrera," *Nueva sociedad* 238 (2012): 148–58.
93. Ávila "La utilidad de la sangre," 155. In addition, see Moraña, *El monstruo como máquina*, particularly "El hombre-lobo y el poder político (Agamben y el psicoanálisis)," 245–53.
94. José Serrato Córdova cites Juan Pablo Villalobos's novel *Fiesta en la madriguera* (2010) as clearly influenced by *Trabajos del reino*, given that Villalobos also references a Court and a palace that belong to narcos. Yolcaut is a capo who lives in the luxurious rabbit warren of the title, which he calls the "Castle," surrounded by underlings, women, and other characters drawn to the narco world. Told from the point of view of his naïve child the narrative incorporates irony and humor. Also present in this novel is the same laconic quality of Herrera's other work along with the desire to recreate the local language of the individuals and areas he represents.
95. Herrera, *Trabajos del reino*, 26; *Kingdom Cons*, 20.
96. Herrera, *Trabajos del reino*, 24; *Kingdom Cons*, 18.
97. Herrera, *Trabajos del reino*, 37–38; *Kingdom Cons*, 30.
98. Herrera, *Trabajos del reino*, 36; *Kingdom Cons*, 29.
99. Herrera, *Trabajos del reino*, 108; *Kingdom Cons*, 87.
100. Herrera, *Trabajos del reino*, 15; *Kingdom Cons*, 11.
101. Herrera, *Trabajos del reino*, 17; *Kingdom Cons*, 13.
102. Herrera, *Trabajos del reino*, 24; *Kingdom Cons*, 19.
103. Valenzuela, *Jefe de jefes*, 13.
104. According to Rosado Marrero: "La realidad presentada por el protagonista se transforma, por tanto, en una visión contra-hegemónica y contra-imaginativa: la misión de la narración de Herrera es mostrar cómo se subsiste realmente en la frontera, es decir, dentro de esta 'narcocultura.' De tal forma que la mirada de Yuri Herrera acaba por ser un replanteamiento político y cultural; y, en este sentido, la recepción crítica que ha tenido su obra en el extranjero ha sido fundamental para la constitución de esa 'otra' realidad que se banaliza constantemente en el territorio mexicano." (The reality that Herrera's narrative presents is thus transformed into a counterhegemonic and counterimaginative

vision. His fictional vision shows how we survive on the border, within this "narcoculture." In this way, Yuri Herrera's gaze presents a political and cultural rethinking. In this sense, the critical reception his work has received outside of Mexico has been fundamental for the configuration of this "other" reality that is constantly represented as banal within Mexico.) Rosado Marrero, "La consagración," 190.

105. In order to keep fools entertained with clean lies, the Journalist had to make them seem true. But the real news was the Artist's job, the stuff of *corridos*, and there were so many yet to sing that he forgot whatever didn't serve the King. Herrera, *Trabajos del reino*, 35-6; *Kingdom Cons*, 28.
106. Herrera, *Trabajos del reino*, 15; *Kingdom Cons*, 11.
107. Herrera, *Trabajos del reino*, 16; *Kingdom Cons*, 11-12.
108. Muelen la hoja entre rodillos de insomnio, avisan, hurgan la blancura baldía en el papel y en el mirar. ¿Y qué habría sido la hoja sino un trasto del jale, como el serrucho si armara mesas, como la fusca si arreglara vidas? Qué, pero nunca este despeñadero de arena con brío y propósitos a saber. Tantas letras ahí. Son. Son un destello. Cómo se empujan y abrevan una de otra, y envuelven al ojo en un borlote de razones. Herrera, *Trabajos del reino*, 39; *Kingdom Cons*, 31.
109. Herrera, *Trabajos del reino*, 39; *Kingdom Cons*, 31.
110. Herrera, *Trabajos del reino*, 39-40; *Kingdom Cons*, 32.
111. Herrera, *Trabajos del reino*, 68; *Kingdom Cons*, 57.
112. ¿Quién era el rey? Un todopoderoso. Un haz de luz que había iluminado sus márgenes porque no podía ser de otro modo mientras no se revelara lo que era. Un pobre tipo traicionado. Una gota en un mar de hombres con historias. Un hombre sin poder sobre la tersa fábrica en la cabeza del artista. (El Artista se permitió sentir esa potencia de un orden distinto al de la Corte, la maña con la que desprendía las palabras de las cosas y creaba una textura y un volumen soberanos. Una realidad aparte). Herrera, *Trabajos del reino*, 117-18; *Kingdom Cons*, 96.
113. Herrera, *Trabajos del reino*, 119; *Kingdom Cons*, 97.
114. Herrera, *Trabajos del reino*, 109; *Kingdom Cons*, 87.
115. José Manuel Valenzuela summarizes the most frequent *narcocorrido* themes including the generally black and white representation of drugs; different forms of power (political institutions, police, religious or the power of money); gender relations; machismo; regionalism; "the gringo" as consumer of drugs, partner and oppressor or protector of the narco; advice or aphorisms that the *corrido* includes as a corollary to its main narrative; and the successful or tragic climax of the antihero. Valenzuela, *Jefe de jefes*, 13-14.
116. Valenzuela, *Jefe de jefes*, 10
117. Well-known studies of this type include those by Américo Paredes, María Herrera-Sobeck, José E. Limón and Vicente Mendoza who have analyzed the *corrido*'s origins, its characteristics, styles, and social function. Hermann

Herlinghaus has carried out a more theoretically complex study in which he analyzes the theme of affect that emerges in the *corridos* in relation to the concepts of sovereignty and "bare life" in the work of Agamben.

118. Américo Paredes, *With His Pistol in His Hand: A Border Ballad and its Hero* (Austin: University of Texas Press, 1958).
119. Herrera, *Trabajos del reino*, 63; *Kingdom Cons*, 52.
120. Herrera, *Trabajos del reino*, 98; *Kingdom Cons*, 79.
121. Valenzuela, *Jefe de jefes*, 10.
122. Herrera, *Trabajos del reino*, 57; *Kingdom Cons*, 47.
123. Herrera, *Trabajos del reino*, 61; *Kingdom Cons*, 51.
124. Herrera, *Trabajos del reino*, 63; *Kingdom Cons*, 52.
125. Herrera, *Trabajos del reino*, 64; *Kingdom Cons*, 52.
126. Habría que tomarlos de la crin y restregarles la cara contra esta verdad puerca y áspera y maloliente y verdadera, que les dé tentación. Hay que sentarlos en las púas de este sol, hay que ahogarlos en el escándalo de estas noches, hay que meterles nuestro cantadito bajo las uñas, ha que desnudarlos con estas pieles. Hay que curtirlos, hay que apalearlos.... Mejor quisieran oír nomás la parte bonita, verdá, pero las de acá no son canciones para después del permiso, el corrido no es un cuadro adornando la pared. Es un nombre y es un arma. Herrera, *Trabajos del reino*, 64; *Kingdom Cons*, 53.
127. Herrera, *Trabajos del reino*, 87; *Kingdom Cons*, 71.
128. Herrera, *Trabajos del reino*, 95; *Kingdom Cons*, 77.
129. Herrera, *Trabajos del reino*, 124; *Kingdom Cons*, 101.
130. Herrera, *Trabajos del reino*, 15; *Kingdom Cons*, 11.
131. Estas eran las cosas que fijaban la altura de un rey: el hombre vino a posarse entre los simples y convirtió lo sucio en esplendor. Al acercarse, el Palacio reventaba un confín del desierto en una soberbia de murallas, rejas y jardines vastísimos. Una ciudad con lustre en la margen de la ciudad, que sólo parecía repetir calle a calle su desdicha. Aquí la gente entraba y salía, echaba los hombros para atrás con el empaque de pertenecer a un dominio próspero. Herrera, *Trabajos del reino*, 20; *Kingdom Cons*, 15.
132. Herrera, *Trabajos del reino*, 31; *Kingdom Cons*, 24.
133. Herrera, *Trabajos del reino*, 31; *Kingdom Cons*, 24.
134. Herrera, *Trabajos del reino*, 129; *Kingdom Cons*, 99.
135. Salieron a los jardines, pasaron junto a una fuente en cuyo centro un dios con tenedor tiraba agua por la boca, siguieron por el laberinto de arbustos trazado con las letras del nombre del Rey.... Luego miró más allá, hacia el fin del jardín, la reja electrificada, el desierto.... Caminaron hasta donde estaba la colección del Rey. Había serpientes, tigres, cocodrilos, un avestruz, y en una jaula más grande, casi un jardín, un pavo real. Herrera, *Trabajos del reino*, 51-2; *Kingdom Cons*, 43.
136. Herrera, *Trabajos del reino*, 127; *Kingdom Cons*, 103.

137. Herrera, *Trabajos del reino*, 127; *Kingdom Cons*, 103.
138. Martín Lombardo, "Autoridad, transgresión y frontera (sobre la narrativa de Yuri Herrera)," *Inti: Revista de Literatura Hispánica*, no. 79/80 (2014): 193–214, 208.
139. Herrera's second novel, *Señales que precederán al fin del mundo* (Madrid: Editorial Periférica, 2009) was translated into English by Lisa Dillman as *Signs Preceding the End of the World* (Sheffield, UK: And Other Stories, 2015).
140. podemos afirmar que estamos ante una literatura de los márgenes comunitarios. No tanto porque sus personajes sean marginales ni tampoco porque algunos de los personajes sean inmigrantes sino más bien porque se interroga al grueso de la comunidad a partir de esos espacios en donde la comunidad empieza a borrar sus fronteras y construir otras formas de vínculos comunitarios: se interroga a la comunidad entera a partir de sus bordes. Lombardo, "Autoridad, transgresión, 194.
141. Lombardo, "Autoridad, transgresión, 196
142. Joseph Campbell, *Hero with a Thousand Faces*, 3rd ed. (1949; Novato, CA: New World Books, 2008).
143. According to Campbell, "A hero ventures forth from the world of common day into a region of supernatural wonder: fabulous forces are there encountered, and a decisive victory is won: the hero comes back from this mysterious adventure with the power to bestow boons on his fellow man." Campbell, *Hero with a Thousand Faces*, 25. Here Campbell outlines the idea of the monomyth or common myth that many literary works share, in which the hero's journey can be distilled to this outline.
144. Vladimir Propp, *Morphology of the Folk Tale*, trans. Laurence Scott (1928; Austin: University of Texas Press, 1968).
145. Herrera, *Señales que precederán*, 36.
146. The inheritance alluded to in the novel seems to be a fraud from the outset and the topic is shrouded in ambiguity and suspicion. The inheritance's documentation, location, and legitimacy all seem questionable as always happens with the recognition of land rights in the case of poor rural workers. However, her brother continues to pursue this remote possibility and Makina's journey is also guided by this motive. Herrera, *Señales que precederán*, 31.
147. Herrera, *Señales que precederán*, 13; *Signs Preceding*, 13.
148. Herrera, *Señales que precederán*, 16–17; *Signs Preceding*, 16.
149. Herrera, *Señales que precederán*, 68; *Signs Preceding*, 61.
150. Herrera, *Señales que precederán*, 16; *Signs Preceding*, 16.
151. Nathan Richardson, "Jarchar: Reading Makina / Makina Reading in Yuri Herrera's *Señales que precederán al fin del mundo*," *Ciberletras: Revista de Crítica Literaria y de Cultura*, no. 41 (2019): 12–23, 17.
152. Herrera, *Señales que precederán*, 19; *Signs Preceding*, 18.
153. Henri Bergson, *Key Writings*, ed. Keith Ansell Pearson and John Mullarkey (New York: Continuum Books, 2002).

154. Herrera, *Señales que precederán*, 38.
155. Herrera, *Señales que precederán*, 89.
156. Herrera, *Señales que precederán*, 13; *Signs Preceding*, 12.
157. Herrera, *Señales que precederán*, 18; *Signs Preceding*, 17.
158. Herrera, *Señales que precederán*, 20; *Signs Preceding*, 19.
159. Herrera, *Señales que precederán*, 53; *Signs Preceding*, 48.
160. Herrera, *Señales que precederán*, 118–19; *Signs Preceding*, 106.
161. Lombardo, "Autoridad, transgresión," 194
162. Here Richardson follows the argument of Sánchez Becerril and Rioseco regarding Makina's descent into the Mexican underworld of Mictlán. Richardson, "Jarchar," 18.
163. Aaron Bady, "Border Characters," *Nation*, Feb. 12, 2015, https://www.thenation.com/article/archive/border-characters.
164. In a skilled but, in my opinion, slightly extreme interpretation, Richardson explains: "If Makina then is incomplete, un-rounded as a protagonist, it is because she is not, in fact, the sole protagonist. Using traditional plotting jargon, Makina is merely the tag—the Peripetia, or restoration—in a three-part Aristotelian plot where not Makina but her brother enacts the Hamaratia (sin), and not Makina but her mother Cora plays the role in the central moment of Anagnorisis (recognition). This is a familial tragedy, not an individualistic bildungsroman. Makina's brother abandons the family, her mother sees that this mustn't be, and Makina sallies forth with the aid of helpers and guides to restore unity. The entire novel with the exception of two brief analepsis is Peripetia." Richardson, "Jarchar," 18.
165. Diego Erlan, "El lenguaje como frontera: Entrevista a Yuri Herrera," *Revista Ñ—Literatura*, Sept. 9, 2011, https://www.clarin.com/rn/literatura/Entrevista_Yuri_Herrera_0_BJKMGU6nDXx.html.
166. Herrera, *Señales que precederán*, 11; *Signs Preceding*, 11.
167. Santiago Navarro Pastor, "La violencia en sordina en *Señales que precederán al fin del mundo* de Yuri Herrera," *iMex Revista* 1, no. 1 (2012): 93–126.
168. Cecilio E. Robelo, *Diccionario de mitología náhuatl* (México: Imprenta del Museo Nacional, 1905).
169. See Michael E. Smith, *The Aztecs* (Oxford: Blackwell Publishing, 2009); and Michael E. Smith, "The Aztlan Migrations of the Nahuatl Chronicles: Myth or History?" *Ethnohistory* 31, no. 3 (1984): 153–86.
170. Herrera, *Señales que precederán*, 49; *Signs Preceding*, 45.
171. Herrera, *Señales que precederán*, 50; *Signs Preceding*, 45.
172. Giovanna Rivero, "*Señales que precederán al fin del mundo* de Yuri Herrera: Una propuesta para un *novum* ontológico latinoamericano," *Revista Iberoamericana* 83, no. 259/260 (April–Sept. 2017): 501–16.
173. Rivero, "*Señales que precederán*," 511.
174. Rivero, "*Señales que precederán*," 509.
175. Rivero, "*Señales que precederán*," 514.

176. Herrera, *Señales que precederán*, 56; *Signs Preceding*, 51.
177. Herrera, *Señales que precederán*, 56; *Signs Preceding*, 52.
178. Herrera, *Señales que precederán*, 56; *Signs Preceding*, 52.
179. Herrera, *Señales que precederán*, 73; *Signs Preceding*, 65.
180. maleable, deleble, permeable, un gozne entre dos semejantes distantes y luego entre otros dos, y luego entre otros dos, nunca exactamente los mismos, un algo que sirve para poner en relación. . . . Más que un punto medio entre lo paisano y lo gabacho su lengua es una franja difusa entre lo que desaparece y lo que no ha nacido. Pero no una hecatombe. Makina no percibe en su lengua ninguna ausencia súbita, sino una metamorfosis sagaz, una mudanza en defensa propia. Herrera, *Señales que precederán*, 73–74; *Signs Preceding*, 65.
181. En medio del llano de concreto y varilla, sin embargo, luego sintió otra presencia, espolvoreada como remaches caídos de una banqueta; efímeras miradas de reconocimiento que de inmediato se ocultaban para convertirse en huida. Era el paisanaje armado de chambas: albañiles, vendedores de flores, estibadores, choferes; depurando el disimulo para no delatar ningún propósito común sino nomás, nomás: que estaban ahí para recibir órdenes. Eran como allá pero menos chifladores, y ninguno pordioseraba. Herrera, *Señales que precederán*, 63; *Signs Preceding*, 57.
182. Herrera, *Señales que precederán*, 65; *Signs Preceding*, 58.
183. Herrera, *Señales que precederán*, 67; *Signs Preceding*, 60.
184. Herrera, *Señales que precederán*, 67; *Signs Preceding*, 59.
185. Herrera, *Señales que precederán*, 90; *Signs Preceding*, 81.
186. Herrera, *Señales que precederán*, 90–91; *Signs Preceding*, 82.
187. As Herrera explains: "en la literatura mexicana la frontera aparece como un espacio con múltiples significados (el trabajo al otro lado, la panacea al otro lado, el enemigo al otro lado, la línea que transfigura nombres y negocios, por ejemplo), mientras que en la literatura estadounidense el espacio que se delinea tras la frontera es básicamente de decadencia o una ruta de escape" (in Mexican literature the border is a space of multiple meanings [working on the other side, the panacea of the other side, the enemy on the other side, the line that transfigures names and businesses, for example] while in US literature the space beyond the border is basically one of decadence or a place of escape). Colanzi, "En la frontera."
188. Herrera, *Señales que precederán*, 119; *Signs Preceding*, 106.
189. Herrera, *Señales que precederán*, 119; *Signs Preceding*, 107.
190. Herrera, *Señales que precederán*, 119; *Signs Preceding*, 107.
191. Herrera, *Señales que precederán*, 107; *Signs Preceding*, 97.
192. Nosotros somos los culpables de esta destrucción, los que no hablamos su lengua ni sabemos estar en silencio. Los que no llegamos en barco, los que ensuciamos de polvo sus portales, los que rompemos sus alambradas. Los que venimos a quitarles el trabajo, los que aspiramos a limpiar su mierda, los que anhelamos trabajar a deshoras. Los que llenamos de olor a comida sus calles

tan limpias, los que les trajimos violencia que no conocían, los que transportamos sus remedios, los que merecemos ser amarrados del cuello y de los pies; nosotros, a los que no nos importa morir por ustedes, ¿cómo podía ser de otro modo? Los que quién sabe qué aguardamos. Nosotros los oscuros, los chaparros, los grasientos, los mustios, los obesos, los anémicos. Nosotros, los bárbaros. Herrera, *Señales que precederán*, 109–10; *Signs Preceding*, 99–100.

193. In "Del sueño americano a la utopía desmoronada," Edith Mora has pointed out how the novel associates el Norte with wealth and opportunities but also with cold, hunger and barrenness. Moreover, Mictlan's northern location links el Norte with death. Edith Mora, "Del sueño americano a la utopía desmoronada: Cuatro novelas sobre la inmigración de México a Estados Unidos," *Latinoamérica* 54, no. 1 (2012): 269–95.

194. Herrera, *Señales que precederán*, 109; *Signs Preceding*, 98.

195. Walter Benjamin, *Illuminations*, trans. Harry Zohn (New York: Schocken Books, 2007): 256.

196. As the author himself has declared, the theme of epidemic was inspired by the massive spread of H1N1 in Mexico and other parts of the world in 2009. Read during the coronavirus pandemic, Herrera's 2013 novel obviously assumes prophetic connotations. Eduardo Ramos-Izquierdo and Sandra Acuña, "Entrevista a Yuri Herrera: 'Caos más tiempo' se convierte en una cierta armonía intangible," *Les Ateliers du SAL*, no. 6 (2015): 161–76, 170.

197. Yuri Herrera, *La transmigración de los cuerpos* (Madrid: Editorial Periférica, 2013).

198. Gómez Michel has followed this line in his reading of *La transmigración de los cuerpos*, interpreting the novel as a sharp critique of the political warfare waged against drug traffickers during Felipe Calderón's government in 2006. The mobilization of more than 40,000 soldiers on Mexican soil resulted in the deaths of 35,000 people and brought about an escalation of terror, the image of a failed government and the idea that the logic of the narco-State had triumphed and remove all institutional legality from the government. Gerardo Gómez Michel, "Nuda vida y espacio límite en *La transmigración de los cuerpos* de Yuri Herrera," *Iberoamericana* 18, no. 2 (2016): 271–95.

199. Looking at home for a drop of water at the beginning of the novel and finding that there's only a tiny trace in the toilet tank el Alfaqueque clearly imitates the Colonel scraping the bottom of the coffee jar in a scene that inserts an air of lack and aggrieved resignation into the plot that begins to unfold. There is a similar narrative rhythm in which social drama combines with a certain lightness that invokes the common spirit, anchored in misfortune, and that in both cases makes the characters, who move between tragedy and farce, equally winning. In both texts, a narrator who seems to have inside knowledge of the fictional world skillfully manages these extremes.

200. Herrera, *La transmigración*, 49; *The Transmigration*, 35. In this regard, Betina Keizman correctly points out that the character displaces the role of language

from the realm of truth to the realm of efficiency in "Transmigraciones y desaparición del trabajo en dos novellas latinoamericanas recientes," *A Contracorriente* 16, no. 3 (2019): 161–83.
201. Herrera *La transmigración*, 50; *The Transmigration*, 36.
202. Herrera *La transmigración*, 21; *The Transmigration*, 15.
203. Herrera, *La transmigración*, 59; *The Transmigration*, 43.
204. sintió por primera vez la presencia del perro negro, que ya nunca se iría; sólo a ratos se echaría fuera de su vista, pero siempre estaría ahí. Aprendió a vivir con él, e incluso a convocarlo en ciertos momentos. Algo le quebraba por dentro, pero a la vez le permitía meterse en lugares y en decisiones que no soportaría a solas. Era un núcleo oscuro que le permitía hacer cosas o dejar de sentir cosas, era algo físico, tan real como un güeso del que uno no se hace consciente hasta que está a punto de reventarle la piel. Herrera, *La transmigración*, 108; *The Transmigration*, 81.
205. Sánchez Becerril has also noted the character's role of mediator, not only in terms of the conflict over the restitution of the corpses but also in terms of "his role as narrative mediator; as such he describes the dynamic established by the state of exception imposed by the government on the grounds of the ongoing health crisis, the fomenting of fear as the reason for the collapse of social connections." Ivonne Sánchez Becerril, "Insólitos estados de guerra: *La fiesta vigilada*, de Antonio José Ponte, y *La transmigración de los cuerpos*, de Yuri Herrera," in *La posición sesgada: Miradas a la narrativa reciente en América Latina*, ed. Ivonne Sánchez Becerril and Alexandra Saavedra Galindo, 199–227 (Mexico City: CIALC-UNAM, 2017).
206. Keizman, "Transmigraciones y desaparición," 179.
207. In this regard, see Lukácas's *Theory of the Novel* (1916/1920), trans. Anna Bostock (Boston: MIT Press, 1974), and *The Historical Novel* (1937/1947), trans. Hanna Mitchell and Stanley Mitchell (Lincolon: University of Nebraska Press, 1983).
208. Georges Bataille, *Erotism: Death and Sensuality*, trans. Mary Dalwood (San Francisco: City Lights Books, 1986), 61.
209. Ramos-Izquierdo and Acuña, "Entrevista a Yuri Herrera," 171.
210. Modernity has celebrated and recognized the iconic value of dead bodies. In Mexico, the rituals associated with the Día de Muertos / Day of the Dead commemorate the memory of deceased family members and friends with gatherings, music, and food, and it has become an established cultural trait that has institutionalized the celebration of a symbolic coming together with the departed. Paradoxically, the aggression wielded against the corpse has often become a frequent practice connected to the proliferation of violence associated both with drug trafficking as well as other forms of organized crime and with actions carried out by the army. These types of acts, also studied in other countries that have withstood periods of terrorism as well as bloody dictatorships (Peru, Colombia) are laden with social, cultural, and symbolic meaning. Incited by tumultuous political struggle, the profanation of corpses expresses

desire for vengeance and the will to carry out extreme and intimidating acts directed toward society.
211. Herrera, *La transmigración*, 130; *The Transmigration*, 98.
212. Jean Baudrillard, *Symbolic Exchange and Death*, trans. Ian Hamilton Grant (London: Sage, 2017), 147.
213. Baudrillard, *Symbolic Exchange*, 147.
214. Kristeva, *Powers of Horror: An Essay on Abjection*, trans. Leon S. Roudiez (New York: Columbia University Press, 1982), 3.
215. Kristeva, *Powers of Horror*, 2.
216. On the representation of work in contemporary narrative see Keizman "Transmigraciones y desaparición."
217. como intermediario, Alfaqueque es el trabajador del presente, aquel que no lucra con objetos materiales sino, sobre todo, con material simbólico y performativo. Es un trabajador de baja gama, porque su terreno es el de las ideas menores que surgen como pompas de jabón, se utilizan y luego explotan. . . . El personaje de Alfaqueque es transversal, por una parte, brinda ese servicio de contacto cara a cara con sus empleadores, un verdadero "comercio de pieles" (o servicio personal, según John O'Neill) que provee un bálsamo para los males que aquejan a sus clientes. Paradójicamente, es un cuidado insustancial: un favor, un acuerdo, un consejo, algo que en muchos casos pertenece al orden de lo simbólico. Keizman, "Transmigraciones y desaparición," 175.
218. Keizman, "Transmigraciones y desaparición," 176.
219. Herrera, *La transmigración*, 8; *The Transmigration*, 10.
220. Herrera, *La transmigración*, 51; *The Transmigration*, 37.
221. Herrera, *La transmigración*, 70; *The Transmigration*, 52.
222. Herrera, *La transmigración*, 78; *The Transmigration*, 56.
223. Herrera, *La transmigración*, 74; *The Transmigration*, 54.
224. era amplia y blanca, y tenía un porche de madera, como si alguien no hubiera podido renunciar a su casa en el trópico, aunque ya viviese en un cerro a miles de kilómetros del mar. . . . Nomás pasar la puerta lo encandiló un salón enorme iluminado por una docena de ventanas altas. En el centro del salón había una mesa y, sobre la mesa estaba tendida la Muñe. Herrera, *La transmigración*, 58; *The Transmigration*, 42.
225. Los Castro tenían unos añitos dándoselas de finos y guapos pero la Muñe les malograba el estilo. También los Fonseca se habían hecho de dinero, pero a ellos no les preocupaba el estilo. Tan parecidos y tan distintos, los Castro y los Fonseca, pránganas un par de décadas atrás, muy sácalepunta hoy en día, y ninguno había abandonado el barrio. Herrera, *La transmigración*, 46; *The Transmigration*, 33.
226. Herrera, *La transmigración*, 59; *The Transmigration*, 43.
227. Herrera, *La transmigración*, 131; *The Transmigration*, 89.
228. Era algo duro, pero sin forma, ese silencio. ¿Cómo describir lo que no está ahí? ¿Qué nombre se le da a lo que no existe y que precisamente por eso existe?

Capos de capos los que habían inventado el cero, pensó, le habían dado nombre a aquello y hasta lo habían metido en una fila de números, como si pudiera quedarse ahí, obediente. Pero cada tanto, como en ese momento frente a la Muñe, el cero se levantaba y se tragaba todo. Herrera, *La transmigración*, 125; *The Transmigration*, 99.
229. Herrera, *La transmigración*, 45; *The Transmigration*, 33.
230. Herrera, *La transmigración*, 59; *The Transmigration*, 42.
231. Herrera, *La transmigración*, 103; *The Transmigration*, 77.
232. Roberto Esposito, "Inmunidad, comunidad, biopolítica," *Papeles del CEIC / International Journal on Collective Identity Research* 2018/1 (March), paper 182, https://ojs.ehu.eus/index.php/papelesCEIC/article/view/18112/17020.
233. Esposito, "Inmunidad, comunidad, biopolítica," 1.
234. Esposito, "Inmunidad, comunidad, biopolítica," 1.
235. Esposito, "Inmunidad, comunidad, biopolítica," 5.
236. Esto puede valer para los individuos singulares, pero también para las mismas comunidades, tomadas en este caso en su dimensión particular, inmunizadas respecto a todo elemento extraño que pareciera amenazarlas desde el exterior. De ahí el doble nudo implícito en la dinámica inmunitaria—ya típico de la modernidad y hoy cada vez más extendido en todos los ámbitos de la experiencia individual y colectiva, real e imaginaria. La inmunidad, aunque necesaria para la conservación de nuestra vida, una vez llevada más allá de un cierto umbral, la constriñe en una suerte de jaula en la que acaba por perderse no sólo nuestra libertad, sino el sentido mismo de nuestra existencia—o bien aquel abrirse de la existencia hacia fuera de sí misma a la cual se ha dado el nombre de communitas. . . . Si la inmunidad tiende a encerrar nuestra existencia en círculos, o recintos, no comunicados ente sí, la comunidad, más que ser un cerco mayor que el que los comprende, es el pasaje que, cortando las líneas del confín, vuelve a mezclar la experiencia humana, liberándola de su obsesión por la seguridad. Esposito, "Inmunidad, comunidad, biopolítica," 5.
237. Esposito, "Inmunidad, comunidad, biopolítica," 7.
238. Esposito, "Inmunidad, comunidad, biopolítica," 11.
239. From the perspective of the analysis of violence, we could add to what was said earlier the idea that the legacy of drug trafficking has imposed a habitus that is today ensconced particularly in the areas close to big cities, in what Hubert de Grammont calls the "nueva ruralidad" (new rurality), which reveals the modification of customs, values, and languages. According to de Grammont, "La nueva ruralidad es . . . una nueva relación campo-ciudad en donde los límites entre ambos ámbitos de la sociedad se desdibujan, sus interconexiones se multiplican, se confunden y se complejizan" (the new rurality is . . . a new relationship between the countryside and the city where the limits between both social areas are blurred, their interconnections are multiplied, confused

and complicated). Qtd. in Sánchez Godoy, "Procesos de institucionalización," 83, 83n20.

CHAPTER 2

1. Fernanda Melchor, *Temporada de huracanes* (Mexico City: Random House, 2017); Fernanda Melchor, *Falsa liebre* (Mexico City: Almadía, 2013); Fernanda Melchor, *Aquí no es Miami* (Mexico City: Random House, 2019).
2. From the outset, Melchor has received praise for her journalistic work. Among other prizes, she has won the Premio Nacional de la Crónica Dolores Guerrero, 2011; the prize awarded in 2018 by the Pen Club for Journalism and Excellence in Literature, for *Aquí no es Miami*; the Internationaler Literaturpreis 2019, Haus der Kulturen der Welt, and the Anna Seghers Prize for *Temporada de huracanes*, 2019. In addition, she was shortlisted for the International Booker Prize in 2020 for the same novel along with the Argentine writer, Gabriela Cabezón Cámara.
3. Included in the group of female authors from Veracruz, among whom Fernanda Melchor counts herself, are Ester Hernández Palacios (born 1952), Celia del Palacio Montiel (1960) and Norma Lazo (1966), among others. Closer to her generation are Itzel Guevara del Ángel (1976) and Magali Velasco (1975), Viridiana Anzures (1985), Norma Blanco (1973), Maricarmen Delgado (1959), Gloria Domínguez (1963), Dolores Dorantes (1973), Mary Carmen Gerardo (1969), Juditzin Santopietro (1983) and Esperanza Tural (1968). For the study of women writers, see Adriana Pacheco Roldán's *Romper con la palabra: Violencia y género en la obra de escritoras mexicanas contemporáneas* (Mexico City: Ediciones y Gráficos Eón, 2017), in which these criteria are evaluated in terms of literary quality, which is a concept that is, of course, open to debate.
4. ¿Qué significa escribir hoy en ese contexto? ¿Qué tipo de retos enfrenta el ejercicio de la escritura en un medio donde la precariedad del trabajo y la muerte horrísona constituyen la materia de todos los días? ¿Cuáles son los diálogos estéticos a los que nos avienta el hecho de escribir literalmente rodeados de muertos?" Cristina Rivera Garza, *Los muertos indóciles: Necroescrituras y desapropiación* (Mexico City: Tusquets Editores, 2013) 16–17; Cristina Rivera Garza, *The Restless Dead: Necrowriting and Disappropriation*, trans. Robin Meyer (Nashville, TN: Vanderbilt University Press, 2020), 2.
5. Rivera Garza, *Los muertos indóciles*, 17; *The Restless Dead*, 2.
6. Kristeva, *Powers of Horror*, 1.
7. Judith Butler, *Gender Trouble* (New York: Routledge, 1999), 169.
8. Martín Guerra Muente "Poderes de la perversión y estética de lo abyecto en el arte latinoamericano," *Guaraguao* 14, no. 34 (2010): 71–88, 71.
9. Guerra Muente, "Poderes de la perversión," 73.
10. Pero lo abyecto no sólo es la forma que se le da, o que se le atribuye, a lo que quiere ser retirado de la circulación, sino que es, también, la forma que

tiene de volver lo que ha querido ser borrado, una política de restitución que objeta el poder perverso y represivo del Estado ... el horror termina siempre por emerger, ya sea como parte de una mercancía visual o como el inconsciente hórrido que nos persigue. Guerra Muente, "Poderes de la perversión," 73

11. Rocha wrote his manifesto just after his cementing his celebrity with the film *Deus e o Diabo na Terra do Sol* (1964), that positioned him as central within the Cinema Novo movement. Rocha speaks of political poetics that counteract the idyllic images promoted by Hollywood and present a close-up view of the economic situation in peripheral and dependent countries. The continuity between these aesthetics and the literary representation of promiscuity and violence emphasized here is connected to the same idea of presenting situations that, although fictional, elude the utopian formulations of democratic integration, popular participation and the benevolent State so as instead reveal the circumstances, languages and sensibilities of marginalized sectors who have been devastated by precarity and inequality. The main difference between the aesthetic and ideological movement of the 70s and the representation of abjection and promiscuity in Melchor's work is connected, above all, to the lack of a political articulation and/or a theory of action that could connect the political consciousness related to this kind of representation to a social and political transformative project.
12. Guerra Muente, "Poderes de la perversión," 75.
13. Guerra Muente, "Poderes de la perversión," 76.
14. Guerra Muente, "Poderes de la perversión," 76.
15. On the genre of the chronicle, see for example, Beth E. Jörgensen, ed., *The Contemporary Mexican Chronicle: Theoretical Perspectives on the Liminal Genre* (Albany: SUNY Press, 2002). On the work of Carlos Monsiváis, see Mabel Moraña and Ignacio Sánchez Prado, eds. *Carlos Monsiváis: El arte de la ironía* (Mexico City: Ediciones Era, 2007).
16. Translated into English as *This Is Not Miami* by Sophie Hughes (New York: New Directions Press, 2023). While translations of story titles are drawn from Sophie Hughes's version, translations of the text are my own.
17. The Zetas came into being in the 1990s when commando deserters from the Mexican army joined the Cartel del Golfo. In 2010 they broke away from the Cartel del Golfo, declaring a territorial war against the organization to whom they had up until this point belonged and also against the Sinaloa Cartel. The Zetas began their activities in Veracruz in 2005.
18. Melchor, *Aquí no es Miami*, 10.
19. El conjunto de relatos que el lector tiene en sus manos fue escrito en un intento por contar historias de la forma más honesta que reconozco posible: aceptando este carácter oblicuo del lenguaje y aprovechándolo a favor de la propia historia. No importa que sea imposible "reproducir" la realidad con una herramienta que deja las manos astilladas; no importa que cualquier imagen en nuestra computadora, por fútil que sea, valga más de mil palabras. Las his-

torias nacen en el lenguaje y en él alcanzan su sentido más profundo, el que se le escapa a las grabadoras y a las cámaras, el que se encuentra enmarañado en las voces y los gestos de la tribu. Melchor, *Aquí no es Miami*, 10.
20. Melchor, *Aquí no es Miami*, 10.
21. Melchor, *Aquí no es Miami*, 11.
22. Melchor, *Aquí no es Miami*, 11.
23. Melchor, *Aquí no es Miami*, 11.
24. Melchor, *Aquí no es Miami*, 18–19.
25. Habitado durante el periodo colonial por libertos de origen africano que levantaron sus viviendas en las márgenes del río Tenoya con los maderos provenientes de los naufragios, el Barrio (a secas) fue durante muchos siglos el único hogar posible para las miles de personas que arribaban al puerto huyendo del hambre y la miseria de las zonas rurales, para invariablemente pasar a engrosar la nómina del muelle, el comercio y el contrabando. Melchor, *Aquí no es Miami*, 25.
26. Melchor, *Aquí no es Miami*, 29.
27. Melchor, *Aquí no es Miami*, 31.
28. Melchor, *Aquí no es Miami*, 35.
29. Melchor, *Aquí no es Miami*, 37.
30. Cuando se da a conocer el crimen de Evangelina, la "buena" sociedad veracruzana se convirtió en Torquemada. Fernanda me dice que "ella padece de sus facultades mentales, la envían a un psiquiátrico, pero los mismos periodistas de la época, la sociedad, los políticos, todo el mundo estaba muy concentrado en castigarla. La idea de la época es: Evangelina Tejera no está loca, es solamente una mujer depravada, que asesinó a sus hijos por mala madre y merece ir a prisión.... Quise cambiar no la historia sino el enfoque, porque empecé a pensar que lo que me interesaba era no sólo hablar de lo que había hecho Evangelina, de su crimen y de su historia, sino del clima que la rodeó: del linchamiento mediático y político que sufrió. Irma Gallo, "Atreverse a la crónica de la violencia con sentido del humor: El caso Fernanda Melchor," *Literal: Latin American Voices*, March 19, 2018, https://literalmagazine.com/atreverse-a-la-cronica-de-la-violencia-con-sentido-del-humor-el-caso-fernanda-melchor.
31. arquetipos opuestos pero complementarios, máscaras que deshumanizan a mujeres de carne y hueso, y que funcionan como pantallas en donde se proyectan los deseos, los temores y las ansiedades de una sociedad que se pretende un enclave del sensualismo tropical pero que en el fondo es profundamente conservadora, clasista y misógina. Melchor, *Aquí no es Miami*, 60, 64.
32. Melchor, *Aquí no es Miami*, 64.
33. Melchor, *Aquí no es Miami*, 65.
34. Melchor, *Aquí no es Miami*, 68.
35. Melchor, *Aquí no es Miami*, 77.
36. Melchor, *Aquí no es Miami*, 75.
37. Melchor, *Aquí no es Miami*, 75.

38. Melchor, *Aquí no es Miami*, 127.
39. In an interview with Mixar López, Melchor explains: "Para mí lo más importante en una novela es, primero, los personajes y sus conflictos, y en ese sentido mi postura ante este género es la misma que la de Kundera: la novela es una exploración de lo que es, o puede ser, o ha sido, la existencia humana en esta trampa que es el mundo, y para mostrar esto necesitas personajes que funcionen como egos experimentales. Y lo segundo más importante son las palabras: el ritmo, la respiración, la atmósfera que pueden llegar a producir. El personaje es el motor de la novela y el lenguaje la carrocería. El argumento es simplemente el movimiento 'natural' que hace un motor bien calibrado bajo el cofre" (In my opinion, the most important aspect of a novel is firstly, its characters and conflicts, and in this context I share Kundera's feelings about the genre, that the novel is an exploration of what is, what might be, or has been human existence in the trap that is the world and to show this you need characters that serve/function as experimental egos. And the second most important thing are the words: the rhythm, the breath, the atmosphere that they can produce. The character is the novel's motor and language is the bodywork. The plot is simply the natural movement that a well-calibrated motor makes under the hood.) Mixar López, "Fernanda Melchor: La novela es una llave de yudo," *Yaconic*, April 19, 2017, http://www.yaconic.com/fernanda-melchor-temporada-de-huracanes.
40. The concept of "pornomiseria" (poverty porn) was coined by the Colombian filmmakers Luis Ospina and Carlos Mayolo, who directed the documentary *Agarrando Pueblo* (1977), considered the clearest example of the genre that flourished in Latin American in the 1970s.
41. On the theme of "fractured" masculinity, see Luis Alfredo Román Nieto, "La masculinidad rota: *Falsa liebre* de Fernanda Melchor" (undergraduate thesis, Universidad Veracruzana, March 2018), https://www.academia.edu/40757892/LA_MASCULINIDAD_ROTA_Falsa_liebre_de_Fernanda_Melchor.
42. Aurelia odiaba a su padre: lo describía siempre como un hombre anticuado y enfermo de celos a quien debía mentir todo el tiempo para poder salir a la calle. La madre de Aurelia era un fantasma: vivía en otro estado, ya tenía otra familia, no se hablaban más que una vez al año, el día de la madre, y eso sólo porque el padre de Aurelia marcaba el número y ponía el auricular contra la oreja de la chica. Melchor, *Falsa liebre*, 97.
43. "The phenomenological idea of the lived body appears first in Husserl and then is developed by Merleau Ponty and other philosophers (José Gaos, José Ortega y Gasset, among others). It is built on the idea that the body cannot be conceived of as independent from experience or separated from the existential space. In this sense, 'the truth of the body' is not based on its empirical nature but rather in its condition as a 'lived body,' that is, in the interactions and interiorization of the experiences that it occupies in the time-space in which it moves. . . . In this way, the body is not seen from a solipsistic viewpoint—as

a self-contained and self-sufficient entity—but rather from a relational viewpoint in that everybody is a situated body." Mabel Moraña, *Pensar el cuerpo: Historia, materialidad y símbolo* (Barcelona: Herder Editorial, 2021).
44. Fernanda Melchor, *Falsa liebre*, 53.
45. It is quite clear to me that Melchor's narrative, in particular *Falsa liebre*, is heavily inspired by Inés Arredondo who, for example, engages with homosexuality in her short story "Opus 123," in which, alongside their mutual attraction, the gay youths share a common interest in music. Mario Muñoz, ed. *De amores marginals: 16 cuentos mexicanos* (Veracruz, Mexico: Universidad Veracruzana, 1996). In Melchor's novel, drawing fulfills this type of mediation and represents an intangible link that indicates a higher symbolic plane and nuances the queer materiality. Many other authors and critics have taken up the theme of homosexuality in Mexican literature and culture. See, for example, Robert McKee-Irwin, *Mexican Masculinities* (Minneapolis: University of Minnesota Press, 2003); León Guillermo Gutiérrez, "Arquetipo y homofobia en el relato mexicano de temática gay," *Anales de Literatura Hispanoamericana* no. 44 (2015): 319–31; and Teresa Valdés and José Olavarría, eds. *Masculinidad/es: Poder y crisis* (Santiago, Chile: ISIS/FLACSO, 1997). At a more general level, see Pierre Bourdieu, *Masculine Domination*, trans. Richard Nice (Palo Alto: Stanford University Press, 2002), and Raewyn Connell, *Masculinities* (Berkeley: University of California Press, 1995).
46. Luis Román Nieto identifies four types of violence in *Falsa liebre*: thwarted violence (Vinicio), subjugated violence (Pachi), disturbed violence (Zahir), and inverted violence (Andrik), although, of course, this classification refers to types of behaviors whose distinctions are relative. These behaviors are instead fluid and build on each other, creating a tense and extreme atmosphere that unsettles the reader. Within this framework, Román Nieto analyzes masculinity as the product of the social, political, and economic structural violence that affects the region. The murder of journalists in 2017, multiple mass graves that uncover the tremendous tensions involving organized crime and the complicity of the police, the presence of drug trafficking, and political and economic pressures that characterized Javier Duarte's time in office serve as a breeding ground for the development of unhinged lives like those that *Falsa liebre* exposes through fiction. Nieto, "La masculinidad rota."
47. Bolívar Echeverría, *La modernidad del barroco* (Mexico City: Ediciones Era, 1998).
48. In this regard, see Echeverría and Rubem Barboza Filho, "La occidentalización barroca de América," in *Modernidad iberoamericana, cultura, política y cambio social*, ed. Francisco Colom González, 121–54 (Madrid, Iberoamericana / Vervuert/CSIC, 2009). Invoking Severo Sarduy, and as a way of illustrating the possible meaning of our current use of baroque, in both *La modernidad de lo barroco* and *Modernidad, mestizaje cultural, ethos barroco* (Mexico City: UNAM/El Equilibrista, 1994), Echeverría rejects the idea that it represents a

call to luxury in language and an elitist taste for obscurantist language. Instead, he sees the return of the Baroque as a modern *ethos* and a way of expressing the combination of tradition and progress, localism, and worldliness. Sarduy himself had already spoken about the meaning of the baroque as a political and ideological positionality with regard to capitalism, as well as an aesthetic possibility: "ser barroco hoy significa amenazar, juzgar y parodiar la economía burguesa, basada en la administración tacaña de los bienes, en su centro y fundamento mismo: el espacio de los signos, el lenguaje, soporte simbólico de la sociedad, garantía de su funcionamiento, de su comunicación" (To be baroque today means to threaten, judge and parody the economic bourgeoisie-based on the miserly distribution of goods at the very heart of its being: the space of signs, language, symbolic societal support, guarantees of its functioning and communication). Severo Sarduy, *Antología* (México: Fondo de Cultura Económica, 2000), 99.

49. Félix Guattari, "La producción de subjetividad del capitalismo mundial integrado," *Revista de crítica cultural*, no. 4 (Nov. 1991): 5–10.

50. Felix Guattari, *Chaosmosis: An Ethico-Aesthetic Paradigm*, trans. Julian Pefanis (Bloomington: Indiana University Press, 1995) 9.

51. Bourdieu, *Masculine Domination*, 49–50.

52. Los hombres no lloran, y por eso, Vinicio había aprendido a contener las lágrimas, primero sólo ante su padre, luego también ante las maestras de la escuela y ante los otros chicos. No podía evitar que los ojos se le aguaran, pero sí podía hacer que las lágrimas nacientes se congelaran en sus ojos, que no brotaran, sino que fueran absorbidas por los tejidos oculares. El truco era mantener los ojos abiertos, la mirada fija; no pestañear; no pensar en nada, especialmente en eso: no pensar en el dolor, no pensar en el significado de las palabras. Contenerlo todo en la garganta y luego tragárselo a buches dolorosos que le dejaban el vientre inflamado, el pecho oprimido por los ojos secos, libres de las abyectas y cobardes lagrimitas. Melchor, *Falsa liebre*, 87–88.

53. Las calles estaban extrañamente vacías, a pesar de que aún no era tarde; incluso las tiendas estaban cerradas y no hallaba a nadie que pudiera explicarle el camino hacia la avenida de los semáforos averiados, el camino de regreso a la casa del hombre. El cielo se volvió completamente negro; la tormenta llegó minutos más tarde. Melchor, *Falsa liebre*, 16, 32.

54. Melchor, *Falsa liebre*, 38.

55. Los monstruos los rodeaban; ahora podía comprobar que no tenían ojos, ninguno de ellos; sólo un par de llagas vivas arriba de las fauces.... Sintió una dentellada en la espalda, en el cuello. Vinicio, a unos metros, ya estaba en el suelo. Los monstruos le sacaban las tripas, pero él no gritaba, sólo miraba a Pachi. Melchor, *Falsa liebre*, 39.

56. Melchor, *Falsa liebre*, 41.

57. La fiebre lo atacaba y transmutaba la sangre de su cabeza por plomo fundido y el dolor era martirizante. Después llegaban los temblores y al último la paráli-

sis. Entonces tenía la certeza de que moriría, de que ya había muerto, de que yacía no sobre la cama de su cuarto, sino encima del suelo duro, bajo un cielo salpicado de estrellas. Había muerto y ya no sentía nada, lo único que quedaba de él era su esqueleto desperdigado por los animales. Y cuando estaba a punto de desaparecer, cuando ya no recordaba quien era, quién había sido, la voz de su padre lo alcanzaba, desde un lugar muy lejano, como hecha de hebras de viento. Melchor, *Falsa liebre*, 102–3.

58. Melchor, *Falsa liebre*, 106.
59. Regarding masculinity, see Bourdieu, *Masculine Domination*, and Raewyn Connell, *Masculinities* (Berkeley: University of California Press, 1995), as well as Tony Coles, who discusses both models of gender interpretation. Tony Coles, "Negotiating the Field of Masculinity: The Production and Reproduction of Multiple Dominant Masculinities," *Men and Masculinities* 12, no. 1 (2009): 30–44.
60. Connell, *Masculinities*, 75.
61. Terry Eagleton, *On Evil* (New Haven, CT: Yale University Press, 2011), 16.
62. Melchor, *Falsa liebre*, 27
63. [Vinicio] quería dibujar a Pachi pero necesitaba distraerlo. Y la mejor forma de hacerlo era ponerlo a contar algo, arrastrarlo al relato de alguna aventura. Entonces Pachi, cosa rara, se perdía en sus historias y daba igual que uno lo dibujara, lo fotografiara o se riera de él haciendo muecas porque apenas se daba cuenta, perdido en sus propias mentiras (porque todo lo que contaba se lo sabía de oídas y no era raro que exagerara), y entonces Vinicio podía observarlo a sus anchas y luego traducir la forma de su cara y cuerpo al cuaderno, sin tener que soportar sus burlas o su retiro indignado del cuarto. Melchor, *Falsa liebre*, 81.
64. Examinó el rostro de su padre: la piel prieta, el cabello lacio, sin canas, embarrado hacia un lado, untuoso de aquella crema especial que compraba en las boticas del centro. Miró luego su rostro infantil: los carrillos sonrosados, las cejas y pestañas invisibles, la mata de cabellos del color del oro antiguo, las pupilas zarcas. "Igual que él," pensó Vinicio, con amargura. Idénticos. Melchor, *Falsa liebre*, 108.
65. Melchor, *Falsa liebre*, 200.
66. Melchor claims to have based this on a real event that appeared in the *crónica roja*, and that she reworked in a literary fashion so as to get at the truth of what happened: "A mí me gusta decir que es una exploración de la sinrazón que hay detrás de un crimen pasional. Una exploración a través de la ficción. . . . Hace varios años seguí un suceso policíaco que tuvo lugar en Veracruz y que me llamó mucho la atención: en una ranchería de la zona cañera, un grupo de personas halló el cadáver putrefacto de la que era la curandera del pueblo, asesinada a manos de su examante, quien estaba convencido de que la víctima le estaba haciendo brujería para que volviera. . . . Sé que las prácticas de hechicería y este tipo de creencias son muy omunes en todo México, pero había

algo en esta historia que me generaba mucha curiosidad: ¿realmente así habría ocurrido? ¿No era aquello una exageración por parte del reportero? ¿Un chisme contado por los policías? ¿Una excusa que el asesino había dado para encubrir el motivo verdadero? ¿Cuál era la verdad de aquel crimen?" (I like to say that it is the exploration of the injustice behind a crime of passion. A fictional exploration.... Several years ago, I followed a police case that took place in Veracruz and that really caught my attention: in a small rural settlement in the sugar cane region, a group of people found the rotting body of a woman who'd been the town's healer and who had been killed by her ex-lover who was convinced that she'd been practicing witchcraft on him so he'd get back with her.... I know these types of practices and beliefs are quite common in Mexico, but there was something about this story that made me very curious: Was that what really happened? Was the reporter exaggerating? Was it police gossip? Or an excuse the perpetrator used to cover up his true motive? What was the truth behind this crime?). López, "Fernanda Melchor."

67. Walter Benjamin, *The Arcades Project*, trans. Howard Eiland and Kevin McLaughlin (Cambridge, MA: Harvard University Press, 1999), 466n5.
68. Moraña, *Pensar el cuerpo*.
69. Benjamin, *The Arcades Project*, 462n2a–3.
70. Le decían la Bruja, igual que a su madre: la Bruja Chica cuando la vieja empezó el negocio de las curaciones y los maleficios, y la Bruja a secas cuando se quedó sola, allá por el año del deslave. Si acaso tuvo nombre, inscrito en un papel ajado por el paso del tiempo y los gusanos, oculto tal vez en uno de esos armarios que la vieja atiborraba de bolsas y trapos mugrientos y mechones de cabello arrancado y huesos y restos de comida, si alguna vez llegó a tener un nombre de pila y apellidos como el resto de la gente del pueblo fue algo que nadie supo.... Era siempre tú, zonza, o tú, cabrona, o tú pinche jija del diablo cuando quería que la Chica fuera a su lado, o que se callara, o que simplemente para que se estuviera quieta debajo de la mesa y la dejara escuchar las quejas de las mujeres. Melchor, *Temporada*, 13; Melchor, *Hurricane Season*, trans. Sophie Hughes (New York: New Directions, 2020), 6.
71. Gloria Luz Godínez and Luis Alfredo Román, "De torcidos y embrujos: *Temporada de huracanes* de Fernanda Melchor," *Anclajes* 23, no. 3 (2019): 59–70.
72. Melchor, *Temporada*, 14; Melchor, *Hurricane Season*, 6.
73. In this regard, see Lucinda Garza Zamarripa's "De Misisipi a Veracruz: La influencia del gótico sureño en *Temporada de huracanes*, de Fernanda Melchor," *Armas y Letras*, September 2020, http://armasyletrasenlinea.uanl.mx/2020/09/missisipi-veracruz.
74. La Matosa no existe como pueblo. Había un lugar que se llamaba así, era una comunidad a orillas de los lagos de Alvarado (Veracruz), pero muere cuando construyen el fraccionamiento Punta Tiburón (residencial de marina y golf).... Para mí, pensar en La Matosa es pensar en esa selva jarocha donde no hay bosque, sino que es puro pasto, pasto, pasto, verde, verde, que crece y

crece y hay que andar cortando. Casi vas abriéndote paso con un machete y se vuelve a cerrar tras de ti, y no ves nada porque la caña es altísima y está solitario como la chingada . . . esa era la imagen que tenía de ese pueblo. Pero no existe. Gloria Luz Godínez and Luis Alfredo Román, "En el corazón del crimen," *Revell: Revista de estudos literários da Uems* 3, no. 20 (2018), 188–95, 189.

75. Godínez and Román, "En el corazón del crimen," 189.
76. Godínez and Román, "En el corazón del crimen," 190.
77. Empecé a construir a La Bruja como un brujo, pero la situación se parecía mucho a la de *Falsa liebre*, y no quería repetir (la historia de un hombre que se enamora de un muchacho y amenaza con matarlo). En ese tiempo había leído también un libro (no recuerda el título) de cómo la criminología habla del crimen sin perspectiva de género. De cómo la violencia que se hace en la sociedad normalmente la ejecutan los hombres y, sobre todo, la violencia a la mujer. Y me dije, por qué no hablar . . . ahora que se nombra tanto el tema del feminicidio—, por qué no convertir al brujo en mujer. . . . Pero cuando el personaje era mujer había algo en el misterio que no cuadraba, no quedaba bien resuelto. Y de repente se me ocurrió. Ya sé. Vamos a jugar con que es mujer y al final volvemos a sacar la historia original. En el fondo, se trata de un amor homosexual. Godínez and Román, "En el corazón del crimen," 192.
78. Se trata de un ser humano que llega al mundo con una madre que obviamente está perturbada por las violencias que recibió y queda entonces sin la posibilidad de elegir: la bruja es bruja porque la mamá era bruja, nadie le preguntó si quería serlo, y la cuestión de que se presenta como una niña tampoco es algo donde tuvo opción, digamos que la bruja-madre odiaba tanto a los hombres que le prohibió a su hijo ser uno, y por eso lo trató así. Godínez and Román, "En el corazón del crimen," 190.
79. Entre las viejas ruinas que según los del gobierno eran las tumbas de los antiguos, los que habitaron antes estas tierras, los que llegaron primero, antes incluso que los gachupines, que desde sus barcos vieron todo aquello y dijeron matanga, estas tierras son de nosotros y del reino de Castilla, y los antiguos, los pocos que quedaban, tuvieron que agarrar pa' la sierra y lo perdieron todo, hasta las piedras de sus templos. Melchor, *Temporada*, 15; *Hurricane Season*, 7.
80. cuando el huracán azotó contra la costa con furia y encono y relámpagos estentóreos tupieron de agua el cielo durante días enteros, anegando los campos y pudriéndolo todo, ahogando a los animales que pasmados por el viento y los truenos no pudieron salir a tiempo de los corrales y hasta a aquellos niños que nadie alcanzó a tomar en brazos cuando el cerro se desgajó y se vino abajo con un fragor de rocas y encinos desenraizados y un lodo negro que arrasó con todo hasta derramarse sobre la costa y convirtió en camposanto tres cuartas partes del poblado. Melchor, *Temporada*, 2; *Hurricane Season*, 16.
81. Melchor claims to have notebooks full of newspaper clippings in which mentions of individuals who were arrested appear (in the case of the killing of the *brujo* in Cardel) and she mentions journalists killed in Veracruz (Gabriel

Huge Córdova "el Mariachi" and Yolanda Ordaz). The faces in the newspaper present traits that the writer (in a perilous exercise in profiling) registers as criminal (dark, sunburnt, dirty, red eyes) and in which she believes she sees "the look of a psychopath" and in whose features she finds inspiration for her characters. Godínez and Román, "En el corazón del crimen," 191.

82. Hasta entonces nadie le había dicho que la tal Bruja era en realidad un hombre, un señor como de cuarenta o cuarenta y cinco años de edad en aquel entonces, vestido con ropas negras de mujer, y las uñas bien largas y pintadas también de negro, espantosas, y aunque llevaba puesta una cosa como velo que le tapaba la cara, nomás con escucharle la voz y verle las manos uno se daba cuenta de que se trataba de un homosexual. Melchor, *Temporada*, 92; *Hurricane Season*, 83.

83. Melchor, *Temporada*, 91–92; *Hurricane Season*, 82.

84. Godínez and Román, "En el corazón del crimen," 192.

85. Melchor, *Temporada* 32; *Hurricane Season*, 24.

86. Melchor, *Temporada*, 29; *Hurricane Season*, 21.

87. Melchor *Temporada*, 31; *Hurricane Season*, 23–24.

88. Melchor, *Temporada*, 29; *Hurricane Season*, 21.

89. Eagleton, *On Evil*, 81.

90. Eagleton, *On Evil*, 80, 82.

91. Eagleton, *On Evil*, 85.

92. Eagleton, *On Evil*, 85.

93. Silvia Federici, *Caliban and the Witch* (New York: Autonomedia, 2004), and Silvia Federici, *Witches, Witch Hunting and Women* (Oakland, CA: PM Press, 2018).

94. In their essay "De torcidos y embrujos: *Temporada de huracanes* de Fernanda Melchor," Godínez and Román have written about this aspect of the novel. In their article, they engage with the theme of the witch in light of Federici's work and signal a connection between Shakespeare's *The Tempest*, inspired by the colonization of America and some aspects of the character of la Bruja in Melchor's novel, specifically in relationship to the figure of Sycorax, Caliban's mother, and her lecherous connection to incubae (demons who assume a masculine form). In particular, these critics highlight the possibility that such relationships will produce children of demonic stock. The same topic is raised as they point out, about the topic of the viability of la Bruja's child, an "issue" whose survival surprises the community. Godínez and Román, "De torcidos y embrujos," 63.

95. Federici, *Witches, Witch Hunting*, 12.

96. Federici, *Witches, Witch Hunting*, 28.

97. Federici, *Witches, Witch Hunting*, 30.

98. Ellas le suplicaban que les prestara ayuda, que les hiciera los brebajes aquellos de los que las mujeres del pueblo seguían hablando, los brebajes que amarraban a los hombres y los dominaban por completo, y los que los repelían para siempre jamás, y los que se limitaban a borrar su recuerdo, y aquellos que concentraban el daño en la simiente que esos cabrones les habían pegado an-

tes de huirse en sus camiones, y aquellos otros, todavía más fuertes, que supuestamente liberaban los corazones de los resplandores fatuos del suicidio. Melchor, *Temporada*, 30–31; *Hurricane Season*, 23.

99. Melchor, *Temporada*, 31; *Hurricane Season*, 23.
100. Melchor, *Temporada*, 32; *Hurricane Season*, 25.
101. As Derrida points out, the given or proper name serves as a mask because it hides what is below, imposing an identity on the person that is not their own. Jaques Derrida, "Aphorism Countertime," in *Acts of Literature*, ed. Derek Kittridge (New York: Routledge, 1991), 427.
102. Ávalos Reyes connects gossip to abjection as residual elements that create "a putrid text," confusing in this statement the narrative material with the text itself. It is interesting to note that the idea of the abject, frequently represented in Latin American literature, constitutes above all a symbolic space that speaks as much about death as it does about life. It channels the vision of a body, in this case a woman's body, demonizing her and representing her as excessive and anomalous through the figure of a character—la Bruja—who emits a powerful and mostly pleasurable albeit counter-normative vital force that is then crushed by male power. Marcos Eduardo Ávalos Reyes, "*Temporada de huracanes* de Fernanda Melchor: Una lectura del cuerpo desde el terreno del chisme y la abyección," *Connotas: Revista de crítica y teoría literarias*, no. 19 (2019): 53–70, 55.
103. Melchor, *Temporada*, 23–25.
104. Melchor, *Temporada*, 17, 29.
105. que a partir de entonces iba a haber tarifas según la dificultad del encargo, según los recursos de la madre debiera emplear y el tipo de magia requerida para lograr el cometido, porque cómo iba a ser lo mismo curar unas almorranas que hacer que el hombre ajeno se rindiera por completo a los pies de una, o permitirles hablar con la madre muerta para saber si les ha perdonado el abandono en que la tuvieron en vida. Melchor, *Temporada*, 19; *Hurricane Season*, 11.
106. Melchor, *Temporada*, 21.
107. Patricia Meyer Spacks, *Gossip* (New York: Knopf, 1986).
108. Meyer Spacks, *Gossip*, 8.
109. According to Josefina Ludmer, "tretas del débil" (tricks of the weak) or the representational strategies mobilized by the subaltern subject, include not only the forms it uses to navigate power relations, but also the fictitious gestures with which the author or narrator of a literary text names that which is defined through lack (lack of resources, recognition, voice), allowing them to express themselves directly in their own language. In this way, the literate voice disguises itself in the fictional world through a pluralizing of perspectives. In *Temporada de huracanes*, the voice undergoes a polyphonic modification, but in general all the characters who "speak" in the text represent voices usually silenced by dominant discourses. Ludmer writes, "The stratagem (another characteristic tactic of the weak) consists in changing, from within one's

assigned and accepted place, not only its meaning but the very meaning of what is established within its confines. Josefina Ludmer, "The Tricks of the Weak," in *Feminist Perspectives on Sor Juana Inés de la Cruz*, ed. Stephanie Merrim (Detroit, MI: Wayne State University Press, 1991), 93.
110. Cited in Federici, *Witches, Witch Hunting*, 39.
111. Edgardo Cozarinsky, *Nuevo museo del chisme* (Buenos Aires: La bestia equilátera, 2012), 21.
112. Jacques Rancière, *The Politics of Aesthetics: The Distribution of the Sensible*, trans. and ed. Gabriel Rockhill (New York: Bloomsbury: 2022).
113. Federici, *Witches, Witch Hunting*, 41.
114. Federici, *Witches, Witch-Hunting*, 88.
115. Ávalos Reyes, "*Temporada de huracanes*," 55.
116. Ávalos Reyes, "*Temporada de huracanes*," 56.
117. Ávalos Reyes, "*Temporada de huracanes*," 57.
118. Jorge Luis Borges "La intrusa," in *El informe de Brodie* (1970; Barcelona: Delbolsillo, 2012); "The Intruder," in *Dr. Brodie's Report*, trans. Norman Thomas di Giovanni in collaboration with the author (New York: Bantam Books, 1973), 67–76.
119. Dicen que en realidad nunca murió. . . . Dicen que en el último momento . . . ella alcanzó a lanzar un conjuro para convertirse en otra cosa: en un lagarto o un conejo. . . . Dicen que muchos se metieron a esa casa a buscar el tesoro después de su muerte. Dicen que la plaza anda caliente, que ya no tardan en mandar a los marinos a poner orden en la comarca. Dicen que el calor está volviendo loca a la gente. . . . Que la temporada de huracanes se viene fuerte. Que las malas vibras son las culpables de tanta desgracia. . . . Dicen que por eso las mujeres andan nerviosas, sobre todo las de La Matosa. . . . Eso es lo que dicen las mujeres del pueblo: que no hay tesoro ahí dentro, que no hay oro ni plata ni diamantes ni nada más que un dolor punzante que se niega a disolverse. Melchor, *Temporada*, 205–6; *Hurricane Season*, 215–18.
120. Italo Calvino, *Six Proposals for the Next Millennium* (Cambridge, MA: Harvard University Press, 1988), 40.
121. Bolívar Echeverría, *Modernidad y blanquitud* (Mexico City: Ediciones Era, 2010).
122. Different approximations to the theme of community can be found in the work of Jacques Lacan, Ernesto Laclau, Chantal Mouffe, Jacques Rancière, Jacques Derrida, Roberto Esposito, Alain Badiou and Jean-Luc Nancy, whose work is perhaps the most relevant for my discussion here.
123. Leela Gandhi, *Affective Communities: Anticolonial Thought, Fin-de-Siècle Radicalism, and the Politics of Friendship* (Durham, NC: Duke University Press, 2006).
124. Jean-Luc Nancy, *The Inoperative Community*, trans. Peter Connor, Lisa Garbus, Michael Holland, and Simona Sawhney (Minneapolis: University of Minnesota Press, 1991).

125. Carlos Roa Hewstone and Vania Albornoz Lagos, "De la comunidad mítica a la comunidad de las finitudes: Una introducción al pensamiento de *La Comunidad Inoperante* de Jean-Luc Nancy," *Revista Observaciones Filosóficas*, no. 10 (2010), https://www.observacionesfilosoficas.net/delacomunidadmitica.htm.
126. As Hewstone and Lagos point out in "De la comunidad mítica a la comunidad de las finitudes": "La comunidad está en los contactos, en los gestos en los que se revela lo común finito, no en las obras ni en los contratos cuya verdad transitoria se halla en el dictamen final de la muerte. Ni inmanencia ni trascendencia, la comunidad, en su desobramiento o en su inoperancia es, para Nancy, lo único que permite una relación originaria con el otro en su propia muerte-fuera-de-sí. Sólo así es posible una comunidad de seres finitos soberanos o una comunidad de los sin comunidad" (Community is found in contacts, in gestures that reveal a finite common ground, not in works or contracts in whose transitory truth death's final report can be found. In its inoperative and unworkable nature, community is neither immanence nor transcendence but for Nancy is instead the only thing that permits an originary relationship with the other in their death-outside-of-themselves. Only in this way is a community of finite sovereign beings or a community of those without community possible). Hewstone and Lagos, "De la comunidad mítica."
127. Nancy, *The Inoperative Community*.
128. Considering these differences, from this point of view La Matosa's type of communitarian construction evokes José María Arguedas's representation in *El zorro de arriba y el zorro de abajo*, when he refers to the inhabitants of the fishing village of Chimbote and the social dynamics that are produced following the commercialization of fish meal, Peru's chaotic internal migrations, and the convergence of cultures, languages, and subjectivities demonized by capitalism that for its part rocks the traditional structures of Andean society. José María Arguedas, *El zorro de arriba y el zorro de abajo*, ed. Eve-Marie Fell, Colección Archivos 14 (Madrid: CSIC, 1990).
129. Maurice Blanchot, *The Infinite Conversation*, trans. Susan Hanson (Minneapolis: University of Minnesota Press, 1993).

CHAPTER 3

1. Winner of a series of important literary prizes, Valeria Luiselli occupies a prominent place in today's global literary panorama. She won the American Book Award (2018) for her book *Los niños perdidos (un ensayo en cuarenta preguntas)*. Her novel *La historia de mis dientes* won the Metrópolis Azul prize. In 2020, she was awarded The Rathbones Folio Prize for her book *Lost Children Archive*. The National Book Foundation gave her the "5 Under 35" award and in 2016 she was a finalist for the US's National Book Critics Circle Award.
2. Ángel Rama, *La ciudad letrada* (1984; Hanover, NH: Ediciones del Norte, 2002).
3. Foucault explained that the dialectic between the said and the unsaid is a characteristic of the apparatus or *dispositif*. For a discussion of this topic, see the

interview he gave to Alain Grosrichard in 1977 "Le jeu de Michel Foucault," *Dits et écrits*, vol. 3, 1976–1979, ed., Daniel Defert, François Ewald, and Jacques Lagrange (Paris: Gallimard, 1994), 298–329.

4. Su obra naturaliza las coordenadas del neoliberalismo a tal grado que las invisibiliza precisamente porque ya no quedan residuos resistentes del paradigma nacional ahora rebasado . . . [lo cual] no sólo deslocaliza la condición nacional de su autora, sino que le permite habitar legítimamente otros espacios de significación cultural más allá del entorno geopolítico mexicano. La obra de Luiselli se construye en una deliberada correspondencia entre referentes de alta cultura y la biografía de la autora en un único plano postnacional donde la Ciudad de México se dispersa cómodamente entre los pliegues de la globalización transnacional. Zavala, *Volver a la modernidad*, 153.

5. In this regard, see Zavala, *Volver a la modernidad*, 23.

6. Valeria Luiselli, *Papeles falsos* (México: Sexto Piso, 2010). The text was translated into English by Christina MacSweeney as *Sidewalks* (Minneapolis: Coffee House Press, 2014).

7. In this respect, see María Paz Oliver's "La mirada aérea de la flâneuse," where she gives an excellent account of the idea of the gaze that constructs the urban landscape from a gendered perspective. "La mirada aérea de la flâneuse: El paisaje vertical en *Papeles falsos* y 'Swings of Harlem' de Valeria Luiselli." *Revista Letral* 22 (2019): 13–29.

8. Luiselli, *Papeles falsos*, 25; *Sidewalks*, 19. Translator's note: As in other of the translations of Luiselli's works, the English version at times diverges from the original. A translation of the phrase "el silencio y quietud del territorio abstracto" does not appear in *Sidewalks*; the translation is mine.

9. Patrick O'Connor suggests that Rebecca Solnit's *Wanderlust: A History of Walking* (New York: Viking, 2000) can be seen as the antecedent of intellectual mapping vis à vis physical movement (walking, traveling, or riding a bike while thinking). "Riding a Tandem Bicycle: Valeria Luiselli Maps the Sidewalks of Mexico City," in *Mapping the Megalopolis: Order and Disorder in Mexico City*, ed. Glen David Kuecker and Alejandro Puga, 211–32 (Lanham, MD: Lexington Books, 2017), 216.

10. Luiselli, *Papeles falsos*, 29; *Sidewalks*, 23

11. Luiselli, *Papeles falsos*, 34; *Sidewalks*, 28. On the topic of verticality and horizontality in Luiselli, see Oliver, "La mirada aérea de la flâneuse."

12. Néstor García Canclini, *Culturas híbridas: Estrategias para entrar y salir de la modernidad* (Mexico City: Grijalbo, 1989).

13. Valeria Luiselli, *Papeles falsos*, 15; *Sidewalks*, 9.

14. Valeria Luiselli, *Papeles falsos*. Translator's note: the use of the word *referentialism* is used here as a descriptor for Luiselli's repeated technique of citing lists of canonical authors and works.

15. Valeria Luiselli, *Los ingrávidos* (Mexico City: Sexto Piso, 2012).

16. Translator's note: in MacSweeney's *Sidewalks* there is no subtitle included; the essay's title is simply "Permanent Residence"
17. Jean Baudrillard, *Simulcra and Simulation*, trans. Sheila Glaser (Ann Arbor: University of Michigan Press, 1994), 1. See also Héctor Zarauz López, who analyzes the relationship between ideology, religion and politics vis-à-vis ideas on reality and simulation. Héctor Zarauz López, *La fiesta de la muerte* (México: Conaculta, 2000), 1.
18. Baudrillard, *Simulcra and Simulation*, 1.
19. Benjamin, *The Arcades Project*, 10.
20. Rama, *La ciudad letrada*.
21. In this regard, María Paz Oliver recalls that Mariana Enríquez's book *Alguien camina sobre tu tumba* (Buenos Aries: Editorial Anagrama, 2014), published after Luiselli's, is also organized around visits the narrator makes to cemeteries in different parts of the world. As far as the urban meander goes, Oliver also references *Flâneuse: Women Walk the City* (New York: Farrar, Straus and Giroux, 2017) by Lauren Elkin and *The Dead Ladies Project* (Chicago: University of Chicago Press, 2015) by Jessa Crispin. María Paz Oliver, "La mirada aérea de la flâneuse: El paisaje vertical en *Papeles Falsos* y 'Swings of Harlem' de Valeria Luiselli," *Letral*, no. 22 (2019): 14–29, 22.
22. Luiselli, *Papeles falsos*, 65; *Sidewalks*, 63.
23. Luiselli, *Papeles falsos*, 65; *Sidewalks*, 63.
24. Zavala, *Volver a la modernidad*, 21.
25. Zavala, *Volver a la modernidad*, 21.
26. A calculated attempt to open the literary sphere as a recurrent practice among upper-middle class authors that began to publish in Mexico toward the end of the 90s with the same globalizing desires that prompted the implementation of NAFTA in 1994. Zavala, *Volver a la modernidad*, 29.
27. John Simpson, Chloe Aridjis, Ólafur Elíasson, Valeria Luiselli, et al. *Where You Are: A Collection of Maps that Will Leave You Feeling Completely Lost* (London: Visual Editions, 2013).
28. el mapa, así, funciona como señal de vigilancia y control frente a la intimidad del cuaderno de notas que acompaña las fotografías, es decir, como una manera de regular y normar el espacio, y los modos en que estos se ocupan. La confrontación entre la libertad de la escritura cotidiana en torno a las caminatas por Nueva York y el espíritu objetivo del mapa fotográfico, resitúa el relato en otra perspectiva y relee la emotividad de aquellos textos desde un ojo mediado por la tecnología del *street view*. Oliver, "La mirada aérea de la flaneuse," 22.
29. Luiselli, *Los ingrávidos*, 20; Valeria Luiselli, *Faces in the Crowd*, trans. Christina MacSweeney (Minneapolis, MN: Coffee House Press, 2014), 10.
30. Luiselli, *Los ingrávidos*, 63; *Faces in the Crowd*, 57.
31. Critics have drawn attention to the presence of methods and themes drawn from Bolaño, Cortázar, Gide and Paul Auster among others. See for example

Ilse Logie. "Escritos en la traducción y para la traducción? Dos ejemplos: Valeria Luiselli y Mario Bellatín," in *Literatura latinoamericana mundial: Dispositivos y disidencias*, ed. Gustavo Guerrero, Jorge J. Locane, Benjamin Loy, and Gesine Müller, 207–318 (Boston: De Gruyter, 2020); and Regina Nelky Cardoso, "Fantasmas y sosías en *Los ingrávidos*, de Valeria Luiselli," *Escritoras mexicanas del siglo XXI: Miradas líquidas fragmentadas*, special issue, *Romance Notes*, no. 54 (2014): 77–84.

32. Zavala, *Volver a la modernidad*, 30.
33. Born in El Rosario, Sinaloa (Mexico), Gilberto Owen was an important member of the Contemporáneos group, together with authors like Salvador Novo, Celestino Gorostiza, Xavier Villaurrutia, Jaime Torres Bodet, Jorge Cuesta, and prominent painters. He was the founder of the magazine *Ulises*, where he worked in different capacities as translator and dramaturge, using the magazine as a platform for the promotion of avantgarde works. He dedicated himself to the renewal of literary genres that he practiced in all forms, making particular contributions to experimental forms of prose poetry. Interested in the literary Baroque, he was also influenced by Rimbaud, T. S. Eliot, and surrealism in general. Among his principal works are the poem "Sinbad, el varado" (published in *Perseo vencido*, 1948), *Desvelo* (1923, but published posthumously), *La llama fría* (1925), *Novela como nube* (1928), *Línea* (1930), and *El infierno perdido* (1978), among others. Owen was also a professor and diplomat.
34. El contexto histórico de Owen está borrado esencialmente al igual que el de la mujer narradora. En su lugar, vemos una única ciudad de Nueva York, contemporánea, habitada por artistas irónicos, desinteresados de lo político, distraídos por cuestiones personales y sin trascendencia más allá de su proyecto intelectual y su entorno inmediato. El espectro de Owen no tiene un verdadero pasado: sólo pertenece al presente de la narradora. Zavala, *Volver a la modernidad*, 168.
35. Sylvia Molloy, "La politica de la pose," *Cuadernos LIRICO*, no. 16 (2017), https://journals.openedition.org/lirico/3576.
36. Molloy, "La politica de la pose."
37. *Los ingrávidos* es una novela sobre dos personajes que se van desdibujando hasta convertirse en espectros de sí mismos, en tiempos y espacios diferentes. La narradora escribe desde su vida presente. No puede respirar: tiene un niño mediano, una bebé y un marido entrometido. Su válvula de escape es la escritura. En las noches de insomnio, escribe párrafos larguísimos sobre otra vida, una vida que es y no es la suya, mientras el fantasma de Gilberto Owen empieza a ocupar los espacios que ella deja vacíos. Liliana Muñoz, "Reseña de *Los ingrávidos*," *Criticismo*, April–June 2012, https://criticismo.com/los-ingravidos/2.
38. During the Harlem Renaissance of the 1920s, there was a flourishing of Black culture in this part of New York, particularly in the realms of literature, painting, and music, especially jazz. Jazz musicians included Louis Armstrong and Duke Ellington, for example. Important literary works that mark this mo-

ment of the renewal and recognition of African American culture are *Harlem Shadows* (1922) by Claude McKay, *Cane* (1923) by Jean Toomer, and *Confusion* (1924) by Jessie Fauset.
39. Regarding this duplication see María Pape "El pasaje como *modus operandi*: Perspectivas simultáneas y recíprocamente excluyentes en *Los ingrávidos* de Valeria Luiselli," *Revista Chilena de Literatura*, no. 90 (2015), and especially Nicolás Licata's "Doble, fantasma y madre: Vasos comunicantes en *Los ingrávidos*, de Valeria Luiselli," *Brumal: Revista de investigación sobre lo fantástico* 8, no. 1 (2020): 71–92. Here, Licata develops the idea of the double and the examples found in the novel of this familiar literary device. Of particular importance here is the comparative reading he does of the two editions of *Los ingrávidos*, in which he traces changes that reinforce a reading of the alter ego: Owen / the narrator on the one hand and Luiselli / the narrator on the other.
40. Licata, "Doble, fantasma y madre," 82.
41. En *Los ingrávidos*, el desdoblamiento y el afantasmamiento de la narradora-protagonista se hacen eco y reflejo de las peripecias de su vida de madre en la medida en que la gestación hace fluidas las fronteras de su cuerpo y en que ella aparece simbólicamente como un Yo escindido, dividido entre pasado y presente, entre trabajo y cuidado de los hijos, entre vida personal y responsabilidades maternas. Licata, "Doble, fantasma y madre," 78.
42. Licata, "Doble, fantasma y madre," 89
43. In "El pasaje como modus operandi," María Pape reads *Los ingrávidos* alongside Benjamin's notion of landscape.
44. Luiselli, *Los ingrávidos*, 65; *Faces in the Crowd*, 60.
45. Anthony Stanton, "Un poeta mexicano se apropia de las vanguardias europeas en Nueva York: Autorretrato o del subway de Gilberto Owen," *Revista Iberoamericana* 74, no. 224 (July–Sept. 2008): 741–50, 742.
46. Qtd. in Stanton, "Un poeta mexicano," 743.
47. Gilberto Owen, "Perfil" and "Vuelo," *Contemporáneos*, no. 12 (1930): 120–22; Gilberto Owen, *Línea* (Buenos Aires: Editorial Proa, 1930).
48. Luiselli, *Los ingrávidos*, 22; *Faces in the Crowd*, 13.
49. En esa misma estación el poeta Ezra Pound había visto un día a su amigo Henri Gaudier-Brzeska, muerto unos meses atrás en una trinchera en Neuville-Saint-Vaast. Pound estaba apoyado contra una columna del andén, esperando, cuando por fin se aproximó el tren. Al abrirse las puertas del vagón vio aparecer ente la gente el rostro de su amigo. Luiselli, *Los ingrávidos*, 23; *Faces in the Crowd*, 14.
50. Cuando abrí los ojos vi a mi lado a William Carlos Williams con unos anteojos enormes, revisando la vagina de una mujer miniatura acostada en una servilleta sobre la barra; dirigiendo una orquesta imaginaria estaba el poeta Zukofsky parado en una mesa; colgado dentro de una jaula en la esquina del bar, Ezra Pound; y García Lorca aventándole cacahuates que él recibía con júbilo. Luiselli, *Los ingrávidos*, 39; *Faces in the Crowd*, 31.

51. Translator' note: A translation of this derogatory term does not appear in *Faces in the Crowd*. Era un españolito bien comido, sobreprotegido, que se quejaba virtuosamente de su vida bohemia en la urbe: palomas y enjambres de monedas, edificios en obra perpetua, multitudes que vomitan, la enajenación, la soledad. El problema con los poemas de Federico es que todos terminaban siendo afedericados. Luiselli, *Los ingrávidos*, 87; *Faces in the Crowd*, 83.

52. Luiselli, *Los ingrávidos*, 16.

53. Luiselli, *Los ingrávidos*, 33; *Faces in the Crowd*, 24.

54. Luiselli, *Los ingrávidos*, 63; *Faces in the Crowd*, 57.

55. desde el día en que empezaron a llegar todas estas cosas—la ceguera, los gatos, el fantasma y, más adelante, las visitas esporádicas de gente que yo no había invitado, las apariciones de muebles y decenas de libros que no había adquirido, desde luego las moscas y cucarachas, y sobre todo el árbol plantado en una maceta que un día encontré—supe que había empezado el final. No el mío, sino el final de algo con lo que yo me había identificado tan estrechamente que acabaría también conmigo. Luiselli, *Los ingrávidos*, 71; *Faces in the Crowd*, 66–67.

56. una manera de integrarse orgánicamente al presente neoliberal de la cultura occidental. Es, en suma, una manera de ser reconocida por esa cultura neoliberal y no para protestar en contra de ella. Con su novela *Los ingrávidos*, Luiselli depura su inscripción en esta genealogía literaria para establecer con mayor claridad su pertenencia al orden cultural global, es decir, su integración decidida en el campo literario mexicano y estadounidense como intelectual orgánica de la modernidad capitalista neoliberal. Zavala, *Volver a la modernidad*, 161.

57. Oswaldo Zavala has highlighted these moments in *Volver a la modernidad* (156 and 164–66).

58. Luiselli, "Gilberto Owen, narrador," *Letras libres*, Jan. 31, 2009, https://letraslibres.com/revista-mexico/gilberto-owen-narrador.

59. Luiselli, "Gilberto Owen."

60. Luiselli, "Gilberto Owen."

61. Luiselli, "Gilberto Owen."

62. Qtd. in Luiselli, "Gilberto Owen."

63. Luiselli, "Gilberto Owen."

64. La fuerza de la mirada de Owen está en su capacidad de ver entre las cosas. Owen no ve los momentos sucesivos que componen una escena sino esos breves espacios entre un momento y otro: ahí clava el ojo.... Esta, en una palabra, podría entenderse como una inteligencia particular para entender las distancias.... Owen mira desde un lugar intermedio. Luiselli, "Gilberto Owen."

65. No es descubrimiento ni paranoia mía: vivimos en un tiempo obsesionado con la voz del autor. Un escritor dedica todo su empeño. a esa búsqueda de la voz propia—sea lo que esto sea—, como si un día fuera de veras a encontrarla en alguna parte. ¿Por qué no en vez, como Owen, cultivar la mirada? Es la norma,

además, que la voz del escritor suene ahora despreocupada, culta, irónica, quizás un poco cínica, definitivamente simpática. Refiriéndose a Owen, Segovia escribe que los sentimientos son cosa bastante desacreditada en nuestros días. Nada podría ser más cierto. Y Owen podría repeler, sin duda, a algunos lectores para quienes lo emotivo sea sinónimo de afectación o cursilería. Luiselli, "Gilberto Owen."

66. Le dije que había encontrado, en la pequeña y desordenada biblioteca de la Casa Hispánica de la Universidad de Columbia, un original anónimo torpemente mecanografiado y apenas legible, donde había una serie de traducciones comentadas de poemas de Owen. Era muy probable que las traducciones fueran de Zukofsky: estaban firmadas JZ&GO. Era la mentira menos verosímil de todas las posibles mentiras en torno a Owen, pero White decidió darme por mi lado. Le prometí llevarle avances de una transcripción literal que yo misma haría. Luiselli, *Los ingrávidos*, 45–46; *Faces in the Crowd*, 38.

67. Luiselli, *Los ingrávidos*, 19; *Faces in the Crowd*, 10.
68. Luiselli, *Los ingrávidos*, 17; *Faces in the Crowd*, 7.
69. Luiselli, *Los ingrávidos*, 17; *Faces in the Crowd*, 7–8.
70. Luiselli, *Los ingrávidos*, 57–58; *Faces in the Crowd*, 50.
71. Rebecca Walkowitz, *Born Translated: The Contemporary Novel in an Age of World Literature* (New York: Columbia University Press, 2015).
72. Logie draws on *Los ingrávidos* as well as Mario Bellatín's *Jacobo el mutante* and *Jacobo reloaded*. In the latter's case, the theme of mutation is contained within the very texts that include multiple apocryphal elements, rewritings, additions, multicultural elements and the insertion of the author's previous works. The question of the original's cohesion and translation are inherent to Bellatín's writing. Logie correctly describes the relationship between Luiselli's work and Roberto Bolaño's *Detectives salvajes*, in which he employs "las vanguardias como ancla de una lectura 'globalizada'" (the avantgardes as the anchor for a "globalized" reading) and when she explains that "En Luiselli la traducción aparece por doquier, pero funciona más como un tropo que como una práctica vinculada a la especificidad de una lengua determinada" (In Luiselli, translation is scattered throughout, but functions more like a trope than a practice linked to the specificity of determined language). Ilsa Logie, "Escritos en la traducción y para la traducción? Dos ejemplos: Valeria Luiselli y Mario Bellatín," in *Literatura latinoamericana mundial: Dispositivos y disidencias*, ed. Gustavo Guerrero et al., 207–22 (Berlin: De Gruyter, 2020), 220.
73. Logie, "¿Escritos en la traducción," 208.
74. Logie, "¿Escritos en la traducción," 209.
75. Logie, "¿Escritos en la traducción," 209.
76. Logie, "¿Escritos en la traducción," 209.
77. As Logie explains, *The Story of My Teeth* includes the chapter titled "Chronologic," which was written solely by MacSweeney, in an addition that critics, such as Jorge Téllez, have assessed negatively, indicating that we now have two

different books: "en la edición en inglés cambian los nombres de personajes, un par de acontecimientos y se agrega un capítulo. Este nuevo capítulo, una cronología de la obra, escrito por la traductora, sitúa la vida y obras de Gustavo Sánchez Sánchez 'Carretera' [Highway] en perspectiva con acontecimientos históricos y anecdóticos/personales del siglo XX mexicano. La vida del protagonista aparece enmarcada, por citar un ejemplo, por la expropiación petrolera, por un lado, y por el destino fatal de uno de los peces rojos del libro de cuentos de Guadalupe Nettel" (In the English edition, character names and a couple of events have been changed, and a chapter added. Written by the translator, this new chapter is a chronology of the novel's events and places the life and works of Gustavo Sánchez Sánchez "Carretera" [Highway] in relation to historical events and anecdotes/figures of twentieth century Mexico. The protagonist's life is framed, to cite one example, by the State's oil expropriation, on the one hand, and by the tragic end of one of the red fish from Guadalupe Nettel's short story collection on the other). For Téllez, it is not simply a question of "libros diferentes" (different books) but also "públicos diferentes" (different publics). Jorge Téllez, "La otra historia de mis dientes," *Letras libres*, February 19, 2016, https://letraslibres.com/revista-espana/la-otra-historia-de-mis-dientes.

For me, the addition is, in effect and as Téllez says, a normalization, which speaks to the book's positioning for a public that supposedly lacks the historical-cultural context that the work evokes. In other words, the measure serves to support the commodification of the symbolic product. At the same time, this is an issue of little relevance in a book itself of little relevance, that tries to gain ground with the iconoclastic gesture of violating the original (as if Benjamin hadn't already explained decades ago what the loss of the aura signified). Logie's generous analysis gives the gesture more credit than it deserves when she says: "Se podría aducir que, al adaptar la novela, Luiselli y su traductora insisten en que el mundo, antes que aparecer como un contenedor homogéneo en el que las obras literarias son 'lo mismo' en varias lenguas, es un colectivo polifónico" (On adapting the novel, we perhaps see that Luiselli and her translator see the world not as a homogenous container in which literary works are just "the same" in different languages but are instead polyphonic collectives). Logie, "¿Escritos en la traducción y para la traducción? Yes and no. In my opinion, this is more a question of "editorial freedom" that occurs with the intent of perhaps desacralizing or demystifying the "Literary Work" and is something that many different authors have successfully undertaken at different periods in history. In Luiselli's case, perhaps the intention was to give the novel an iconoclastic twist. This is also a strategy of little consequence that is less significant than the judgement we can levy as to the quality of a book that contains these and other market-driven gestures that, while not a sin, are certainly a weakness. The book's neoliberal commercialization promotes ambiguous reactions and strategies in which the cultural operator marks out a positionality that vacillates between being inside and outside of commerce (all of which is material for a separate book). I agree with Téllez who, drawing on Bady's excellent review of the book, explains that the "renaissance" of Mexican literature owes much—but not all—to the "nueva ola de traducción que han [sic] llegado gracias al interés y éxito editorial de las traducciones de Bolaño" (new wave of translations that has arrived due to the interest in and the commercial success of translations of Bolaño's work). Téllez, "La otra historia de mis dientes." Of course, this does not negate the talent of many great contemporary writers whose works speak for themselves.

78. Logie, "¿Escritos en la traducción," 211.
79. With regard to the translation of *Desierto sonoro*—published first in English as *Lost Children Archive*—Luiselli collaborated directly with Daniel Saldaña París to produce a Spanish version. The fact that two of her works were originally published in English, just before their appearance in the author's mother tongue, proves that there are works that are "born translated."
80. *Los ingrávidos* has a chiastic structure: the text possesses a translatability that it itself calls into question. We see this in its anxiety to express a multilingual modus operandi that at the end of the day operates as the framework of its thought and affect, as well as the need to write in a single language for publication purposes. Logie, "¿Escritos en la traducción," 214.
81. Christopher Domínguez Michael, "Dos cajas de Valeria Luiselli," *Letras Libres*, Feb. 9, 2014, https://letraslibres.com/libros/dos-cajas-de-valeria-luiselli; Roberto Pliego, "Mero parloteo '*La historia de mis dientes*,'" *Milenio*, Feb. 15, 2014, https://www.milenio.com/cultura/mero-parloteo-la-historia-de-mis-dientes.
82. Susan Sontag, *Notes on "Camp"* (1964; Penguin Modern: London, 2018).
83. Although both terms are connected and often used interchangeably, collage is more strictly used to describe the combination of materials of different types (writing, visual elements, found objects, clippings) that are used to form a piece of art whose aesthetic value derives from the combination's effectiveness. For its part, pastiche is a fusion of different styles, of genres or narrative lines that come together to form something new that can give the appearance of heterogeneity or perhaps incongruence.
84. Valeria Luiselli, *La historia de mis dientes* (Mexico City: Sexto Piso, 2013), 36; Valeria Luiselli, *The Story of My Teeth*, trans. Christina MacSweeney (Minneapolis: Coffee House Press, 2015), 25.
85. Luiselli, *La historia de mis dientes*, 75; *The Story of My Teeth*, 79.
86. Luiselli, *La historia de mis dientes*, 93; *The Story of My Teeth*, 102. The character of Roberto Bálser, or "Beto," is called "Jacobo de Voragine" in the English translation.
87. Luiselli, *La historia de mis dientes*, 97; *The Story of My Teeth*, 110.
88. Translator's note: I've been unable to locate an equivalent phrase in *The Story of My Teeth*. The translation is mine.
89. Empecé a escribir la autobiografía dental del mayor héroe de nuestro barrio hace casi un año. Carretera fue uno de esos espíritus enormes, eternos. Su

presencia era a ratos amenazante, no porque supusiera una amenaza real para nadie, sino porque contra su libertad feroz todos los parámetros que solemos medir el mundo parecían frágiles, perecederos y triviales. Luiselli, *La historia de mis dientes*, 107; *The Story of my Teeth*, 150. Translator's note: Although the phrase "dental autobiography" can be found in other parts of the novel, the first sentence of the quote from the Spanish original here is not reproduced in the English translation.
90. Luiselli, *La historia de mis dientes*, 110; *The Story of My Teeth*, 150.
91. Cuando lo conocí Carretera estaba enfermo y débil. Si se miraba en algún espejo decía que parecía gallina prieta y se propinaba un generoso cacareo. En efecto, tenía pocos pelos, perennemente erizados hacia el cielo; las patas venosas y muy flacas, la barriga redonda y abultada, Había perdido su amada dentadura postiza, de manera que incluso una actividad tan cotidiana como hablar resultaba, no imposible, pero sí una batalla constante contra la humillación. Luiselli, *La historia de mis dientes*, 108; *The Story of my Teeth*, 149.
92. Luiselli, *La historia de mis dientes*, 19. Translator's note: translation mine. I've been unable to find an equivalent phrase in the English translation.
93. durante las subastas alegóricas no se subastaban objetos, sino las historias que les daban valor y significado. Los objetos se aluden, pero sólo tangencialmente; no son el eje en torno al cual gira la subasta. Las alegóricas eran, según Carretera, "las subastas poscapitalistas de reciclaje radical que salvarían al mundo de su condición de basurero de la historia. Luiselli, *La historia de mis dientes*, 121; *The Story of My Teeth*, 156–57.
94. Jean Baudrillard, *The System of Objects*, trans. James Benedict (London: Verso Books, 1996), 92.
95. Baudrillard, *The System of Objects*, 98–99.
96. Baudrillard, *The System of Objects*, 91.
97. Baudrillard, *The System of Objects*, 97.
98. Luiselli, *La historia de mis dientes*, 20. Translator's note: as we can see, the translation moves extremely far away from the original here. Luiselli's Spanish phrase describes the baby as "black as oil" (6).
99. Baudrillard, *The System of Objects*, 97.
100. Baudrillard, *The System of Objects*, 98.
101. Baudrillard, *The System of Objects*, 2.
102. Baudrillard, *The System of Objects*, 89.
103. Baudrillard, *The System of Objects*, 84.
104. Baudrillard, *The System of Objects*, 84.
105. Baudrillard, *The System of Objects*, 92.
106. Baudrillard, *The System of Objects*, 106.
107. Fredric Jameson, *Postmodernism, or, The Cultural Logic of Late Capitalism* (Durham, NC: Duke University Press, 1992). See also Dino Felluga, *Critical Theory: The Key Concepts* (New York: Routledge, 2015).
108. Jameson, *Postmodernism*, 17.

109. Jameson, *Postmodernism*, 18.
110. In this vein, Jameson presents a convincing series of examples drawn from architecture, cinema and the historical novel. See chapter 1 of *Postmodernism, or, The Cultural Logic of Late Capitalism*.
111. En este sentido, *La historia de mis dientes* es una forma errante, como las que describe Speranza: una encrucijada estética, un cruce entre geografías diversas (del escritorio de la "autora" Luiselli en Nueva York a la lectura de sus colaboradores en un barrio marginal del D. F., o de las calles de ese barrio a las grandes avenidas y monumentos destruidos de la historia europea) y también entre géneros artísticos y literarios (la autobiografía que se vuelve biografía, la picaresca, las biografías breves que acompañan el gesto de la subasta, las fotografías de un recorrido "turístico," el catálogo artístico). Graziela Speranza, *Atlas portátil de América Latina: Arte y ficciones errantes* (Barcelona: Anagrama, 2012). Lorena Amaro Castro "Autobiografía, fábula biográfica y deconstrucción del espacio literario en *La historia de mis dientes*, de Valeria Luiselli," *Revista Laboratorio*, no. 16 (July 2017), https://biblat.unam.mx/hevila/Revistalaboratorio/2017/no16/7.pdf.
112. Amaro Castro, "Autobiografía, fábula biográfica."
113. Amaro Castro, "Autobiografía, fábula biográfica."
114. Amaro Castro, "Autobiografía, fábula biográfica."
115. Marco Ramírez Rojas, "*La historia de mis dientes* de Valeria Luiselli: El relato como mercancía, colección y propuesta de archivo," *Hispanófila*, no. 183 (June 2018): 333–49.
116. Ramírez Rojas, "La historia," 339.
117. In this regard see Téllez, "La otra historia de mis dientes" and Zavala, *Volver a la modernidad*.
118. Referencing Blom, Ramírez Rojas alludes to the fact that collectible objects in many cases become reliquaries, with the "lógica de transferencia" (logic of transference) in which these objects are inscribed essential for understanding this. Blom qtd. in Ramírez Rojas, "La historia," 337.
119. Luiselli, *La historia de mis dientes*, 114; *The Story of my Teeth*, 151.
120. Ramírez Rojas, "La historia," 340.
121. Translator's note: the phrase is used in auctions and means "any more bets" or literally "who'll give more." In English, of course, the auctioneer declares "Going once, going twice" before closing bidding.
122. Luiselli, *Los niños perdidos (un ensayo en cuarenta preguntas)* (Mexico: Sexto Piso, 2016).
123. Valeria Luiselli, *Tell Me How It Ends: An Essay in Forty Questions*, trans. Lizzie Davis (Minneapolis: Coffee House Press, 2017).
124. Son, si acaso, fugaces destellos de esperanza en ese limbo oscuro donde chillan las ruedas metálicas y constantes de La Bestia—como si en su ascenso al norte mallugaran racimos de pesadillas. México se ha vuelto una gran aduana custodiada tanto por criminales de cuello blanco como por criminales con fuscas

y trocas, y los migrantes centroamericanos que cruzan la frontera sureña del país entran al infierno. Luiselli, *Los niños perdidos*, 28; *Tell Me How It Ends*, 27–28, 80.
125. Luiselli, *Los niños perdidos*, 15–16; *Tell Me How It Ends*, 7.
126. *Los niños perdidos*, 44. Translator's note: this phrase does not appear in the English translation. It means "a crack, a fissure, the long continental scar."
127. Las causas y raíces de la situación actual tienen vínculos hemisféricos; y las consecuencias, por ende, tienen un alcance también hemisférico. Es urgente empezar a hablar de la guerra del narco como una "guerra hemisférica" que abarca cuando menos el territorio que empieza en los Grandes Lagos del norte de Estados Unidos y termina en las sierras de Celaque, en el sur de Honduras. [Esta perspectiva] obligaría a repensar el lenguaje mismo en torno al problema y, por lo tanto, la posible dirección futura de políticas públicas para enfrentarlo. Los niños que cruzan México y llegan a la frontera de Estados Unidos no son "migrantes," no son "ilegales," y no son meramente "menores indocumentados": son refugiados de una guerra y, en tanto tales, tienen derecho al asilo político. Luiselli, *Los niños perdidos*, 76–77; *Tell Me How It Ends* 80, 90.
128. Luiselli, *Los niños perdidos*, 76–83; *Tell Me How It Ends*, 55.
129. Los relatos oficiales en Estados Unidos—digamos, lo que circula como información cotidiana en los periódicos o la radio, así como el mensaje desde Washington y la opinión pública más general—casi siempre ubican la línea divisoria entre la "civilización" y la "barbarie" abajo del río Bravo. Luiselli, *Los niños perdidos*, 75; *Tell Me How It Ends*, 83.
130. Frente al alucinante clima político actual, en donde ideas intolerantes y sectarias sobre la identidad nacional y la raza han adquirido una prominencia hasta un grado no visto durante muchas décadas en distintos lugares del mundo . . . y ha quedado claro que los miedos y el odio que ha desatado no serán fáciles de superar. Luiselli, *Los niños perdidos*, 11; *Tell Me How It Ends*, 3.
131. Luiselli, *Los niños perdidos*, 87; *Tell Me How It Ends*, 95–96.
132. Estados Unidos integra al inmigrante que decide asimilarse. Pero ¿habrá que integrarse, sin importar el costo? ¿Sin importar el costo de la leche, la renta, los cigarros? ¿El de las humillaciones, las guerras? Tal vez algunos nos lleguemos a convencer de que la integración es sólo una etapa pasajera, y que volver a ser nosotros mismos es sólo cuestión de tiempo; de que sin duda volveremos a ser quienes éramos, incluso a pesar de todas las capas de extranjería que se nos adhirieron a la piel y a la personalidad. Aunque es posible, también, que llegue un día en que ya no queramos volver a ser quienes éramos. Luiselli, *Los niños perdidos*, 89; *Tell Me How It Ends*, 99.
133. For an analysis of the rise of microhistory, see Georg Iggers, *Historiography in the Twentieth Century* (Middletown, CT: Wesleyan University Press, 1977), in which he explains that it arose as a reaction to social science methodologies whose generalizations regarding processes of struggle and social change excluded "small scale" actors and developments. Studies of microhistory iden-

tify Carlo Ginzburg's *The Cheese and the Worms: The Cosmos of a Sixteenth-Century Miller*, trans. John Tedeschi and Anne C. Tedeschi (Baltimore: Johns Hopkins University Press, 1980), as a pioneering text in the development of the micro-historical method. Ginzburg published a series of articles in *Quaderni Storici*, criticizing the wide scope of quantitative analysis and traditional historiography and proposing in its place a study of smaller lives, experiences, and events in which social actors moved away from dominant norms. See also Giovanni Levi, "On Microhistory," in *New Perspectives on Historical Writing*, ed. Peter Burke, 97–119 (College Park, PA: Pennsylvania State University Press, 2001).

134. Quizá la única manera de empezar a entender estos años tan oscuros para los migrantes que cruzan las fronteras de Centroamérica, México y Estados Unidos sea registrar la mayor cantidad de historias individuales posibles. Escucharlas, una y otra vez. Escribirlas, una y otra vez. Para que no sean olvidadas, para que queden en los anales de nuestra historia compartida y en lo hondo de nuestra conciencia, y regresen, siempre, a perseguirnos en las noches, a llenarnos de espanto y de vergüenza. Luiselli, *Los niños perdidos*, 32; *Tell Me How It Ends*, 30.

135. Luiselli, *Los niños perdidos*, 63; *Tell Me How It Ends*, 69.

136. Lo más probable es que la historia de las dos niñas de los vestidos, por ejemplo, nunca salga del archivo y se convierta en un "caso." Son muy pequeñas, y aún si tuvieran un relato para justificar una intervención legal a su favor, no cuentan con las palabras que se requieren para narrarlo. Es difícil que dos personas de su edad puedan generar—en una segunda lengua, además, traducida a una tercera—un discurso que las inserte exitosamente en el sistema de la corte migratoria. Luiselli, *Los niños perdidos*, 60; *Tell Me How It Ends*, 66.

137. Durante las entrevistas, a veces anoto las respuestas de los niños en primera persona, y a veces en tercera: Crucé a pie. Cruzó nadando. Es de San Pedro Sula Soy de Guatemala. Nunca ha conocido a su papá. Pero no se acuerda cuándo fue la última vez que la vio. No sabe si lo abandonó. Se fue cuando yo tenía cinco años. Luiselli, *Los niños perdidos*, 57; *Tell Me How It Ends*, 62.

138. Jason De León, *The Land of Open Graves: Living and Dying on the Migrant Trail* (Berkeley: University of California Press, 2015).

139. Luiselli, *Los niños perdidos*, 21; *Tell Me How It Ends*, 15.

140. Drones, cámaras de vigilancia en los trenes y puntos estratégicos como túneles, puentes, cruces ferroviarios o centros urbanos; bardas y alumbrado en los patios de maniobras de los trenes; brigadas de seguridad privada e instalación de sistemas de geolocalización simultánea en los trenes; equipos de alarma y movimiento en las vías; centros de mando de seguridad en puntos estratégicos; y last but not least, los famosos "Grupos Beta" que, bajo el disfraz de brigada de ayuda humanitaria, localizan y luego denuncian a los migrantes con oficiales de migración, para que éstos puedan "asegurarlos"—eufemismo mexicano para decir "capturar y deportar migrantes." En suma: el Programa

Frontera Sur de Peña Nieto convirtió a México en las puertas de bienvenida a Trumplandia. Luiselli, *Los niños perdidos*, 29; *Tell Me How It Ends*, 78.
141. Valeria Luiselli, *Lost Children Archive* (New York: Knopf, 2019). The Spanish translation, carried out by the author in collaboration with Daniel Saldaña, is entitled *Desierto sonoro* (New York: Vintage Español, 2019). Translator's note: because the novel appeared first in English, I am not going to cite the Spanish translation.
142. William Golding, *Lord of the Flies* (1954; reis., London: Faber and Faber, 2011); Cormac McCarthy, *The Road* (New York: Knopf, 2006).
143. Pierre Schaeffer, *Traité des objets musicaux: Essai interdisciplines* (Paris: Éditions Du Seuil, 1966).
144. Se necesita recuperar y reivindicar la importancia de lo sonoro en la vida cotidiana como elemento de comunicación sensorial y de transmisión de emociones. El concepto de ecología acústica descansa sobre la relación que mantienen las personas con su entorno acústico, planteando, por ejemplo, si dicha relación es equilibrada o no, si facilita la integración del individuo dentro de la comunidad o si resulta ajena e insostenible. José Luis Carles, "El paisaje sonoro, una herramienta interdisciplinar: Análisis, creación y pedagogía con el sonido," Centro Virtual Cervantes, accessed March 12, 2024, https://cvc.cervantes.es/artes/paisajes_sonoros/p_sonoroso1/carles/carles_01.htm.
145. En definitiva, el sonido, con su gran capacidad de evocación, adquiere un valor que va más allá de las características reales del momento, y con su poder puede hacernos recordar otras situaciones. A través de unos índices sonoros que la acústica tradicional ha considerado básicamente en términos físicos—niveles sonoros, frecuencias, espectro—el sonido nos muestra nuevas dimensiones del medio ya que puede activar instantes y experiencias ya olvidadas y "transportarnos" a otras situaciones. El sonido ayuda a "reconstruir" el lugar resultando, por tanto, determinante en la evaluación que el sujeto realiza del espacio y en la preparación y realización de sus acciones en el medio. José Luis Carles, "El paisaje sonoro."
146. Giorgio Agamben, *Infancy and History: On the Destruction of Experience*, trans. Liz Heron (London: Verso Books, 2007), 51.
147. Agamben, *Infancy and History*, 55.
148. Agamben, *Infancy and History*, 54 (emphasis and ellipsis in original).
149. Agamben, *Infancy and History*, 53–54.
150. Agamben, *Infancy and History*, 54–55.
151. Luiselli, *Lost Children Archive*, 28.
152. Luiselli, *Lost Children Archive*, 111.
153. Walter Benjamin, "The Storyteller: Reflections on the Works of Nikolai Leskov" (1936), in *Illuminations*, ed. Hannah Arendt, trans. Harry Zohn, 83–109 (New York: Schocken Books, 1969), 83.
154. Walter Benjamin, "Experience and Poverty" (1933), in *Walter Benjamin: Selected Writings, vol. 2, 1931–1934*, ed. Michael W. Jennings, Howard Eiland, and

Gary Smith, trans. Rodney Livingstone, 731–36 (Cambridge, MA: Harvard University Press, 1999).
155. Agamben, *Infancy and History*, 14.
156. Agamben, *Infancy and History*, 17.
157. Jacques Derrida, *Archive Fever: A Freudian Impression*, trans. Eric Prenowitz (Chicago: University of Chicago Press, 2017).
158. Derrida, *Archive Fever*, 2.
159. Jorge Luis Borges "Funes, el memorioso" (1942), in *Ficciones* (Madrid: Alianza, 1997).
160. Eduardo Ismael Murguia, "Archivo, memoria e historia: Cruzamientos y abordajes," *Iconos: Revista de Ciencias Sociales* no. 41 (2011): 17–37. Alongside his mentions of Derrida, Murguia also refers to Borges.
161. No es una novela que hable de mi vida, pero habla de extranjería... la narradora ve el mundo como un mundo a veces horroroso, abandonado, un mundo que se comporta de manera brutal con aquellos que llegan a pedir asilo porque... están enfrentados a una crisis migratoria y la realidad de esta frontera México-Estados Unidos, que de alguna manera es el corazón oscuro de ese país. Luiselli was interviewed by Carlos Puig on a program entitled *Bote Pronto*, broadcast by Milenio Televisión, Mexico City. Luiselli appeared on the show on Feb. 15, 2020.
162. Me resulta imposible separar la experiencia vivida de la experiencia interna de un libro. Las dos cosas están siempre nutriendo mutuamente. No vemos siempre igual el mundo después de haber leído algunos libros.... Es una división ficticia. Yo pienso de esa manera y consigo así mis libros, son espacios que están formados por la experiencia completa. Luiselli interview with Carlos Puig.
163. En otras palabras, las referencias a las fuentes—textuales, musicales, visuales o audiovisuales—no fueron pensadas como marginalia, o como ornamentos que decoran la historia, sino que funcionan como marcadores interlineales que apuntan a la conversación polifónica que el libro mantiene con otras obras.... No me interesa la intertextualidad como un gesto explícito y performativo, sino como método o procedimiento compositivo. Luiselli interview with Carlos Puig.
164. Paul de Man, "Autobiography as Defacement," *Modern Language Notes* 94, no. 5 (Dec. 1979): 919–30.
165. Philippe Lejeune, *On Autobiography*, trans. Katherine Leary (Minneapolis: University of Minnesota Press, 1989).
166. Leigh Gilmore, *Autobiographics: A Feminist Theory of Women's Self-Representation* (Ithaca, NY: Cornell University Press, 1994).
167. Anthony Cummins, "*Lost Children Archive* by Valeria Luiselli," *Guardian*, March 3, 2019, https://www.theguardian.com/books/2019/mar/03/lost-children-archive-valeria-luiselli-review.
168. Pierre Bourdieu and Jean Claude Passeron, *Reproduction: In Education, Society and Culture*, trans. Richard Nice (London: Sage Publications, 1977).

169. Pierre Bourdieu and James S. Coleman, eds. *Social Theory for a Changing Society* (New York: Routledge, 2019).
170. Luiselli, *Lost Children Archive*, 26.
171. Luiselli, *Lost Children Archive*, 79.
172. Luiselli, *Lost Children Archive*, 145.
173. Luiselli, *Lost Children Archive*, 146.
174. Luiselli, *Lost Children Archive*, 139.
175. Luiselli, *Lost Children Archive*, 113.

www.ingramcontent.com/pod-product-compliance
Lightning Source LLC
Chambersburg PA
CBHW051207300426
44116CB00006B/458